Ways of Learning to Teach

Ways of Learning to Teach

A Philosophically Inspired Analysis of Teacher Education Programs

Shlomo Back
Kaye College of Education, Beer-Sheva, Israel

SENSE PUBLISHERS
ROTTERDAM/BOSTON/TAIPEI

A C.I.P. record for this book is available from the Library of Congress.

ISBN: 978-94-6091-850-6 (paperback)
ISBN: 978-94-6091-851-3 (hardback)
ISBN: 978-94-6091-852-0 (e-book)

Published by: Sense Publishers,
P.O. Box 21858,
3001 AW Rotterdam,
The Netherlands
https://www.sensepublishers.com/

Printed on acid-free paper

Dedicated to Hagit, my wife and partner,
and to our children Yonatan and Aya

Once our master Rabbi Hayyim of Zans [19th century] told a parable:

A man had been wandering about in the forest for several days, not knowing which was the right way out. Suddenly he saw a man approaching him. His heart was filled with joy. "Now I shall find out which is the right way," he thought to himself. When he neared one another, he asked the man, "Brother, tell me which is the right way. I have been wandering in this forest for several days."

Said the other to him, "Brother, I do not know the way either. For I too have been wandering about here for many, many days. But this I can tell you: do not take the way I have been taking, for that will bring you astray. And now let us look for a new way out together."

Our master added: "So it is with us. One thing I can tell you: the way we have been following this far we ought following no farther, for that way leads us astray. But now let us look for a new way."

S.Y. Agnon. (1948). *Days of Awe*. NY: Schoken Books. p. 22)

TABLE OF CONTENTS

PREFACE

This book arises out of a deep concern about teaching and teachers. Involved in Israel's teacher education system for the last thirty years, I have been a teacher educator (philosophy of education), an academic administrator (Rector of Levinsky and President of Kaye Colleges of Education), teacher of teacher educators (MOFET Institute) and a researcher. After so many years, I feel that the formal education system is heading in the wrong direction, and that the preparation of teachers is endangered. This state of affairs characterizes many western countries, including my own, and it is my professional and civic responsibility to understand its causes and suggest what can be done about it.

The book has two major aims. The first is to suggest a meta-theory of teacher education, which enables a fruitful discussion of its characteristics. This meta-theory (presented in chapter 2) has two interrelated features. On the one hand it is descriptive in so far as it proposes a set of concepts and ideas which might be used to analyze Teacher Education Programs (TEPs), discuss their features and assess their strengths and weaknesses. On the other hand, it has normative aspects so far as it addresses and evaluates the program's moral commitments. This feature is justified because education has an inherent normative aspect which cannot be ignored in any discussion of its essence. Furthermore, I claim that some TEPs are more favorable than others because of their normative stance.

The second aim of the book is to prompt the reader to rethink his or her own ideas about education, teaching, and teacher education, and to offer my ideas on these issues as stimulation for this process.

As the subtitle of the book discloses, it is written from a philosophical point of view. However, it is not a philosophical inquiry. It is not intended to present a new philosophical theory, but to suggest an exercise in applied philosophy. Philosophy, for me, is not about building grand theories but about critical analysis of belief systems. My basic attitude is skeptical. Any idea has to be checked for its reasonableness; every theory needs to question its soundness. Such an inquiry attests the relevance and importance of the philosophical dimension to educational practice, and demonstrates that without it, there can be no serious discussion of education, teaching, and teacher education.

The book contains a philosophical reconstruction of the conceptual framework of some approaches to teacher education, so they can be discussed and criticized. A major aspect of this reconstruction is the principle that in order to see the full force of any approach, it is critical to look for its practical manifestations, in our case, its influence on TEPs. Thus, although the theoretical analysis, by itself, might seem to be fairly remote from practical realities, it will enable the presentation of a broad spectrum of the practices of teacher education. It is vital to see the complex relationship between theory and practice, both because theory plays a major role in academic TEPs, and because going back from practice to theory enables the reevaluation of the theory in light of its practical outcomes.

The book's structure

The book can be compared to a journey. The first chapters present the preparation for the trip (Its reason, its ends, and the various travelling possibilities). Next come three different ways in the journey can take place, and the end displays the map of the area traveled followed by a recommended sightseeing explorations.

Less dramatically, the first chapter of the book presents three aspects of the struggle in which teacher education programs find themselves: the postmodern challenge, the neo-liberal world-view, and the professional debates about the teacher that teacher-educators want to prepare.

Chapter 2 introduces the main ingredients of a meta-theory of teacher education, in which the notion of "identity" plays a major role. The notion of identity is based on three underlying theories: A philosophical theory about the "sources of the self" (based on Charles Taylor's theory); a psychological theory about humans' "Modes of Existence" (based on Erich Fromm's theory extended by Jacob Rand); and a sociological theory (based on Axel Honneth's "Modes of Recognition" theory).Taylor posits three 'moral sources', Enlightenment, Romanticism, and External-Belief, as three moral stances which define one's identity in the modern era. Fromm and Rand describe three psychological attitudes of the self toward life: HAVING, BEING, and DOING. These attitudes (or Modes of Existence) determine three ideal types of human behavior in the modern era. Honneth connects identity with recognition, because for him self-identity presupposes the phenomenon of self-recognition. In modern societies, recognition involves three modes: *Love, Law,* and *Social-Esteem.*

I suggest that the notion of identity can be extended to include programs and institutions. I assume that each TEP has an identity, which can be used to understand its vision and aims, its content, and structure. The test of this theoretical extension will be its fruitfulness. It will be justified if it enables a better understanding of what is happening in teacher education. Understanding TEPs identity, in terms of how it is shaped by a moral source, a certain mode of existence and a mode of recognition, enables to analyze and understand various visions of "the good teacher", as each vision represents a specific mixture of the three stances. The second chapter presents the three theories, deals with the complex interrelations between them, and focuses on their implication to a meta-theory of Teacher Education.

The three theories have a strong philosophical flavor, and all of them address the issue of the meaning of life. Therefore, the moral source theory will serve as the basis for our subsequent discussion, while the other two will augment and expand it. Throughout the book, the theoretical framework presented in the second chapter will be used to: (1) further analyze the moral source's philosophical background and its relations to the various Modes of Existence and Modes of Recognition; (2) present its implications to education in general and to teacher education in particular; (3) exemplify how various TEPs implement it; and (4) critically discuss the pros and cons of each approach.

The bulk of the book takes each of the three moral sources, the Enlightenment (chapters 3-6), the External-believer (chapter 7), and the Romantic (chapters 8-9), as terrains to be explored. (A more detailed description appears at the end of chapter 2.)

The last chapter of the book, chapter 10, presents a summary of the book from its meta-theory perspective. Although seemingly contradictory, the three moral-source approaches might share significant mutual traits, and can even be seen as various angles of a "balanced", multifaceted way to advance teaching, teachers, and teacher education. To conclude the discussion, I briefly propose a first sketch of a synthesis of these approaches, which, hopefully, might deal with the postmodern challenge, the neoliberal threat, and the professional identity crisis.

I want to thank the numerous colleagues and students with whom I discussed many of the ideas presented in this book. Their encouraging and critical remarks make me think time and again about the ideas and the arguments presented along these pages. Kaye Academic College of Education has been my professional home for the last two decades. It is a fascinating multicultural environment of teaching, research, and social reform activities. I am especially grateful to Lea Kuzminsky, the President of the College for enabling me the time and the facilities to complete this book. MOFET Institute for research and development of teacher education provides another friendly and critical environment in which the ideas in this book have been presented and discussed. Special thanks to John Loughran, Monash University, for the wonderful opportunity to spend a Sabbatical in Melbourne and for the encouragement to write the book. Due to Angie Avittan, my English language editor, this book became much more readable, although the mistakes remain my own.

Last but not least, special thanks to my family, my son Yonatan, my daughter Aya, and Hagit my wife and partner, with whom I discussed every idea in this book. Her insights and sensitivity improved the book enormously. Her patience and support are my security net, and our love and friendship – give my life the extra flavor it has.

Throughout the book I use the third person pronoun "he". It applies, of course to both genders, and I apologize in advance if someone might be offended by this usage.

THE END OF THE JOURNEY: REVEALING THE PRESENT CONDITION OF TEACHER EDUCATION

A MULTIFACETED STRUGGLE

Teacher Education Programs (TEPs) find themselves in the midst of a multifaceted struggle. In an era in which a frequently asked question is: "How critical is a teacher-preparation program in determining the future effectiveness of a teacher?" and a frequently heard answer is "not very" (Feistritze, 2011), their very existence needs to be argued for and justified. Simultaneously, TEPs (1) face the postmodern challenge, (2) confront the neoliberal threat, and (3) have to overcome a professional identity crisis. Put together, the first two issues raise the question whether TEPs, in their current format, should persist. The third issue suggests that any argument for the merits of TEPs, provided by TEPs proponents, might presuppose some questionable ideas about teaching and teachers. In this chapter, I present this compound struggle, and introduce what is required in order to deal with it. Since the first two issues are frequently discussed in the literature, I will summarize the prevailing arguments concerning their impact on TEPs and expound on the third one.

The Postmodernist Challenge

The postmodern challenge is the charge that TEPs fail to prepare teachers who can deal with the educational needs of today's pupils. This condemnation is a side effect of a much broader argument, discussed, for instance, by Zygmunt Bauman (2000, 2003; 2005; 2008), which states that formal education is irrelevant or even destructive to what our next generation really needs and deserves. We live in a postmodern (or "liquid") society, which questions all the fundamental presupposition of education because it glorifies the idea of change. Everything around us is in a permanent flux, and the pace of the changes accelerates daily. In our consumerist era, what is new is always better. The last upgrade is always an improvement, and the "just arrived" is indubitably preferable. In this postmodern culture, everything has an expiration date. The minute you obtain something, it already becomes "old fashioned" and has to be thrown away and forgotten as quickly as possible. As Bauman (2008, p. 157) puts it, "… in a society of consumers, the pursuit of happiness tends to be refocused from making things or acquiring them to *disposing of* them." There is no "past" that has to be sustained, because past experiences are totally irrelevant to current situations. And no tradition has to be maintained, because tradition may prevent one's chances to adjust oneself to the ever-novel circumstances.

Formal education, to the contrary, is by its very nature conservative, steady, and stable. The name of its game is persistence. It looks to the past, and aims to preserve, and pass on to the new generation those long-established ideas, ideals, values, or attitudes, which seem to have an everlasting significance. But if none of those ideas, ideals, values, or attitudes are really viable, if they cease to be relevant and cannot survive the day, formal education loses its raison d'être. Its aims become dubious, its legitimization suspicious. In the secular, postmodern world, the status of knowledge is debatable, ethically driven principles are doubtful, esthetical valuations are highly questionable, and even God is dead. Consequently, every "ism" is suspected to lead to exertion of power, oppression and humiliation. But if one cannot rely anymore on any durable conception of the "True", the "Good", the "Beautiful", or the "Divine", it may be questioned whether education, in the traditional and common sense of transmitting the past for the future's advantage, still has something constructive to offer. As Bauman noticed: "Loading oneself with information, absorbing and retaining information, struggling for a completeness and cohesion of the information stored—it all looks suspiciously like offering oneself as a dumping site for prospective waste, and thus like an outrageous waste of time" (Bauman, 2005, p. 313). No wonder that the "crisis" of education is a widespread phenomenon in the Western world.

The only thing we do know for sure about the coming future is that it will be erratic and very challenging. Among other things, we face an ecological crisis (the planet gets warmer and suffers irregular weather changes; and we exploit too much energy), massive migration, immense unemployment, huge socio-economical gaps, terrorism, high rate of crime, violence, drugs and alcohol consumption, and daily violations of human rights. For Bauman, "the future, now largely out of control and unpredictable, is increasingly turning from a land of hope into a major source of apprehension... The blows come suddenly, with irregularity; and their nasty ability to appear from anywhere and at any moment makes them unpredictable, and renders us defenseless. …we are their sitting targets—we can do little, if anything at all, to prevent their arrival. Such hopelessness of ours is frightening. Uncertainty breeds fear." (Bauman, 2005, p. 304) This state of affairs encourages an emphasis on the "present". There is no reason to prepare for the unknown, to get ready for what you cannot expect. Live the moment and enjoy life as far as you can. The impact of this "here and now" attitude upon education is straightforward. It makes it futile and pointless.

The postmodern challenge has yet another aspect. Due to the ICT (Information, Communication Technology) revolution of the last decades, the world becomes "flat". The "global village" is virtually in everyone's room. The TV, the computer, the internet, and the cellular phone radically transform our life. Their influence is felt everywhere. More exactly, everywhere, except in the classrooms[1]. Teaching is still a "talk and chalk" routine, in which teachers act as "performers", representing and presenting valuable "material", while pupils act as passive recipients of their prudence and wisdom. Teaching seems to be immune tothe ever-changing world outside school. It does not adjust itself to the new "cut and paste" culture, in which the hard disc replaces memory, and the web replaces the library. In an era in which knowledge comes from Wikipedia, ethical principles are learned from Facebook, aesthetics relies on YouTube, and the new worship is dedicated to TV stars, schools remain the same as they were centuries ago. In an age in which the "word" has lost its priority to the "image", and everything should be as colorful, noisy, and energetic as possible in order to be recognized, classroom experiences seem to be outdated, boring and tiring to most of the children. Once they cannot zip between classes and lessons, and once the school does not resemble a huge mall or an inviting website, classroom learning seems to them outdated and old-fashioned. The price for this anachronism is huge. Schools become more than ever irrelevant to real life, and teachers have lost their authority and their influence on the children lives. It is neither what the pupils want nor what they need and deserve.

In a word, the accusation is clear cut. Formal education simply misses its target. It fails to successfully prepare the children for their future. Partly, because the only thing we know about this frightening future is that it will not resemble anything present; partly because current education cannot assimilate present innovations. It is possible, however, to answer this blame. In such a liquid world, we do need something solid. In an ever-changing reality there has to be an anchor that provides meaning and significance to our life. This response may be true, but it just postpones the challenge. For who will decide what this anchor should look like in these turbulent waters. Having no valid criteria of "true" or "good", the only available compass is fashion, but fashion is a very shaky anchor, because it is constantly changing. I will return to this point toward the end of the book (see chap. 10), and in the meantime let me briefly mention the implications of this argument to education in general and TEPs in particular.

Formal education has to change in order to stay viable. It has to become a light speedboat instead of a heavy huge vessel. However, such a transformation means that teaching itself has to change in order to support it. It is clear that for the "Teacher" to survive, his aims, roles, and responsibilities have to be re-conceptualized and redefined. His place in his pupils' lives should be reconsidered. The "what" and "how" of teaching should be revisited. Teaching methods and practices should be adjusted to the digital environment. The "classroom" concept has to be replaced by new learning environments[2].

But, for such a major renewal to occur, it is necessary that teacher education will be transformed as well. Otherwise, it will be impossible to prepare the prospective teachers to the updated environment. Moreover, since teacher education usually takes place in an academic environment, it may even be expected that TEPs will guide the educational revolution and provide the leaderships of the needed and long expected change.

Does TEPs meet this challenge? Not thus far. Teacher education remains, by and large, indifferent to it. TEPs adhere to what they have always done. They still prepare the teachers of the past. Can Teacher Education meet the challenge? It is one of the purposes of this book to examine critically this option. However, another factor disparages the likelihood that TEPs will effectively deal with the postmodern challenge. TEPs struggle for their very survival because of our current neo-liberal world.

The Neo-Liberal Threat

In the closing chapter of the *Handbook of Teacher Education*, Richard Bates and Tony Townsend claim that "In Anglo-Saxon countries the New Right political ascendancy has constantly belittled teacher education, seeing it as both unnecessary and, indeed, corrupting" (Bates & Townsend, 2007, p. 729). If true, the implication of this situation is obvious. TEPs are facing a real threat to their existence.

The rational of the neo-liberal attitude against TEPs can be easily traced. It is, once again, a side effect of a more general accusation, this time against public education as a public service. The keywords of the argument are free-market economy and privatization. Assume, to begin with, that humans seek happiness. Then accept the supposition that material wealth is critical to attain happiness. These assumptions are, of course, controversial, but they represent a major philosophical trend in the western thought (following, e.g., Jeremy Bentham or Adam Smith). Moreover, they represent what the majority of the people in the western world take to be an unquestionable truth (e.g., Solomon et al., 2007, p. 130). To these ideas, add the ethical principle that every human being has the equal right to attain material wealth. This is what social justice really means. Now you face a problem. Since the material resources are scarce, there is a competition regarding who will achieve them. This competition has to be fair and open to all. And there should be a proper way to decide how to distribute the resources. The neo-liberal ideology maintains that the free market-economy is the only conceivable means that ensures that everybody will have an equal opportunity to participate in the competition. Only in such an environment, humans can act rationally and choose the best available means for them to prosper.

To achieve happiness is an individualistic project. It is up to each individual to do his best to fulfill his desires. Although any individual should have the right to advance his own interests, achieve his ends, and be fully responsible for his own actions. Freedom, which means lack of imposed restrictions, is an essential feature of the free market society. Market economy is driven by the private sector. Individual people just mind their own business, and do what is good for them, and the "invisible hand" of the market ensures that, taken as a whole, society will be more affluent. Freedom, however, is feasible only in a political regime in which government involvement is minimal. Any external force should not hinder the market's invisible hand. Any intervention, especially if it comes from the government, will have the negative effects of freedom restrictions and prevent prosperity.

This kind of reasoning should be applied to the public services. The public sector breeds impotence, waste, and corruption. Its ever-growing bureaucracy, which is unable to deliver any promised goods, can only empower laziness, dependence, and obedience. It perilously diminishes human freedom, and may even lead to totalitarianism. Taken to the extreme, according to the free-market principle, it is mandatory to get rid of the public services sector (health, social insurance, security, transportation, prisons, etc). In order to improve society, you have to privatize the public services. You have to provide every service by non-government organizations, not-for profit and even for-profit organizations. Competition itself, supplemented by limited but necessary regulations to assure the quality and the accessibility of the service, will ensure that it will be much more effective, efficient, and accountable than the corresponding public one.

Note that the tendency to privatize the public services is not only profit-oriented. Referring to the place of the private sector in education, Patrinos and Sosale attest the "need for the private sector to share a public responsibility: that of financing and/or providing education" in times where there is "increasing and competing demands on the state" (2007, p. 1).

According to Saltman (2009, p. 54), the underlying supposition of this argument is that if privatization works for businesses and make them prosper, it should be the model for schooling as well. Private schools will be more flexible, and less burdened by endless regulations and constraints (e.g., obeying the teachers-union dictates). Moreover, they are much more attentive to their pupils (clientele) needs and responsive to society's requirements; because if they fail to meet the highest educational standards, they will disappear. The bare need to compete with other schools will make them inevitably better. They are the only sites in which the long awaited educational superman can prosper (K. Weber, 2010).

This line of reasoning may end with a much more radical approach to public education. Education needs to be privatized, but such transformation is barely possible unless demonstrated (in an evidence based, and credible statistical method, which is transparent to the public) that it is in a critical condition and there is no other choice but to replace it altogether. But the public suspicions that only the private entrepreneurs will benefit from this transformation can be calmed down only if there is a clear-cut manifestation that "things cannot get worse". It is necessary to ascertain that public education is in a real crisis. This, however, is not such a difficult task (see, for example: K. Weber, 2010).

As Noami Klein argues in her book *The Shock Doctrine* (2007), what happens is reminiscent of the biblical story about the Israelites in Egypt which complain: "...There is no straw given unto thy servants, and they say to us: Make brick" (Exodus, 5, 16). First, the government cuts the budget of the public service until it cannot properly function. Thereafter, it can easily validate the claim that the (deprived) system malfunctions because it cannot deliver the required goods. Thereafter, the door is open to invite the private sector to be charitable and rescue the service. As Saltman puts it: "Around the world, disaster is providing the means for business to accumulate profit" (2008, p. 187). That this strategy may further enrich the rich is not a counterargument, if the outcome is that the service benefits more people more efficiently.

Public education provides no exception. According to Saltman, the logic of the "shock doctrine" is fully applicable to it (2008, p. 187). The case of Australia provides a typical example[3].According to Davis: "amid scaremongering about low teaching standards and substandard facilities at government schools, private schools received around double the total amount of federal government funding received by public schools (two-thirds of children attend public schools)..." (Davis, 2008, p. 118).

No wonder that the children in the private school systems fare much better, and in order to make this point evident, it is necessary to create a comprehensive (and expensive) system of quality assurance, which includes standards, benchmarks, and national and international exams. Using these tools, justified by the name of transparency, and the "right to know" principles, it is quite easy to demonstrate that the public system is inefficient and unaccountable. It clearly causes social injustice to too many children, especially those who learn in urban schools and do not receive a proper education (K. Weber, 2010). The public system's failures are remarkable; its malfunctions are notorious. So much so, that even pouring a lot of money into it will not rescue the system. As the Mckinsey report documented, "Between 1980 and 2005, public spending per student increased by 73 percent in the USA, after allowing for inflation... Actual student outcomes, however, as measured by the Department of Education's own national assessment program, stayed about the same" (2007). The only remedy to this malaise is to privatize education. Public education has to be replaced by private sector enterprises.

This line of reasoning may seem exaggerated. Many liberals still appreciate the need for public education. They still believe that only public education, in which everyone has an equal right for a proper education, regardless of the tuition he can afford to pay, can ensure social justice and cultivate a democratic citizen (Saltman 2009, p. 55). Nevertheless, the neo-liberal argumentation proved to be very influential in instilling the business terminology into the educational discourse. As stated by Gandin (2007), the market ethic replaces the public good ethics. A new set of economic considerations replaces the pedagogical discourse of education. As a result, contemporary schools behave like businesses. They must be competitive, present a "plan" for action, have a budget, and need to look for additional income resources (including commercial ads and products), hire seasonal teachers to minimize their expenses, and have to fare well in the achievement league.

The very idea of private education needs to be revisited and discussed, and I will return to the ideological background of the neo-liberal agenda (see: chaps. 6; 10). In the meantime, let us see the impact of this ideology on teachers and teacher education. Teachers enter the scene because the "quality of the system cannot exceed the quality of its teachers" (McKinsey&Company, 2007). As the McKinsey report emphasizes, "The available evidence suggests that the main driver of the variation in students learning at school is the quality of the teachers..." (2007). A lower teachers-pupils ratio or smaller class-size does not elevate the students' outcomes. If a system's achievements are poor – it is because its teachers are not as good as they should be. This stance is, of course, just another manifestation of the privatization spirit, in which every individual must be responsible and accountable for his achievements, notwithstanding any social or economic factor.

Now we reach the punch line. Teachers fail because they receive poor preparation. Instead of cultivating expert technicians, who will prepare their pupils to meet the required standards and pass the high-stake exams, too many TEPs prepare teachers whose aim is to revolutionize schools. Instead of training teachers to observe competently that "No Child Left Behind", they produce inapt pseudo-professionals, who replace accountability to outcomes with endless chats about immeasurable "processes". The teachers they train pretend to "educate" the pupils.

They disguise their inability or reluctance to teach the "basics" by using a pedagogical jargon about "constructive" knowledge, and "meaningful" or "relevant" learning. It is of no wonder that their pupils achieve poor academic outcomes.

These malfunctioning teachers are the product of academic programs, which are clearly ineffective. TEPs are too long for such an easy occupation as teaching, and their academic setting makes them too costly. In addition, this academic setting is destructive to proper teacher training because it attracts mediocre students and is too "theoretic" so it fails to prepare the students for school's realities. It is preferable to find "alternative routes" for teacher preparation, which will be shorter, cheaper, "field-based", more attractive, and more efficient, for the student-teachers, for the schools, and for the system (see the papers in: Grossman & Loeb, 2008). Alternatives like "Teach For..." programs in the States and elsewhere indicate the right direction for teacher preparation in the coming decades[4].

There are two alternatives for TEPs to deal with this threat. They can accept the terms of reference of the discussion, and try to demonstrate that, after all, they are efficient and accountable programs. If properly conducted, they prepare the needed teachers, i.e., the teachers whose pupils succeed to meet the standards and pass the exams. In that case, the answer to the neo-liberal threat should demonstrate that teacher education programs are evidence-based, and that the programs have their own experts who genuinely know how to prepare teachers, and really provide the best and only viable way to prepare teachers. (See, for example, Darling-Hammond, et al. 2005, [Does teacher preparation]; Grossman & Loeb, 2008). Alternatively, to this "if you cannot beat them join them" strategy, TEPs can argue that the neoliberal ideal of education is flawed and has to be replaced by a different ideology altogether (See, for example, Hobbel, 2009; Ravitch, 2010). In that case it will be harmful to adjust TEPs to the ruling but misguided ideology. TEPs struggle is not just about questions of efficiency, accountability, and success. It is a about the criteria of what counts as efficiency, accountability, and success, and about the proper ways to verify that these criteria have been met. Moreover, it is a fight about the very use of these terms in the educational discourse and about what counts as proper education at large.

This is an ongoing debate within teacher education itself. Teacher educators simply do not agree on how a proper TEP should look. Let me now address this "internal" debate, which renders the very possibility to deal with the "external" difficulties much more problematic.

The Professional Identity Crisis

Teacher educators do not have a common answer to the question, "What should characterize the teacher they prepare?" Although most of them reject the popular 'teacher as transmitter' conception, they do not agree on what should be his professional identity. What may be even more disturbing is that they lack an accepted method of how to deal with this question. After years of attempts to identify "The Teacher", there are many competitive and even contradictory ideals of "The Teacher", and teacher educators do not have any agreed way of how to choose between them.

7

If teacher educators do not agree on their graduates' characteristic, it is because teaching itself lacks a common vision of its essence. This state of affairs generates an "internal" conflict within teacher educators, and has a weakening impact on the possibility of TEPs to deal with the two "external" struggles mentioned before. Moreover, it points to a major problem with the idea that teaching is a profession. In the opening sentence of their seminal book *Preparing Teachers for a Changing World*, Darling-Hammond and Bransford declare, "All professions at some point of their development have worked to achieve consensus about the key elements of a professional educational curriculum" (2005, p. vii). However, the content and the structure of any TEP become dubious if its aims are debatable. For how can you prepare someone to be a teacher if your picture of "The Teacher" may be suspect?

On the face of it, that there is no acceptable ideal of "The Teacher" may be a surprising state of affairs. It seems that all of us – teachers, pupils, parents, politicians, and the general public –"know" who the teacher is. We all have shared beliefs about his identity. We all can recognize him. After all, we all have been pupils, and some of us continue to visit schools as parents or caretakers. We observe what the teacher is doing; we are familiar with how he looks. Otherwise, we would have been surprised to find an academic research whose title is *That's funny, you don't look like a teacher* (Weber & Mitchell, 1995). In their research, the authors find that "Even a cursory analysis of drawings done by children and teachers reveals the persistence and pervasive presence of traditional images of teaching as transmission of knowledge from all-knowing teacher into empty vessel student" (p. 28). When they ask: "Quick! Think of 'teacher'. What do you see? What does what you see mean? Where does what you see come from?" (p. 20), the respondents' answers expose "…common stereotypes of teachers as drab, asocial, and asexual creatures whose sole mission is to make children learn, whether they want or not" (p. 4). Admittedly, this is a negative prejudice, but even the teachers who take part in the research embrace it.

Teacher students enter teacher education programs "knowing" about teaching and teachers from their own "apprenticeship-of-observation" experience (Lortie, 1975, p. 61 – 65). Many of them want to resemble a "good" teacher they love or differ from a teacher they hate. These presuppositions suggest that they have a model to identify with. Nevertheless, Lortie finds that "the descriptions …respondents gave of remembered teachers point to variety rather than similarity" (p. 66; cf.: Wideen et al., 1998). As he points out: "There is little reason to expect that any group of teachers-to-be will share common images or proclivities… Education students have undergone diverse prior experiences and their assessments will presumably reflect personal differences, varieties of social experience, and the different contexts within which their assessments were made" (Lortie, 1975, p. 66). However, this divergence is within a narrow range. As Darling-Hammond notices, many people who enter teaching believe that teaching is only about transmission (2006, p. 36; cf.: Hammerness et al., 2005, p. 369).

Teacher educators have a very different characterization of the professional activity of the teacher. But although they do not see the professional teacher as a transmitter[5], they cannot offer to this prevalent image any shared alternative. If you ask teacher educators the same "Think of teacher" questions, you will not get one prevalent view regarding his professional identity. Once teaching is not seen solely as transmission, the debate, on what it really is, is open.

It is quite easy to demonstrate the claim that teacher educators do not have a common vision of "The Teacher" they prepare. The variability of Teacher Education Programs is remarkable. Some of them are located within universities or academic colleges. Some are provided by various agencies, school districts, and even schools. Some TEPs are extremely long. Others are notoriously short. Some of them prepare high-school graduates. Others prepare only post graduates prospective teachers. Some of them are stand-alone programs. Others are part of a broader course of academic study. Some of them are pre-service programs. Others include an in-service course of study. The program's curricula are no less diverse. Some programs include constituents that others neglect. Some of the programs are theory focused or research oriented. Others are field based or practice oriented. Some of them address only educational or methodological issues. Others concentrate on subject-matter studies, and still others focus on general knowledge or on the student's personality. In various programs there are different teaching and learning methods and strategies. The criteria of the student's evaluations are as diverse as the programs. The student's entry and exit requirements are different. The programs obey varied regulations. The teacher-educators have different characteristics as well. Some of them have school experience. Others are university faculty without any in-school teaching experience. In sum, the program's aims, and the ways they perceive the role of the teacher, and the meaning of teaching and learning are very different from each other.

The research of TEP reveals a similar picture. A brief look at the three successive editions of the *Handbook of Research on Teacher Education* (Houston, 1990; Sikula, 1996; Cochran-Smith et al., 2008) discloses significant differences between TEPs about the required characteristics of the teachers they educate. In the opening paper of the *Handbook*'s first edition, Doyle (1990, p. 5 – 6) presents five major paradigms underlying TEPs. His list, based on previous studies by Zeichner (1983) and Joyce (1975), includes: The Good Employee, "who can efficiently cope with the 'real world' of schooling"; The Junior Professor, whose focus is on the subject matter he is going to teach; The Fully Functional Person, who facilitates student's personal development; The Innovator, who acts as a source of renewal and innovative practices for schools; and The Reflective Professional, who inquires into teaching and thinks critically about his work. Doyle does not mention the criteria for selecting these paradigms, and it is not clear how to compare them with each other. While the Good Employee, the Innovator, and the Reflective Professional may characterize any professional in any occupation, the other two paradigms are much more restrictive and deal specifically with the way teachers function. Moreover, these paradigms are not mutually exclusive. It is quite possible, for example, that the fully functional person will be at the same time innovator, and the junior professor can be a reflective professional as well. Doyle does not examine the relations between these paradigms and various conceptions of teaching and learning. While the first two paradigms seem to be well-suited to the transmission model, it is not clear which theory of teaching and learning is presupposed by the others.

Feiman-Nemsser (1990, p. 220 – 228), partly relying on the same sources, describes in the *Handbook*'s same edition, five "conceptual orientations" in teacher education. An orientation, she defines, is "a set of ideas about the goals of teacher preparation and the means for achieving them... [It] includes a view of teaching and learning and a theory about learning to teach." Her list includes: The Academic Orientation, in which the teacher is primarily concerned with the transmission of knowledge and the development of understanding; The Practical Orientation, which concentrates "on the elements of craft, technique, and artistry that skillful practitioners reveal in their work" in the particular context in which they teach; The Technical Orientation which emphasizes "the acquisition of principles and practices derived from the scientific study of teaching"; The Personal Orientation which "places the teacher-learner at the center of the educational process... [So that] the teacher's own personal development is a central part of teacher preparation"; and, The Critical/Social Orientation, which "combines a progressive social vision with a radical critique of schooling", according to which, the teacher is an educator and a political activist. Unlike Dyole, Feiman-Nemsser maintains that reflection is not a separate orientation, but rather "a generic professional disposition" embedded in all the orientations. She concedes, however, that these orientations "do not represent a set of equally valid alternatives from which to choose", because none of them "offers a fully developed framework to guide program development." Once again, the various orientations are not exclusive. Howey and Storm (1987), for example, put them all in one bag, requiring that each teacher education program "should have as its basic goal of development of teachers as persons who have conceptual systems characterized by the qualities of being adaptable, questioning, critical, inventive, creative, self-renewing and oriented to moral principles"[6] (cited with approval by Zumwalt and Craig in the *Handbook*'s third edition (2008, p. 416)).

Neither Doyle nor Feiman-Nemseer mention Fenstermacher and Soltis' influential book "*Approaches to Teaching*", whose first edition appeared in 1986. Fenstermacher and Soltis discuss three "basic approaches" to teaching: "The executive approach views the teacher as a skillful manager of learning who brings about high levels of student's achievements – features a new emphasis on competence; the therapist approach views the teacher as an empathetic, caring person who helps students reach a high level of self-actualization – features a new emphasis on caring, nurturing, and fostering achievement of each student's potential; the liberationist approach views the teacher as a liberator of the mind and a developer of the student's intellectual and moral virtues – features a fuller treatment of emancipator/critical pedagogy and a broader view of teaching as initiation" (Fenstermacher & Soltis, 1998, p. 4 – 5).

The *Handbook*'s second edition begins with an introductory paper by Schwartz (1996). She states that: "...teacher education is a complex production with many voices" (p.5). Nonetheless, she expresses the need for a "codification" which "allows questions about effectiveness and quality control". Towards this end she adopts the five ideal profiles suggested by Doyle (1990). In another paper, Christensen analyses documents of 42 American institutions applying for National Council for Accreditation of Teacher Education (NCATE) accreditation in 1993.

She notes that "The overwhelming impression gained from the review was the diversity of approaches" to teacher education. Within the various "program design themes" she finds: "Effective liberally educated teacher; Empowered person and professional; Lifelong scholar; Practicing professional; Professional educator; Reflective practitioner, Reflective decision maker; Skilled and reflective practitioner. Teacher as a catalyst for change; Teacher as an active learner and decision maker; Teacher as the developer of human potential; Teacher as an effective leader in a diversified society..." Christensen emphasizes that even: "programs with similar theme statements had substantially different approaches" in their actual practice (1996, pp. 38 – 52). In the succeeding paper, Henson (1996) extends the reflective professional paradigm, and examines the teacher as researcher profile, which refers to "teachers who each day pursue relevant topics to improve their teaching" (p. 54).

In the *Handbook*'s third edition, Sockett (2008) identifies four models of the "professional teacher", each of them presupposing a different moral and epistemological purpose. His list includes: the scholar-professional, which regards knowledge as the purpose of education; the nurture-professional, which focuses on the development of the individual; the clinician-professional, which emphasizes the learning processes and the teacher's adaptive expertise; and the moral-agent professional, which focuses on teaching as a moral activity, integrating academic content with intellectual and moral virtues. Each model, he explains, "is seen as an ideal type, with the label acting as a rough and ready descriptor of emphasis, and not carrying exclusivity". For Sockett, each of the models supports a different view of the teacher's professional[7] identity, and has its specific impact on teacher education programs, due to the different aspects the teacher may emphasize in his work (the subject-matter; the pupil; the process of learning; and the moral dimension), and the different weight he assigns to each of the above components.

This brief survey attests that although teacher educators reject the pervasive opinion that teaching is an easy and simple job, they do not have an agreed conception of The Teacher they prepare. It also indicates that they do not even share a general framework (or a 'meta-theory') which articulates a common vocabulary to discuss this issue. Each of the above proposals seems to presuppose a different set of values, relies on a different epistemology, uses different terminology, and makes use of different classificatory criteria. As a result, it is hardly possible to compare the various proposals. It is not even obvious that they present the only possible options to define the Teacher, so it is not clear why one has to choose between them, and how such a choice can be justified. Teacher Education desperately needs a principled method to deal with this issue, a method that will rely on some general ideas about what can be counted as a reasonable discussion on the aims of education, regardless of any specific content they may have.

Thus, instead of generating list after list of possible characteristics of The Teacher, it will be more productive to approach this issue from a different angle. What is needed is not another specific theory about what constitutes the "good" teacher regardless of any ideological biases, but a meta-theory of how to address the topic. If such a framework can be constructed, it will enable a fruitful dialogue about teaching, its essence, and its aims. At the core of such a meta-theory lays questions such as: What are the prerequisites of the discussion? What are the questions one has to ask? What are the keywords that one has to use? Only after the articulation of such a meta-theory, will it be possible to explain the vast diversity of TEPs, look for the communalities between them, and examine the question "Is there something common to all the possible approaches to teacher-education?" Thereafter, the possibility to address the external threats and challenges will be much more grounded and persuasive.

The Search for a Meta-Theory

The following question may provide the first clue as to the direction we have to follow: "Why is it that after so many attempts to identify The Teacher, it still lacks a generally accepted characterization?" Part of the difficulty arises because the 'what for' of teaching is, in principle, controversial. Each of the above characterizations of "The Teacher" seems to presuppose different ethics; each of them depends on a different ideology. Consequently, beside the vague slogan, that the teachers should "prepare the children for the future", everything else is disputable. Teacher educators have different pictures of this future. Feiman-Nemser justly remarks that the plurality of orientations of teachers and teaching demonstrates a plurality of values. "People", she says, "hold different expectations for schools and teachers" (1990, p. 220). The different paradigms, orientations, or models reflect different and sometimes conflicting ideological backgrounds.

This point is crucial. As put by Goodwin, "the heart of the concern [about teacher's quality] is not simply *that* teachers should be capable or qualified, but *what constitutes* capableness or qualification. Thus, each constituency comes at the question with different definitions of teacher quality and different ideas about what teachers should know and be able to do, ideas and definitions that are framed by different values, socio-cultural norms, and aims." (2008, p. 399)

Different ideological stances advance different models of the ideal teacher and his professional mission. Consequently, different ideals of the "good" or the "ideal" teacher lead to different TEPs. This reasoning indicates that the meta-theory we are looking for has to address the question of how one justifies the ideology which guides one's personal and professional life. In other words, it addresses the issue of the teacher's personal and professional identity, since having a certain ideology is part and parcel of one's identity.

As I understand it, to have a certain identity means to endorse a certain philosophical worldview, to psychologically adjust one's life to a certain world view in the midst of one's social environment. Thus, the notion of personal identity has philosophical, psychological and sociological dimensions. This notion of personal "identity" captures three levels of reference: the personal, the professional, and the program. So it will be congenial to refer to a TEP's identity, its background and its impact.

GETTING THE EQUIPMENT: THE THEORETICAL FRAMEWORK

Identity is a slippery notion. I am looking at the mirror and recognize myself. Somebody I know recognizes me on the street. These acts of recognition are based on physical similarity (to look like…). But this is barely a sufficient condition for identity, as can be seen from cases of identical twins that physically look identical. Similarly, I recognize myself albeit the fact that I am quite different from what I was (physically) yesterday, a week ago, a year ago, a decade ago. Almost every cell in my body has been replaced and still it is me. Thus, self-Identity does not mean that I am identical to myself but that I am sufficiently similar to what I used to be, that I preserve my continuity with the person I was. On the other hand, it possible for me to declare, after an exceptional experience, that I am not the same person as I was before. "Recognizing yourself in a mirror is a far cry from having a sense of a unique life story, of being conscious of being conscious, and being able to contemplate your own demise" (Greenfield, 2008, p. 133). Self-identity is the narrative I tell about myself, and my life, a story in which I am the hero (MacIntyre, 1984; Ricoeur, 1992, Taylor, 1989). It is a manifestation of mine unique belief-system, which includes the statements I believe to be true and the values I treat as good (cf.: Greenfield, 2008, p. 217). This essential connection between someone's self-identity and one's belief-system indicate that the notion of (professional) identity may provide a first clue as to how to penetrate the troublesome terrain of TEPs.

The notion of identity fuels many philosophical, sociological, anthropological, and psychological discussions and leads to various controversies. Thus, it is necessary to explicate the meaning of the notion in our context. In very broad terms, personal identity is about similarity and difference, i.e., comparing individuals, addressing the similarities between them and characterizing the distinctive traits of each of them. It is commonly held "(1) That identity is dependent and formed within multiple contexts which brings social, cultural, political, and historical forces to bear upon that formation; (2) that identity is formed in *relationship* with others and involves emotions; (3) that identity is *shifting, unstable* and *multiple*; and, (4) that identity involves the construction and reconstruction of meaning through *stories* over time" (Rodgers & Scott, 2008, p. 733). Thus, identity formation combines external factors such as contexts and relationships as well as internal factors such as narratives and emotions (p. 733). The 'self' concept is composed of many dimensions such as content, positivity, intensity, stability, and accuracy (Solomon et al. 2007).

As mentioned in the previous chapter, the notion of personal identity has philosophical, psychological and social dimensions. Thereafter, I shall rely on three different theories that explicate the notion. (1) A philosophical theory based on Charles Taylor's "sources of the self" concept; (2) A psychological theory based on Eric Fromm's "Modes of Existence" (elaborated by Jacob Rand); and; (3) A sociological theory based on Axel Honneth's theory of Recognition which analyses the social prerequisites for a having a personal identity. Admittedly, the last two approaches have a strong philosophical flavor as well. They both have an essential moral or normative component. On one hand, what distinguishes me from any other human being can be perceived as something factual.I compare myself to others, and ask myself: do I resemble them, and in what ways do I differ from them? On the other hand, those same issues may be framed in normative terms: Is it good to be like them? Is it better to be different, in what aspects, to what extent? How can I justify my personal beliefs, desires, and attitudes?

These three theoretical approaches enable to suggest a coherent and extensive theory, which can deal with the multifaceted notion of identity. In what follows I shall briefly present the three theories, as a preparatory stage to the discussion of their impact on the possible professional identities of The Teacher and the TEP.

THE MORAL DIMENSION

The first theory is strictly philosophical. Such a theory is necessary because as we have seen, personal identity is defined by reference to one's belief system, or by the philosophy, which directs one's life. The normative aspect of personal identity connects identity and morality. According to Taylor, morality is about what type of people we want to be. It specifies our ideal about the morally good. His main tenet is that each person defines his identity with reference to the "good" he identifies with:

> My identity is defined by the commitments and identifications which provide the frame or horizon within which I try to determine from case to case what is good, or valuable, or ought to be done, or what I endorse or oppose… it is the horizon within which I am capable of taking a stand. (Taylor, 1989, p. 27)

Wishing to define his identity, and decide what he wants to identify himself with, the individual needs some kind of orientation in this quest. Some kind of map is needed in order not to be completely lost in this strange territory. Otherwise, he will be completely perplexed as to what should be counted as right or wrong, good or bad, justifiable or dreadful. Such a map is offered by what Taylor calls a "moral source", a source which acts as a compass, helping the individual to navigate through life.

According to Taylor, our era acknowledges more than one available compass . There are three distinct moral sources, and the question of which them one chooses has an overall importance to one's identity. The first source is external to the individual. The other two, reason and feeling, are internal.

According to the external-source, morality is prescribed by a transcendental power that is beyond human command, such as God, "the Law of History", "The law of Evolution", or some other eternal force. This external power directs humans to their absolute duties and obligations. This is so because the very existence of an external power fulfills the world with meaning. It is an organized Cosmos and not a mechanical Universe (Taylor, 2007, p.59 – 61). What happens in the world is a process in which human agents play a definite and all-important role. Usually, the name of the process is salvation. If only humans will do their duties, the fate of the world will be entirely different, and humans will return to the lost heaven.

To rely on an external moral source, the individual has to believe that it exists. He must assume that there is a divine entity, or a supreme (secular) force, whose dictates needs to be observed. Thereafter, this source will shape his notions of "The True" and "The Good", specify his absolute duties, and render his life meaningful. Each of his activities will have special significance; each of them will contribute to the fulfillment of the holy mission he takes upon himself.

This is a Sisyphean and never-ending mission. It cannot be carried on by any single human being. Only within a community of believers it is possible for the individual to have the strength to cope with it. The decisive role of the community cannot be underemphasized. The community empowers the individual, and ascertains that, albeit laden with difficulties, he will not turn away from the enormously hard mission he must undertake. Consequently, community has a major influence on his self-identity as well, because in such a context identity is strictly defined in terms of belonging. There is clear sense of "we" and "they" which provide the terms of reference. However, this attitude can be very perilous, as the religious or ideological wars can testify.

In sum: the believer defines his identity in terms of his identification with his divine mission. He sees himself as a devotee and a missioner, and feels that he is responsible for the cosmos as a whole, for the future of the human race, for the fate of his society. An essential part of this identity is his identification as a member in the community of devotees who share the same commitments.

Unlike the believer, the enlightenment person is an individual who believes the source of the "True" and the "Good" is to be found within himself, or more precisely, within his rational mind. The enlightenment person believes that science alone can reveal nature's secrets and that only the thinking faculty, by using the scientific method, enables man to know himself, and the physical and social world which surround him. Knowledge has practical implications. "Knowledge is power," says Francis Bacon, as early as 1597. Rational thinking is practical as well. It helps humans to utilize knowledge in order to conquer the world. It enables them to invent technologies that bring progress and prosperity. For this to happen, the human being has to be free. He has to be liberated from any external impositions in order to act according to what his own reason dictates as "true" and "good".

Rationality has four important characteristics. First, being rational is something individual. Each individual should exercise his own reasoning faculty. He cannot rely on other's wisdom because he has a personal responsibility for his choices and actions. Nevertheless, and this is the second characteristic, reason is not something subjective or arbitrary. To the contrary, reason is objective, universal, and eternal. Given the same premises of a valid argument, its conclusion is logically proven. It is crucial that the validity of any given argument does not depend on its specific content but only on its form. (This is why logic texts are full of formulae and variables.) Formal reasoning does not deal with discovering the truth but with the examination of the coherence and consistency of a certain sequence of statements. However, for many philosophers, consistency is a necessary condition of truth, for an inconsistent argument cannot be reliable. Third, as far as possible, the rational thinker has to be disengaged. His deliberations should not be influenced by his emotions or desires, because such an intervention might bias the process, and lead to faulty outcomes, due to wishful thinking. Fourth, reason is analytic. To have an explanation for a phenomenon, it is necessary to analyze its constituents and the way its whole behavior is defined by them, by their interconnection and by the way these constituents react to external forces.

Practical rationality can be substantive or formal. While substantive rationality deals with the reasonableness of the aims we want to achieve, formal or "instrumental" rationality deal with relations between aims and means (cf., M. Weber, 1947, p. 184 – 186). Formal rationality seeks after the best available means to achieve a certain given aim, regardless of the question of what count as a proper aim. However, it is generally supposed that the highest human aim is happiness, and that any action should contribute to it. Thus, the ethics behind instrumental rationality is utilitarianism, and we will examine it in a later chapter (chap. 3)

Instrumental rationality has one all-imported aspect that had to be spelled out. In order to perform utility calculations it is necessary that the different values, attached to each of the preferences, will be commensurable. Otherwise, it will not be possible to compare them. Therefore, there needs to be a certain scale on which it will be possible to locate all the different values. For such a scale to be efficient, all the values must share a common denominator. This denominator has to be defined in quantifiable terms to enable a comprehensible and unequivocal comparison. Knowledge itself has to be quantified, as it is clear to every pupil at school and to every academic who want to pursue his career. It is no incident that money becomes the main mechanism of measuring values (while in education grades replace money). The outcome of this characterization is that even personal identity has to be defined in measurable terms. As Fromm suggested, for many people, "I am what I have" defines who they are (Fromm, 1976, p. 82). I will return to this attitude in the next section.

The third moral source is irrational. Its representative is the Romantic individual. (The term, with a capital R, designates a European philosophical and cultural movement in 18-19th centuries.) The Romantic person despises the detached individual and its cold calculative mind, which distance humans from nature and alienates them from their real selves. Reason can only lead to estrangement and depression. It may provide "explanation" but not "understanding"; it may analyze the constituents of happens, but it loses the holistic aspect of the phenomena and its hidden meaning. Although its technocratic achievements render life much easier than ever before, life becomes miserable as well. To be reasonable is to sell one's soul to the Devil.

Instead of reason, one has to rely on one's irrational inner self. A new idea enters the scene: each and every man has a unique "deep inborn nature" (Taylor, 2007,

p. 257; cf. Bruford, 1975; Seigel, 2005; Gergen, 1991) to which he should be loyal. The Romantic person believes that deep inside himself there is an authentic self that has to be uncovered and expressed, and that it is this irrational seat of genuine feelings and desires which gives his life meaning and direction. Man has to be attentive to his inner voice and be innovative in the ways he expresses it. The main purpose of life is to get in touch with this inner self, to recognize its passions, and to act for its self-fulfillment. Humans have to be authentic. They must preserve their integrity. They have to obey neither God nor Reason nor even society's conventions, because they all may oppress their genuine nature. While society is eager to disregard the inner self, repress its manifestations, and control its expressions, the true self must rebel against the oppression, be imaginative and creative, and express himself as sincerely as possible.

The first spokesman of this philosophy was Rousseau, who tells us that our life would be much more satisfying if only we could be brave enough to free ourselves from any external convention and habit. For Rousseau, the inner self reveals the Truth and the Good. Despite the fact that what we find is necessarily subjective and relative, it teaches us something deep about our human condition in general, as long as its expression is sincere and authentic. To understand another human, and to sympathize with him, is more important than to have a scientific explanation of his behavior, because it enables us to understand ourselves, and to make sense of our experiences. In this sense, art is much more revealing than science. Art is a mean to connect us with our own inner reality. Hermeneutical self-study, dialogue with others, and creative (often artistic) activities are the main venues to reveal and develop man's unique identity. Towards this aim, it is necessary to look at the "dark" sides of life. Man's life should be meaningful even if it turns out to be miserable (in utilitarian terms, e.g., Socrates) or wicked (in deontological terms, e.g., Dostoievsky's (1866/1996) Raskolnikov), because such a life reveals his own genuine self.

As we will see in a later chapter of the book (chap. 8), the idea of authenticity has its own problems. One of them concerns the question whether the hidden self is something already there or something the individual creates or invents. This issue has important implications, because, if innate, it raises the idea of childhood as the locus in which the authentic self is at its best, because the socialization process threatens to alienate the individual from its inner nature.

How can the irrational inner self act as a moral source? For many scholars, the slogan "ethics of Romanticism" is an oxymoron. Its individualism, emotionalism, and subjectivism may seem to make it self-contradictory. For others, subjectivity does not necessarily imply egocentricity. To the contrary, the Romantic person should have a dialogue with the Other. He has to face him as "thou" and not as "it". As formulated by Buber, Gadamer, Levinas, Logstrup, Taylor, Honneth, and other philosophers, for someone to fulfill himself, he has to be in a constant dialogue with his fellows. He has to recognize that they are human beings who have their own inner selves in order to be recognized by them. This principle is presupposed, for example, by the ethics of the other (Levinas), the ethics of caring (Noddings), or the ethics of recognition (Honneth). It entails the feeling that the Other is a human being whose life is as important as yours, that you care about his well-being, that you search his intimacy. It is the love to the other which is at stake. Love is, therefore, an all-important relation in this Romantic framework. As Schlegel (1982) declares: "Only because of the power of love and the conscience of love - a man becomes a man." Love is a major driving force that can change the world. Reason attempts to oppress it (see Freud's, Eros and Civilization), but it has gone too far.

Differently put, Romanticism advances a new ethics of authenticity, based on the ideal that "each one of us has his/her own way of realizing our humanity, and that it is important to find and live out one's own, as against surrendering to conformity with a model imposed on us from outside..." (Taylor,2007, p. 475). The ethical theory underlying this approach centers on values like authenticity, integrity, truthfulness, sincerity, courage, and originality. The more connected the self will be to himself and to others, the better this self will be.

There is still another sense in which subjectivity does not imply selfishness. For many thinkers and artists it becomes evident that when you pursue subjectivity you finally find yourself in a position where you feel that you are part of a much broader reality. You feel that there is a whole, which is more than the mere sum of its part, and in which you can find your proper place. While still remaining a unique individual, you belong to something bigger than yourself, a unity that you want to identify with, because it endows your life with meaning. However, this Romantic feature has its own backslashes, since such a unity can be defined in a narrow nationalistic terms (see chap. 8).

The modern individual has three alternative moral sources to choose from, the external power, the enlightened rational mind, and the irrational Romantic soul. Each of these alternatives leads to a different worldview and a different way of life. Each of them has enormous impact on the way people identify themselves. Each of them may be represented by very different figures. Thus, for example, the enlightened individual may be the rational scientist, the professional manager, or the rich businessperson. The Romantic individual may be the authentic artist, the caring fellow, the passionate lover. The believer individual may be the faithful devotee, the missioner, or the pioneer.

There is, however, a fourth possibility from which to choose. The postmodern individual referred to in chapter 1 (first section). The postmodern individual believes that any meta-narrative presents a dangerous illusion which has to be abandoned (Lyotar, 1979). Hence, he does not want to be guided by any moral source. Once God is dead, the postmodern man lost his faith in any religion. Europe of the early modern era can attest that religions lead to intolerance, wars, and ignorance. Even the contemporary believer may regard all those who do not share his faith as heretics to be isolated from or disposed of. The postmodern individual is disappointed from reason as well. The malaise of modernity (the holocaust, the nuclear weapons, or the deployment of people and nature) made him suspect whether reason can provide happiness. And he is afraid of the dangers of Romanticism, of its nationalistic and fascistic disastrous outcomes (Nazism, world-wars, concentrations camps, genocide).

The postmodern individual loses his faith in any moral source. Consequently, he loses his identity, because he finds himself in a situation of "not knowing who is", a situation which Taylor refers to as 'identity crisis' (Taylor, 1989, 27). The disappointment in the three moral sources characterizes a new type of individual, which, following Bauman, we can call the 'liquid' individual. For him, everything is relative, and anything may be justified because there is no reliable compass, which can direct his life. Taylor regards this fourth alternative as an absurd. He sees it as a dead end road because it contradicts itself. To oppose any meta-narrative is, in its self, just another meta-narrative. But the obvious answer to the Taylor concern might be "who cares?" The liquid individual can choose to endorse an inconsistent belief system, because he deconstructs the modern logocentric approach.

Now, we can better understand the current education crisis. Education presupposes one of the three sources, so that their collapse delegitimizes its aims, and renders its whole *raison d'être* highly problematic. Unless we can vindicate some kind of moral source, education will be a in a hopeless state. I shall return to this crucial issue in the last chapter of the book (suggesting a possible fourth moral source, which might resolve the problem).

Two main implications of the three sources classification are important for the following discussion. The first is that each of the three sources entails a different characterization of human knowledge. The slogan of the enlightenment individual is "know your world". He wants to have a broad and valid picture of the physical, social and psychological aspects of his world. He regards scientifically approved knowledge as the only tool enabling him to exploit Nature for human benefits. The slogan of the Romantic individual is "know yourself". He looks after the meaning of life, and feels that this existential question can be answered only if he will be sensitive to Nature, to his human fellows, and to artistic creations of human spirit. The slogan of the believer is "know your God". Knowledge is, for him, "knowledge of good and evil". He has to know the divine laws and acknowledge their spirit in order to be to be a loyal missioner. Science, art, and faith denote the respective methods of acquiring the desired knowledge.

The second implication is that each of the three sources advances a different type of moral justification. Reason identifies good with happiness and suggests utilitarian ethics (do not lie because it may harm you). Romanticism suggests an ethics of authenticity (Taylor, 1991) in which the good is identified with sincerity, caring, dialogue, and solidarity (you do not lie because you love the Other and want to be sincere to yourself (cf. Stout, 2008)). The external source dictates a deontological ethic, directing to a life of musts and duties (you tell the truth because to lie is not permitted by some divine law). Moreover, each of the moral sources has a different criterion of what has to be checked in order to be counted as morally acceptable. Utilitarian reason stresses the outcome of our action; Romanticism emphasizes the process, while for the external source the all-important moral feature of any action is the intention that leads to its execution.

This normative aspect of the different moral sources is reflected in the different vocabulary that is typical to each. The major notions of the enlightenment source are: reason, rationality, progress, competition, success, efficacy, efficiency, transparency, accountability, proficiency, expertise, input-output, aim-means, profit, or career. The major notions of the Romantic source are authenticity, self-expression, self-fulfillment, dialogue, process, feelings, or creativity. The major notions of the external source are: mission, duty, fulfillment, obedience, devotion, sacrifice, solidarity, or modesty.

The picture is, of course, much more complicated. I present the three sources, as if they are mutually exclusive. Nevertheless, there are, as I shall examine below, interesting interconnections between them. The different ethical theories have complex influences on each other. Thus, for example, Kant offered a secular and individual notion of duty, based on "pure" reason, Utilitarianism might get support from the Protestant ethics, and religious thinkers such as Buber advances an ethics of authenticity, so that the suggested account will serve only as a first approximation.

When applied to the TEP level, the three diverse epistemological and ethical conceptions lead to different educational systems, which have diverse and sometimes contradictory, aims, curricula, and structure. Moreover, they entail quite different conceptions of the aims of teaching and the identity of the Teacher. The definition of a successful teacher is value laden, so that the various criteria of the "good" teacher reflect the relevant moral source. Thus, there is a difference between (1) the teacher who teaches biology or literature because he wants the students to succeed in the exams, or because he believes that what they learn will help them in life (the enlightenment moral source); (2) the teacher who teaches these same subject-matters to enhance the pupils self-understanding; or (3) the teacher who teaches these subjects because they attest the divine nature of God or Nature, so that the pupils' faith in their life long mission will be strengthened (the external moral source).

Not surprisingly, each one of these conceptions advances a different characterization of the good teacher:

1. Teaching can be regarded as a profession, and the teacher, as an enlightenment individual, is an expert practitioner, whose main aim is that the pupils will be knowledgeable.

2. Teaching can be regarded as an art, and the teacher, being a Romantic individual, is an authentic creator who loves his pupils and enhances his pupils' ability to self-fulfill themselves.

3. Teaching can be regarded as a duty, and the teacher, as a devoted believer, is a missioner whose obligation is to ascertain that the new generation will share his faith.

Each of these concepts puts forward a different question to be addressed in the preparation-to-teach process. The enlightened TEP's question is "what the teacher should know and be capable of"; the Romantic TEP's question is "who is the teacher and what is his personal and professional identity"; the externally driven TEP question is "what is the mission that the teacher should undertake and how to ascertain his loyalty to it". Clearly, each of these conceptions requires a different kind of TEP, in terms of the educational environment, the curriculum, the faculty, and the sought after students.

Enlightened TEPs will highlight the theoretical and practical knowledge that the teacher should acquire (Darling-Hammond & Bransford, 2005), and will emphasize the outcomes. Romantic TEPs will emphasize the empowerment process and highlight the dialogue between teachers and learners. The externally driven TEPs will emphasize the personal example that the teacher provides, and his devotion to his mission.

Hence, the importance of having a moral source is decisive to any TEP, and should be presented in the meta-theory I will endorse. However, once again it is necessary to remember that there is no "pure" TEP, and in reality, there is an interchange between the conceptions within any program. An interesting issue is to inquire how different TEPs have a different mixture of these contradictory conceptions.

THE PSYCHOLOGICAL DIMENSION

One fruitful way to articulate the links between a person's moral commitments and his self-identity is provided by Eric Fromm's (1976) theory of "Mode of Existence" (MoE)[8]. According to Fromm, the individual displays consistency in his reactions to its inner and outer world. This steadiness is influenced by a certain system of beliefs that he adopts (cf. Rand, 2009). The notion MoE refers to this steady system, which directs the individual's attitudes, priorities, aims, decisions, actions. It displays a potential human orientation toward self, society, and world, which determines his individual and social character (Fromm, 1976, p. 26).

Fromm postulates two such broad orientations: HAVING and BEING. Jacob Rand (2009) adds DOING as a third mode of existence. From the outset, it should be emphasized that although the three modes represent three different mutually exclusive orientations, in reality one barely finds a case of any "pure" orientation. The three Modes classification represents three "ideal type" distinctive categories, which cannot be found in their "pure" form. In fact, humans combine all the three and create a personal mode of existence, which displays their comparative significance (in terms of ranking their relative importance and impact on their life). Each typology is by its very nature simplistic and misleading. Reality is always more complex and complicated than any conceptualization. The merit of the theory comes from the fact that is directs our view of a certain phenomenon and enables a better understanding of what happens.

HAVING   In the HAVING mode of existence the self identifies himself according to what he possess. "*I am what I have*", says Fromm, meaning that "my property constitutes myself and my identity" (Fromm, 1976, p. 82). According to Rand, this mode characterizes the individual whose basic motive in life is to acquire things. For example, the desire to earn more and money reflects such an attitude. HAVING, however, is not restricted to material objects. An individual can have non-material objects if he feels that he owns them. For example, "I have a wife", "I have knowledge", "I have high status in the community", could be manifestations of HAVING in as much as the attitudes towards humans, knowledge, or society are part of the formula "I have more and therefore I worth more". In this MoE, the self reificates everything in terms of the value they add to his life.

BEING   This term designates the self, whose main motive in life is the search for meaning. It refers to an inclination to be conscious about the world and the self. Thus, BEING reflects becoming, in the sense of authentic self-fulfillment, regardless of the specific occupation or practices with which the individual is involved.

DOING   Represents the individual's inclination to partake in an active role in designing his environment. While activity itself is the important factor, its aim is to accomplish a socially important mission, and not self-egoistic benefits or his own self-fulfillment. Thus, DOING differs from BEING which concentrate on the inner self. It differs from HAVING as well, because its activities are not directed towards acquisition of wealth or of social status.

The similarity between this psychological theory and Taylor's views is apparent. The BEING MoE presupposes the Romantic moral source, while the DOING MoE presupposes the external moral source. As to HAVING, its origin is clearly within the instrumental rationality of the enlightenment source, but it gives to this source a predominant utilitarian interpretation, for it emphasizes its material manifestations.

Before we go on, let me clarify that these BEING, DOING, and HAVING notions are very different from a widespread conception of them. (A Google search contains no less than 2,610,000 items of the sequence Be-Do-Have in its list (26/06/2010.)) The following web site presents a dialogue between the author, Neale Donald Walsch, and "GOD", in which according to GOD:

> Most people believe if they "have" a thing (more time, money, love -- whatever), then they can finally "do" a thing (write a book, take up a hobby, go on vacation, buy a home, undertake a relationship), which will allow them to "be" a thing (happy, peaceful, content, or in love). In actuality, they are reversing the Be-Do-Have paradigm. In the universe as it really is (as opposed to how you think it is), "havingness" does not produce "beingness," but the other way around (http://www.taketheleap.com/create.html, 29/06/2010)[9].

Thus:

> Most of us have been taught that we need to HAVE things in our life to allow us to DO what we want, allowing us to BE who we want to be (i.e., 'When I HAVE more time, I will be able to DO the activities with my children therefore I will BE a better father'). In reality, we will never be the person we want to be if we wait to HAVE first. If you really want to HAVE ultimate success in ALL areas of your life (personal and in business) you really need to start BEING the person you want to be right from now. If it is financial freedom and happiness you are aiming for, then start being the person who is financially free and happy. Imagine that you are already financially free and start being that person. Walk like a person who is financially free. Make the choices that a person who is financially free will make. Do the things that a financially free person will do. Live like a financially free person will live. Feel like you are financially free! (http://www.squidoo.com/ BE_DO_HAVE_Principle; retrieved: 29/06/2010)

This "new age" approach to life may be profitable not only to spiritual or business coaches, but it clearly puts BEING as a mean to HAVING rather than as an aim in itself. Be-Do-Have becomes "a formula for success":

> In order to HAVE amazing customers, and amazing businesses, you must develop your business into one that will attract amazing customers. What is an amazing customer? It is specific to your business. Only you can define for yourself the characteristics of your amazing customer. Perhaps it includes a customer who always pays cash. Maybe one who sends you lots of referrals. You must identify who your amazing customers are and what these customers want. You must know how these customers shop. You must BE the place where these customers want to shop. (http://www.evancarmichael.com/Business-Coach/5/Be-Do-Have-a-Formula-For-Success.html; retrieved: 26/06/2010)

If HAVING means "what can I benefit from you", DOING signals "what can you do for me", and BEING denote "how can my/your being serve my having", the BE-DO-HAVE sequence has an entirely different meaning. The last point illustrates that MoE is not only a descriptive psychological theory. It is not value-neutral, because the factual question "what is the MoE of an individual?" should be supplemented by the normative question: "what should be his MoE"? The reason is that Fromm himself warned against the dominance of the HAVING MOE in the modern world. For him, the BEING MoE alone can salvage the individual from the malaise of modernity, in which the other human being is, almost necessarily reified. Fromm was not the first to endorse the dichotomy between BEING and HAVING. It was the young Karl Marx who declares in his *Economic-Philosophic-Manuscripts-1844*, that "The less you are, the less you express your own life, the more you have" (Marx, 19322000). As Trilling summarizes, "There was no question at all of what diminished the experience of self – the great enemy of being was *having*" (1972, p. 122).

The relationships between the moral sources and the modes of existence are quite complex. To a first approximation, Enlightenment can justify HAVING through the utilitarian ethics. It may support BEING if the individual sees the attainment of knowledge as self-fulfillment, and although it opposes religion, it may legitimize DOING in its secular version, when theory becomes ideology. Romanticism strongly supports BEING, although it may legitimize DOING, if the individual's inner feeling reveals that he is part of a sublime reality, while HAVING is usually seen as an obstacle to genuine authentic life. External belief can legitimize HAVING (as in Protestant Ethics). It can support BEING as is the case in some religious sects. However, its natural MoE is DOING. I shall return to these observations in later chapters of the book.

MoE theory has a special relevance to teachers. First, empirical studies reveal that Israeli teachers, including teacher-students, share a dominant MoE, which integrates, the three Modes in the hierarchical order: BEING > DOING > HAVING (Reichenberg & Sagy, 2003; Rand & Shkolnik, 2009). The respondents in these studies sympathize with Aoki who claims that "…Teaching is fundamentally a mode of being… What matters most in the situated world of the classroom is how the teachers' "doings flow from who they are, their beings" (T. Aoki, 2005, p. 160). They share with Palmer the conviction that "…We teach who we are… As I teach, I project the condition of my soul onto my students, my subject, and our way of being together… Teaching holds a mirror to the soul… and knowing myself is as crucial to good teaching as knowing my students and my subject" (1998, p. 2). Palmer just reiterates Janusz Korczak, who recommends that educators "Be what you are – find your own way – Know yourself before you get to know the children" (1929/1974, I, p. 285). They do not hesitate to mention that they love the children, care about them, and want to enhance their development. (In this respect, they do not differ from other teachers around the globe. See, for example, Alexander, 2010, p. 408, for an account of how British teachers view their job.)

Second, and a bit less important, teachers view teaching as devotion. They endorse the claims that the teacher should be a moral guide for the children, and serve as a model of the "correct" behavior. (Interestingly enough, but clearly anticipated, religious teachers reverse the order of modes. DOING is more important for them than BEING.) Only then, they are interested in HAVING aspects such as their salaries, or their social status as teachers.

Reichenberg and Sagy claim that this is not only a descriptive finding about the MoE of those who choose to be teachers. For them this factor suggests a main reason for choosing teaching as an occupation. In their opinion, "the hierarchical pattern is pragmatically useful because it enhances the correspondence between the teacher's personality and his system of values and the educational needs he want to address in his work" (2003, p. 68).

This research discloses the intimate connection between the personal and the professional identity of the teachers. It casts doubt on the widespread sociological accounts that insist on a sharp demarcation between spheres of activity (Webb, 2006, p. 170). Labaree points out that even professions devoted to human improvement, demand that the professionals will keep an emotional distance from their clients (2004, p. 45 – 51). However, such a professional distance may be a hindrance to good teaching (p. 46 – 50).

The teachers' typical BEING > DOING > HAVING MoE centers on the ideal of self-fulfillment (I fulfill myself when I educate others), which the teachers interpret as a mission they have on behalf of their pupils and their society. If this attitude can be generalized it may explain the uneasiness of teachers and teacher educators in the prevailing HAVING climate of the educational system (besides being paid relatively low salaries in this society). So now, we face the normative question: Should the BEING > DOING > HAVING sequence characterizes the teachers' MoE? Is it appropriate for a society in which HAVING MoE is the ideal MoE? Maybe the negative neo-liberal attitude towards TEP, discussed above, is, after all, justifiable?

Moral source theory provides a hint which can help us understand why the postmodern condition is perilous to education as a human endeavor. MoE theory points to the problematic state of the teacher in a HAVING driven society. Many teachers, who, as professionals, endorse the BEING > DOING > HAVING MoE, confront the HAVING society with which they identify as individuals. This troubled situation leads to an identity crisis. In many western countries, there is a profound gap between the way teachers and educators see their vocation, and the way it is regarded by today's consumer society. While society wants them to be efficient in preparing pupils to succeed in the exams, the teachers desire to develop their pupils' personality. These are two opposing conceptions of what it means to prepare the pupils for life. However, nobody is attentive to the teachers' professional voice. Society does not recognize the right of the teachers, as professionals, to decide about their professional work. Consequently, the teachers struggle for recognition, but their lack of power leads to submission and frustration. It is this struggle for recognition which explains why it is so important for teachers and teacher educators to win the battle, and why do they not give a "who cares?" or a "so what?" response to this challenge.

The teachers' poor social status in many countries is not only a question of low salaries. Salaries are just the symptom. It is mainly a question of recognition. Contempt and disrespect cause frustration and abuse. No wonder in many western countries it is hard to recruit good candidates to the profession, and that so many beginning teachers leave their occupation during the first years of work. To address the issue, of how recognition affects identity, I turn to Axel Honneth's "struggle for recognition" theory.

THE SOCIAL DIMENSION

In the context of Honneth theory (1995; 2002; 2003; 2004; 2008), the term recognition (*Anerkennug*) refers to granting of social status. The main tenet of his theory is that the dominant drive of humans, both as individuals and as collectives, is their craving for recognition. Hobbes claims that humans are involved in a constant "war of all against all", and form a society because they are forced to. Honneth, to the contrary, follows Hegel, and believes that humans, by their very nature, are social animals who seek the proximity of others. Man can properly grow and attain self-fulfillment only if he is recognized by his society. He cannot develop his personal identity without receiving a feedback to his actions from society. The self assimilates this external recognition and transforms it into self-recognition. Self-recognition, and hence self-identity, crucially depends on the self being recognized by others. Honneth believes that any individual, in order to have normal development, must gain confidence in his cognitive capacities and trust his feelings and emotions towards others. The very possibility to become a fully autonomous and independent person depends on an attitude of acceptance of the self by himself. However, recognition is not something "given". It has to be fought for by the individual. The "struggle for recognition" is the major cause of human social behavior.

Today, according to Honneth, there are three different modes of recognition, and each of them nurtures a different kind of self-recognition. The first mode is addressed toward certain individuals, being singular in some respect (e.g., being my partner, child, or friend). The second mode is addressed toward any person *qua* being human, and the third one is addressed toward a particular person because he has certain characteristics or features (e.g., being famous, rich person, or professional expert).

The manifestations of these three modes of recognition are emotional. The feelings of: self-confidence is an outcome of love relationships; self-respect is an outcome of institutional relations of respect for the autonomy, dignity, and human rights; and self-esteem is the outcome of having publically acknowledged social value. Lack of recognition is critical to human well-being, and results in dreadful feelings of being abused or raped (denial of love), excluded (denial of rights) or insulted (denial of esteem) (Honneth, 1995, p. 129). Without love, rights, and esteem, the possibility to become an autonomous person is seriously impaired.

Love Honneth learns from Donald Winnicott's object-relations psychoanalytic theory that love is essential to self-confidence. For Honneth, "Love relationships are to be understood… as referring to primary relationships insofar as they – on the model of friendships, parent-child relationships, as well as erotic relationships between lovers – are constituted by strong emotional attachment among a small number of people" (p. 95). As Honneth emphasizes, "We assert nothing less than that the human relationship to the self and the world is in the first instance not only genetically, but also categorically bound up with an affirmative attitude, before more neutralized orientations can subsequently arise" (Honneth, 2008, p. 35).

As the individual moves from the safe surroundings of his family to the much larger and less intimate society, it becomes impossible that love will continue to provide the basis for recognition. The individual must enter society and seek after another kind of recognition, which will not depend on intimate personal relationships. Honneth believes that there is a crucial difference between the familial-based and the societal-based modes of recognition. In contradistinction to love, which is a universal and almost socially unchangeable feeling towards certain individuals, the societal types of recognition are culturally dependent, and have different characteristics in different societies.

In fact, the modern era witnessed a major change in these characteristics. The societal-based kind of recognition in the pre-modern era had been dignity. Dignity had been granted to a person because of his social status. Usually this status had nothing to do with the person himself. It had been awarded to someone because he had some inherited characteristics. "Being the son of…" was the important factor. The stratum to which the person was born was an innate feature which dictated his proper social position, his estate, his occupation, his marriage options, etc. It also dictated his social merit and the rights he would attain Different social classes accord their members with different rights. Granting dignity to a certain individual shows that the he knew his proper place in his social world.

All this has changed in the modern era. The rise of the nation state, industrialization and secularization processes assign a definite role to the individual *qua* individual. In a climate, in which the individual's fate depends on what he does, the notion of dignity has to be modified as well. According to Honneth, it has been bifurcated into two different notions. The first, respect, signifies that the individual has to be recognized as a human being, who has certain rights and duties. The second, esteem, means that he has to be recognized according to his contributions to society. The first of these new modes of recognition is universal and impersonal. The second – is particular and personal.

Law Every human being, regardless of his social stratum, gender, occupation, political ideas, race, religion, etc., is an autonomous individual who has certain human rights which have to be protected. In the modern era this protection is provided by the juristic system in which the law, the court, and the police guard the autonomy of the individual and avert the threat that he will harm others' autonomy. The basic value behind modern law is equality. Everyone is equal to any other because everyone has the same human nature to be respected and protected. To be equal to everybody else, to have the same status before the law, presupposes that there is a certain relation of mutual recognition, in which the individual unconditionally respects the others as human beings and is respected by them as well. Such a reciprocal relationship develops the individual's self-respect. He respects himself as an autonomous human being. Otherwise, if the individual's rights are violated, he feels oppressed, discriminated or excluded, and justifiably can claim for his rights.

The struggle for recognition is, again, a struggle for autonomy and independence. Unlike the former notion of dignity, which presupposes conformity and obedience, the legal mode of recognition guarantees that there are individual (and group) rights, which do not depend on who he is or what he does. Every individual has the right to be authentic, to do it "his own way", as far as he does not hinder this right from the other, thus advancing the enlightenment spirit of fairness, equity, and justice.

Social value The second mode of societal recognition, which evolved in the modern era, refers to persons *qua* individuals. Once the predestined dignity is no longer available, the need for a new mode of recognition emerges, which has to do with how the person is acknowledged for what he does as an individual. Thus, while the legal mode of recognition is egalitarian and prescribes equal respect to any person *qua* person, the social value mode differentiates between people according to some criterion of merit. The more the individual meets this criterion, the more social esteem he is granted, and the more social esteem he is given, the more he develops his self-esteem. "To have the sense that one has nothing of value to offer is to lack any basis for developing a sense one's own identity" (Anderson, 1995, p. xvi).

This mode of recognition raises the question of what counts as worthy in a given society. Not everything a man does bears the same social esteem. Homemaker work or certain low paid occupations get relatively little esteem in our society, while big tycoons or TV stars get enormous public appreciation. Thus, this mode of recognition is related to society's values, preferences and priorities (van den Brinck & Owen, 2007, p. 14).

For Honneth, in today's capitalistic society, the underlying principle of social esteem is the "achievement" principle:

> With the gradual establishment of the new value model asserted by the economically rising bourgeoisie against the nobility, the estate-based principle of honor... lost its validity, so that the individual social standing now become normatively independent of origin and possession. The esteem the individual legitimately deserved within society was no longer decided by membership in an estate with corresponding codes of honor, but rather by individual achievement within the structure of the industrially organized division of labor... Each was to enjoy social esteem according to his or her achievement as a "productive citizen."... (Honneth, 2003, p. 141)

The modern principle of achievement, in our capitalistic, neo-liberal regime is one-dimensional. It emphasizes life's financial aspect, and especially, it intermeshes payment and respect. Material success becomes the one all-important factor of esteem. The fate of the poor becomes highly awkward. Unlike the dignified place of the poor in the traditional Christian society, in today's attitude, to be poor, is to be miserable, because to be poor is a shame. It is the consequence of the individual's own failures since (as the second mode of recognition ascertains) he has been given an equal opportunity to prosper.

Thus a struggle of recognition arises, which presents a struggle about the interpretation of the achievement principle (Honneth, 2003, p. 137). The fact that teachers, being mostly women, have lower social status (p. 154) and have to wrestle to be recognized as equal to men in their contribution to society, is just an example of this kind of struggle.

The achievement principle does not have to be based on financial criteria, and award social esteem to those who are more affluent. It can be based on merit and award social esteem to the experts, the professional specialists, or the outstanding performer, sportsman, musician. But both criteria are problematic for teaching because they emphasis the outcome and not the process. Teaching does not have an immediate impact on pupils. The only way to evaluate the immediate results of teaching is to focus on measurable achievements of pupils at tests, but this is a limited aspect of the teachers' work.

In many countries, the social esteem of the teachers is relatively low. Teaching is mainly a feminine vocation, and it is seen as an easy occupation because it deals with children. A common belief is that everyone can be a teacher, and consequently, teaching is not recognized as genuine profession (Labaree, 2004). Teachers have restricted professional autonomy, and their salary is relatively small. Teachers lack the autonomy and the prestige of genuine specialists. (For example, in many Hollywood films, model teachers enter a problematic class, for the first time in their career, and succeed to rescue their excluded pupils exactly because they lack any professional preparation.)

TEPs fair no better. Even when located within the academic environment, the status of the faculty of education is one of the lowest in the entire academic sphere (Clifford, & Guthrie, 1988; Lagemann, 2000; Labaree, 2004). The status of TEP is even worse, being the weakest part of the education faculty. In many academic institutions, the TEP does not have a full academic status, as it is only a supplementary program leading to a professional certificate and not to an academic degree. Many teacher educators do not have full university staff status. They are "practitioners" who are not research oriented, and lack academic recognition.

The denial of recognition, in all of its three modes, leads to possible damages to the individual's physical, psychical, and social integrity. Hence, it may hamper the very possibility of his self-fulfillment (Honneth, 1995, p. 129). Moreover, in a recent augmentation of his theory, Honneth suggests that lack of recognition threatens to impair the individual cognitive development, because "cognition presupposes recognition", and when there is no recognition (especially, but not exclusively, of the first mode) the individual reificates human relationships, and his ability to cognize the social world is severely damaged (Honneth, 2008). While this theoretical expansion can be contested (see the exchanges ibid), it provides another indication for the theory breadth and fruitfulness.

Honneth theory has an essential normative aspect. "The recognition of human dignity", he claims, "comprises a central principle of social justice" (Honneth, 2004, p. 352). This aspect is partly descriptive. The experience of social injustice is explained in terms of the withholding of some type of recognition held to be legitimate. However, the theory also has an evaluative component:

> The turn to the normative becomes necessary as soon as we are no longer discussing how present-day social struggles are to be appropriately analyzed theoretically, but turn to the question of their moral evaluation. It is obvious that we cannot approve of every political uprising as such, nor hold every demand for recognition to be morally legitimate or defensible. Rather, in general we judge the objectives of such struggles to be positive only when they point in the direction of a societal development that we can grasp as coming closer to our notions of a good or just society… [Therefore] a political ethics or societal morality must be tailored to the quality of societally guaranteed recognition relations. The justice or wellbeing of a society is measured according to the degree of its ability to secure conditions of mutual recognition in which personal identity formation, and hence individual self-realization, can proceed sufficiently well. (Honneth, 2004, p. 354)

A struggle for recognition can be of two different kinds. It can arise out of an agreement with the hegemonic criteria of recognition, and the problematic issue is, accordingly, the feeling of not getting the proper respect. In that case, the struggle for recognition is a sign of existing problems in a given society. It is not about inventing a different mode of recognition or a novel criterion of esteem, but about the fair distribution of the agreed upon criteria of recognition. Alternatively, the struggle can arise out of a rebel against the hegemonic criteria of recognition, believing that other criteria are more suitable to Man's life. This possibility is revolutionary. It aims to change society's moral source or its prevalent Mode of Existence, because therein lies the justification of the revolt. What are at stake are the values of the society, its ideals, and its preferences.

The various modes of recognition and their ideal interconnections require justification, which presupposes a certain moral source (E.g.: Enlightenment can justify both the achievement principle (a utilitarian means-end ethics), and the *law* (universal Kantian rule-case ethics); Romanticism can justify *love* and caring; and the external believer can justify the traditional notion of honor).Therefore, it seems appropriate that in what follows I will address the modes of recognition theory mainly when there is a need to shed light on a certain problematic situation in which teachers and teacher educators struggle for recognition.

For example, it is generally recognized that teachers' vocation is highly important to society's future. The problem is that teachers have a very different criterion of self-esteem which has to do with the first mode of recognition. Teachers care for their pupils. They love them. They want them to grow up and develop. However, teaching as an act of love is quite problematic in an age in which love is interpreted in sexual terms (in some countries the teacher is prevented from hugging the children even in kindergarten), and showing one's emotions is seen as unprofessional act. In many modern societies the teachers' work is not recognized as professional. It has to do with children who do not, yet, accomplish anything valuable, and being mainly a feminine work, it becomes *in loco parentis* in another sense whatsoever; it merits the same, relatively low social esteem.

THE MERGING EFFECT

The philosophical, the psychological, and the sociological aspects of identity formation interact in various ways and influence different ideals of personal identity. For instance, a common possibility to mix the three is to rely on the enlightenment moral source, with a strong emphasize on rational instrumentality and utilitarian ethics, to add to it the HAVING mode of existence and the wish to be recognized according to the achievement principle of self-esteem. This combination is, of course, just a formula. To be a basis for personal identity characterization, it has to be filled with a detailed analysis of what that person means by each of these terms. He has to explicate his utilities and preferences. He has to state what HAVING amounts to. He has to define the meaning he gives to the notion "achievement". This example is quite straightforward because the three aspects are complementary. It is easy to conceive of a continuous link between the idea that everyone should fight for his own interests combined with a materialistic world-view in which happiness depends on wealth, a desire to have more resources, and a belief that material success is responsible for social esteem Another individual believes in Romantic ideals of self-development, creativity, caring, and dialogue. He connects them to the BEING mode of existence, and regards his social esteem as being dependent upon his being sincere and loyal to his inner self. Still another person may be part of a community of believers in which one's main target is to fulfill his duties. He is fully obliged to the DOING mode of existence and the social-esteem criterion which accordingly correlates esteem and devotion. The more faithful and loyal he is to the community's beliefs, the more social-esteem he will receive.
.There are much more complex cases in which the three aspects pull toward different or even opposing directions, thus causing inner conflicts and identity crises. A believer who judges himself upon a materialistic achievement principle is a case in point. He may receive social esteem, but, unless he adopts the "Protestant

Ethics", having more money is not necessarily a sign that he faithfully conforms to his moral duties and obligations. This might be so even if he is charitable and generous if these behaviors come from utilitarian beliefs. A man of BEING may believe that the moral source, which prescribes his activities, is divine, and that he has to cultivate his own individuality for God's sake. This attitude may turn out to be problematic if God's demands require a personal sacrifice. Again, an enlightenment individual may feel that he has a duty to rescue a sick child, although it might require that he lose money for no benefit. In all these examples, to understand one's identity, it is important to estimate the relative influence of each of the aspects, and to appreciate their exact blending into a whole.

Such a blending characterizes the TEPs as well. It is possible to create a portrait of some ideal cases, in which there is a full congruence between the three aspects, although it is more common to find blending cases in which inner tensions and conflicts are prevalent. However, to simplify the discussion I shall focus on the following types of TEPs:

1. An Enlightenment inspired TEP: Teaching is regarded as a profession, and the teacher is an expert practitioner, whose main aim is that the pupils will be knowledgeable. It is possible to further differentiate between TEPs which regard the teacher as an "educated" person and those who focus on his being expert in a certain discipline. Usually, the enlightemned TEPs are (i) HAVING driven (knowledge is power), or (ii) BEING driven (through the concept of *Bildung*[10] *durch Wissenschaft* [education through knowledge]). In both cases, the social esteem of teaching is dictated by the achievement principle, although each of them uses a different criterion of esteem.

2. A Romantic inspired TEP: Teaching can be regarded as an art, and the teacher, being a Romantic individual is an authentic creator who loves his pupils and enhances his their ability to self-fulfill themselves. Usually it is BEING driven whose social esteem is dictated by love, caring, and dialogue.

3. An External Belief inspired TEP: Teaching can be regarded as a duty, and the devoted believer teacher, as a missioner whose obligation is to ascertain that the new generation will join his faith. Usually it is DOING driven whose social esteem is dictated by loyalty to the community and its laws and by a faithful devotion to its creed.

The next chapters (3-9) elaborate and expand this preliminary picture:

a) Chapters 3-6 present the Enlightenment inspired TEPs: Chapter 3 introduces the philosophical background of the Enlightenment. It discusses two versions the idea of reason (Formal and Substantial) and clarify their main features with regards to two forms of reasoning (theoretical and practical). The discussion of practical reasoning will disclose two types of ethics (means-ends utilitarian ethics and rule-case deontological ethics), each leading to a different ideals of Modes of Existence and different criteria of Recognitions. Thereafter, chapters 4-6 describe three consecutive phases of development of TEPs in which the Enlightenment's ideals are enacted in different ways.

b) Chapter 7 presents the External-Believer inspired TEPs. It introduces the background of the communalities between the religious and the secular variants of this kind of TEPs and describes various TEPs which implement them.

c) Chapter 8-9 present the Romantic inspired TEPs: Chapter 8 introduces the philosophical background of Romanticism. It discusses its main concepts, tenets, and moral ideals. Chapter 9 describes various TEPs which exemplify this approach.

HAVING REASON

A common approach to analyze a given TEP is to reveal its aims, examine how it reaches them, and estimate its success in achieving them. Trying to understand the program's rationale, we want to learn about its educational philosophy. We want to disclose the connection between what is declared about the prospective teacher and what is actually done to prepare him for the profession. We approach the issues of the scientific basis of the program, and its ethical justification. We evaluate its consistency, efficiency, efficacy, responsibility, and accountability. We postulate that its quality depends on its 'fitness for purpose', and we evaluate whether it is successful.

Notions, such as analysis, aims, rationale, efficiency or accountability, indicate that we are exploring a kingdom whose people speak the language of *logos* (a term whose ancient Greek meaning is both 'word' and 'thought'). In this enlightened kingdom, the only legitimate governor is the human reason, and the only respectable citizen is the independent autonomic individual who enthusiastically obeys the dictates of his own reasoning.

The enlightened man liberates himself from the authority of God and his priests. He rejects the sovereignty of any tradition, and believes that reason alone enables humans to deal with all the problems they face. He sees himself as a free agent who is not afraid to set aside customary dogmas and conventional knowledge. He believes that only because of this world-view, aptly called 'modern', he can gain liberty, progress, and prosperity. Reason enhances the ideals of human rights and democracy, equity, and equality. It gave birth to the French and American revolutions. It enables the rise of science and the achievements of technology. Scientific discoveries and technological innovations empower the industrial revolution and enable the hegemony of the man around the globe. Indeed, the vision, that reason will inevitably enhance improvement and progress, has been realized in the modern era. The world looks very different from how it looked in 500 years ago. Evidently, humans, who are free to use their own reason, conquer the moon, expand their material wealth, and live longer, healthier, easier and happier lives.

The enlightenment's spirit is best captured by H.G. Wells, who says about Mr. Barnstaple, the hero of his novel *Men Like Gods*: "at the back of [his] mind… had been the persuasion that presently everything would be known and the scientific process come to an end. And then we should be happy for ever after" (Wells, 1923).

This picture is oversimplified and too optimistic. As we shall see, there are good reasons to suspect its soundness. A strong case can be made for the claim that the use of reason has detrimental and even dangerous outcomes as well. However, the enlightenment's focus on reason and reasoning has tremendous impact on education and on teacher education. Most TEPs are conducted in academic institutions, the shrines of the enlightenment kingdom of reason, so it is appropriate to examine some of this world-view's notions and tenets.

To begin with, there is the notion of 'reason' itself. It is far from clear what the notion denotes and what is its exact meaning. Some of the conceptual problems around the notion are centered on two basic issues, which are important to our context. The first is the distinction between theoretical and practical reason and the second, the demarcation between formal and substantive reason. In this chapter I examine these two issues, and in the next two chapters I explore their relevance to teacher education.

THEORETICAL AND PRACTICAL REASON

The first conceptual distinction is between theoretical and practical reason. Theoretical reason addresses the descriptive question "what is there?" The theory's outcome is theoretical knowledge ("knowing that" or declarative knowledge), which is centered on the notion of "truth". Practical reason addresses the normative question "what should be done". Its outcome is practical knowledge ("knowing how" or procedural knowledge). It is focused on the notion of "good" (good behavior, good artifact). The difference between the two kinds of knowledge is decisive. It is possible to know that something should be done without knowing how to do it. It is possible to know what is good to do without the possibility or motivation to do it (to stop smoking). From the other side, it is possible to know how to do something (swim, calculate mathematical equations, or write novels) without knowing the theory which explains these activities.

The theory-practice bifurcation has a long history. Its enlightenment salient spokesmen are Hume and Kant, and its prominent ancient Greek representative is Aristotle. Aristotle (1984, E.N.) not only demarcates between theoretical and practical knowledge, but further maintains that each of them is further divided into two types. Theoretical knowledge includes *sophia* and *episteme*. *Episteme* refers to specific knowledge in a certain domain (such as physics, biology, or psychology), while *sophia* refers to general, non-empirical, knowledge (e.g., logic, mathematics, metaphysics). Practical knowledge includes *techne* (proficiency, skill, craft knowledge) and *phronesis* (practical prudence). The difference between *techne* and *phronesis* is that while *technical* knowledge helps to actualize goals that are external to the action, *phronetic* knowledge helps achieve goals that are intrinsic to the action. The *techne*'s artifact or outcome is distinct from the process of its production, and it is attained only after the process of its production is completed. To bake a cake is *techne*. So long as the baking activity continues, the cake is not yet ready, and only after the baking terminates, the cake is ready. The *phrosesis*' outcome is the process itself. Aristotle's typical example of *phronesis* is seeing. One does not look at something, close his eyes and then see. Life is another example. To live, and especially to live well, is life's sole aim. There may be aims in life but not aims of (or to) life. Aristotle claims that man does not live in order to accomplish certain external goals. As soon as someone dies, there is no further purpose that his life can achieve. In a similar manner, following Dewey (1916), if one equates life with education, it is evident that education as such has no external aim.

Another difference between *techne* and *phronesis* is that *techne* provides the answer to the productive question, "How do you do?) ...., in order to yield ...., or effect....?" It is 'know-how' knowledge in a certain definite area. *Techne* has to do with knowledge of effective means-end causal links in a concrete area, so that the *technitas*, the man who possesses *techn*ical knowledge in this area, knows how to achieve certain aims. *Phronetic* knowledge relates to the question, "How can I live my life so that I can achieve my well-being?" It conveys general 'know-how' knowledge that applies to human behavior in all of its aspects, since it relates to the virtues of the "good" man. Thus, *phronesis* is about one's own life in general, and how to make improvements therein. The *phronimon*, the man who has *phronesis*-type knowledge, knows to do "the right things and from the right motive, in the right way and at the right time" (Aristotle, 1984, E.N., III, 7, 1115^b 18, cf.: II, 9, 1109^a 27-28), in order to attain his well-being.

In Aristotelian terms, formal teaching is *techne*. It is an activity whose ends are external to the process of teaching itself. (Teaching mathematics in ninth grade is not the aim of teaching mathematics in ninth grade). It is, however, a very special kind of *techne*, since the aim of teaching might be theoretical knowledge (if one teaches science or logic), or practical knowledge. In the second case, it might be *techne* (if one teaches spelling, driving, or engineering) or *phronesis* (if one deals with moral or political education). While it is controversial whether theoretical knowledge is teachable in the sense of 'being transmitted', it is clear that practical knowledge cannot be simply poured into the learner's head. Experience is an essential ingredient for becoming master (*technitas*) in a special productive domain. Without practice the required skills cannot be mastered. Similarly, *phronesis* can be acquired only through practice, because one becomes morally prudent only by being morally good, and not by talking about beeing moral. Instead of being a 'transmitter' of knowledge, the teacher is responsible for structuring an environment in which moral behavior can be fortified (Aristotle, 1984, E.N., X, 9).

Accordingly, TEPs are complex hybrids which mesh theory and practice. They combine 'knowledge that' and 'knowledge how', and raise questions about the mutual relationships between them, about the proper environment to teach and learn them, and the proper methods to do so. They involve *techne* and *phronesis* and address the perplexing relations between the professional and the personal, between the efficient and the moral.

The modern demarcation between theoretical and practical reason is principled. David Hume (1740/1978, p. 469) famously declares that it is logically impossible to infer an "ought" statement from an "is" one. Individuals, who fully agree about the facts, can reasonably and legitimately infer different conclusions about what they ought to do in a certain state of affairs, if their deliberations begin with different aims and values. Consequently, it is illegitimate to proceed from 'what there is' to 'what should be'. It is logically prohibited to infer the 'good' from the 'true', the normative from the descriptive.

What the teacher does when he faces a decrease in student attendance depends upon his aims and values. He will behave differently if he interprets such a decrease as a sign of the pupils' indifference, as a sign of their autonomy, or as a sign that they have a serious personal or social problem. Similarly, his reaction when his pupils 'copy and paste' some assignment from each other depends on his values and aims. He can ignore the issue, if his only target is that they will achieve good grades. He can be very angry if being honest is the 'name of the game'. He can be more considerate if what counts is learning, and he believes that this special case of 'copy and paste' helps them learn. He can even support it, if collaboration and cooperation is what he wants to cultivate.

The facts by themselves do not entail 'what should be done'. The aims of teaching (the 'ought') cannot be inferred from the context in which they arise (the 'is'). Although these aims are connected to the context (the rate of attendance, the percentage of successful pupils, the amount of violence etc.), they are independent from the facts, in the sense that it is possible to have different reactions to the same state of affairs. Some of the different reactions mirror disagreements about values, aims and preferences. Such disagreements are always normative.

The implication of this tenet to TEPs is obvious. The aims of any program cannot be derived from the real context in which it operates. They are inferred from the values of those involved in the relevant situation. After positing the ends, the means to attain them are disclosed by a reasoning process which involves 'means-end' deliberation. This kind of kind of reasoning is usually called formal or instrumental.

FORMAL AND SUBSTANTIAL REASON

Hume takes sides in another contentious issue. Reason can be a special source of knowledge or merely an instrument to analyze the data gathered from other sources, such as the senses or the desires. In the first case, reason is substantial. It provides a unique type of knowledge. It has certain content. It tells us something *a priori* about ourselves or about the world. In the second case, reason is formal. At most, it tells something about our thinking faculty. It specifies the forms of valid argument, no matter what its specific content is, or who is in favor of the argument.

The debate about the proper function of reason is the core of the philosophical dispute between the Rationalists and the Empiricists. The Rationalists (e.g., Descartes, Spinoza, and Leibniz) hold the first point of view, while the Empiricists (e.g., Locke, Berkeley, Hume), opt for the second. Kant proposes a controversial compromise. He suggests that our perception of the world is constructed by our cognition. This construction is not only formal. It includes substantial categories, principles, and mental schema, which organize the sense-data and provide the building blocks of knowledge. The debate is ongoing. It is reflected, for instance, in different learning theories (Behaviorism [Watson, Skinner], Nativism [Chomsky],

Constructivism [Piaget, Vigotsky]), which strongly influenced the educational arena in the last century. It has a remarkable impact on both the content of TEPs and the learning environment they construct.

Despite the differences, the three philosophies share the tenet that formal reasoning is an essential element in the quest for the "true" and the "good", because it prevents the danger of contradiction.

Formal Reasoning

Contradiction is the bitter enemy of reason. It is the main symptom of irrationality. We cannot comprehend someone, who declares that this piece of paper is simultaneously both white and not white, and literally means what he says. As already mentioned (chap. 2), formal reasoning is individualistic, objective, and disengaged. First, to be rational requires that each individual can think by himself about the implications of his beliefs or values. Second, although individualistic, reason is neither subjective nor capricious. Reason is objective, universal, eternal, and absolute. The axioms of formal logic are valid no matter who performs the calculations, or the specific content of a certain argument[11]. The laws of logic, such as 'a=a' [meaning 'a is identical to a'), are valid exactly as the mathematical statement 1+1=2. The verbal phrase 'my private reason' is as meaningless as the verbal phrase 'a rectangular circle'. Third, this line of thinking justifies the idea of the disengaged mind. Rationality means that given that one's aims, preferences, and beliefs are fully articulated, it is necessary that any other person, who accepts the same premises, will arrive at the same conclusion. It is not important who is thinker but how he thinks. For instance, in science, the focus is on the scientific method: the validity of the scientist's reasoning and his arguments, and the reliability of his experiments (that they can be repeated). Similarly, practical deliberation should be "cold" in the sense that it should be a careful calculation. Rational decision must be justified. It cannot be a mere instance of uncontrolled feelings. It should be taken or understood by anyone who pursues the same process.

Formal reasoning checks the validity of our arguments. It does not deal with their soundness. In other words, it examines whether the conclusions necessarily derived from the premises, not whether they are necessarily true. One can logically derive a false conclusion if one begins with false premises. Thus, one can be rational (in the sense of deriving a correct calculation) but not reasonable (in the sense of deriving a true conclusion). That the laws of logic are formal means that being rational is insufficient for being reasonable. The premises of any argument should be true or acceptable in order to arrive at a sound or reasonable conclusion. Any paranoid is a rational individual who starts from insane premises. But is there a rational method to arrive at true premises? The answer to this question depends on the type of knowledge involved and on the philosophical stance you adopt.

Theoretical formal reasoning

For the empiricists, there is an objective world out there. It consists of facts (Wittgenstein, 1922/1961), which are solely material and their existence is independent of any human mind. The world is ordered. In its very essence, it is but a very huge machine. Like a computer, it can be digitalized and programmed. As for theoretical reason, Empiricism holds that the scientific method, based on induction, is the only path to attain sound knowledge. You carefully gather data, generalize over the facts, test your generalizations, and at last you arrive at a valid theory.

The scientific method encompasses the following features:

1. Scientific knowledge should be transparent, publicly validated, and carefully examined. It should be objective. Mere subjective impressions or casual perceptions cannot be trusted. Careful observations and experiments, combined with valid logical, mathematical and statistical reasoning, enable the scientists to generalize over the facts, discover the laws of nature and disclose the knowledge required to devise technological innovations.

2. Science cannot deal with unobservable, spiritual or mystical realms. It has no access to supernatural worlds or to invisible realities. Material facts (sense-data) are the only phenomena that humans can have knowledge of.

3. The success of science is due to its strategy. It replaces the Aristotelian search for hidden quality with an inquiry of changes in quantities. Instead of asking what the essence of a given phenomenon is, it asks how it changes. (The physicist does not inquire the nature of "force", and the psychologist does not explore the essence of IQ. Both only know how to measure them.)

4. Scientific research does not refer to an overall picture of a certain phenomenon but analyzes its visible constituents (usually called variables). The hallmark of the scientific method is its emphasize on cause-effect (or correlational) relations between its variables, which can be discovered only after a thoughtful analysis of the phenomenon is carried out. This enables a mathematization of the world, which, through the formulation of precise and unequivocal formulas, enables humans to predict events and control the world.

5. To attain a generalizable knowledge, amidst the complexity of any real situation, the data should be simplified. It is necessary to construct a model which ignores certain elements (regarded as "noise") and concentrates on those which promise to be fruitful in finding natural laws and regularities.

Wells predicts that science will disclose all the secrets of nature, and sooner or later, humans will have full knowledge of every phenomenon. This optimistic view has been radically changed in the twentieth century. It has been acknowledged that inductive reasoning cannot guarantee the "truth", and that the scientific process cannot come to an end. Scientific knowledge grows and develops. New areas of research are being established. Better theories replace old ones. Moreover, the scientists seem to utilize a different kind of reasoning than induction. According to philosopher Karl Popper, the definitive feature of a scientific theory is not that it proved to be true, but that it can be empirically refuted. Nevertheless, while no theory can be evidently true, it can be tentatively confirmed, in the sense that it has not been refuted, albeit serious attempts to falsify it.

According to Popper, the scientific discovery is rational if its logic obeys the general formula:

$$P_1 \rightarrow TT \rightarrow EE \rightarrow P_2$$

P_1 represents a problem, TT represents tentative solution or tentative theory, EE is an error-elimination process, which unavoidably leads to a new problem P_2 (Popper, 1972, p. 119)[12].

For Popper, the scientific research is a never-ending, rational problem-solving process. It always ends with new quests as new problems necessarily arise. The scientific method seeks falsification and corrections, and not corroborations or affirmations. This is a rational endeavor because it strives to eliminate mistakes and contradictions. It invites counter examples and criticism. It is reasonable as well because it continuously leads to develop 'closer to the truth' theories. When confronted with refutations (e.g., unforeseen events) the rational scientist is asked to refine or abandon his theory and search for a better one. Although some philosophers of science doubt whether scientists are in fact that rational (e.g., Kuhn, 1970), the ideal–type of inquiry, which science advances, is the paradigm of theoretical rationality.

The "trial and error" problem-solving method of thinking is not limited to scientific inquiry or to theoretical reasoning, for, it is just another manifestation of the principle that humans learn from their experience. John Dewey predates Popper when he characterizes reflective thinking as a problem-solving activity. It occurs in the space between a *pre*-reflective state, which sets the problem to be solved, and *post*-reflective state in which the doubts have been expelled. In between are the following five phases:

> (1) An intellectualization of the difficulty or perplexity that has been *felt* into a *problem* to be solved, a question for which the answer must be sought; (2) *suggestion*, in which the mind leaps forwards to a possible solution; (3) the use of one suggestion after another as a leading idea, or *hypothesis*, to initiate and guide observation and another operations in collection of factual materials; (4) the mental elaboration of the idea or supposition as an idea or supposition (*reasoning*, in the sense in which reasoning is a part, not the whole, of inference); and (5) testing the hypothesis by overt or imagined action... (Dewey, 1933, in Rather, 1939, p. 855).

Dewey further emphasizes that "… any particular overt test need not be final; it may be introductory to new observations and new suggestions, according to what happens in consequence of it" (p. 856). The scientific method may inform humans about the feasibility of their wishes. Moreover it might contribute to finding out whether they are really desired (Biesta, Burbulles, 2003, 78). According to Dewey, moral thinking can imitate the scientific method and bring moral progress, which will bring humans to live according to a system of values which can be attentive to more needs (Rorty, 1994/1999, p. 84). Nevertheless, Dewey's model is a formal model since it does not deal with the content of the process.

Practical formal reasoning and the utilitarian ethics

For the empiricists, reason is unable to prescribe the "good". This stance is, again, best articulated by David Hume, for whom practical reason is but the "slave of passions" (Hume, 1740/1975, p. 415). It is restricted to enable humans to find the best feasible means to fulfill their given aims:

> It appears evident that the ultimate ends of human actions can never, in any case, be accounted for by *reason*, but recommend themselves entirely to the sentiments and affections of mankind, without any dependence on the intellectual faculty. Ask a man *why he uses exercise*, he will answer, *because he desires to keep his health*. If you then enquire, *why he desires health*, he will readily reply, *because sickness is painful*. If you push your enquiries farther, and desire a reason *why he hates pain*, it is impossible he can ever give any. This is an ultimate end, and is never referred to any other object.

> Perhaps to your second question, *why he desires health*, he may also reply, that *it is necessary for the exercise of his calling*. If you ask, *why he is anxious on that head*, he will answer, *because he desires to get money*. If you demand *Why? It is the instrument of pleasure*, says he. And beyond this it is an absurdity to ask for a reason. It is impossible there can be a progress *in infinitum*, and that one thing can always be a reason why another is desired. Something must be desirable on its own account, and because of its immediate accord or agreement with human sentiment and affection (Hume, 1777/1975, p. 293).

The kind of formal reasoning, which is devoted to finding the best feasible means to attain certain ends, is usually called "instrumental" or "technical" rationality. A simplified example of instrumental reasoning is:

> My aim is to lose weight; In order to lose weight it is necessary either to eat fewer sweeties or to run 10 km every day. To run every day will take too much time and effort, while eating fewer sweeties will make me suffer because I will miss them. I prefer to suffer because of lack of sweeties than to lose my time. So I choose to eat fewer sweeties.

This form of reasoning is practical because its conclusion is a decision or an action. The process of practical reasoning is usually called "deliberation". From a logical point of view, the deliberation is sound if and only if its factual statements are true[13]. In such a case the chosen action is 'evidence-based'.

This kind of reasoning is instrumental in the sense that is does not deal with the aims of the activity. The "what for" issue is presupposed by the specific reasoning, and not addressed within the deliberation. While the deliberation is directed to find the best possible means to attain certain ends, it does not question the ends themselves. Already Aristotle maintains that "we deliberate not about ends but about what contributes to ends... Having set the ends they [humans] consider how and by what means it is to be attained..." (Aristotle, 1984, E.N. 1112^{b}13-15; p. 1756). Although the Aristotelian phrase "what contributes to ends" [*ta pro to telos*] includes an analysis of the end or an understanding of what it means (Back, 1987).

Hume assumes that the highest aim of human activity is to feel pleasure and avoid pain. Jeremy Bentham expresses a similar view. In the very first sentences of his seminal book, *The Principles of Morals and Legislation*, he says: "Nature has placed mankind under the governance of two sovereign masters, *pain* and *pleasure*. It is for them alone to point out what we ought to do, as well as to determine what we shall do" (1780/1948, p. 1). For Bentham, the desire to feel "good" and abstain from "bad" feelings is innate. These concepts of "good" and "bad" are not moral. They denote subjective feelings, so that what is good (i.e., pleasurable, enjoyable) for me may be bad for someone else (it may make him suffer). However, Bentham suggests that it is possible to construct a general moral theory based on the human universal strive to feel good. Bentham defines the state in which a human being feels "good" as a state of happiness (1780/1948, p. 70). The classical formulation of this theory is Bentham's principle of utility, which is "that principle which approves or disproves of every action whatsoever, according to the tendency which it appears to have to augment or diminish the happiness of the party whose interest is in question" (p. 2).

Hence, the utilitarian individual is not necessarily egoistic (Hahn & Hollis, 1979, p. 3). He may be altruistic if he believes that such an attitude will be more beneficial for him. He may consider others' happiness as a major contribution to his own well-being. Different versions of utilitarianism have different ideas regarding the issue of the "who" is the "subject whose interest is in question?" (the individual, his relatives, his close friends, those belonging to his tribe/social/religious /nation /race /social class, the entire humankind, or even the whole cosmos).

The utility principle stands behind utilitarianism, a family of ethical theories which are based on two underlying ideas: "First that the results of our actions are the keys to their moral evaluation, and the second, that one should assess and compare those results in terms of the happiness or unhappiness they cause" (Shaw, 1999, p. 2).

For Bentham, the measure of right and wrong is defined by the "greatest happiness of the greatest number [of people]" (Shaw, 1999, p. 8). This definition of happiness is contested. To some thinkers, the feeling of pleasure is too subjective. They prefer to define happiness in terms of an objective measure of desire fulfillment or an objective state of well-being. This state can be an ideal state of complete satisfaction or nirvana, or a socially dependent state in which some of the desires are culturally defined. But whatever the definition would turn out to be, it refers to a state which signifies something desirable. It is even arguable that the longing for happiness enables the very survival of the human being because it motivates all human actions (Layard, 2005, p. 14).

Utilitarianism has one important consequence. In order to calculate the utility of the actions, it is necessary that the various values, representing one's preferences, be commensurable. It is necessary to place all the values on one yardstick because otherwise it will be impossible to compare them and define an order of priority between them. Usually it is practically impossible to simultaneously attain all of them, so there should be a way to decide their relative importance. Consequently, it is necessary to find a denominator into which their respective "values" can be translated. Moreover, this common denominator has to be quantitative, because it is impossible to compare qualities in an objective, transparent, and unequivocal way.

The utilitarian line of reasoning is supported by the success of modern science. Science, we remark, abandons the search for quality and replaces it with the inquiry of the changes in quantities. The desire to develop a "science of values" leads to the interpretation of the values as quantifiable variables, as the very term "value" can attest. It even justifies the conviction that what cannot be quantified cannot be improved. It is of no coincidence that "money" provides the major measure which can comply with this condition. Gradually, the mean becomes an end. Money transforms from being a mean to compare values to a value in its own right. To accumulate money becomes an overriding goal in the materialistic society, which emphasizes financial wealth, and focuses on economic growth. Eventually, a "one-dimensional" society (Marcuse, 1964) develops, in which the social identity of the individual as well as his social power and status are defined by the amount of money he accumulates. As Ayn Rand (1962) predicts, in such a climate, even personal relationships, including intimacy between couples, has to be carefully calculated, formulated in a legal contract, and valued according to commercial criteria without a place for sentiments (Illouz, 2002; Honneth & Hartmann, 2004).

The man on the street usually associates the state of happiness with material wealth. He identifies high life quality with high standards of living, and believes that high standards of living positively correlate with a high level of happiness[14]. Adam Smith, the founder of the modern science of economics, says that: "...An augmentation of fortune is the means by which the greater part of men propose and wish to better their condition" (Smith, 1776/1904, Part II, chap. 3). Many economists agree. They discover that "income buys happiness" (Frey & Stuzer, 2002, p. 9; Bruni, 2007, p. 25).

This conception of happiness can, of course, be challanged. It is arguable that in effect, the struggle for material wealth distances humans from happiness, and that beyond a certain threshold of attaining some basic needs, there is no direct correlation between wealth and happiness (Layard, 2005)[15]. An old Hebrew proverb explicitly connects wealth with anxiety. Too many rich people are unhappy. Not every wealthy man attains well-being or happiness, and there are poor individuals who claim that they are happy. Material affluence cannot be identified with happiness, and it is not a sufficient condition for it either.

Nevertheless, the materialistic interpretation of happiness dominates the current western capitalistic culture. It provides the justification of the HAVING mode of existence, and it enhances the achievement principle of Honneth's third mode of recognition (social esteem). In this culture it is commonly held that those who have material resources have better chances to satisfy their needs, and hence have more means to achieve well-being. After all, a poor man is less able to control his life, because his possibilities to realize his wishes are limited (especially in the privatized society we live in, with its low level of solidarity). Even if wealth is not a recipe for happiness, poverty usually causes distress. The prosperous individuals can more easily live where they want, buy what they wish, spend their time where they desire[16]. Wealth also enables humans to fulfill non-material desires such as good health, personal security, social status, good education, cultural entertainment, etc. The wealthy can even be benevolent if they like, and spend their money on social matters, with or without the intention to receive honor and public esteem. As an advertisement to a new car states: "Whoever said money can't buy happiness, isn't spending it right" (cited in: Layard, 2005, p. 77).

The question whether utilitarianism can provide a justifiable moral theory is contested. For example, imagine that my old car is still working, and a new one costs $30,000.00. I could use my old car and give $20,000.00 to save someone else's life (I keep 10,000 for my old car's maintenance). To give the $20,000.00 to charity seems to maximize utility. So, if it is morally wrong to do anything other than what maximizes utility, then it is morally wrong for me to buy a new car. But, intuitively, buying the car does not seem morally wrong. Another objection to utilitarianism is that it demands the problematic prescription: "if the only way to prevent ten murders is to commit one yourself" you must do it (Scheffler, 1988, p. 3). Yet another objection is that it implies that our obligations to strangers have the same moral weight as our obligations to our friends and relatives. (Slote, 2007). It has been argued (e.g., by Rawls) that utilitarianism gives no directions to consideration of justice in the distribution of goods (so far as an action maximizes an overall satisfaction, it is a good action). These are somewhat counter-intuitive consequences of utilitarianism. Thus, a different moral outlook may be sought after, and the question is whether the faculty of reason can say something substantial about it.

Now it is possible to readdress the distinction between rationality and reasonableness (Sibley 1953; Gewirth, 1983; or Rawls 2001). The two notions have a common semantic origin (the Latin *Ratio*), but each of them implies a different way of looking upon practical issues. Allan Gewirth elaborates the differences between the two notions:

According to many philosophers, there is a sharp distinction and even opposition between rationality and reasonableness. A person is said to be rational when he or she adopts the most efficient means to achieving his or her ends, whatever they may be. Rationality... is held to characterize efficient, self-interested action. A reasonable person, on the other hand, is one who takes due account of the interests of other persons, respecting their rights as well as one's own and maintaining a certain equitableness or mutuality of consideration between oneself and others... This opposition is a version of the traditional conflict between egoism or exclusive self-interest and morality, especially the moral quality of justice (Gewirth, 1983, p. 225).

While it is possible that some action will be rational, in the sense of providing appropriate means to achieve a certain end, it is not always reasonable to execute it. For example, although it may be rational to cheat on an exam, it is not always reasonable to do so, for example, if it will damage others.

To be reasonable, then, is to discuss the intrinsic aims of human activities. It is to acknowledge that the human being is a social animal, that his happiness depends on his being part of society. This notion of *phronesis* is appealing to many contemporary thinkers. The idea that one has to subordinate the efficient technical means (and ends) to moral considerations is embraced by many thinkers who fear that a 'narrow' technological approach does not take into account human well-being in general. Technical thinking is always from a certain domain related instrumental perspective. It cannot incorporate the entire range of implications that a certain action or production can have upon human life in general.

Substantial practical rationality

Utilitarianism presupposes that in order to be morally good it is necessary to have utilitarian reasons to perform certain actions. For the empiricists, practical reason is only means-ends and instrumental; it is formal and the substance (content) of its deliberations comes from irrational sources (feelings, emotions). Thus, there is no principled difference between *techne* and *phronesis*. The same kind of reasoning is required when the aim is how to do or perform something or when it is how to behave prudently and achieve happiness. Quite a different view is endorsed by Kant who, like Aristotle, differentiates between "pure" practical reason and instrumental rationality. Kant fully accepts Hume's 'is-ought' demarcation. He highlights the idea that to be rational means to be consistent, and but he believes that reason itself poses certain limitation on human actions, and prescribes absolute duties, and necessary 'oughts'.

"Pure" practical reason deals with the relationship between the law and the concrete case which implements it. Instrumental reason, which deals with means-end relationships, is the slave of passions, but reason can overcome the ruling of the appetitive faculty. Reason enables humans to construct a system of moral axioms (imperatives) from which any individual can detect his moral duties. Because these axioms can be discovered by any individual, Kant regards the individual as autonomous. He alone can decide what is moral. Reason is universal. Every rational person must reveal the same set of imperatives, so that reason functions like an ultimate moral source. Reason provides *a priori* true moral principles, which are not based on the utilitarian merits of behaving morally, because utility is casual and changeable. Pure practical reason can dictate objective, absolute and universal imperatives which are valid and sound.

One of Kant's favorite examples of how to judge the morality of an action is that of the grocer who does not deceive his clients (1785/1948). This behavior can be performed for different reasons. For sure, the grocer can be honest for purely utilitarian reasons. He may believe that such a behavior will bring him good reputation and attract more clients. It can be seen to accord to the moral "good". But then, the grocer may think, in certain circumstances, it may be more advantageous for him to cheat them. Alternatively, the grocer may be honest because he obeys a moral obligation) not to cheat. He may endorse the moral maxim that in every context one has to be sincere and tell the truth. In this case, his action can be done because of a moral duty. Kant claims that an action is counted as moral only if it is performed because of the moral law. How can the grocer justify this duty without retreating to the notion of utility?

Kant suggests the grocer adhere to the following deliberation. First, suppose a case in which he cheats his clients. This case can be generalized. The grocer can imagine a state of affairs in which everyone is lying to everyone with no exception, so that lying becomes a law of nature. In such a case the word "truth" will be meaningless. Hence the verb to "cheat" will become meaningless as well, because its meaning presupposes the notion of truth. But now the grocer faces a contradiction. He cannot want that the verb "to cheat" will lose its meaning because the very action which starts the deliberation will be senseless. The grocer cannot have it both ways. It is logically impossible to retain the meaning of the verb (to cheat) in action, while at the same time realize that it has no meaning after the required generalization. This contradiction characterizes the original action as immoral. In other words, according to Kant, if the generalization of an action to the level of natural law involves the destruction of the original meaning of the action – it is not moral. This is the essence of Kant's Categorical Imperative which states: "Act only according to that maxim whereby you can, at the same time, will that it should become a universal law" (1785/1948).

For Kant, it is the shamefulness of vice, not its harmfulness, that must be emphasized (1803/1964, p. 156). Not to use reason is disgraceful. It makes one unworthy of happiness. "Since man's consciousness of his own nobility then disappears and he is for sale and can be bought for a price that the seductive inclinations offer him" (p. 156). Kant's theory is an attempt to construct a reason-based non utilitarian ethic. It demands from the individual to be free from his own inclinations and wishes. To be free just means that the individual freely commits himself to the duties imposed on him by his pure reason. In Isaiah Berlin (1958) terms, Kant substitutes liberty "from" with "liberty to". The autonomous individual is a self-regulator, but his regulations are mandatory, and demand compliance. He is not an individual who does whatever he wants. Any individual has the right (and the obligation) to reveal independent thinking. He alone is responsible for his actions, which are not dictated by any supernatural force, and they are not the effect of any law of nature.

At the center of Kant's ethics stands the notion of duty. One should autonomously obey reason's prescription. Thus it encourages the DOING mode of existence. Though secular, it favors the individual who has the inclination to fulfill his duties, overcomes his HAVING or BEING tendencies, if they conflict with his moral obligations, and rejects the hegemony of his utilitarian desires. Obviously, he supports the principles of the legal mode of recognition.

Kant's theory is secular, although he claims that it is instructive to believe in God. For individuals who are not autonomous, it is preferable that they will act according to the moral law being afraid that otherwise they will be punished by the deity. For our purposes it is instructive to see the similarities between Kant's ethics of duties and the religious one. For both, the child is an imperfect adult whose memory precedes reason (Kant, 1803/1964, p. 150). Virtue is learned by practice. It must be cultivated and developed (p. 149) within a community of believers. These similarities explain why Kant's individualistic theory, which emphasizes the individual and his autonomy, could be embraced by those who emphasize the collective and its togetherness. The idea that man's life should be governed by his duties marks the resemblances of the two, seemingly radically different, approaches.

Kant does not give an answer to the question why should the individual be moral? Why should he accept the moral law even when it prescribes self-defeating actions (such as to tell the truth in every context)? Kant's answer is naturalistic: humans have an innate feeling of respect (*Achtung*) to the moral law. The minute they legislate a moral imperative, they have a feeling that they have to obey it. This feeling differentiates between humans and brutes. Although innate, it requires strengthening and it has to be enhanced by proper education. Only an adult is autonomous and can discover the moral imperatives. The child has to be trained to perform moral actions, so that he gets accustomed to moral behavior and thus he cultivates his moral conscience. This training needs to be supported by a dialogue which illuminates the moral thinking presupposed by the behavior. Kant calls such an educational approach moral *catechism* (p. 151). Though based on an exchange between the teacher and the child, it is not a Socratic dialogue between them, because "the teacher alone does the questioning" since the "pupil has no idea what questions to ask" (p. 151).

Kant's approach has its own problems. For example it cannot deal with any grading of activities (every immoral action is as bad as any other immoral action, so that to kill someone is as bad as to cheat him). Another problem is that it cannot accept supererogation as a moral action. To give a donation to a poor person cannot be legitimized in this view.

Kant's ethical theory presupposes that humans want to be rational, that they act to avoid contradictions, that they value their "pure practical reason". As mentioned, Kant explicitly avoids the question of why to be moral because for him this question presupposes a utilitarian answer. If a moral action is "for" something, it cannot be "pure", and the "good" becomes a relative instrumental means-end conclusion of a certain calculation instead of an instance of a categorical imperative.

Following Kant, it is impossible, for purely logical reasons, to defend an argument whose conclusion gives a special privilege to any specific individual or group. The last idea concerning generalization points to a basic similarity between Kant's deontological ethics and Utilitarian ethics. Both share the basic intuition that the notion of morality presupposes generalizability. Equity presumes equality. Look at the statement "I have a right to smoke in public areas". In order to morally justify this statement, I have to show that everyone has the right to smoke in public areas, and therefore I have the same right. Alternatively, I have to demonstrate that there are special and exceptional circumstances, which can be justified independently of my claim, which validates the claim that 'it is permissible, for me alone, to smoke in public areas'. In other words, only if 'I have a right to x' is an instance of the general statement 'everyone has a right to x', I can legitimately perform x. Only then it is "fair". If I cannot separately justify the claim that "'everyone' equals only 'I'", doing x becomes immoral. Moral justification cannot refer to a single case, even if it refers to me, because justice presupposes generalization, fairness, reciprocity, and equality (e.g., Rawls, 1971; 2001). Hence, although instrumental reasoning reveals the means to achieve the ends, logic may put a limit to any purely egoistic behavior. Here surfaces the notion of social justice. The competition should be just, that everyone really has a chance to become successful. There should be a "fair fight". Fairness should be seen. Any process should be transparent and open to legal control.

There are two opposing moral intuitions which are at stake here. The first is the ideal of freedom. The second is that of equality. Both ideals can be grounded in reason, because it is impossible for someone to behave rationally unless he is an autonomous free individual, while the principle of generalization makes it clear that because everyone should be autonomous, his freedom needs to be restricted, to enable the other's autonomy. This tension results in two distinct social and political systems. Capitalism, on the one hand, emphasizes freedom, and competition. Socialism, on the other, emphasizes equality and cooperation. Both, however, emphasize the material aspect of humans. The question which divides them is: what is the just distribution of wealth between the individuals, given the materially limited resources of the environment. Capitalism and Socialism try to justify their conception using reasons. While welfare states seem to give a balanced solution to this problem, for the neoliberals, who believe that personal freedom is more important than social equality, this solution is too extreme.

EDUCATIONAL IMPLICATIONS

The Enlightenment highlights the ideal individual that formal education is supposed to nurture. He is an independent person who uses his reason to know the world and what he should do. He is rational because he obeys the laws of logic. He is reasonable because his beliefs and values can be justified and open to critical discussion. Thus the enlightened person has an inclination to place his reason above any other human faculty. However, the child is an incomplete adult. He cannot be autonomous because his reason is still immature. The adults know what is good for the child. Education is, by its essence, authoritarian and enforcing.

The two conceptions of reason, the substantial and the formal, have different educational implications. Kant, who emphasizes the substantial role of reason, acknowledges that: "The *experimental* (technical) means to the formation of virtue is *good example* on the part of the teacher... For, to the yet unformed human being, imitation is what first determines him to embrace the maxims that he afterwards makes his own..." But, as he immediately emphasizes, "...good example should not serve as a model but only as a proof that it is really possible to act in accordance with duty. Thus it is not comparison with any other man whatsoever (with man as they are), but comparison with the Idea of Humanity (with what man ought to be) and so with law, that must serve as the constant standard of the teacher's instruction" (Kant, 1803/1964, p. 152 – 153). The role of the teacher is not to make the child happy, but worthy of happiness by providing him with exemplary behavior, and cultivation of the child's reason by discussing moral issues with the pupil.

On the other hand, the enlightenment's formal reasoning is strictly utilitarian. It is infused with the HAVING mode of existence as the means to achieve happiness. Education has to provide the child with the necessary tools which will enable him to achieve happiness. Accordingly, the teacher has to teach the child useful knowledge and proper conduct, so that it will be possible for him to achieve happiness. In utilitarian terms, education must prepare the pupil to successfully join his society as a productive adult. In the modern society it seems that basic knowledge (at least of the three R's) and mastery of proper social behavior are the minimal requirements that education has to achieve. Philosopher Herbert Spencer, in the middle of the 19th century, suggests, "Before devoting years to some subject which fashion or fancy suggests, it is surely wise to weigh with great care the worth of the results, compared with the worth of various alternative results which the same years might bring if otherwise applied" (Spencer, 1861/1911, p. 5 – 6). And Spencer continues:

> To prepare us for complete living is the function which education has to discharge; and the only rational mode of judging of an educational course is, to judge in what degree it discharges such function... In bringing up our children we may choose subjects and methods of instruction, with deliberate reference to this end (p. 7).

In an order of subordination, it is rational to have education "which prepares for direct self-preservation..., indirect self-preservation..., parenthood, citizenship... and miscellaneous refinements of life" (p. 9). Such a curriculum will emphasize the worth of knowledge both for purpose of guidance and for purpose of discipline and regulating conduct (p. 37). Not surprisingly, Spencer's favorite subjects are science and mathematics. Science, he adds, is an appropriate tool for moral discipline as well, because it makes constant appeal to individual reason (Spencer, p. 40).

PROFESSIONAL TEACHER EDUCATION

Enlightenment inspired TEPs have two different roads to follow. The TEPs may be grounded on instrumental rationality, or alternatively, they may be based on substantial rationality. The first path takes them into the realm of means-ends deliberations, efficiency, productivity, and accountability. Its main concept of the teacher they prepare is that of a professional agent, who is responsible to prepare his pupils to become useful members of a society, which highlights the achievement-based mode of social recognition.

The second path that TEPs can follow is directed at the teacher as an independent, autonomous and rational agent. It looks at education as a devotion to enhance the pupils' scientific thinking and moral reasoning. Thus, especially because it emphasizes man's duties toward himself and his society, it might promote the DOING mode of existence and focuses on human duties and obligations. The educated man should be able to set aside his own subjective desires, preferences and priorities and be committed to his moral obligations.

Most TEPs in the Anglo-Saxon world choose the first path, and although they incorporate some elements of the second in their curriculum, their main focus is to prepare utilitarian teachers. This, of course has to do with the current *weltanschauung* which is neo-liberal and capitalistic. It is also due to the academic environment in which TEPs are located, which is "is" oriented (science) and is hostile to normative discourse. In other, mostly North European counties (e.g., Finland), there are TEPs which travel along the second path, and although their rationale does not ignore utilitarian considerations, their overall curriculum is attentive to different voices.

It is important to trace the differences between these two types of enlightenment inspired TEPs, as they refer back to the rationalist-empiricist debate. While the North-European TEPs are usually more deductively oriented, the Anglo-Saxon ones are usually more inductive. While the latter focus on "what the teacher should learn and be able to do" (Darling-Hammond & Bransford, 2005), the first deal with the teacher's reasoning as an autonomous agent (Kansanen, 2004). While the second emphasize competencies and teacher's skills, which promote pupils' learning and achievements, the first address his responsibility to empower the pupils' entire personality. Both types of TEPs claim that they prepare the needed professional teacher. Both can present a hopeful outlook, but, as we shall see, both has a threatening potential to society and its future.

PREPARING PROFESSIONALS:
THE TECHNICIAN PHASE

From a utilitarian-enlightened perspective, teacher education combines problem solving with instrumental rationality. The problem it faces is how to produce efficient teachers in the most efficient way. More concretely, any TEP has to respond to the questions: (1) what should the teacher learn and be able to do? (cf.: Darling-Hammond & Bransford, 2005); and (2) how to design an efficient program which produces teachers who know what to do and are able to implement their knowledge? The answers to these questions should provide the most effective means to produce professional teachers in accordance with the instrumental rationality criteria of: soundness, coherence, accountability, efficiency, and efficacy.

In this chapter we begin to explore the programs which adopt this utilitarian variant of the enlightenment stance. The focus will be on United States TEPs, mainly because they offer a good example of this perspective. Beginning at the end of the 19th century, teacher education in the US underwent a process whose aim has been to improve the preparation of professional teachers. This development, however, has not been straightforward. It involves many back and forth steps, and interrelated dialectical tensions between: theory and practice; general education and specialized knowledge; teaching and learning; pedagogy and instruction.

The process can be divided into three phases:

1. The academization of teacher education. The transfer of TEPs to an academic environment can be seen as a shift from the view that teaching is an art (or better, craft) to the view that it is a profession. The idea that teaching can be learned by apprenticeship has been replaced by the idea that it is a technical or applied science profession, which needs academic in-service course of studies. Teaching has a theoretical basis, which should be learned in an academic setting. This move reflects a growing emphasize on instrumental (or technical) rationality, as distinct from substantial practical reasoning (This chapter).

2. In the next phase of the process, teaching is no longer regarded as a technical profession but as a reflective-practical one. The reflective practitioner teacher replaces the technician. The teacher is seen as a knowledge producer, and there is a shift from the view that the teacher is a transmitter of knowledge to a constructivist conception of teaching and learning. This attitude leads to two different types of programs. In the US TEPs, the teacher's knowledge is based upon the "what works" type of evidence, simultaneously, with the view that he is a clinician whose

concern is that every child will learn. A different (non US) type of TEPs breaks the limits of technical rationality towards substantial rationality (chapter 5).

3. The third phase of the process is characterized by a retreat from the idea that teaching is a genuine profession. Academic pre-service TEPs are seen as inefficient and even damaging. Teaching is a vocation which, should be learned from practice. Academic sites are no more seen as needed or even appropriate environments in which TEPs have to be conducted. The relevance of theory to the teachers' knowledge base is questioned, and the role of experience is seen as all important. This phase is dominated by a very narrow concept of the aims of formal education. The professional teacher is no longer seen as an educated person, who has general liberal education, and whose aim to enhance the pupils development, but as a specialist whose success is determined by the academic accomplishments of his students in national and international exams. The proficient teacher is still an expert who masters "what he has to know and be able to do", but especially in the US educational system, this idea is understood in a one dimensional way. In congruence with the social-esteem mode of recognition of the neo-liberal consumer society, the "public" appreciates only the teacher whose professional activities are dictated by the increasing importance of the achievement principle (chapter 6).

In terms of the previous chapters, this path can be seen as a movement from both the DOING and BEING toward the HAVING mode of existence. It is a path from the Believer and the Romantic moral stances toward the Enlightenment one, and within the latter, from substantive to instrumental reason[17]. As we shall see, the picture is not that monolithic. Some TEPs deviate from the dominate path and proceed along different roads. However, especially in the US, the growing hegemony of the HAVING mode of existence, and its materialistic *weltanschauung,* highlights the achievement principle of recognition. This path concentrates on efficiency, effectiveness, and accountability. I believe that this is a problematic position, which threatens to undermine the teachers' professional identity.

To justify these claims, let us have a look at the major kinds of TEPs in the last century, although as we shall see, it is possible to find present-day TEPs which exemplify all the three phases. The following presentation is an oversimplification. As everything else in education, every program is context dependent. My intent, however, is not a historical description but an analysis of the enlightenment inspired ways of teacher preparation. This analysis provides a framework for comparing the programs and understanding the possible advantages and limitations of what they assume about the teacher and his profession.

TEACHING AS A PROFESSION

"Profession" is a salient notion in the vocabulary of the enlightenment's utilitarianism. Societies want to prosper, and prosperity depends on the "division of labor" principle. If everyone will do everything, the outcome will be inefficient and cause waste of time and money. It will be much more fruitful if each individual will be a specialist in some domain. The products of his work will be much better, their quality much higher. As a result, the *wealth of nations* will increase

(Adam Smith, 1776/1904), and it will be easier for their citizens to achieve happiness. The division of labor principle is a paramount example of the technical-rationality, means-end, way of thinking. The noticeable case of the principle is the professional specialist. He is a rational, autonomous, knowledgeable, deliberate, efficient, accountable and responsible individual, whose work is devoted to improve the well-being of his fellows. His activities obey the norms of the instrumental rationality (Evetts, Mieg & Felt, 2006, p. 107).

According to Shulman (1998/2004), four important features characterize any profession(p. 529 – 530):

First, a vocation is a profession if its aims display commitment to society, and if its activities are devoted to serve public needs. Subsequently, the aims of any profession are not decided by the professionals themselves but by the society in which they operate. According to the instrumental rationality way of thinking, the professional's activity should keep the ethical commitment of service to the community, and he should not put his personal interests above any other consideration (p. 530). Within these limits, his actions should be, as far as possible, value-neutral (Parsons, 1968, p. 537).

Second, a profession is an occupation which requires intellectual techniques of problem solving in a certain practical domain[18]. Professional activity provides a special case of the P_1-TT-EE-P_2 Popperian paradigm. It requires "understanding of a scholarly or theoretical kind" which influences a "domain of skilled performance or practice" (Shulman, 1998/2004, p. 530).

Third, any profession has an exclusive knowledge base, which enables the bearer to be efficient in achieving its aims. This knowledge base legitimizes the monopoly that the profession has on the occupational domain. The professional knowledge base combines theory (knowing that) with practice (knowing how). It includes an intellectual ingredient, which is discovered, formulized and theorized within the academic environment.

Fourth, the profession's knowledge base is acquired through a prolonged, pre-service academic course of studies, in which the prospective practitioners acquire the required knowledge-base that any novice, who joins the profession, must have. This preparation includes a necessary component of practicum, in which the theoretical knowledge has to be practiced.

The professional knowledge base

Until the 1970s, the common conception of the professional knowledge-base has been that it contains three layers of knowledge (Schön, 1983, p. 24; 1987, p. 9). These layers are arranged in a pyramid structure, in a hierarchical order, from the bottom up. The pyramid's basis consists of theoretical or "pure" scientific knowledge, and its top consists of the "know how" practical knowledge. In between is an intermediate layer of "applied science". It consists of research which tries to explore the implication of the scientific knowledge on a certain practical domain. Engineering, for instance, is based on physics and chemistry, and medicine is based on physics, chemistry, and biology. In this conception, the flaw of knowledge is "upward": from the "pure" layer, through the "implied" layer, to the practical one. Each layer has its own experts, and the professional practitioner, whose knowledge occupies the topmost layer, knows how to implement the relevant scientific knowledge in his practice.

According to the applied science paradigm there is a sharp division of labor between the researchers and the practitioners. "Although some professional workers carry out the kind of research that adds to our scientific knowledge, it would be unrealistic to expect most of them to do so. Developing, testing and confirming scientific knowledge is not something the practitioner can do as a hobby or in spare moments at work. The discovery of new knowledge is a full time job" (M. Lieberman, 1956, p. 194). "The important thing", Lieberman continues, "is not that the research will be *carried on* in classroom, but that the findings of research will be *applicable* to educational problems..." (p. 195). A claim which is directed against "... the notion that the average teacher should be *expected* to conduct such research" (p. 195).

As we shall see in chapter 5, the last statements are contested. Since the 1970s, a constructivist paradigm of science replaces the positivistic one. It legitimizes the qualitative research, and changes the concept of the profession as an applied science (Schön, 1983). The physician is expected to conduct research and produce knowledge, and the "teacher as researcher" (Kincheloe, 2003) becomes a favorite conception. Accordingly, an important type of TEPs is devoted to prepare to teachers to be researchers (Toom et al. 2010). Nevertheless, albeit these changes, the basic tenet, that any professional knowledge-base includes an essential scientific component which should influence practice, remains intact.

According to the applied science concept, TEP should include "a systematic discussion of selected educational issues in which the focus will be on applied knowledge taken from the theoretical bases of education and its basic sciences" (CHE, 1981). Such a TEP should be carried in an academic setting, and indeed within less than a century, teacher education became academic. Most of today's TEPs are located in universities and academic colleges. But the academization of the TEPs is far from a being a mere change of site. It influences the nature of the preparation process and with it the essence of the profession. To better understand this transformation, a brief discussion of pre-academic TEPs is in order.

THE INITIAL PHASE: THE PRE-PROFESSIONAL PERIOD

At the beginning the idea had been that the teacher is an educated individual, who can influence what children know and how they behave, and both aspects have a "correct", enlightened answer. Two different models of teacher education dominated the field in the 19th and 20th (beginning to middle) centuries: The *seminaristic tradition* [ST] (or the *école normale* [normal school tradition], which prepared teachers for primary schools in specially designed, non-academic institutions, and the *academic tradition* [AT], which prepared teachers for secondary schools in the universities (Buchberger, 1998, p. 54 – 55). Besides being placed in different educational environments, the main difference between the two traditions was that ST considered the teachers to be all-purpose educators of young children, while AT conceived them as transmitters of certain subject matter knowledge to a selective group of able pupils. While ST is concerned with teaching subjects (individuals), AT is about teaching subject (matter).

Buchberger summarizes the two traditions in Europe of the 19th century:

> The focus of ST is on "practical" training (teaching practice, methodology) and [it] devaluates the importance of both educational theory and academic/scientific knowledge. Categories such as "ethos" or the "personality of teachers" *(Lehrerpersinlichkeit)* form integral parts of this tradition. In rather rigid learning environments [prospective] teachers should learn to "model the master" and to acquire some basic skills of teaching (e.g., the "apprenticeship" model)...

> AT emphasizes the high importance of theoretical scientific knowledge. [Prospective] teachers had to acquire scientific knowledge in academic disciplines (cf. the principle *Bildung* [19] *durch Wissenschaft* [education through knowledge]). It is assumed that this scientific knowledge and the competences and attitudes learned during the processes of its acquisition would enable [prospective] teachers to perform the tasks of teaching and of education competently. The importance of educational theory, methodology and teaching practice is devaluated or neglected in this tradition. Initial Teacher Education for teachers at (upper) secondary schools has been strongly influenced by this tradition (1998, p. 54 – 55).

ST: The culture and the learning environment of the *seminars* resembled that of the schools[20]. Most of the students were young (16 females; 17 males), graduates of 10-12 years of studies (without a matriculation). The typical teacher educator had been a former primary school-teacher, without academic background. Teaching had not been regarded as a profession but as a craft or set of techniques which has to be learned from experienced masters (e.g., Fowle, 1867). The students were arranged in cohorts, according to their year of study. The curriculum had been compulsory, almost without any students' choice. The course of studies focused on a broad survey of the primary curriculum, at only a slightly higher level, with no domain specialization (See: Appendix, example 1). It contains everything that the teacher is expected to deliver.

According to popular text-book on teaching, TEP should instill in the prospective teacher the "true spirit of the teacher".

> A spirit that seeks not alone pecuniary emolument, but desires to be in the highest degree useful to those who are to be taught; a spirit that elevates above everything else the nature and capabilities of the human soul, and that trembles under the responsibility of attempting to be its educator; a spirit that looks upon gold as the contemptible dross of earth, when compared with that imperishable gem which is to be polished and brought out into heaven's light to shine forever; a spirit that scorns all the rewards of earth, and seeks that highest of all rewards, an approving conscience and an approving God; a spirit that earnestly inquires what is right, and that dreads to do what is wrong; a spirit that can recognise and reverence the handiwork of God in

every child, and that burns with the desire to be instrumental in training it to the highest attainment of which it is capable, - such a spirit is the first thing to be sought by the teacher, and without it the highest talent cannot make him truly excellent in his profession (Page, 1857, p. 9 – 10).

The school subject-matters had been conceived as the main mean to enhance the pupils' development. The teacher is held responsible (to a degree) for the bodily health of the child, for the intellectual growth of the child; (to a degree) for the moral training of the child and (to a degree) for the religious training of the child (Page, 1857, p. 18 – 34). By himself he has to serve as a model for his pupils. He has to exemplify Personal Neatness; Order; Courtesy; Punctuality; and Habits of study (p. 40 – 46).

The primary teacher of those days was not only interested in the cognitive abilities of his pupils. He used to dance, play and hike with them; he knew how to sing and to grow vegetables and raise hens. He taught house maintenance (boys), cooking, and sewing (girls). Nevertheless, the teacher's major role had been to deliver to his pupils the basic knowledge (the three R's), skills, attitudes, and behaviors required by adult (mainly agriculture) society.

The preparation curriculum had been shallow and uncritical and did not develop subject-matter expertise. It had not been academically oriented and even its subject-matter studies were not intellectually demanding but pedagogically focused. Special attention had been given to nonverbal practical domains like painting, singing, dancing, or physical education, because of their importance to enhance the various skills of the child, or cultivate his desired attitudes and behavior. The main concern was on the "how". The student had to master the methods of proper instruction. Therefore, the professional preparation merged the disciplines and their respective teaching methods (e.g., "mathematics for primary school and how to teach it"), and focused on teaching skills and successful recipes (A representative textbook which addresses these issues is Fowle, 1857).

The practicum had been regarded as the corner stone of the curriculum. It included observation of experienced teachers and conducting actual lessons, preferably in a "model school" (Ogren, 2005, p. 136). The rationale had been that teaching experience should not be a blind imitation of what the student observed but a deliberate "thoughtful and well informed" action (p. 140). In some cases the practicum began at the beginning of the program. In others it was placed towards its end. Experienced school teachers served as "supervisors" or "critic teachers", and the experiences had been followed by reflective discussions in a seminar. According to Ogren, "These discussions were also an opportunity to integrate the experiential knowledge gained in the model school with the technical and liberal knowledge acquired in classes" (p. 142).

ST emphasizes the idea that the teacher should be an educator. It holds that teaching is basically a devotion to children (Hargreaves, 2000, p. 156). Its aim is formative. It has to care for the "proper" development of the child, who has to join his society. Special attention had been given to his moral development which was at least as important as his cognitive achievements. This ideal reflects the substantive enlightenment ideal of cultivation of the pupil's personality. Prospective teachers had to acquire and internalize this mission, so that learning to teach was a formative process as well. It had less to do with educational theories or detailed disciplinary knowledge and more with the personality, attitudes and behaviors of the teacher, which had to serve as a model to his pupils.

AT: Unlike ST, AT focuses on the schools' subject-matters (See Appendix Example 2). A typical TEP includes two ingredients: (i) A complete course of academic studies (at least at a Bachelor level) in one or two subjects, learned in the appropriate academic faculties; (ii) Studies within the faculty of Education, which include: Theoretical courses (e.g., Philosophy, History, and Psychology of Education); Principles of Teaching, General Didactics, Method courses in various disciplinary areas, Field observations and teaching experience. There are two possibilities to combine ingredients (i) and (ii): the concurrent model, in which both ingredients are studied simultaneously within the university, or a consecutive model, in which learning to teach follows the subject-matter studies, either in the university or in special institutions.

Once it had been appreciated that teaching is not an easy job, partly because the high-school became compulsory and includes all children, it became apparent that "knowing the" subject-matter does not imply "knowing how" to teach it. It seemed necessary to supplement the subject matter-studies with a special program of teacher preparation. Nevertheless, TEPs had not been regarded as an academic program but as supplement to the regular academic course of studies. The number of courses devoted to TEP in AT had been usually quite limited[21], and it did not grant an academic degree but a vocational certificate. Teaching, per se, was not seen as a genuine profession.

ST and AT have their respective strengths. ST is close to the field, and emphasizes the formative roles of the teacher. AT focuses on rigid subject-matter and stresses academic rigor and updated knowledge. However, both ST and AT fail to provide an adequate professional preparation (Hargreaves, 2000). ST, because it belittles the importance of theory. AT, because it belittles practice.

ST is not professional for several reasons. First, schools expand and include all the children. Their population is much more diverse and demanding. Teaching can no longer rely only on the intuition and experience of a model teacher or on seemingly established recipes, which are casual, context dependent, and lack scientific foundation. To become a profession, the relevant (behavioral) sciences should inform the processes of teaching and learning in much more subtle ways. Second, the growing emphasize on pupils' academic achievements requires that the teachers should have a deep understanding of the subject-matter. Subject-matter domains should be taught by informed faculty, and not by a former school-teacher. Third, the *seminars* lack the academic tradition of questioning and research. The attitude towards the student teachers tends to replicate the attitude towards the children. In many cases they were seen as immature individuals. Loyal to the school's culture, they do not encourage critical thinking, and prefer instruction and delivery over skepticism and renewal. In a climate of authority and obedience, "Do it that way" has been much stronger than "Find your own way". Imitation is more important than understanding ("You will understand it when you are an experienced teacher"). This attitude is problematic, because it may prevent innovations and entrepreneurship. Last but not least, what renders ST even more problematic is that it seems unprofessional to educate the prospective teachers to passionately love their pupils (Honneth's first mode of recognition). The over caring relationships between students and teachers seems to be too much 'family' like, and leave too little room for professional deliberations. Teachers are required to instruct students or care for them, but they have no professional legitimization to let their personal preferences, attitudes, and emotions to intervene into their decisions. It is expected that they will be objective, rational and emotionally detached as far as possible (Parsons, 1968; Labaree, 2004).

From the beginning of the 20th century, ST enlarged and developed. Its student become older (high-school graduates), its program become longer (2 and later 3 years of study), and its curriculum expanded (to include domain specialization)[22]. Nevertheless, its school-like culture remains intact, and its lack of academic spirit makes the transition of teacher education to an academic setting unavoidable. Its continuance seems a hindrance to recruit good candidates and to elevate the accountability, efficiency, and professionalism of teaching.

But AT seems equally inapt to prepare professional teachers. AT presupposes that teaching is a devotion to knowledge. Learning to teach is subsidiary to learning to be a scholar. But albeit the academic envelope, teaching has not become an academic discipline. The academic ingredient of the AT is devoted to the subject-matter the teacher is going to teach. But this knowledge, which is studied in the relevant faculties, is not specific for teaching as a profession. The prospective researcher should have it as well, so it cannot be a unique characteristic of the teacher. The educational side of AT is academic in the sense that it has been delivered by the faculty of education, but usually its academicians are not teaching oriented (they are experts in various field of educational research), while its teaching specialists are not academics but expert school teachers. The split between theory and practice assures that the practice of teaching is not founded on any scientific theory. This situation is reinforced because the practicum occupies a minimal part of the program, and usually has nothing to do with the theoretical studies. Teaching is, once again, a craft whose knowledge is derived from what experienced teachers know to do. AT seems to be unprofessional.

Thus, both ST and AT do not see teaching as a genuine profession. ST emphasizes the general and the formative aspects of teaching. It is not scientifically based and lacks intellectual curiosity and rigor. AT emphasizes subject-area specialization and theoretical aspects of education. However, its programs demonstrate that there is no integration between theory and practice, so they lack coherence and credibility. For both traditions, educational theory has not been "for action", and serves merely as lip service, hoping that somehow, sometime it may help. Detached from actual practice, the program seems irrelevant to the work of efficient, professional teachers. Both traditions do not lead to a TEP which can develop a professional teacher.

To become a profession, TEP must become fully academic. In the growing hegemony of the achievement principle of recognition, for teaching to remain a non-academic occupation means a dead-end. It can no longer be honored as a respectable "profession", and parents and children alike will lose confidence in their teachers. Indeed, there were some doubts whether teaching should become a profession. For example, many teachers regard as the core of their work the intimate relationships with their pupils, a relationship which is labeled as a not-enough-professional attitude. But the quest for an appropriate mode of recognition, and the demand that the teacher should know what they are doing, ends the combat between the so called "academic" and the "humanistic" camps with a definite answer. The move to the academic world becomes unavoidable.

The universities are the enlightenment temples. They are the locus of scientific knowledge. In an academic culture of autonomy and freedom, knowledge is discovered, developed and transmitted to new generations of scientists. To belong to an academic environment is a sign that a certain domain of knowledge is important and worth inquiry. It also means that the domain's knowledge base is kept up to date, and is innovative and reliable. Belonging to the academic world carries recognition and prestige. Today's universities are multidimensional. They deal not only with "pure" science, as their research includes a growing number of applied science domains, which enables the academic institutions to address the issue of professional preparation (e.g., medicine, social work, engineering, accounting).

However, a TEP cannot look like AT, which is not a 'fit for purpose' professional preparation program. AT is inapt to prepare efficient secondary-school teachers; it is even more inadequate to deal with primary teachers. Given the necessity of the academic relocation of TEPs, the challenge is how to transfer the ST type of TEP to the academic environment without losing the strengths of the *seminaristic* tradition and without becoming absorbed in the problematic non-academic *academic* tradition. Or, alternatively put, how to modify AT so that it will be a genuine academic program, adequate to prepare professional teachers? This turns out to be a very difficult mission. Even today it is still debated whether it has been met successfully. One of the first attempts to face the challenge raised by the necessity to become academic had been to construct specially designed academic programs for teacher preparation

PHASE 1: THE PLAIN VANILLA MODEL

Russell's Proposal (RP)

Toward the end of the 19th century, James Earl Russell, Dean of Education at Teachers College, Columbia University, presents one of the first efforts to meet the challenge of transferring the TEPs to the academic environment. Russell suggests a new program which attempts to bridge the gap between ST and AT, between primary and secondary TEPs, and between theory and practice. RP has been devised as an academic four year bachelor degree program, in which the first two years are devoted to general education and the last two to professional studies.

Russell proposes an integrated academic curriculum for teacher education. It includes four components, which he considered essential to success in teaching: General Culture, Special Scholarship, Professional Knowledge, and Technical Skills. In his own words:

The general culture must be liberal enough to inspire respect for knowledge, broad enough to beget a love for the truth. The special scholarship must be sufficient for the work to be done, it should give that absolute command of the instruction which frees the teacher from slavish adherence to manuals and methods. The right professional knowledge should enable the teacher to view the subjects he teaches and the entire course of instruction in its relations to the child and the society of which the child is a part. The true educator must know the nature of the mind: he must understand the process of learning, the formation of ideals, the development of will, and the growth of character. The artist in every vocation must have consummate skill in the use of his tools. The teacher must be skilled in the technique of his art; he must have the ability to impart his knowledge in a way that shall broaden his pupils' horizons, extend their interests, strengthen their characters, and inspire them to right living. And as every art is most efficient when intelligently directed, the art of teaching should be found on the science of teaching, which takes account of the ends and means of education and the nature of the material to be taught (quoted in Cremin, 1979, p. 12 – 13).

RP "combined a broad general education, a solid command of one or more teaching fields, an inquirer's knowledge of educational theory and practice, gained largely via the history and psychology of education, and scientifically based technical skills, developed through practice under expert supervision" (Cremin, 1979, p. 14).

Cremin notes that by "general culture", Russell means a kind of preparation that would enable the prospective teacher to see the relationships between the various fields of knowledge, particularly between his own field of expertise and all the others. The inclusion of this component in RP reflects the belief that "...the goods intrinsic to liberal education – humane values, critical thinking, historical perspective, broad knowledge – are central for teaching" (Feiman-Nemser, 1990, p. 214). Similarly, Siegel and Delattre state that "It is not likely that students will come to any real understanding of human nature without studying literature and history. It's not likely that 'global perspective' will be informed if they are taught without geography and foreign language" (cited in Howey & Zimpher, 1989, p. 256). NCATE 1970 standards, explains the need for general studies as follows:

Prospective teachers, like all other students, need a sound general education. However, their need is accentuated by the nature of the professioanl responsibilties that they are expected to assume. As teachers, they are destined to play an important role in providing general education for the children and youth they teach, and serve as adequate models of educated persons to their students. Furthermore, the subjects studies in general education may be needed to support their teaching specialities (p. 3).

By "special scholarship", Russell means an academic course of study which develops a kind of reflective inquiry that "would equip an aspiring teacher to select different sequences of material and adapt them to the needs of different students" (Cremin, 1979, p. 13). By "professional knowledge", he means a systematic inquiry into the theory and practice of education "pursued via the same controlled observation and rigorous theorizing that pertained in the natural sciences and medicine" (p. 13 – 14). By "technical skills", Russell has in mind "not the rote knowledge gleaned by the observant apprentice but rather expert ability in determining what to teach and by what methods, when and to whom" (p. 14). These skills should be developed within an experimental school, in which teacher educators will serve as models to schools-teachers, teacher-students, and pupils.

Nothing seems to be missing from this ideal proposal. The preparation of the teacher is intellectual and emotional, theoretical, and practical. The student teacher has to acquire a "respect for knowledge" and "beget the love for the truth". He has to understand the "formation of ideals, the development of will, and the growth of character". He needs to be able to "broaden his pupils' horizons, extend their interests, strengthen their characters, and inspire them to right living" (Cremin, 1979, p. 14). In a nutshell, the teacher should not only instruct his pupils, but educate them. To be able to meet this pedagogical role, teacher education should be as comprehensive as possible. It has to deal with both the knowledge required for teaching and learning, and with the formation of the teacher as a human being who can inspire and educate his pupils. Although teaching is conceived as an art, the preparation to the occupation should be scientifically based. It should take into account the up to date scientific knowledge, which can be developed and tested in the experiential setting of a laboratory school.

RP presents an interesting blend of enlightenment ideals. On the one hand, the teacher is open-minded and has broad knowledge. He is seen as an intelligent, autonomous, free agent. The knowledge he transmits should be related "to the child and the society of which the child is a part". Its aim is to empower his pupils' "growth of character", their learning, and their "formation of ideals". These ideals, which presuppose the vision of humans as enlightenment, well informed, moral being, can be justified by substantial rationality. They do not specify concrete utilitarian targets but a general spirit in which TEP should operate. However, other traits of RP incorporate the instrumental rationality approach. The teacher is free because he masters an "absolute command of the instruction". The theory of instruction is founded on "the science of teaching". This science, "which has been experientially validated", "takes account of the ends and means of education and the nature of the material to be taught" (Cremin, 1979, p. 14). Russell adopts the utilitarian means-end vocabulary and speaks about efficiency and about the teachers' technical skills. This is, clearly, the applied science concept of the profession, although Russell acknowledges that teachers and teacher educators can be involved in knowledge creation. Significantly, RP does not emphasize the HAVING mode of existence. No mention is made in regards to the pupils' prospects of success, any notion such as well-being or happiness does not appear, and material considerations (such as preparing the pupils for the work force) are absent. Knowledge is connected to truth and not to utility.

RP had been generally accepted. It provides the basis for the B.Ed. concurrent TEP (e.g., Conant, 1963, p. 148 – 150) (See: Appendix example 4). Feiman-Nemser calls RP the "plain vanilla" of TE programs (1990, p. 216), and its influence can be seen even in 1970, in which the NCATE standard no. 1 requires that:

> Teacher education curricula are based on objectives reflecting the institution's conception of the teacher's role, and are organized to include general studies, content for the teaching specialty, humanistic and behavioral studies, teaching and learning theory with laboratory and clinical experience and practicum (NCATE, 1970, p. 3).

The problems with RP

Except for some outstanding TEPs (Howey & Zimpher, 1989), RP was not really implemented. As Feiman-Nemser observes:

> Although we can discern the basic structure of Russell's curriculum in the familiar components of the typical undergraduate program, it is the letter, not the spirit, of the proposal that stands out.... Typical undergraduate programs seems more like an organizational compromise, the offspring of an unhappy union between the normal school [ST] and the liberal arts [AT] traditions (1990, p. 216 – 217).

On the face of it, the academic setting presents three main obstacles to RP: (1) The academic setting's structure is based on strong classification; (2) It is value neutral; and (3) It separates theory from practice. Special effort should be made to overcome these obstacles, but such an effort had been rarely made.

1. Strong Classification

The knowledge base of teaching is multidisciplinary. It contains knowledge from various academic domains. While it is quite easy to construct a program of study in which each of the components is studied separately and in isolation, it is much more difficult to build a TEP which will be cohesive and consistent. The difficulty arises because the academic culture is characterized by strong classification (Bernstein, 1975, p. 75). Each domain of knowledge has its own tradition, questions, research method, and language, and due to the 'division of labor' principle, each of them has its own specialists. Strong classification characterizes the educational studies as well. It is divided into areas such as Philosophy, History, Psychology, or Sociology of Education, each of them is more related to its "mother" discipline than to its fellows in education.

With distinct specialists, each delivering his own goodies, TEP looks like a pie, in which each slice is "responsible for its own bit of the overall function" (Combs, 1965, p. 113 – 114):

A pie model program lacks the expected coherence that the "applied science" pyramid structure presupposes. In the pie diagram the disciplines are not arranged in any hierarchical pattern. It is also very different from RP's intent of enabling "the prospective teacher to see the relationships between the various fields of knowledge, particularly between his own field of expertise and all the others" (Cremin, 1979, p. 14). Consequently, time and again, a demand arises "for a more integrated, and hence more meaningful" program (CTE [Commission on Teacher Education], 1946, p. 251), a program that will be more "functional" for educational matters (p. 252)[23].

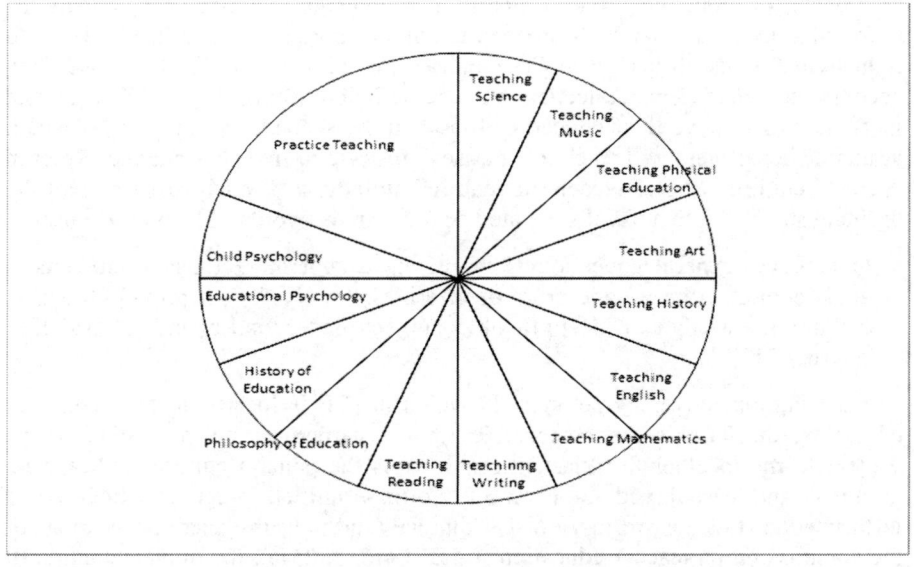

The Pie Model Program (Combs, 1965, p. 114)

Strong classification is problematic for TEPs. It is very difficult to have a coherent view of the profession if each ingredient of its knowledge-base addresses different questions, employs different vocabulary, and has different practical implications. But if there is no mutual academic "space", in which all the participants in teacher preparation can meet and discuss the program, there is no "program". In 1946, a commission on teacher education in the US finds that "The schism between educationists and professors of the various academic subjects constituted a formidable obstacle in the way of achieving anything like integrated programs of teacher preparation... The individual course, half course, or even quarter course, given independently by an individual professor, had become the educational atom..." (CTE, 1946, p. 251). This problem still exists As Darling-Hammond complains in 2006: "Subject-matter courses are disconnected from courses on teaching methods, which are in turn disconnected from courses on foundations and psychology... Student teaching [has] few connections to [theoretical studies]. In the classroom many students encounter entirely different ideas from those they had studied..." (p. 153). "Programs that are largely a collection of unrelated courses without a common conception of teaching and learning have been found to be relatively feeble change agents for affecting practice among new teachers" (Darling-Hammond et al. 2005 [The Design], p. 391 – 392). Given that the student teachers have to develop an integrated professional identity, strong classification is a hindrance to an adequate preparation.

As the RP program has four different ingredients, each of them suggests a special difficulty:
(a) First is the issue of "general studies". Can their studies be similar to that of a regular undergraduate course or, should they "enable the student to see the relationships among the various fields of knowledge", in order to "impart his knowledge in a way that shall broaden his pupils' horizons... and inspire them to right living" (Russell quoted in Cremin, 1979, p. 12 – 13). In the first case, they become an inefficient collection of courses, interesting by themselves but inefficient to achieve their educational task. In the second, the question of which academic department will teach them arises. It is rare to find an academic expert in "general culture" who can teach the required attitude. It is much easier to split the "general studies" into a list of separated courses. In the words of Feiman-Nemser:

> In practice, general education is more like a supermarket where students make choices from a wide array of offerings. Rarely does it provide broad cultural knowledge or deep flexible subject-matter understanding (1990, p. 216 – 217).

In the common university settings, in which a TEP is located in the faculty of education, the TEP is not responsible for the particular choice of courses the student learns in other faculties. In many cases the general culture studies were fractured and casual and could barely form a unified program which could influence the students' world-view. Despite RP (and the subsequent suggestions of the commission on teacher education (CTE, 1946, p. 251)), the implementation of the general culture, interdisciplinary, ingredient of the program misses its target. Thus, RP's general studies component, which supposedly provides the core or unifying theme of any TEP, cannot perform its enlightenment role. Howey and Zimpher (1989) "suggest the possibility of designing specific courses that directly link disciplines traditionally taught in arts and sciences with education..." This can be done "by having faculty in arts and sciences together with faculty in teacher education jointly design courses in different core disciplines..." (p. 257). This is, by no means, as easy task in the current universities' publish or perish climate.

(b) The "special scholarship" is no less problematic. Like "general studies", it can be learned either within the faculty of education or within the relevant disciplinary faculties. In the first case, the studies are not professional enough, because the subject matter experts are not located in the education faculty but in the relevant faculties. In the second case the special scholarship studies can hardly fulfill their educational aims. An academic researcher, who is an expert in a specific domain, does not necessarily know how to "enable the student to select different sequences of material and adapt them to the needs of different students" (Cremin, 1979, p. 13) within each doamin. Although a few departments, especially mathmatics and sciences, offer special courses "for teachers", it may simply mean that these courses are less demanding, not that they are conducted by special experts.

With the growing emphasis on subject-matter specialization (usually in the form of a major or two), the general culture component loses its educational priority, and the time allocated to it becomes more limited (Wesley, 2007). The need for a general overview of human culture and spirit remains unanswered. The prospect of looking at the disciplines from an integrated broad perspective, which focuses on the interactions between various aspects of human knowledge, has been diminished.

One remedy to this problem has been to transfer the integrative role, assigned by RP to the general culture studies, to the foundation of education courses (Arnstine, 1973; Wesley, 2007). Courses, like Philosophy, History and Social aspects of Education, should provide the "broad cultural knowledge" and the general humanistic flavor, needed to the prospective teacher. However, this shift enlarges the gap between the Educational studies and the subject ingredients of the program. The formative role of studying the disciplines becomes a casual side-effect of the program. The justification of their learning becomes purely instrumental (you cannot teach if you do not know what you teach).

There is another detrimental effect of the separation of both general education and special scholarship from education. As pointed by Korthagen, [TEP] is just a model of the learning process which should occur in schools. Ideally, such a TEP requires that the subject-matter component will be part of the responsibility of its faculty. "In this way, the processes involved in learning the subject content can be used as objects of reflection" (Korthagen et al. 2001, p. 96).

Such integration is hardly possible in a strong classification culture, which means that TEPs students should find an opportunity to "reexamine their subject matter courses" (Korthagen et al. 2001, p. 262).

(c) The course of studies in the department of education fare no better, as the theoretical studies have been separated from the didactic and practicum in schools. After all, a professor of educational psychology may not be an expert in Methodology, and a specialist in school reform does not have to know how to supervise a practical experience.

This split intensifies the fragmentation of the program. Again, each ingredient has its own culture, language, faculty, etc. Although this structure implements the pyramid "implied science" conception, it also means that "foundation" courses have no direct connection to the "field". Again, a special effort has to be made for such a connection to take place.

The "foundation" level of the teachers' knowledge-base is not unique to the teaching profession. It is needed for the education of researchers, consultants, educational policy makers, etc. The main area, which calls for a specific professional knowledge, is methodology (both general and domain specific), which should integrate all the teachers' knowledge base into a unified "theory of teaching". Thus the role to connect between the theory and the practice is assigned to the intermediate level of Didactics and Method courses. But it is extremely difficult to establish a viable connection between the "foundation" and the "methods" levels. The foundation courses rarely influence the content and the method of the method courses. It is very demanding to coordinate the content of the method courses, which have their own agenda, with the theoretical ones. The Methods' specialist presents another obstacle. He is usually a former teacher who has a relevant academic background. He is not an expert in all the theoretical domains of knowledge, and he can hardly integrate between them. He can barely fulfill the integrative role of all the program's ingredients.

(d) The practicum raises its own problems. Regularly, it is supervised by a former school-teacher, selected because of his successful experience, and not because of his academic credentials. Usually, his own actions are not theory-based. Barely can he exemplify the implementation of the "applied science" paradigm. Rarely can he provide a good example of the influence of general education to his own practice.

This situation has an important consequence. Teaching is a practical profession. Located at the upper level of the pyramid, the question of "how" is the most important issue to be dealt with. But if this level is detached from its basis, and especially from its foundation level, teaching becomes a set of techniques. Instrumental rationality becomes the only legitimate method of thinking. But then, the entire rationale of RP collapses.

Even from strictly technical-rationality stance, the program ceases to provide an efficient preparation. "Learning is enhanced when learners encounter mutually reinforcing ideas and skills across learning experiences" (Darling-Hammond et al. 2005 [The Design], p. 393). It is, therefore, not a surprise that "A number of studies have offered empirical evidence that teacher education programs that have coherent visions of teaching and learning, and that integrate related strategies across courses and field placements, have a greater impact on the initial conceptions and practices of prospective teachers than those that remain a collection of relatively disconnected courses" (p. 392).

2. Value Neutrality

What remains from the liberal ideal, that the teacher "shall inspire the students to right living" (Russell, cited in Cremin, 1979, p. 13)? Questions of ethics can be dealt with directly (e.g., in Ethics course) or indirectly (e.g., in method courses). Once detached from the subject-matter domain, the burden of dealing with this issue has been given to the "Foundations" courses. Although, again, the strong classification principle prevents both faculty and students from seeing and practicing the implications of inspiring the "right living" in the school environment. Addressing moral issues can be fragmentary, and casual unless specifically designed, but the structure of the academic environment does not facilitate this possibility. Howey and Zimpher, find that even in their sample of outstanding TEPs "rarely did we see strands focused specifically on the *moral* and *ethical* dimensions of what is a highly moral endeavor. Again, the dominant emphasis in most institutions remains on the technical and communicative dimensions of teaching" (1989, p. 258).

This emphasis is not a casual fact. The academic environment emphasizes scientific knowledge and cognitive skills. It highlights the dominance of the rational approach to knowledge, the importance of the scientific way of thinking, and the focus on compartmentalization, specialization, and expertise. The importance of cognitive skills precedes the emotive or social ones. The student is expected to excel according to the single criterion of intellectual abilities and performance.

The academic environment does not support the External-Believer or the Romantic outlook. To maintain "academic freedom" and rational, critical thinking, it requires a suspicious, if not hostile, attitude to any dogma or fixed *a priori* belief, ideology, or faith. It also rejects the Romantic, non-rational and even irrational stance, which concentrate on human imagination and feelings, and not on scientific, detached knowledge. In the former ST environment, the Believer could find a proper space (due to its authoritative, orthodox and uncritical climate, which resembles that of a church). Even the Romantic, who emphasizes the non-cognitive aspects of life, can sympathize with the *Bildung durch Wissenschaft* principle, which had been the basis of the humanistic education. This ideal was at odds in the academic setting. Gradually, it receded into the background, and left the scene. Educated in an environment which favors "objectivity" over "subjectivity", "cognition" over "emotion" and "science" over "tradition", the prospective teachers assimilate the enlightenment outlook, and it becomes a cornerstone in their professional stance. TEPs become one-dimensional in the academic environment, where only cognitive or intellectual virtues are important, and the outcome is a redefinition of the teacher's task. The formative role of education, which is much more salient in both the Believer and the Romantic world-views, diminishes. Step-by-step, the "value-neutrality" scientific ideal pushed aside the ideals of creating a better human being or an improved society.

However, the "value-neutrality" ideal is an illusion, because the very choice of the enlightenment stance is, in itself, value-driven. Moreover, the academic environment, on the applied science level, advances the utilitarian culture in which "knowledge is power". Instead of BEING or DOING, the academic environment, which focuses on knowledge for action, intensifies the HAVING mode of existence, and its utilitarian way of thinking. "How to" becomes the dominant question. Efficiency and efficacy become the cherished values. Technical (instrumental) rationality becomes the favorite paradigm.

3. The Theory-Practice Gap

Yet another outcome of strong classification is that the programs themselves do not implement the theories they advocate. Being an amalgam of courses, their curriculum does not obey any principle of professional or adult learning (Fuller, 1969). Teacher education differs from any other professional preparation programs, because the teacher educators are teachers who perform the same activities they prepare for. While the academic environment of the medical faculty resembles neither a hospital nor a clinic, many aspects of TEP do bring to mind a school. Unlike the physician educators, who do not cure the students, teacher educators teach their students. They should serve as a model for their students, and the program as a whole should provide a model of a proper learning environment and be constructed according to the principles it preaches. This requirement is not met even by the faculty of education itself. Thus, for instance, the teaching methods employed may contradict the learning theory the program promotes. The principle of "practice what you preach" has been frequently violated, as when the students heard a lecture about the weaknesses of the delivery model of teaching or learned in large classes about individualized learning. The hidden message to the students is clear: do not trust the theory, for it is simply not needed.

Moreover, there is a wide gap between what the students learn and the realities of school. The program remains in the "semantics stratosphere" (Peck & Tucker, 1973, p. 970). Darling-Hammond mentions that "one major critique of teacher education, particularly in the years after normal schools were abandoned for university departments, was the apparent separation between theory and practice in many programs" (p. Darling-Hammond, 2006, 153). No wonder that student-teachers regard the theoretical part of their preparation as irrelevant to their job. As *Teacher Man* Frank McCourt remembers:

> Professors of education at New York University never lectured on how to handle flying-sandwich situations. They talked about theories and philosophies of education, about moral and ethical imperatives, about the necessity of dealing with the whole child, the gestalt, if you do not mind, the child's felt needs, but never about critical moments in the classroom (McCourt, 2005, p. 16)... I am not prepared, trained or ready for this. It has nothing to do with English literature, grammar, writing (p. 22)...
>
> In college... there were courses on how to teach by professors who did not know how to teach (p. 25)... The student next to me in the professor's class whispered. This guy [the professor] is so full of crap. He never taught a high school class in his life (p. 41)... 'Professor, how many high school classes have you taught?' 'Oh, I've observed dozens of classes over the years... I've observed and supervised dozens of student teachers'. 'My father is a high school teacher, professor, and he says you know nothing about high school teaching till you've done it' (p. 42)...

The gap between the program and the field is detrimental, because it undervalues the practical impact of the TEP. No wonder too many teachers find their preparation unwarranted. William Ayers comments on the myth that "Teachers Learns to Teach in Colleges of Education":

> Teachers do not believe it for a minute... Teachers know that their journey through teacher education was painfully dull, occasionally malevolent, and mostly beside the point. Some teachers believe that a few college courses could have been useful if they had been offered during the first years of actual classroom experience, instead of being dished out as "truth" disconnected from the messy reality of schools... When teacher education programs structure the separation of theory and practice, this message alone is enough to degrade teaching... (Ayers, 1993, p. 12)[24]

Tom and Valli (1990, p. 390) propose a suggestive explanation to the theory-practice gap. Both teachers and teacher educators still see teaching as a craft. But craft knowledge is usually undervalued within the academic environment. It is seen as something acquired through apprenticeship and not through typical academic preparation. Hence the schism between the two which reflects itself in the way TEPs are formed in AT.

It is time to pose and look at the travelled area. Teaching struggles to be a genuine profession. Teacher education should be conducted within the academic universities and colleges, the shrines of the enlightenment spirit of rationality and liberty, progress and development, scientific discoveries and technological innovations. However, as we have seen, there is a price to be paid. Despite its shortcomings, AT's heritage becomes more dominant than ST. The structure of the programs has not been really that of "applied science". The fragmented nature of the academic programs breaks the necessary interconnections between the different levels of knowledge. In the end, teaching remains a set of techniques to be learned by apprenticeship. In fact, many of the B.Ed. programs have the weaknesses of both ST and AT. They are fragmented and casual. They lack cohesiveness and consistency. They do not have any organizing theme, and they lose RP's broad educational aspirations. While they concentrate on the technical issues of "how to", their ability to effectively deal with the "why" and "what for" questions deteriorated.

Maybe teaching is really but a set of techniques. Maybe Russell was wrong, and teaching should be a content-free, value neutral profession. Maybe it consists of delivery methods which are relatively insensitive to the transmitted material. Such an assumption can legitimize a TEP which completely separate the subject-matter studies from the methods of teaching them. This separation can free the B.Ed. TEPs from the burden of dealing with the subject-matter and general education. But the remaining ingredients should form a consistent and integrated program, which will more faithfully implement the "implied science" pyramid of knowledge. The theory will inform the practice, the academic "ivory tower" will meet the schools, and the studies will merge into a coherent whole. This intention motivates the design for new models of TEPs.

To become an applied science, teaching should be based on scientific theories, and especially on psychology. In the majority of the 20th century, the dominant psychology theory was behaviorism (Watson, Skinner, Hull), with its focus on overt behavior. Teacher education should be constructed accordingly. TEPs should condition the overt behavior of the prospective teachers, who will thereafter condition their pupils. The example of a behaviorism based TEP is CBTE, which, in the early 1980s, had a widespread influence in the United States and some other countries.

Competency Based Teacher Education Model (CBTE)[25]

CBTE[26] enthusiastic adherents believed that it brought, to the educational domain, "whole new worlds of opportunity" (Houston & Howsman, 1972, p. 3). They were sure that the rapidly growing movement will transform the entire field. The model, usually a concurrent B.Ed. program, withdraws the attempt to incorporate the subject-matter studies into TEPs, and focuses solely on the education element of teacher preparation. It focuses on developing skills instead of cultivating the personality of the teacher (See Appendix, example 5).

CBTE is an archetype of a TEP which strictly implements the implied science, technical-rationality rationale. CBTE fully adopts the positivistic stance according to which scientific research does not refer to an overall look of a certain phenomenon, but analyzes its constituents and emphasizes the cause-effect (or correlational) relations between its variables.

In December 1971, the American Association of Colleges of Teacher Education (AACTE) initiated a survey on "the state of the art" of the CBTE movement. Written by Stanley Elam, the survey addresses the question "What is PBTE and why some authorities consider it potentially superior to traditional strategies for developing the teacher knowledge, skills, and attitudes necessary to facilitate pupil learning?" (Elam, 1971, p. 1). The existing TEPs "do not specify what prospective teachers need to be able to do or accomplish" (p. 1). In contrast:

> In performance-based programs, performance goals are specified, and agreed to, in rigorous detail in advance of instruction. The student must either be able to demonstrate his ability to promote desirable learning or exhibit behaviors known to promote it. He is held accountable, not for passing grades, but for attaining a given level of competency in performing the essential tasks of teaching; the training institutes is itself held accountable for producing able teachers. Emphasis is on demonstrated product or output. Acceptance of this basic principle has program implications that are truly revolutionary (p. 1 – 2).

CBTE programs are founded on "new concepts of management, used in the planning, design, and operation of more efficient, product-oriented programs" (p. 3). (Elam is referring to the "system approach" as providing a new paradigm for educational system management; cf., Le Baron, 1973.)

CBTE assumed that teaching is composed from a given set of competencies (attitudes, understandings, skills and behaviors), which enable the intellectual, social, emotional and physical growth of children" (Cooper, Weber, 1973). These competencies, which can be scientifically discovered, provide the basis for effective teaching. They should be the basis of TEPs as well.

While existing TEPs focus on the programs input (coursework, field experience), CBTE programs emphasize their outcomes. They relate teachers' behavior to student learning, college success to vocational success, and theory to practice. As summarized by Elam (1971, p. 6 – 7), a TEP is a CBTE program if:

1. Competencies (knowledge, skills, behaviors) to be demonstrated by the students are:
   a. Derived from explicit conceptions of teacher roles,
   b. Stated so as to make possible assessment of a student's behavior in relation to specific competencies, and
   c. Made public in advance;

2. Criteria to be employed in assessing competencies are:
   a. Based upon, and in harmony with, specified competencies,
   b. Explicit in stating expected levels of mastery under specified conditions, and
   c. Made public in advance;

3. Assessment of students' competency:
   a. Uses his performance as the primary source of evidence,
   b. Takes into account evidence of the student's knowledge relevant to planning for, analyzing, interpreting, or evaluating situations or behavior, and
   c. Strive for objectivity;
4. The student's rate of progress through the program is determined by demonstrating competency rather than by time or course completion;
5. The instructional program is intended to facilitate the development and evaluation of the student's achievement of competencies specified.

Most CBTE programs share the following principles:

– There is a (preferably, scientifically discovered) list of competencies that comprise the work of any successful teacher. These competencies should be formulized in operative terms, which enable the specification of clear objectives that the prospective teacher should master.
– A TEP is not an amalgam of courses. It should be viewed as a whole, coherent and cohesive program, encompassing theory and practice, campus and field cites.
– The program is divided into study units (modules), each of them devoted to a specific competency, with the aim of achieving specific objectives. The modules form a hierarchical learning path. Corresponding to the list of competency and objectives, there are evaluation criteria which specify in advance and operational terms what it means to have a mastery of a given competency, and how it can be examined.
– The learning process is individualized. Each student learns each module for mastery by himself and at his own pace. He can proceed from one module to another only after successful accomplishment of the requirements of the preceding one. The evaluation of his success is criteria based, and the grades are not normalized. Every student who masters the module passes.
– The modules are "teacher proof", and they contain scientifically valid content. Each module has seven ingredients: rationale, explaining the 'what for' of the module; a list of the module's objectives stated in operational terms (the student will be able to...); prerequisite knowledge; initial test (learn what you do not know); acquisition activities; achievement test (criterion test); remediation activities (if necessary). Each module uses various learning strategies and a different learning environment. To facilitate the learning process, there is a resource center in which the student can find the relevant material, and where he can consult an informed faculty member.

This brief survey of the CBTE principles and methods attests to why it can be viewed as an archetype of a TEP which aims at suitable professional preparation. It fully incorporates the 'applied science' pyramid. It is a target oriented, scientifically based, program which merges all the necessary ingredients of the professional knowledge base into a coherent whole. It emphasizes the outcomes of the process, and evaluates the students' mastery of the required competencies. It also demonstrates that a coherent and cohesive program should incorporate a unified, transparent and effective method of instruction and evaluation.

What is significant about the CBTE Model is that it has been congenial to develop and embrace. Under this model the teacher is an efficient technician. Given that he masters the competencies and has a complete set of learning modules, his job becomes restricted to an effective instruction of pre-planned and well-packed material. Today, more than 40 years later, and with the advent of the digital technology, there is once again a widespread search "for ways to somehow "teacher-proof" our classrooms" (Berry et al., 2011, p. xv). It is believed that "virtual schools" will be more efficient and cheaper than teachers (Moe & Chubb, 2009; cited by Berry et al., 2011, p. 84). According to the applied science approach to teaching, the role of the teacher becomes to intelligently apply the scientific knowledge about teaching and learning. His activities should be planned and rational, and like many other crafts of the past, a proper technology may either change his role or render his job redundant.

Nonetheless, within a decade or two, all the CBTE programs disappeared[27]. It is instructive to diagnose the reasons for this collapse:

First, it was impossible to scientifically justify the set of competencies (especially those of the novice teachers). The empirical research does not reveal any agreed upon list of competencies which characterize the effective teacher. Second, it becomes evident that the scientific framework of the model is mistaken. During the eighties, it became clear that the behavioristic learning theory is suspected. The emergence of the cognitive sciences undervalues the scientific merit of the model. A behaviristic approach, like the CBTE, cannot deal with the thinking processes which underlie learning, as prospective teachers were not asked to explain why they would make a particular decision. If prospective teachers are not reflective about their own thinking and activities, they will neither be prepared to understand their students thinking and activities, nor will they be able to enhance reflective thinking in their pupils. Another example of the CBTE shortcomings is that a proper use of the competencies means to know when to apply them. But this knowledge cannot be a competency in itself, because it cannot be operationally defined, nor operationally assessed. No module can be designed to acquire it. What is at stake is not a collection of competencies but the way they are integrated into one's whole behavior. While CBTE focuses on the analysis part of the process, it lacks the means to address the synthesis part. In the end, the assessment of the student as a teacher should be holistic, but as such, it lacks valid objective criteria. It seems that after all, the teacher's personality is what matters, but as such it lacks objective measurements. Third, the spirit of the program runs counter to the tradition of academic freedom. A very structured and closed program seems at odds and out of place in the academic environment. Moreover, the uncompetitive culture of the program (everyone who masters the competencies passes), and the collaboration it demands from the faculty (designing the program and creating the modules), seems antagonistic to the climate of competition which is part and parcel of the academic culture.

SUMMARY

In this chapter we follow the first steps of the TEPs in the academic arena, from the pre-academic ST and AT through Russell's suggestion, the B.Ed. model to CBTE. We have seen that this process changes the essence of the programs so that they could be incorporated into the culture of the academic institution. This entails:

- A focus on theoretical knowledge, as teaching is conceived of as an applied science profession (Education for high-school teachers, Subject-domains for primary teachers)
- A gap between theory and practice
- A narrowing of teaching to address mainly cognitive elements of teaching and learning
- A growing withdrawal of the TEPs from the formative and moral aspects of preparing a teacher.

In the language of the previous chapters, this phase encourages a technical-rationality approach, which embraces the utilitarian ethics, the HAVING MoE and the "achievement principle" as a professional mode of recognition. This approach culminates in the CBTE programs.

CBTE, however, did not rescue the TEPs. At the end of this phase, teacher education seems to be drowning in troubled water. The National Commission on Teaching and America's Future (NCTAF, 1996) identified several problems with the then current pre-service teacher preparation programs. Among them are:

- Inadequate time: 4-year undergraduate degrees make it difficult for prospective elementary teachers to learn subject matter and for prospective secondary teachers to learn about the nature of learners and learning.
- Fragmentation: The traditional program arrangement (foundation courses, developmental psychology sequence, method courses, and field experiences) offers disconnected courses that novices are expected to pull together into some meaningful, coherent whole.
- Uninspired teaching methods: Although teachers are supposed to excite students about learning, teacher preparation method courses are often lectures and recitation. So, prospective teachers who do not have hands on, "minds-on" experiences with learning are expected to provide these kinds of experiences for students.
- Superficial curriculum: The need to fulfill certification requirements and degree requirements leads to programs that provide little depth in subject matter or in educational studies, such as research on teaching and learning. Not enough subject-matter courses are included in teachers' preparation (1996, p. 31 – 32).

The commission, however, forgets to mention a further shortcoming of the TEPs. As summarized by Zeichner (2010):

The traditional model of college-recommending teacher education emphasizes academic knowledge for teacher candidate learning (about learning, development, the social context of schooling, content area teaching methods and curriculum, assessment and so on). Candidates are supposed to learn what and how to teach in their campus courses and then go out and "apply" what they learn during their practicum and internship experiences in schools. Historically, very little success has been achieved in coordinating what is done in the campus and field components of teacher education programs (Zeichner, 2010).

PREPARING PROFESSIONALS: THE REFLECTIVE PRACTITIONER ERA

PHASE 2.THE TEACHER AS A *TECHNITAS*

Three interrelated changes characterize the next phase of academic TEPs: First, a new conception of social science emerges: positivism, has lost its hegemony and qualitative research methods, become legitimate. Second, behaviorist learning theories are replaced by cognitivist and constructivist ones. Piaget and Vygotsky substitute Watson, Skinner, and Hull. The focus shifts from teaching (as instruction) to learning (as construction), as social constructivism and activity theory emphasize learning from action within communities of practice. It is also a shift in focus from "common processes for all schools to common outcomes for all children" (Levine, 2006, p. 18). Third, teaching is not seen as an applied science but as a practical vocation. In Aristotelian terms, it moves from the concept of the teacher as a techn*ician* to the teacher as a *technitas*. Thus, we face a paradigm shift, in which teaching in general, and teacher education in particular, has its own scholarship[28].

A new research paradigm

In the last decades, qualitative research gained scientific legitimacy. According to Gadamer (1960/1989), there is a genuine problem with social or human science theories which try to imitate natural science theories. Not every phenomenon can be observed and measured. There can be a legitimate qualitative research which deals with unobservable and immeasurable aspects of reality. The natural sciences provide explanations for human behavior (e.g., learning or developmental theories), but they do not help people to understand each other. They provide explanation to a concrete phenomenon only when they see it as a special instance of a general law (Hempel, 1935/1980). This kind of explanation is not sufficient when one wants to find the singularity of what happens, or understand it from "within". Such an understanding is necessary if one presupposes that there is a free will and humans are autonomous and not merely "objects". This kind of understanding is a necessary condition for the teachers' educational work. Without proper understanding of the pupils, their beliefs, values, and attitudes, there can be no efficient process of teaching and learning, because there can be no dialogue between teachers and pupils.

Instead of the "objective" scientific method, Gadamer and his followers locate the process of interpretation at the center of the scientific inquiry, and hermeneutics becomes a scientific method. In the hermeneutic quest, which is a search after meanings and interpretations, the special case becomes highly important, for it raises concrete questions of values and beliefs and helps us understand each other. Hermeneutics recognizes the variability of different perspectives, and sees them as legitimate sources of knowledge which are connected to different social powers (Flyvbjerg, 2001).

The academic legitimation of this kind is strengthened by postmodern views of science. Postmodern criticism discloses that science cannot be "positive". It cannot discover absolute eternal truths. Knowledge is culturally defined, and the accumulation of knowledge has normative and evaluative aspects. Like any other human activity it is cannot be conducted in a detached and cold manner. The rigid dichotomy between researchers and practitioners disappears. Practitioner research (e.g., action research or self-study) becomes not only legitimate but a required ingredient of the professional performance.

Learning as social construction

For most of the 20th century, behaviorism had been the hegemonic psychological paradigm. In the field of learning, classical and operant conditioning provided the models of the processes of learning in brutes and humans. This paradigm lost its credibility in the last decades of the century. First was the cognitive revolution, inspired by Chomsky and the rise of computer sciences. Then was the constructivist turn, inspired by Piaget and Vygotsky. Learning becomes activity. You learn by doing and reflecting. And you learn by checking what you know against the critical feedback you receive from others in your community of learning. It becomes widely recognized that the role of formative assessments is to improve learning and not to grade it (e.g., NRC [National Research Counsil], 2000). The "learning environment" becomes decisive. Problem based learning (one of Dewey's favorite themes) and project based learning regain approval. Action research, self-study, case study, reflective journals, and portfolios are accepted as main vehicles of learning. As this conception of learning gains scientific credibility, it changes not only the content of TEPs, but the way they perceive the role of the professional teacher and the processes of learning to teach.

From Techni to Techne

In the 1980s, it became evident that teaching is not an applied science profession. Usually, when a teacher faces a problem he does not turn to scientific knowledge but consults his colleagues. His community of practice is much more relevant than the research. Experience outweighs any theory. One reason for this common attitude is that today there is not a sound scientific theory on which teaching can be based (Lam, 2000, p. 68). The discipline of education is full of many rival theories, but none of them seems to be adequate. None of them effectively deals with the realities of teaching and learning in schools. If there is no available science of teaching, the concept of teaching as an applied science has to be revisited. There is no significance to psychological, sociological, or anthropological theories by themselves, beyond the point that they widen the general background knowledge of the student teacher. Unless connected to the practitioner's daily problems, they will barely affect his worldview, attitudes or actions. Of course, it will be mistaken to ignore theoretical knowledge in education, and it should be taken into account, but only in so far as it is relevant to the actual educational activity. Even then, the implementation of any theory requires special deliberation to evaluate its applicability in a specific context (Shulman, 1998/2004, p. 534; Johnson, 1975, p. 50).

Teaching is a complex profession. It has different and often contradictory aims. It is performed in a class which is composed of many pupils and each of them has different abilities, learning styles, and previous knowledge. It necessitates integration of knowledge from various subjects, and it requires variable teaching methods, and adjusting the curriculum requirements to the children wishes (Darling-Hammond, 2006, pp. 39 – 40). Teaching is based on practical, contextual knowledge, grounded in what actually happens in the classrooms. It is not an implementation of "external" knowledge revealed by researchers who may never have worked in the profession (Remember: McCourt, 2005). It is never a routine activity which can be performed in a context-free environment.

Teaching requires practical knowledge based on experience which grows from the field up, rather than reaching the field from scientific theory. Practical knowledge is highly contextual since each situation is unique and requires special consideration and deliberation. It is usually tacit, and includes the professional's situated knowledge (Polanyi, 1962). However, it can be disclosed, formulated and discussed by the practitioner with the help of the community of practice to which he belongs. When it has successful outcomes, it can even be offered to others as an example of "a best practice".

Korthagen et al. (2001) term the teacher's practical knowledge a "theory with a small t". They erroneously connect it with the Aristotelian notion of *phronesis*. More correctly it refers to his notion of *techne*: quintessential professional knowledge that relates to the specific connection between goals and means in a definite area in a given context. The Aristotelian *Techne* differs from the modern *Techni*. *Techni* is an applied science concept. The teacher as technician implements procedures and routines discovered and designed by non-teachers. *Techne* is the practical knowledge of the expert practitioner. It is often tacit and intuitive. Like the craftsman skill, this knowledge is constructed (rather than acquired) by the novice through a reflective process upon his professional experience.

For Aristotle, *techne* involves a cluster of features, which includes:

(1) A productive-theoretical knowledge about the ends of the profession and the common ways in which it is possible to attain them;

(2) An excellence in deliberation about the means-end relationships in concrete situations of a certain practical domain;

(3) A mastery of 'knowing how', the practical skills and competencies, necessary to execute the appropriate means in this practical domain; and

(4) Practical *nus* (intuition) which is the ability to perceive the uniqueness of the concrete situation while at the same time to see it as a 'case of...' a certain practical domain.

The *technitas*, such as the physician or the ship-builder (and probably the teacher as well), is an agent who has general knowledge in a specific productive domain (e.g., medicine, engineering). Each productive domain is characterized by a set of aims (e.g., the ends of medicine are to cure sick people and to prevent illness). In each case there is a certain theory (or more precisely, a productive-theory) about the essence of the ends (e.g., what does it mean to be healthy), and about how it is possible, in general, to achieve them (possible healing methods for a disease, etc.). (Aristotle, 1984, Rhet., I, 2, 1356b 28-32; cf.: Pos.An., II, 13, 97^b 26-27). Such a productive-theory resembles scientific theory since it is learned from experience (*empeiria*) by the method of induction (Aristotle, 1984, E.N., II, 1, 1103^a 30-31)[29].

Productive-theory, is essential but insufficient for a genuine *technitas*.

"...actions and productions are all concerned with the individual; for the physician does not cure a man... but Callias or Socrates... If, then, a man has theory without experience, and knows the universal but does not know the individual included in this, he will often fail to cure; for it is the individual that is to be cured" (Aristotle, 1984, Meta., I, 1, 981^a 16-24; cf.: E.N., VI, 7, 1141^b 7-21).

Aristotle's remark has its point. Productive-theory contains general statements, and it is, therefore, possible to publicly formulized these general statements (e.g., it is possible to write handbooks about 'how to make...' etc.). Hence, the productive-theory is teachable (Aristotle, 1984, Meta., I, 1, 981^b 8). It is possible to learn these principles without being engaged in any activity (e.g., by reading a handbook or listening to a lecture). Aristotle, however, makes it clear that 'theoretical' learning alone cannot convert someone to be a genuine *technitas*. Someone might replicate others' "knowledge why" theoretical principles, but lack the expert's "knowing how". Such a man does not have genuine practical knowledge, for although his knowledge can be formulated, it is, in a sense, not 'his' knowledge. He cannot reach the induction's conclusions by himself (because induction starts from experience), and as he is not sensitive to the particulars, he cannot identify those problematic situations in which his general knowledge can be applicable. He does not have an essential characteristic of the *technitas*, which is the ability to 'perceive' that a particular action is of a certain kind. This kind of intuition is the practical *nus*. The practical *nus*, however, is developed on the basis of the other ingredients of the *technitas* knowledge, as practical theory can instruct him on 'what to look at'.

Again, as Aristotle emphasizes, it is impossible to develop practical knowledge without learning by doing:

"...but the virtues we get by first exercising them, as also happens in the case of the *techne* as well. For the things we have to learn before we can do them, we learn by doing them, e.g., men become builders by building and lyre-players by playing the lyre..." (Aristotle, 1984, E.N., II, 1, 1103^a 30-1103^b 1)[30].

The genuine *technitas* cannot remain in the theoretical sphere. He should act as well:

> "A man will be a grammarian, then, only when he has both done something grammatical and done it grammatically; and this means doing it in accordance with the grammatical knowledge in himself" (Aristotle, 1984, E.N., II, 4, 1105ª 24-2).[31]

The process of learning to teach cannot ignore the teachers' practical knowledge. Instead of cultivating a good technician (or a "routine" expert), a TEP has to nurture an "adaptive" expert (NRC, 2000). It has to develop the "*techne*" of the prospective teachers, relying on what successful teachers do (their best practices) and not only on what the theory says they should. Like a physician, the teacher has to be cultivated as a clinician who is engaged in problem solving and in research about his actions. Teaching is a knowledge creation profession. And the practitioner research (such as action research or self-study) is not less important than research on teaching conducted by professional academics.

Aristotle supports an inductive process of professional preparation. Teaching education should include cycles of action – reflection – action (case studies and simulations can replace real life experiences), in which the reflection should be raised to the level of practical theory construction. This concept of TEP proliferated in the 1990s under the title of reflective teacher education (see, for example, Valli, 1992; Tabachnick & Zeichner, 1991)[32].

Reflective Teacher Education

Being reflective substitutes the technician as a sign of being professional. Professional teachers "reflect on their work to assess the outcomes of their efforts and the reasons for their successes and failures" (Porter et al., 2001, p. 266). Valli (1997) suggests that professionalism means that:

> ...Teachers had to demonstrate the ability to make thoughtful and reflective decisions about classroom incidents. Fostering teacher thinking promotes teaching as a profession. Teachers do not, and should not be, unthinking conformists. Rather, they are decision makers and problem solvers who work in an extraordinarily complex environment with multiple and simultaneous demands on their time and attention... We cannot take for granted that prospective teachers will become reflective practitioners with experience (p. 71 – 72).

There are many interpretations of what reflection means. Under the title of "reflective teacher", different TEPs are constructed around different conceptions of the nature of the required "reflection". Though each of them highlights the importance of the reflective teacher, there is no agreement about the "content" or the aims of the intended reflection. These conceptions range from a "narrow" meaning of reflection as a mean to enhance technical-rationality deliberation, to a "broad" outlook of reflection as a mean to reform society (Zeichner, 1992).

Almost every account, of the reflective practitioner, traces its origin to Dewey's notion of reflective thinking (e.g., Zeichner & Liston, 1996, p. 8 – 14). As Valli (1997) recognizes, "…Dewey's language is so powerful that one wonders how teacher education could be based on anything other than reflecting thinking" (p. 69).

According to Dewey, one of the major differences between technical rationality and reflective rationality has to do with the nature of the means-end relationship:

> We have spoken as if aims could be completely formed prior to the attempt to realize them. This impression must now be qualified. The aim as it first emerges is a mere tentative sketch. The act of striving to realize it tests its worth…[U]sually - at least in complicated situations - acting upon it brings to light conditions which had been overlooked. This calls for revision of the original aim; it has to be added to and subtracted from. An aim must, then, be flexible; it must be capable of alteration to meet circumstances. An end established externally to the process of action is always rigid… Such an end can only be insisted upon. The failure that results from its lack of adaptation is attributed simply to the perverseness of conditions, not to the fact that the end is not reasonable under the circumstances. The value of a legitimate aim, on the contrary, lies in the fact that we can use it to change conditions. It is a method for dealing with conditions so as to effect desirable alterations in them… A good aim surveys the present state of experience of pupils, and forming a tentative plan of treatment, keeps the plan constantly in view and yet modifies it as conditions develop. The aim, in short, is experimental, and hence constantly growing as it is tested in action.
>
> In contrast with fulfilling some process in order that activity may go on, stands the static character of an end which is imposed from without the activity. It is always conceived of as fixed; it is something to be attained and possessed. When one has such a notion, activity is a mere unavoidable means to something else; it is not significant or important on its own account. As compared with the end it is but a necessary evil; something which must be gone through before one can reach the object which is alone worthwhile. In other words, the external idea of the aim leads to a separation of means from end, while an end which grows up within an activity as plan for its direction is always both ends and means, the distinction being only one of convenience. Every means is a temporary end until we have attained it. Every end becomes a means of carrying activity further as soon as it is achieved… Every divorce of end from means diminishes by that much the significance of the activity and tends to reduce it to a drudgery from which one would escape if he could…(1916, p. 54 – 55).

This process is evident, for instance, in TEPs like PROTEACH. Although PROTEACH has a very detailed account of what "reflection" means (Ross et al.,

1992, p. 27), "our definition of reflection is still evolving…" an "ongoing process of evaluation… leads to clarification of its goals, and to changes in instructional strategies. It is this recursive, reflective process that is the core of PROTEACH" (p. 37 – 38). Another TEP claims that "the very conception of reflection itself should be open to growth and transformation" (McCaleb et al., 1992, p. 64).

The end-in-view can be decided only by an analysis of the action. The starting point is the action and not the end, and the question is what could be the consequences of the action. The important point is, according to Dewey, if the desired end is fixed beforehand, in a precise and unequivocal manner, the thinking process is not reflective but technical. "We do not know what we are really after until a *course* of action is mentally worked out" (Dewey, 1922/1930, p. 36 – 37). This means that ends are always contextual (e.g., what is wanted for one child may be wrong for another). It also means that it is impossible to separate the descriptive (is) from the normative (ought), since the "ought" emerges (although not deduced) from the "is", and the "is" is interpreted in the light of various "oughts":

> As far as it [the notion "end"] means consequences actually reached, it is clearly dependent upon means used, while measures in their capacity of means are dependent upon the end in the sense that they have to be used and judged on the ground of their actual objective values. On this basis, as *end-in-view* represents or is an *idea* of the final consequences, in case the idea is formed *on* the *ground of the means that are judged to be most likely to produce the end.* The end-in-view is thus itself a means for directing action – just a man's *idea* of health to be attained or a house to be built is not identical with *end* in the sense of actual outcome but is a means for directing action to achieve that end (Dewey, 1939, p. 52).

Sennett takes Dewey's ideas one step further. "Pragmatism", he says, "has argued that to work well people need freedom from means-ends relationships" (Sennett, 2008, p. 288). This is because to work well means to do the best work you can, "to do it for its own sake", regardless of any external limitations (such as time or budget), and this might be in conflict with the external constraints (p. 9). In other words, to work well is a mode of BEING and not an instrument for HAVING. (In some approaches, like protestant ethics, it is a sign of DOING because that is what God expects from you.) According to Sennett, experience has two undividable meanings. It names something that makes an emotional inner impression, and at the same time, something which turns one outward and requires skill rather than sensibility. Without the inner monitor of "how it feels", "you may succumb to the vice of instrumentalism" (p. 288). But the outer aspect is what defines an expert: "we would try to make the particular knowledge we possess transparent in order that others can understand and respond to it" (p. 289)

For Sennett, the emphasis on the connection between means and ends is the Pragmatism contribution to ethics. "Pragmatism wants to emphasize the value of asking ethical questions during the work process… (p. 295). Curiously enough, Valli asserts that "Although Dewey discussed the importance of reflective dispositions – wholeheartedness, responsibility, and open mindedness – he was mostly preoccupied with the cognitive, systematic aspects of reflection. He gave much less attention to intuition and moral urgency" (Valli, 1997, p. 69).

As the above discussion clarifies, Valli's interpretation cannot be justified.

Following Dewey's insight, Van Manen (1977) differentiates between three levels of reflectivity of "deliberative rationality",

> On the first level of deliberative rationality, the practical is concerned mainly with means rather than ends... On this level, the practical refers to the technical application of educational knowledge and of basic curriculum principles for the purpose of attaining a given end.

> On [a] higher level of reflectivity, it is assumed that every educational choice is based on a value commitment to some interpretive framework by those involved in the curriculum process. The practical then refers to the process of analyzing and clarifying individual and cultural experiences, meanings, perceptions, assumptions, prejudgments, and presuppositions, for the purpose of orienting practical actions.

> But in order to deliberate the worth of educational goals and experiences, a still higher level of reflective rationality is needed. It is on this highest level of deliberative rationality that the practical assumes its classical politico-ethical meaning of social wisdom. On this level, the practical addresses itself, reflectively, to the question of the worth of knowledge and to the nature of the social conditions necessary for raising the question of worthwhileness in the first place. The practical involves a constant critique of domination, of institutions, and of repressive forms of authority (p. 226 – 227).

Valli elaborates on van Manen's typology, and stipulates six levels of "Reflective Teacher Preparation", the first two represent "technological rationality" and the other four "reflective practice":

1. Technical rationality, of the behavioral kind, in which there is no reflection about generic instruction and management behaviors derived from research on teaching, because they are *prescribed.*

2. Technical decision making, in which the reflection is about generic instruction and management behaviors derived from research on teaching and how performance matches to external guidelines.

3. Reflection-in-action whose content is personal teaching performance and its focus is on conceptualizing craft and propositional knowledge.

4. Deliberative (social efficiency, cognitive) whose content is a range of teaching concerns and the focus is weighing claims and viewpoints

5. Personalistic (developmental, narrative) whose content is personal growth and relational issues, and it focuses on hearing one's voice.

6. Critical whose content is social and political dimensions of schooling, while its focus is on problematizing the goals and purposes of schooling in light of justice and other ethical criteria (Valli, 1992 Afterword, p. 221).

While the first two levels of reflection are not that different from the previous phase of the "applied science, technical rationality" conception[33], the other four suggest that the process of educating teachers should deal with broader contexts. (e.g., Ciriello, Valli, Taylor, 1992)[34]. Given this hierarchy, it is often contentious to what level TEPs should orient themselves (Calderhead, 1992, p. 145 – 146). Some teacher educators claim that reflection is only efficient once initial skills have been established. This means that novice teachers, such as those in initial training, may use reflection to improve on specific and immediate skills. Other teacher educators disagree. They believe that the reflective attitude to teaching has to be learned and it is the job of TEPs to instill it in the prospective teacher. Moreover, it is not enough that the students "fell prey to a prevailing mentality which justified using any management or survival strategy as long as it 'worked'." They want students to think "about principled action or the ethical issues of schooling" (Ciriello, Valli, Taylor, 1992, p.107).

Usually, the reflective practitioner approach has been limited to the practicum and their associated method courses. But Valli (1992) and Korthagen (2001) provide examples of TEPs which, as a whole, try to enhance the reflective teacher concept. In most of these programs it is possible to find pedagogies such as inquiry based learning, journals, narratives and biographies, action research, self-study, cases, and supervised practicum, as well as focus on workshops, cohorts, students presentations and PDS[35]. Depending on the content of the reflection, each of the programs emphasizes different philosophical, historical and scientific theories which seem to be necessary to improve the process of reflection by adding different voices to the framework (See Appendix, example 6).

There are some concerns about the effectiveness of reflection in TEPs. Calderhead (1992, p. 145 – 146), we have seen, questions whether and what type of reflection can be promoted in pre-service course of studies. According to Tomlinson (1999), the teachers do not confirm the importance of reflection. Many of them have "an antipathy towards deliberate reflection generally and formal 'theory' in particular" (p. 408). Richardson and Placier (2001) survey a number of researches which found that "students who come into the program without reflective orientations do not gain very much from teacher education courses that emphasize reflection" (p. 915)[36]. Possibly the problem is that the students should have some real teaching experience in order to see the merits of this approach. "Some students resist becoming reflective rather than develop reflective capacities" (p. 915). Does it mean that these students will not be professional teachers, or that they have not received adequate preparation? These findings pose a dilemma "between believing on the one hand that there may be substantial numbers of teachers who are professionally lacking, in that they are not and do not wish to be reflective, and on the other hand admitting that there may be many teachers who manage to become professionally competent without being reflective" (Tomlinson, 1999, p. 408). These findings might be justified if it is found that teachers who critically reflect on their work are less or as efficient as non-reflective ones, or if non-reflective teachers are equally or more effective than the reflective ones.

So here we are at the crossroad. On the one hand we can understand reflection in a technical-rationality manner. In this option, reflection might produce deliberative teachers who can improve "what works". On the other hand, we can understand reflection in substantive-rationality manner so that it will deal with the reasonable, and not just the rational. In that case it might lead to critical teachers which will question the entire education system. The choice between the two paths goes back of course, to the ideological, ethical and epistemological presuppositions of the TEP. While the first option conveys the HAVING mode of existence, the second is primarily that of BEING (although it might turn out to be of the DOING mode if the individual has a concrete ideology he wants to implement).

Given these possibilities, the prevalent choice to date is to embrace the technical rationality approach but augment it with some ingredients of social awareness. Before looking closely at this option, it is interesting to pursue the other way, and look at TEPs which embrace the substantial rationality option, by following Dewey, van Manen (third level of reflectivity) or Valli's (levels 4-6). It is even possible to intensify the reflective attitude of the teacher's work and emphasize that to be a professional teacher just means to be engaged in an ongoing rigid and thoughtful research about the ends and the means of teaching. The paradigm of such a view can be found in the Finnish teacher education system.

Research-Based Approach to Teacher Education

TEPs in Finland aim to be effective: "Good teaching takes place according to a curriculum and a good teacher is able to achieve the results set forth in the curriculum. According to this rationale, a utilitarian criterion was adopted: effectiveness" (Kansanen, 2003, p. 92). However, this criterion should not mislead us, for in Finland the teacher is responsible for the curriculum (both aims and means), so that effectiveness becomes an inner criterion, and the rationality is substantive.

The research based approach is "an organizing theme" of the program (Toom et al., 2010, p. 334; Jyrhama et al. 2008, p. 2). Research is integrated in the program from its start, so that students "have opportunities for self-directed reflection and developing a personal practical theory of the instructional process" (Toom et al., 2010, p. 334). The students are required to conduct their own research (Bachelor and Master theses), but the aim is not to produce researchers but "to provide students with skills and knowledge to complete their own studies, observe their pupils, and analyze their thinking" (2010, p. 334). They should be able to base their pedagogical decision-making on a theoretical foundation and reflect on their work as teachers. As summarized by Toom et al., "the aim is to educate autonomous and reflective teachers who are capable of using research in their teaching and can be defined as pedagogically-thinking teachers" (p. 333).

The research-based approach is preferred to the conventional "everyday practice and mastering general teaching skills, acquisition of practical skills and fundamental knowledge that typify the whole instructional process as well as a variety of subject matter pedagogical content knowledge courses" (Toom et al., 2010, p. 338), which is quite limited. It significantly improved student achievements, but only up to a threshold… "Beyond which further effect is minimal… However, beyond this level, there is a need for a conceptual level whose goal is the sustained development of a teacher's work…" (p. 338).

According to Toom et al. (2010), "Teachers are able to analyse and develop their work. Teachers' pedagogical thinking means the ability to conceptualize everyday phenomena, to look at them as part of a larger instructional process and to justify decisions and actions made during this process" (p. 339). They are engaged in three levels of acting and thinking: the action level: planning, realizing and evaluating actions; the practical theory of education level; and the meta-theory of education based on practical theory.

The Research-Based Approach encompasses the enlightenment concept of scientific inquiry and its Deweyan/Popperian problem-solving attitude, based on a cycle of self-responsible planning, action and reflection/evaluation in dealing with professional tasks and problems. All the courses of the TEP are integrated with research. The structure and the curriculum of teacher education in Finland are focused on academic disciplines, research studies, pedagogical studies, communications, and language and ICT studies (Niemi & Jakku-Sihvonen, 2011, p. 35) (See Appendix example 7).

The amount of time allocated to the practicum reflects a "deductive-rational" approach: extensive academic studies, including methodological studies, are more valuable than practical teacher training (Toom et al., 2010, 334). However, teaching practice is integrated into all levels of teacher education time. In the first year it is integrated with theoretical studies, in second and third years, it is conducted mainly in university teacher-training schools. It starts with specific subject-areas, and moves towards more holistic and pupil centered activities. In the fourth and fifth years, usually conducted in municipal field schools, there are different options for developing expertise, which can be connected with the MA thesis (Niemi & Jakku-Sihvonen, 2011, pp. 43 – 44).

Niemi and Jakku-Sihvonen describe the main principles of teaching practice: It should start as early as possible, it integrates theory and practice and, gradually, it supports students to take holistic responsibility (2011, p. 44). As pointed out by Sahlberg: "Over the five-year program, candidates advanced from basic teaching practice, to advance practice, and then to final practice. During each of these phases, students observe lessons by experienced teachers, practice teaching while being observed by supervisory teachers, and deliver independent lessons… Practicum experiences comprise about 15 to 25 percent of teachers' overall preparation time" (Sahlberg, 2011, 36).

An important characteristic of the Finnish model is its notion of 'Didaktik'. Westbury notes that "Didaktik is centered on the forms of reasoning about teaching appropriate for an autonomous professional teacher who has complete freedom within the framework of the *Lehrplan* to develop his or her own approaches to teaching". Thus, "*Didaktik*, as a system for thinking about the problems of the 'curriculum,' is not centered on the task of directing and managing the work of school systems or of selecting a curriculum for this school or this district. Instead, *Didaktik* provides teachers with ways of considering the essential what, how and why questions around their teaching of their students in their classrooms... Every teacher must, necessarily, assume a role as reflective educational (and curriculum) theorist in order to teach anything, anywhere" (Westbury, 2000, 17-19). So that teaching becomes a substantive-rationality endeavor.

The German tradition, from which this notion is taken, links "*Didaktik*" with "*Bildung*". In the words of Wilhelm von Humboldt, one of the founders of the *Bildung* ideal, we, humans are born with a "concept of humanity in our person". The *Bildung* process mainly concerns human "inner improvement and elevations" as he "seeks to grasp as much world as possible and bind it as tightly as he can to himself" (von Humboldt, 1793/2000, p. 58 – 59). The human being has to "reflect back into his inner being the clarifying light and the comforting warmth of everything that he undertakes outside himself..." (p. 59). This process is not done in a vacuum, but always within a given culture. The individual, guided on his journey by a certain inner picture (*Bild*), tries to attain his self-fulfillment through his encounters with his cultural heritage. In the process of *Bildung,* the universal concept of humanity, , has to be uncovered and given a personal interpretation. For this to happen, the human has to undergo as many different life-experiences as possible, to recognize the cultural heritage of the society he is born into, and be acquainted with its knowledge as it is manifested in the art and the sciences.

Bildung is a holistic process, based on the individual's experiences and reflections upon them. Experiences, however, contain what happens to others, real or imaginative, including historical or artistic happenings, and heroes with whom the individual can identify. Humboldt emphasizes that "Within him are several faculties to represent one and the same object to himself in various guises: now as a concept of reason, now as an image of the imagination, now as an intuition of the senses. Using all of these... he must try to grasp Nature, not so much in order to become acquainted with it from all sides, but rather... to strengthen his own innate power... its own self-determination" (von Humboldt, 1793/2000, p. 59).

The notion of *Bildung* has its enlightenment origin. As we shall see in chapter 8, it has also a strong Romantic flavor because it emphasizes the BEING mode of existence[37]. As Seigel stresses, *Bildung*, is "a process... in which the singular potential inherent in particular individuals could find realization in the world: life in society helped bring the self to cognizance of its own needs and powers because the persons and conditions it encountered there help to reveal the inner structure of its own being" (2005, p. 333). *Bildung* is, therefore, a never-ending process. It is a life-long-learning process, and it does not have any external aim. "The result of *Bildung* is not achieved in the manner of a technical construction, but grows out of the inner process of formation and cultivation and therefore remains in a constant state of further continued *Bildung*." (Gadamer, 1960/1989, p. 12).

According to Gadamer, the general characteristic of *Bildung* is "to keep oneself open to what is other, to other, more universal points of view... To distance oneself from oneself and from one's private purposes means to look at these in the way that others sees them" (1960/1989 p. 17). As Gadamer emphasizes, it involves cultivating a universal sense, and not the universality of concepts (p. 18).

Didaktik is the method of conducting the process of *Bildung* in the educational system. According to Kansanen, this means that there are "general aims and goals that are common to all teachers and all subject matters and that can be expressed in all teaching and all other activities in school, all the time" (2004, p. 216). In a way which resembles van Manen's or Valli's typologies, Kanansen maintains that

> In this curriculum, there are two levels, one focusing on a basic domain of teacher education, i.e., methodology, subject matter instruction, pedagogical content knowledge, et cetera. This level is enriched by a second level which is identified as general teacher education. In this respect, teacher education focuses on the intricate mix of normative and descriptive elements in the interaction between teaching and learning, on the combination of declarative and procedural knowledge and their relation to professional beliefs and attitudes, on ethics of education, et cetera (2004, p. 207).

The layer of everyday practice includes the mastering of common teaching methods. In basic teacher education, the programs usually concentrate on practical skills and the fundamental knowledge of the whole instructional process. The general level of teacher education is a kind of metacognition, discovered by looking at one's own work and decisions concerning teaching. This level addresses issues such as:

– teacher thinking and student thinking, in accordance and in disagreement;
– teachers' declarative and procedural knowledge and their belief systems;
– good teaching and good teachers;
– descriptive and normative thinking;
– teachers' professional morality and their moral dilemmas;
– students' moral perspectives;
– promoting moral learning in students;
– reflection in counseling situations (Kanansen, 2004, p. 213).

This kind of Didaktik might clearly lead to "reflective progressivism" and to TEPs which aim to "change committed approach" (Simola, 1998, p. 333). Substantive rationality has an important place in this approach.

Toom et al. emphasize that the research-based approach is part of the academic university curriculum (2010, p. 334). It belongs to the pedagogy of higher education and the principles of how academic studies are organized (p. 335)[38]. University teachers conduct research on the subject they teach. Students are provided with the means to carry out research and they behave like researchers during their studies. They develop an understanding of educational research with a positive attitude, and enhance student teachers' pedagogical thinking. "Instead of providing ready answers and tips, a research-based approach encourages student teachers to make independent pedagogical judgments. This calls for autonomy, which in turn, requires sufficient educational knowledge and professional self-assurance..." (p. 335). Moreover "Inquiry orientation is also transmitted from the teacher to the students... Teachers serve as an example and guide their students towards inquiring learning" (p. 340). In light of the *Bildung* ideal, it is quite clear why children have to be able to develop their inquiring learning. Without it, they will not be able to make sense of the changing world.

Kansanen reports that a common criticism against research-based teacher education is that "it is simplistic idealism and has nothing to do with reality". He responds with "We need idealistic thinking" (2006, p. 21). The Finnish model is much more responsive to the enlightenment ideal of the "educated man" or to Russell Proposal. It suits the country's educational system, which is focused on broad learning, and gives equal value to all aspects of an individual's growth in personality, moral, creativity, knowledge and skills (Hautamaki et al., 2008). As teachers are educated to become autonomous actors, with the ability to make rational theory-based decisions and to consume as well as produce research, they are able to meet the challenges of the future.

Two questions remain open: First, TEPs in Finland recruit the best graduates of BA studies. Can a program like *Research-Based Approach* be successful with less talented students? Probably the answer is positive, because the approach is the archetype of the schools as well, but it may be suspected that such a program might not suitable to less developed countries, in which the educational system cannot rely on the autonomy of the teachers (McKinsey, 2010). Second, the program is quite expensive. Finland, which is a well-fare state, has the required resources. Can it be implemented in a country which does not supply enough funds to the education system?

The National Academy of Education Model (NAEM)

What is feasible in Finland might be a dream for TEPs in the US and elsewhere (Darling-Hammond, 2009; Sahlberg, 2011). The basic difference is that while TEPs in Finland incorporate the substantial rationality approach, the US TEPs prefer instrumental rationality. One of the most ambitious attempts to offer a general guideline to TEPs along the latter approach has been made in 2005 by the US National Academy of Education's Committee on Teacher Education. The NAE model presents a detailed picture of "what teachers should learn and be able to do" (Darling-Hammond & Bransford, 2005), and suggests the content and the structure of the TEPs that can ensure their graduates will be effective teachers.

The NAE committee, comprised of researchers, teachers, and teacher educators, asks how could what is known about learning inform the curriculum and the design of teacher education programs. This question discloses the entire message. According to the committee, the focus of any TEP should shift from teaching to learning, from the teacher to the learner, and from the teacher's input to the pupil's achievements. Issues such as how children learn and how to assess their learning become of an utmost importance, since the teacher's aim is primarily that all pupils will learn.

This transformation is reflected in the following figure:

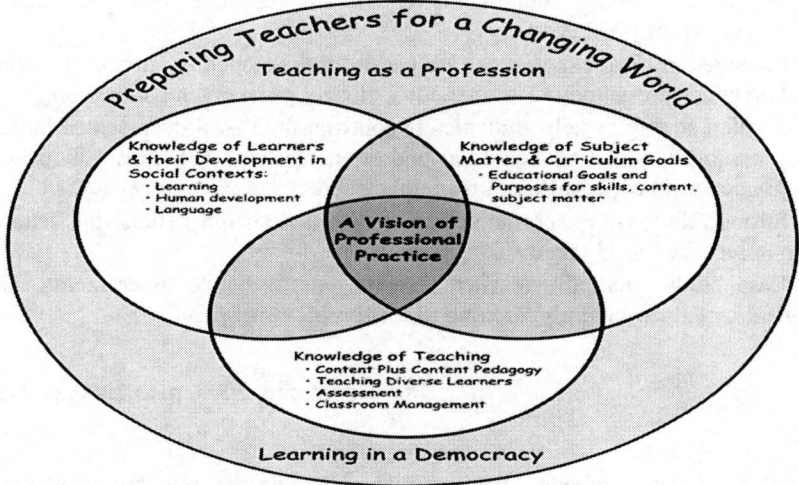

(Darling-Hammond, Bransford, LePage, 2005, p. 11)

NAEM requires that any TEP should be cohesive and coherent and not a casual list of courses supplemented by loosely connected practicum. Teaching is seen as *techne*, and the teacher as knowledge-creator practitioner, who has to be involved in reflection and research about his work. The clinical approach is encouraged, as well as the establishment of Professional Development Schools (PDS). The teacher's work should be evidence based, and utilize the "best practices" to promote learning and enhance equity and social justice.

To be professional, the teacher's activities should be evidence based, but the evidence should not be restricted to academic, theoretical knowledge. It includes the "what works" practical knowledge of experienced teachers, and the data the teacher accumulates on his pupils' learning. These ingredients should be integrated into the teacher's knowledge-base. Hence, the pyramid construction of the knowledge base, in which the scientists inform the teachers about their findings, has to be replaced by a much more complex structure, in which teachers themselves become knowledge-creating.

After a "set of case studies about extraordinary teacher education programs" (Darling-Hammond, 2000, p. v), Darling-Hammond finds that the following features characterize "strong programs of teacher preparation":

– A common, clear vision of good teaching permeates all course-work and clinical experiences;
– Well-defined standards of practice and performance are used to guide and evaluate coursework and clinical work;
– Curriculum is grounded in knowledge of child and adolescent development, learning, social contexts, and subject-matter pedagogy, taught in the context of practice;
– Extended clinical experiences are carefully developed to support the ideas and practices presented in simultaneous, closely interwoven coursework;
– Explicit strategies help students (1) confront their own deep-seated beliefs and assumptions about learning and students and (2) learn about the experiences of people different from themselves;
– Strong relationships, common knowledge, and shared beliefs link school- and university-based faculty;
– Case study methods, teacher research, performance assessments, and portfolio evaluation apply learning to real problems of practice.

(Darling-Hammond, 2000, p. x; 2006, p. 41)[39]

To implement these methods, TEPs must develop their own "signature pedagogies". According to Shulman, "Signature pedagogies are… the forms of instruction that leap to mind when we first think about the preparation of members of particular professions" (2005, p. 52). As mentioned, these can be student teaching, performance assessments and portfolios, analyses of teaching and learning, case methods, autobiographies, and practitioner inquiry" (Darling-Hammond et al. 2005 [The Design], p. 441). They should build the new teacher's ability to reflect and analyze his performance.

The last mentioned pedagogies should be realized in all the courses (theoretical and practical). They will help the student to formulate his own productive theory (theory with a 't'), and demonstrate that theoretical knowledge (theory with a 'T') might have practical relevance and the potential to change the prospective teacher's attitude toward teaching and learning. Such pedagogies might overcome the three basic challenges that any TEP must face: The apprenticeship of observation, the problem of enactment, and the problem of complexity (Darling-Hammond, 2006, pp. 34 – 40). They might also narrow the gap between the ways the students understand the "field" and the way their teacher educators grasp it (See: Appendix, example 8 for an Israeli variant of this approach.)

NAEM presents another step towards more professional preparation programs. It replaces the "applied science" approach in favor of the "evidence based" one. It favors the *technitas* over the technician, the "clinician" over the "provider". It is much more focused and target oriented. It is cohesive and coherent, although it seems to abandon the attempt to incorporate the subject-matter studies into the TEP. It is much more practice oriented and the question of social justice (i.e., that all the children will learn) has an important place in its curriculum (e.g., addressing diversity).

In particular NAEM presupposes a certain scientific theory of how to develop an "adaptive expert". According to this theory, there are two axes, efficiency and innovation which characterize the adaptive expert. On the one hand he is an efficient agent "who can rapidly retrieve and accurately apply appropriate knowledge and skills to solve a problem or understand an explanation" (Schwartz et al. 2005). On the other hand, he is innovative and creative in face of change. An efficient TEP should do both: the "just do that" must be supplemented by "letting go" (Bransford et al. 2005, p. 77).

What kind of reasoning stands behind the NAEM? Again, it is just another instance of the familiar technical-rationality mode of thinking. TEPs should be efficient and accountable. This time, the reasoning has two layers. First it relates to the teacher. He is a professional who knows the "best practices", and able to implement them adaptively in his activities. Research informs us that to promote the student teacher achievements, it is necessary to construct a learning environment in which he will have opportunities to experience teaching, and reflect on his experiences, by themselves, with a supervisor, and within a community of practice. In this process, the concept of "evidence based activity" replaced the "applied science" one. The student has to learn to work like a clinician who can efficiently diagnose and treat his clients. This is an improved version of the teacher as a technician because it is more tailored to how teachers actually work. The teacher is viewed as an agent who has his own practical theory. In the second layer, it relates to the TEPs. Efficient TEPs recognize the "best practices" of teacher education, and are able to implement them, in adaptive manner, in their environment and activities. The aforementioned listed characteristics of the "strong programs of teacher preparation", is an example of an evidence based approach to TEPs.

Nevertheless, NAEM presupposes a problematic worldview. In Aristotelian terms, it focuses on the *technitas* aspects of the teacher's work and the *phronetic* side of his mission is undervalued. Take the clinical model, which is borrowed from medicine. The preparation should simulate cases in which the practitioner is requested to solve a professional problem on the basis of his theoretical knowledge, productive theory, and practical skills. The clinical model deals with the practitioner's instrumental behaviors. It might inspire deliberations on 'what works', it might even inspire innovative thinking about what might work, but usually it does not ask what can be the value of 'what works', and thereby ignores van Manen's or Valli's upper levels of reflection. The clinical model ignores Dewey's concept of end-in-view. What is missing here are the pedagogical aspects of teaching. The teacher could become a good *technitas*, but he is not prepared to be a *phronimon*, a teacher for life. The child, however, does not only need a competent clinical teacher who knows to diagnose his academic situation and find a suitable remedy. He deserves a mature friend who can support him as he deals with the complexities of his life. He wants to have a pedagogue, who can reliably guide him amidst and toward the frightening future. This is especially problematic today, in a society like ours, in which the teacher is requested to function *in loco parentis*, because in too many cases there is no family that can support the child (van Manen, 1991, p. 8).

Like any other technical rationality deliberation, TEPs do not question their aims, but concentrate on their "hows". The clinical approach, the case studies method, and the PDS are all based on the "best practice" paradigm. But "what works" does not always work. Learning from "what works" presupposes that we have already found the best means to achieve certain ends, and that we have to learn from our successes and failures. But it also means that the "is" is regarded as "ought". The "what works" approach presupposes that the current educational system is basically acceptable. Although it has its flaws, they are correctable, and it is possible to improve the system if the teachers will work as they should (i.e., as efficient teachers). This approach is conservative and conformist. The question, to what extent the educational system itself can be justifiable, is not being asked. The system's reasonableness is not questioned. Nowhere in the NAEM can one find a triggering question about the system's aims, or about its vision of the good teacher. Instrumental rationality is again the dominant hegemonic strategy.

But as Gert Biesta says,

> The most important question for educational professionals…is *not* about the effectiveness of their actions but about the potential educational value of what they do, i.e., about the educational desirability of the opportunities for learning that follow from their actions (Biesta, 2010, 36-37).

Oancea and Pring (2009) argue that the 'what works' approach is not value-neutral. Accepting the here and now, it neglects the problematic normative agenda which underlies the research, and tends to support the current policy makers ideology. A TEP, whose aim is to enhance the prospective teachers' critical thinking, cannot be based only on 'what works' research or experience. Lee Shulman (2007) distinguishes between the practitioner and the *praxitioner*. The *praxitioner* deliberates like a *phronimon*. He considers not only how to improve his actions, but also how his actions will improve his world (Kincheloe, 2004; Weglinsky, 2004).

There are two different intuitions here. One: The teacher cannot act against the society which he represents. He should be a loyal to his society, its norms, its *Weltanschuung*. In particular, he should faithfully implement the educational policies and regulations of the political system. The teacher must remain practitioner or *technitas*. As a professional agent he should not be involved in any social debate outside school. The second intuition sees the teacher as the representative of a still-to-be ideal society. His job is to educate his students to improve society, and his responsibility, as an educator, is to act as *praxitioner*. In that case he will act according to substantial rationality, and become a "transformatory intellectual" (Giroux, 1988).

NAEM favors the practitioner teacher. As the NAEM figure displays, the socio-political sphere envelops the program. It is not placed in its center. NAEM addresses the social issue by emphasizing the role of the teacher as a "change agent", in the sense that he has a responsibility to "create new conditions for learning that provide more equal access to challenging curriculum and more engagement in decision making" (Darling-Hammond et al., 2005 Educational, p. 170). In her TEPs survey, Darling-Hammond finds that "the view that education is a social force and that teachers are moral change agents is evident throughout the programs we studied" (Darling-Hammond, 2006, p. 238). This theme is characterized by a "concern for social justice and educational equity", not only in foundation courses but "also in those on methods of teaching and child development and the advisement process" (p. 238). "In all these programs", Darling-Hammond discovers that "students are repeatedly asked to think about the consequences for students' individual and social development of teaching decisions, means of organizing the classroom, and choices of curriculum materials... Students teaching placements are typically well-developed sites for democratic practice in which antiracist and egalitarian norms are pursued" (p. 238). In some of the institutions faculty members believe that "teaching can change the world – child by child" (p. 241). Student teachers are infused with "willingness to struggle with issues of race, class, gender, and social inequality" (p. 242), as they appear in their experiences. And special attention is given to skills for teaching diverse learners (p. 246).

One problem of the piecemeal "child by child" approach is that, if the educational system is itself the problem and not the treatment of social injustice and inequality, the teacher's job becomes frustrating and he might become exhausted and desperate. It might be rewarding to change the lives of individuals, but it becomes a Sisyphean mission to do so time and again without a prospect to radically transform the situation that causes the problems in the first place. This is especially true if the society adopts the achievement principle as the only type of social esteem.

NAEM, as might be expected from a national institution, does not consider the option of the teacher as *praxitioner*. Its concept of *phronesis* is, therefore, quite limited: its notions of good and bad uncritically coincide with that of the establishment. For example, NAEM presupposes the US vision that the main aim of teaching is that (all) students will succeed in their academic studies (as mandated by the No Child Left Behind legislation). Hence, social justice is understood in terms of giving every child an equal opportunity to achieve high scores. Teaching as a profession is directed to achieve this target, and it disregards other social factors which can contribute to the children's well-being. The larger questions of the how society distributes its wealth, and how the educational system itself contributes to (besides being an outcome of) social inequality is not addressed (Darling-Hammond et al., 2005 Educational, p. 174). Just as though, if only the teachers will be professional enough, the social justice problem would be solved.

In NAEM, teaching is interpreted as preparing all students for "equitable participation in a democratic society" (Darling-Hammond, Bransford, LePage, 2005, p. 11):

> In a democratic society, teachers must evaluate their teaching decisions against the goals of preparing students to be equitable participants in a society that lies on interdependence... This includes a commitment to eliminate disparities in educational opportunities among students, especially those students who have been poorly served by our current system. It also includes ambitious learning opportunities and, in today's society, equitable access to the technological tools that citizens need to succeed (Darling-Hammond, Bransford, LePage, 2005, p. 35).

Though eliminating disparity is seen as an important mission of democratic public education, it is interpreted in strictly utilitarian terms: we need to eliminate disparity because the productiveness of society depends on the contribution of every citizen to its economy. This interpretation is focused on the HAVING mode of existence and advances academic achievements as the only criterion of success and social recognition.

For Dewey, this concept of democracy is too narrow:

> Translated into specific aims, social efficiency indicates the importance of industrial competency... There is, however, grave danger that, in insisting upon this end, existing economic conditions and standards will be accepted as final. A democratic criterion requires us to develop capacity to the point of competency to choose and make its own career. This principle is violated when the attempt is made to fit individuals in advance for definite industrial callings, selected not on the basis of trained original capacities, but on that of the wealth or social status of parents (Dewey, 1916, p. 61).

Substituting "industrial competency" with "ICT competency" will bring his claim up to date. Democracy means much more than equal opportunity in education. It is based on the principle that public contests can be legitimately solved only by dialogue between rival ideas and interests. It is a regime which enables and even encourages diversity by recognizing the equal right of each citizen to participate in and influence the public discussion of mutual problems:

> If democracy has a moral and ideal meaning, it is that a social return be demanded from all and that opportunity for development of distinctive capacities be afforded all ...the adoption of the narrower meaning of efficiency deprives it of its essential justification (Dewey, 1916, p. 64).

John Goodlad (1984, pp. 51 – 56) lists four "big" goals for schooling in the US: academic, vocational, social and civic, and personal goals. Darling-Hammond at al. agree (Darling-Hammond et al., 2005 Educational, p. 172). But NAEM does not meet the challenge of "articulation of [the goods] and commitment to them"

(Goodlad 1984, p. 56). It only emphasizes that, in order to be efficient, the teacher should "understand the social context of schools as organizations… if the members of the school are to accomplish their jobs effectively" ((Darling-Hammond et al., 2005 Educational, p. 175). Adjusting to the expectations of the community (p. 173) and society at large is not the same as being an educational leader in the community.

It is instructive to compare the NAEM worldview with an earlier attempt to construct the teacher's function. In 1956, AACTE published a book called *Teacher Education for a Free People* (Cottrell, 1956). According to the authors of this report, the goal of teacher education is to "prepare teachers to contribute to the improvement of society (sic!) in a threefold manner – as active citizens, as educational leaders in their communities, and as guides who help children and youth become informed, active citizens" (Stratemeyer, 1956, p. 232). Teacher education should prepare teachers which can enhance civic education (Cottrell, 1956 Facing, p. 385). A theme such as "education as a social force in a democracy" (Stratemeyer, 1956, p. 251), from a critical point of view, should underlie any TEP. Although this approach can provide a "midway" position, between the conservative practitioner and the revolutionary *praxitioner*, it is absent from NAEM.

Art Levine notes that "Outcome-based systems, concerned with what students learn, have a single measure of success—student achievement" (Levine, 2006, p. 18). A school system which emphasizes only one, relatively limited, aspect of academic achievements cannot adequately prepare the child to live in a democratic society, because it neglects the dimension of the *phronetic* empowerment of the child. If there is no questioning of the 'what for' of schooling, the school becomes a training institution instead of educational one. A TEP which does not address this aspect cannot prepare the teacher to foster "education in a democracy". In an education system, which recognizes only one criterion of success (academic achievements), schools cannot promote social justice. The very basis of the system is not based on dialogue, but dictated by those who know what is good for the child and not by the genuine desires of himself, his culture, or his environment. NAEM, however, barely addresses this question, though the burden to cure society is placed on the shoulders of the teachers.

NAEM, which shifts the focus from teaching to learning from delivery to construction, and from the teacher to the child, might be problematic for other reasons. There is a growing criticism against constructivist instruction (Tobias & Duffy, 2009). Rosenshine, for example, finds that in mathematics, "direct instruction is particularly important for students from low SES backgrounds (2009, p. 212; cf. NMAP, 2008, p. XXII). This means that constructivist instruction might present an obstacle to the 'social justice' endeavor. The question of diversity raises another facet. It is arguable that the constructivist paradigm of teaching and learning is problematic from a normative point of view (Bowers, 2005, p. IX; Jardine, 2006, pp. 105 – 126; Jardine et al. pp.123 – 135). It promotes the neo-liberal agenda, because it neglects the cultural heritage of the individual. There is only one legitimate culture (WASP) which is democratic, progressive, and liberal, while all the rest are primitive, oppressive, and dangerous. Despite the pluralistic cover, the reflective-rational approach is utterly modern in its trust of reason and science.

The clinician attitude might distance the teacher even further from his pedagogical mission. Like a physician who is more interested in the illness than in the sick person, the child may become a "case" which has to be studied instead of an individual who has to be empowered. Almost every child becomes a "problem" which has to be treated. The child is no more a human being but an object of a persistent process of diagnosis (testing) and evaluation. We have already seen the rational "trial and error method" in which every activity is problem solving. While this method is rational and reflective, it leaves little room for spontaneous emotional relationships. "Cold" deliberation means that empathy and sympathy is replaced by rational, professional thinking.

NAEM is caught in the 'teacher as professional' model, in which the major role of the teacher is to care that the child will learn (i.e., attain high grades on the exams). It does not prepare him, however, to care for the child. This model does not concentrate on the emotional or social aspects of the teacher-child relationship, as if the sole aim of these relations is to enable learning. (Moral and community issues are dealt with under the title of "Classroom Management".) The criticism is that the clinical approach, if focused only on the child as learner, and the teacher as expert, ignores the pedagogical role of the prospective teacherFor sure, there are many TEPs which avoid falling into these traps.

NAEM is located at the continental divide between the teacher as autonomous professional technitas and the teacher as proficient technician. The "what works" attitude might signify the importance of the teachers' practical knowledge, their ability to create knowledge, their ability to evaluate their successes and failures. It might, however, point to the opposite direction as well. For, there are two basic answers to the questions: who decides 'what works' and according to what criteria? The first one is that the teachers themselves, especially as community of professionals, know what works. They have the practical *nus* which enables them to identify successful professional activities. And they might perform the research (e.g., action research or self-study), which explains why they are successful. The second is that success is defined by outcomes, and the outcomes are defined by educational policies. Thus, if the major aim is that all students will pass a certain exam, the 'what works' research should objectively locate the variables which tend to facilitate the achievement of this outcome. Although 'what works' reflects the teachers' activities, the evaluation of these activities is not left to the teachers. Both the definition of the standards and the ways of measuring their attainment is accomplished by non-teachers. The first answer, adopted for example in Finnland, strengthened the professional autonomy of the teachers. The second weakened it (even if it is accepted by the teachers themselves). The first is essential to the teacher's well-being, the second threatens to corrupt his professional identity (Sennett, 1998).

NAEM favors the first interpretation of 'what works'. "The recommendations for teacher education discussed in this volume represent the considered judgments of a large number of experienced practitioners and scholars in the field of education" (Darling-Hammond, Bransford & Lepage, 2005, p. 21). Although it recognizes the important role of external standards and regulations in defining the aims of education (Darling-Hammond, Banks et al. 2005, p. 172), it tries to preserve the teacher educators' professional autonomy.

Arne Duncan, the US Secretary of Education, favors the second. The to-date focus on the TEPs' outcomes, as they are measured by their graduates' success to bring their pupils to high achievements in standardized exams, might explain why many politicians are not satisfied with NAEM. They want programs that "have a shared vision of what constitutes good teaching and best practices including a single-minded focus on improving student learning and using data to inform instruction" (Arne Duncan U.S. Secretary of Education, Speech at Teachers College, October 22, 2009). For them, the NAEM professional outlook is too little too late. Duncan accuses:

> ...by almost any standard, many if not most of the nation's 1,450 schools, colleges, and departments of education are doing a mediocre job of preparing teachers for the realities of the 21st century classroom. America's university-based teacher preparation programs need revolutionary change—not evolutionary tinkering... (Arne Duncan, October 22, 2009)

Duncan claims that "I taught it—but the students didn't learn it" cannot be an excuse for failure, and adds:

> My good friend, Congressman George Miller, the chair of the House Committee on Education and a great reform advocate, points out that America's taxpayers already generously support teacher preparation programs. And it is only right that this investment should be well spent (Arne Duncan, October 22, 2009).

In the climate of a neo-liberal regime of privatization, accountability, and efficiency, it is quite tempting to prefer "programs committed to results: programs that use data, including student achievement data, to foster an ethic of continuous improvement for students and teachers" (Arne Duncan, October 22, 2009). What is needed is that states and districts "carefully track the performance of teachers to their teacher preparation programs to identify which programs are producing well-prepared teachers—and which programs are not turning out effective teachers" so that it will be possible to study and copy "the practices of effective teacher preparation programs—and encourage the lowest-performers to shape up or shut down" (Arne Duncan, October 22, 2009).

The newly established (beginning in summer 2011) TEP called TERI (Teacher Education Redesign Initiative at the University of Minnesota) seems to meet Duncan's requirements (See Appendix, example 9). In the TERI website, the University proudly claims that "We will measure progress made by the students taught by teachers who have completed preparation with us and guarantee that these P–12 students will experience at least one year of academic growth in one year of instruction". (http://conservancy.umn.edu/bitstream/90574/1/Race%20to%20the%20Top%20Funds.pdf; retrieved 8/8/2011).

Interestingly enough, TERI clearly bases its strategy on NAEM. It stresses four "Key areas": (1) Partnerships: Professional development schools in partnership districts that improve student performance through research-based teaching; (2) Adaptive Expertise: Teachers with an expert knowledge base, defined as a balanced combination of efficiency, and ability to differentiate instruction for students' needs; (3) Performance driven curriculum: focus on both what we teach (content) and who we teach (English Language (ELLs), special education, culturally diverse communities); (4) Research agenda: Questions centered on effectiveness of our program in preparing teachers who make a difference for students.

The program's "Pedagogies of Performance include: Performance assessment strategies: Microteaching; Performance tasks; Teaching portfolios; Analysis of teaching and learning: Video analysis and Student work analysis; Case methods; Autobiography; Inquiry and action research" (http://conservancy.umn.edu/bitstream/90574/1/Race%20to%20the%20Top%20Funds.pdf; retrieved 10/08/2011).

SUMMARY

Teachers' knowledge has a vital component of practical knowledge, which has to be at the core of any TEP. There are two different paths along the way to become a reflective practitioner. The first is to follow the substantial rationality stance, and to define the teachers' role as *Bildung* facilitators. The teacher should become a well-educated, research oriented practitioner. He is a *phronimon* whose long term aim is to educate an independent, autonomous human being. The second is the technical rationality ideal in which the teacher is merely a *technitas*. His short term aim is that children will learn (i.e., achieve high grades in standardized exams). His hope is that this will render them productive citizens in the future.

The first, the *phronimon* oriented path, leads to the enlightenment ideal of the educated person. In the second, the *technitas* oriented one, the enlightenment vision is understood in strictly utilitarian terms. In that path, the HAVING mode of existence becomes dominant and pushes aside both BEING and DOING. The teacher's role is restricted to enhancing the academic achievements of his students. Thereafter, it is possible to define his functioning in rational problem solving terminology, and utilize 'what works' methods to find what he can do, as an adaptive expert, to solve various practical difficulties. Once again the teacher is seen as a mere technician. This approach, as we shall explore in the next chapter might be detrimental to the teacher as professional ideal, and to the academic TEPs as its prerequisite preparation environments.

PREPARING (PSEUDO) PROFESSIONAL: THE PROVISIONAL EMPLOYEE ERA

PHASE 3. "STANDARDS-AND-ACCOUNTABILITY" MODELS

In 1999, The Thomas B. Fordham Foundation publishes a manifesto entitled *The Teachers We Need and How to Get More of Them*. With no word of reluctance, it claims that:

...America is beginning to adopt a powerful, commonsensical strategy for school reform. It is the same approach that almost every successful modern enterprise has adopted to boost performance and productivity: set high standards for results to be achieved, identify clear indicators to measure progress towards those results, and be flexible and pluralistic about the means for reaching those results. This strategy in education is sometimes called "standards-and-accountability" (Thomas B. Fordham Foundation, 1999).

Consequently, the manifesto suggests that:

A better solution to the teacher quality problem is to simplify the entry and hiring process... Instead of requiring a long list of courses and degrees, test future teachers for their knowledge and skills... Focus relentlessly on results, on whether students are learning. This strategy, we are confident, will produce a larger supply of able teachers and will tie judgments about their fitness and performance to success in the classroom...

Rather than buttressing an orthodoxy that does not work, the common sense approach embraces pluralism. In a deregulated environment, good teacher education programs will thrive and prosper. Those that do a poor job will not, once they lose the protection that the regulatory monopoly confers on them... The popularity of such programs as Teach for America, which places liberal arts graduates without formal education course work in public school classrooms in poor rural communities and inner cities, indicates that the prospect of teaching without first being obliged to spend years in pedagogical study appeals to some of our brightest college graduates (Thomas B. Fordham Foundation, 1999).

The main problem with present academic TEPs is that they are ineffective and inefficient. They do not take into account the realities of schools, and the systems' priorities, policies, and regulations. For example, they ignore the fact that the most important ingredient in the preparation of teachers is the practicum. The recently published "*Transforming Teacher Education through Clinical Practice: A National Strategy to Prepare Effective Teachers*" tries to meet this challenge. It calls for "a fundamental shift in how we conceptualize, deliver, monitor, evaluate, oversee, and staff teacher preparation" (NCATE, 2010, p. 12):

> The education of teachers in the United States needs to be turned upside down. To prepare effective teachers for 21st century classrooms, teacher education must shift away from a norm which emphasizes academic preparation and course work loosely linked to school-based experiences. Rather, it must move to programs that are fully grounded in clinical practice and interwoven with academic content and professional courses (NCATE, 2010, p. ii).

In the following table, NCATE maps the shift from the "current model" to "the model we need":

Feature	Current Model	The Model We Need
Basic approach	Largely focused on content knowledge, theory and, and pedagogy with clinical experience added on to course work, or just clinical with no rigorous academic components.	Clinical preparation developed by partnerships of preparation programs, A&S faculty, school districts and unions is the centerpiece; course work is woven around and into clinical experiences.
Providers	Largely institutions of higher education.	Multiple forms of partnerships involving all teacher preparation programs, including higher education institutions, in partnership with school districts.
Curriculum	Focus on content preparation, theory, child development, and methods developed in course work; loosely linked to practice and student teaching experience.	Course work and clinical preparation woven together throughout programs to emphasize translation of knowledge into practice. Multiple opportunities to study practice through simulations, case studies, and other laboratory based experiences utilizing available technologies; extensive school embedded clinical practice under the guidance of qualified clinical educators. Focus on development of assessment strategies founded on strong findings from learning research, uses of data for decision making, and incorporation of technology into teaching.

Measures of Effectiveness	Programs are not always held to same standards by state departments of education; variability of standards and licensure requirements among states.	All programs held to same standards; data-driven accountability based on measures of candidate performance and student achievement, including gains in standardized test scores. Data drives reform and continuous improvement.
Staffing	Academic faculty with content and pedagogical knowledge; clinical supervision often by untrained graduate students and P-12 faculty.	Academic faculty and specially prepared clinical faculty, drawn from preparation program faculty and P-12 schools.
Roles and Relationships	Higher education institutions and school districts have limited interaction and separate responsibilities for teacher preparation and development.	Joint responsibility for preparation and induction; differentiated staffing and new boundary spanning roles created for clinically based programs.

(NCATE, 2010, p. 12)

While in phase II (chapter 5) the TEPs ask "what teachers should learn and be able to do", in phase III they ask how to meet the standard of "data-driven accountability based on measures of candidate performance and student achievement, including gains in standardized test scores". According to the NCATE (2010) report, the recommended program should implement the following principles:

1. Student learning is the focus: P-12 student learning must serve as the focal point for the design and implementation of clinically based teacher preparation, and for the assessment of newly minted teachers and the programs that have prepared them. Candidates need to develop practice that advances student knowledge as defined by, for example, the Common Core State Standards, for those subjects for which they have been developed.

2. Clinical preparation is integrated throughout every facet of teacher education in a dynamic way: The core experience in teacher preparation is clinical practice. Content and pedagogy are woven around clinical experiences throughout preparation, in course work, in laboratory-based experiences, and in school-embedded practice.

3. A candidate's progress and the elements of a preparation program are continuously judged on the basis of data: Candidates' practice must be directly linked to the Interstate New Teacher Assessment and Support Consortium (INTASC) core teaching standards for teachers and Common Core Standards, and evaluation of candidates must be based on students' outcome data, including student artifacts, summative and formative assessments; data from structured observations of candidates' classroom

skills by supervising teachers and faculty; and data about the preparation program and consequences of revising it.

4. Programs prepare teachers who are expert in content and how to teach it and are also innovators, collaborators, and problem solvers: Candidates must develop a base of knowledge, a broad range of effective teaching practices, and the ability to integrate the two to support professional decision-making. To be successful teachers in challenging and changing environments, candidates must learn to use multiple assessment processes to advance learning and inform their practice with data to differentiate their teaching to match their students' progress. Further, effective teachers are innovators and problem solvers, working with colleagues constantly seeking new and different ways of teaching students who are struggling.

5. Candidates learn in an interactive professional community: Candidates need lots of opportunities for feedback. They must practice in a collaborative culture, expecting rigorous peer review of their practice and their impact on student learning.

6. Clinical educators and coaches are rigorously selected and prepared and drawn from both higher education and the P-12 sector: Those who lead the next generation of teachers throughout their preparation and induction must themselves be effective practitioners, skilled in differentiating instruction, proficient in using assessment to monitor learning and provide feedback, persistent searchers for data to guide and adjust practice, and exhibitors of the skills of clinical educators. They should be specially certified, accountable for their candidates' performance and student outcomes, and commensurately rewarded to serve in this crucial role.

7. Specific sites are designated and funded to support embedded clinical preparation: All candidates should have intensive embedded clinical school experiences that are structured, staffed, and financed to support candidate learning and student achievement.

8. Technology applications foster high-impact preparation: State-of-the-art technologies should be employed by preparation programs to promote enhanced productivity, greater efficiencies, and collaboration through learning communities. Technology should also be an important tool to share best practices across partnerships, and to facilitate on-going professional learning.

9. A powerful R&D agenda and systematic gathering and use of data supports continuous improvement in teacher preparation: Effective teacher education requires more robust evidence on teaching effectiveness, best practices, and preparation program performance. A powerful research and development infrastructure – jointly defined by preparation programs, school districts, and practitioners – supports knowledge development, innovation, and continuous improvement. While not every clinically based preparation program will contribute new research knowledge or expand

development, each must systematically gather and use data, and become part of a national data network on teacher preparation that can increase understanding of what is occurring and evidence of progress in the field.

10. Strategic partnerships are imperative for powerful clinical preparation: School districts, preparation programs, teacher unions, and state policymakers must form strategic partnerships based on the recognition that none can fully do the job alone. Each partner's needs can be met better by defining clinically based teacher preparation as common work for which they share responsibility, authority, and accountability covering all aspects of program development and implementation (NCATE, 2010, p. 5 – 6) (remember: Appendix, example 9).

One message is clear. Extended clinical experience is necessary for it is the best means to ensure that the evaluation of the candidates will be based "on students' outcome data, including student artifacts, summative and formative assessments". An even more radical outlook is prescribed by the recently suggested *NCTQ* [National Counsil on Teacher Quality] *Standards for Rating the Nation's Education Schools*, which formulates "its standards… first and foremost on the basis of research". The standards aim to assure that "every child will have an effective teacher". Among others, the standards include:

A. Grounded Clinical Practice:

Standard 1: Classroom Management. The program ensures that teacher candidates learn and practice specific techniques for managing the classroom.

Standard 2: Practice Planning Instruction. The program requires teacher candidates to design and adjust instruction to enhance the academic performance of all students.

Standard 3: Measurement. The program requires that teacher candidates gain a thorough overview of student assessment that includes practice analyzing student performance data to drive instruction.

Standard 5: Student Teaching. The program ensures that the student teaching experience includes the essential components for success: a full-time placement of sufficient length that is aligned with the school calendar, adequately supervised, and attendant to the qualifications of the cooperating teacher.

B. Preparation of Elementary School Teachers:

Standards 6: Early Reading. The program consistently prepares candidates in the essential components of effective reading instruction. [Similar standards apply to Mathematics (standard no. 7), core curriculum content (no 8), English (no. 9), and Reading skills to students at risk (no. 10).]

C. Entry into Program and Profession:

Standard 16: Selectivity. The program selects candidates of high academic caliber using a screen that enables comparison of their academic achievement to that of college-attending peers.

Standard 17: Outcomes. The institution collects data related to its graduates' performance in the classroom (NCTQ, 2011).

NCTQ provides a detailed set of indicators which check the attainment of these standards. For example, the programs should:

10.1 Specifically address the student teacher's ability to establish a positive learning environment and standards of classroom behavior.

10.2 Specifically address the student teacher's appropriate use of low profile desists for managing minimally disruptive behavior.

10.3 Specifically address the student teacher's appropriate use of disciplinary action to handle significant student misbehavior.

10.4 Require comments by the supervisor to support each rating.

10.5 Allow the cooperating teacher to document his/her evaluation of the candidate's classroom management techniques...

12.1 The instructional role of standardized tests, particularly the program state's standardized tests, is addressed.

12.2 Teacher candidates are required to prepare formative and summative classroom assessments.

12.3 Individually and in teams, teacher candidates are taught how to interpret and apply data from both standardized and classroom assessments in order to inform instruction...

17.2 The institution surveys its graduates' employers about their professional performance.

17.3 The institution secures data from teacher performance assessments (e.g., California's PACT) administered to candidates just prior to or at graduation.

17.4 Unless state data systems preclude access to meaningful data, the institution secures value-added performance data on its graduates' students, including any teacher evaluations which are based at least partially on such data.

17.5 All forms of data noted are collected on an established timetable that supports regular program evaluation.

18. (Applied only to institutions in states with adequate student data systems): On average, institution's graduates have a positive impact on student learning (NCTQ, 2011).

The lesson of these standards and indicators is straightforward. The NCTQ suggests a model of one dimensional instrumental rationality. The language of accountability and efficiency, of standards and evaluation, of tests and outcomes is its only language. HAVING (good grades in the exams) is its one and only recognized aim. Instrumental rationality is its sole mode of reasoning. The achievement principle is its single mode of recognition. The child is seen as an 'achievement driven' machine which the teacher should be able to put in motion. Questions of ends, such as can this policy promote genuine learning, enhance the student's personality, or narrow the social gaps, are not even mentioned.

This outlook can be hardly met by an existing academic TEP, especially if its faculty is hostile to the measurement and accountability regime. We shall shortly examine other types of TEPs, like TFA, RGSE, or UTR which try to meet these standards and indicators. Together with TERI (which had been discussed at the end of the previous chapter),they all belong to the "standards-and-accountability" movement. They all want their preparation-to-teach program to be directly beneficial to pupils' achievements.

Homo Economicus

The race towards output driven TEPs, where the outcome is the short term academic achievements of the pupils, requires justification. On the face of it, it is so removed from the enlightenment ideal of the educated person, that it demands a principled excuse. The rationale of this approach comes from the tenet that the ideal individual is the "Economic Man" (*Homo Economicus*). The first characterization of the notion has been suggested by J. S. Mill, though Mill himself did not use the term. For Mill, "Political Economy presupposes an arbitrary definition of man, as a being who inevitably does that by which he may obtain the greatest amount of necessaries, conveniences, and luxuries, with the smallest quantity of labor and physical self-denial with which they can be obtained in the existing state of knowledge" (Mill, 1874/2000, p. 101). Since Mill, this notion has encountered many modifications, and its meaning became increasingly narrow to encompass less and less aspects of human behavior. Currently, the term *Homo Economicus* usually denotes the individual who wishes to maximize his material profit in a certain context, although as we shall see, this limited notion is contested.

Homo Economicus presents a special case of instrumental rationality. While the economical agent is still concerned with means-ends relationships, he acts rationally if "given the set of available actions, there is no other action available to him, the consequence of which, he prefers to that of the chosen action" (Hahn & Hollis, 1979, p. 4). In economic theory, a rational decision maker is an agent who "chooses an alternative after a process of deliberation in which he answers three questions: "What is feasible?"; "What is desirable?"; "What is the best alternative relative to what is desirable, given the feasibility constraints?" (Rubinstein, 1998, p. 7). *Homo Economicus* is an ideal type of an individual who knows what he is looking for. He has preferences with regard to the consequences of each of the alternative courses of action. He has abundant information about the opportunities to realize his preferences as well as about the constraints, both natural and institutional, which limit his ability to achieve his predetermined goals. When he has to choose what to do, he asks what alternatives he faces and what the consequences of each of them are. Consequently, he chooses the alternative which best suits his preferences (Rubinstein, 2009, p. 42 – 43). This kind of deliberation does not mean that the individual's actual goals are themselves reasonable in some larger ethical, social or human sense, only that he tries to attain them at minimal cost.

In a bit more technical language, the main aspiration of *Homo Economicus* is that of utility maximization. Utility in this context is a measure of relative satisfaction. It is usually defined by economists as the price an individual is willing to pay for the fulfillment or satisfaction of his desires. Utility maximization means that the individual seeks to attain very specific and predetermined goals to the greatest extent with the least possible cost (in game-theory terms this attitude is called the "maxi-min" strategy). The main question that the economical man asks himself is: "how should I spend my resources in order to maximize my utility?" Or "how will I get the greatest value possible from expenditure of the least amount of money?".

A closer look on this approach reveals some of its presuppositions:

1. *Homo Economicus* is an individual who finds himself in a constant struggle for survival in a permanent state of scarcity of resources. His life is a continuous process of problem solving, the most important of them is to sustain his existence and well-being. (This is a Hobbesian approach supported by Darwin's 'survival of the fittest' theory). Reason is the main weapon which enables the individual to succeed in this struggle.

2. The starting point of *Homo Economicus'* deliberation is always his self-interest. He always tries to find out what will bring him the biggest utility. It might seem that he is an egoistic individual who cherishes only material profits and behaves like a "cold" computer. But *Homo Economicus* need not be selfish and antisocial, for he might believe that being selfish runs against his self-interest (Hahn & Hollis, 1979, p. 3). "Socially acknowledged norms may act as additional restrictions on his behavior because their violation often brings about only small costs in the short-run, but possibly considerable ones in the long-run" (Kirchgassner, 2008, p. 32)[40]. However, even in this case, his reasoning takes his own interests as the starting point of his deliberation.

3. Society is a community of Economic Men. It should enable each individual to do his best to attain maximum utility. The ideal political regime should ensure that any individual has the opportunity to exercise his free choice, and the government has to interfere in his actions only if they violate the free choice of his fellow citizens. Contemporary western thinkers believe that only democracy can provide the security net in which the individual might be secured from tyrannical, suppressive and authoritative regimes. Neo-Liberals further believe that only a

capitalistic economy, based on a self-regulated free-market, can prevent the negative intervention of the state in the individual's freedom.

This individualistic attitude has another important feature. Any organized group of people (the state, the nation) is seen as a mechanical aggregate of individuals. Following Hobbes, the state or the nation is not an organism which has thoughts, desires, soul or spirit of its own. It is no more than a necessary, though useful, arrangement which should promote the individual's well-being by securing their independence and autonomy. The basic presupposition is that humans "are in a situation of scarcity" (Kirchgässner, 2008, p. 11), so that without a political arrangement (a social "contract"), they would be involved in a constant "war of all against all". But such a contract has to impose as few limitations as possible to human activity.

4. Even interpersonal relationships, including love relationships between adults, should be carefully calculated, formulated as a legal contract according to commercial criteria. (It is not casual that in a society, in which everything is a commodity, everything, including education, should be open to judicial consideration.) Ayn Rand faithfully presents this ideal:

> Man—every man—is an end in himself, not the means to the ends of others. He must exist for his own sake, neither sacrificing himself to others nor sacrificing others to himself. The pursuit of his own rational self-interest and of his own happiness is the highest moral purpose of his life. The ideal political-economic system is *laissez-faire* capitalism. It is a system where men deal with one another, not as victims and executioners, nor as masters and slaves, but as *traders*, by free, voluntary exchange to mutual benefit (A. Rand, 1962).

5. One of the prevalent ideas of the individualistic approach is that it attributes the lure of the individual to his talents and efforts. Everyone can be successful, and it depends only on his labor and on his being an innovative entrepreneur. In the spirit of Protestant Ethics (Weber, 1905/1958), achievement becomes the major criterion of social merit (Honneth, 1995). Success, especially material success, turns out to be only measure of the individual's worth. To be "number one" becomes the aim of every person. But since only one individual can be "number one", society becomes extremely competitive. The to-date trend of TV reality programs (such as Survival, American Idol, or the Amazing Race) provides another mark of this principle, as well as the "publish or perish" academic prerequisite. In such a climate, the most important notions are: efficiency, efficacy, progress, development, growth, improvement, competition, and upgrade. To ensure a fair competition everything should be transparent, so that the public right to know will be preserved.

6. *Homo Economicus* is an informed individual. To function efficiently, he has to rely on facts. His activities should be evidence-based. Education enlightens the individual, and provides him with the knowledge necessary to be successful. Meritocracy, the ideology that society should be governed by those who know and

are able to act according to their talents and acknowledged knowledge, attributes a major weight to formal education and to the credentials it supplies.

The implications of these ideas to teacher education are straightforward. TEP should be run like a business whose aim is to produce teachers which will improve their pupils' chances to achieve immediate and measurable outcomes. TEPs should educate a teacher who acts in accordance with the *Homo Economicus* ideal so he will be able to educate his pupils toward the same ideal. If grades substitute money as the main criteria for success, it means that:

1. The teacher should ascertain that each child will strive to achieve the highest possible grade, regardless any other aim he might have. To meet the social justice criteria, he has to ascertain that by all means each child will have a minimum rate of success.

2. The teacher ignores other needs or desires of the pupils because "there is not enough time" to deal with them in a climate of high stake testing.

3. Since schools become commercially competitive institutions, the chance to recruit the pupils and retain them depends on the achievements of the schools in the exams. A good teacher must absorb the schools' priorities, and uncritically adopts them. Teacher education must prepare the prospective teacher to function in such a climate.

The same approach applies to the aims of the teacher educator with regard to his students:

1. Each singular TEP should be in a constant struggle for its survival. Fighting for its very existence will improve it. Privatization and competition should be imported to education, so that every institution would accommodate itself to the "free market" environment.

2. To survive, TEP should be successful and accountable. Its self-interest dictates that it will be attenuate to the markets' demands and responsive to the clients' needs. TEP's course of studies is best seen as a set of contracts between the state, or other financial supporters, and the educational provider; the provider and the students; and the TEP and the schools. Its major aim is to see that all the "stakeholders" will be pleased with the program's outcomes.

3. To survive, TEP should be economically efficient. Its budget should be balanced, if not profitable, and its resources spent in a cost-effect way. However, as providers of public service, TEPs should serve the public good. They have to comply with a certain set of rules and regulations, which define the necessary outcomes of the program, assure that it maintains high quality, albeit its financial interests, and guarantee that it will not be "selfish" and compromise quality for profits. Especially, the provider has to see that its products (the teachers) can meet the market requirement (i.e., that each of their pupils will learn).

4. Assessment becomes the critical notion. Under the title of "quality management", a proper measurement should indicate "where the institution stands" and whether it deserves to survive. This will enable the stakeholders to

decide which institution to finance, and the prospective teacher to choose where to study.

To include the TEP in the market economy will make them competitive, accountable and better institutions. However, it is vital to see what the market expects from teachers in general and TEPs in particular. As we have already seen, the answer is that in the short run the product should be a teacher whose pupils gain high scores on exams. In the long run, it is believed that achieving this end will enable the pupils to become productive citizens. Each of these aims is, of course, highly susceptible. To have HAVING (grades) as the only aim of the entire educational system might raise many objections. I will shortly return to deal with these objections, but first let us examine the implications of this approach to current TEPs.   The last decades flood of committees and tank forces, reports and manifestos, standards and indicators, which become more and more detailed, indicate that the "public" lost its trust in the academic-based TEPs. The idea that informed "policies" will enforce the "correct" type of TEP conveys the message that the best, though not really feasible, way to deal with the academic TEPs is simply to get rid of them (Levine, 2010; Zeichner, 2010). The proliferation of "alternative routes", favored by officials (such as Duncan) and financed by the US government, might be seen as the first steps in the actualization of this attitude.

It might even indicate that the public withdraws from the idea that teaching is a genuine profession, which requires prolonged academic preparation. If any university graduate can become a licensed teacher after 40 hours of pre-service training and another 200 hours of in service training, accompanied by a full-time mentor for the first 20-day period of teaching (Humphrey & Wechsler, 2008, p. 71), it means the idea that teaching necessitates a pre-service course of studies is no longer widely accepted. Academicians, for sure, firmly reject this attitude, but their reaction might be just like a cat which is asked to protect the cream. Maybe, in order to be efficient, TEPs should really look different and provide a totally different kind of preparation.

Teach For...

From the early 1990s there is a growing tendency towards "alternative routes" to teacher preparation. Motivated by a shortage of teachers in urban and rural areas, and by the aims to recruit better candidates for teaching, and place apt new teachers in deprived areas, the "Teach For" programs (starting in 1990 with "Teach for America" (TFA), and "Teach First" in UK (2002)), spread to another 16 countries (2011), including Israel, and constitute the "Teach for All" organization (launched in September 2007) (http://www.teachforall.org/network_locations.html).

According to the official website of TFA (http://www.teachforamerica.org accessed at 16.3.2011), "TFA provides a critical source of well-trained teachers who are helping break the cycle of educational inequity. These teachers, called corps members, commit to teach for two years in one of 39 urban and rural regions across the country, going above and beyond traditional expectations to help their students achieve at high levels". Similarly, "The social enterprises in Teach for All recruit outstanding university graduates and young leaders of a variety of disciplines and career interests to commit two years to teach in high-need areas, providing a critical source of additional teachers who ensure their students have the educational opportunities they deserve, despite socioeconomic factors".

Teach for America promises that:

Our training is designed to give corps members the foundational knowledge and skills they need to become highly effective teachers. Teach for America provides rigorous pre-service training during the summer institute, one-on-one coaching throughout the two-year teaching commitment, and an extensive bank of online resources to help corps members succeed in the classroom. [See: Appendix example 10].

The "Teach For..." model takes teaching to be a temporary vocation. It is designed as a preparation for a social mission, and not for professional life. Nevertheless, its adherents claim that the outcomes of the children with whom the graduates of this model work are at least as good as the outcomes of children of teacher who has been prepared in a regular TEP.

This claim is not really justified. Heilig and Jez (2010) review of the literature about TFA reveal that "a simple answer to the question of TFA teachers' relative effectiveness cannot be conclusively drawn from the research; many factors are involved in any comparison. The lack of a consistent impact, however, should indicate to policy-makers that TFA is likely not the panacea that will reduce disparities in educational outcomes".

Studies have found that, when the comparison group is other teachers in the same schools who are less likely to be certified or traditionally prepared, novice TFA teachers perform equivalently, and experienced TFA teachers perform comparably in raising reading scores and a bit better in raising math scores. The question for most districts, however, is whether TFA teachers do as well as or better than credentialed non-TFA teachers with whom school districts aim to staff their schools. On this question, studies indicate that the students of novice TFA teachers perform significantly less well in reading and mathematics than those of credentialed beginning teachers (Heilig and Jez, 2010).

However, since

Experience has a positive effect for both TFA and non-TFA teachers. Most studies find that the relatively few TFA teachers who stay long enough to become fully credentialed (typically after two years) appear to do about as well as other similarly experienced credentialed teachers in teaching reading; they do as well as, and sometimes better than, that comparison group in teaching mathematics. However, since more than 50% of TFA teachers leave after two years, and more than 80% leave after three years, it is impossible to know whether these more positive findings for experienced recruits result from additional training and experience or from attrition of TFA teachers who may be less effective (2010).

In an earlier survey, Johnson and Birkeland find contradictory assessments of TFA graduates with regard to their effects on students' scores (2008, p. 104).

Even if the surveys' findings had been conclusively positive, there is a real difficulty here, because the very logic of the research is upside down. It is clearly a mean-ends checking, which presupposes the policy makers' terms of reference. What about other roles that the teacher might have aside from preparing children to high-stake exams? Is it possible to find out the long-term consequences of employing unprepared teachers? And what about the broader issue of social justice, if it is accepted that provisional and inexperienced teachers will always be places in poor or deprived schools? Is it not an excuse to claim "we do what we can" without dealing with the real, but probably more costly, issue of how to place the best teachers in such schools for longer periods.

A related problem is straightforward. It is simply unjust and not proper to judge the quality of the TEPs as a function of children achievement in standardized exams. Beside the many problems of devising proper exams (Nichols & Berliner, 2007 or Ravitch, 2010, p. 149 – 167), it is clear that they are not specifically designed to test teachers' achievements. Ravitch (who had been one of the supporters of *The Teachers We Need and How to Get More of Them* (Fordham Foundation, 1999, p. 20), and since has changed her mind) notes that "Testing experts reminds that standardized test scores should be used not in isolation... but only in conjunction with other measures of student performances... The [experts] also warn that test scores should be used only for the purpose for which the test was designed: For example, a fifth grade reading test measures fifth-grade reading skills and cannot reliably serve as a measure of the teacher's skill" (Ravitch, 2010, p. 152 – 153). To say nothing about his pedagogical skills or the way he cares for his pupils.

TFA does not see teaching as a lifelong career. Usually, it is seen as a relatively short period of service, in which the most talented graduates are ready to serve their country for a couple of years, in urban and rural schools. Hess (2009) suggests that this attitude reflects the present day tendency of youngsters to constantly change their work places. He also notes that many individuals who begin their career elsewhere are ready to enter teaching later in their lives. TFA, he suggests, fits those who do not want to see teaching as a lifelong career. Advocates of this approach diminish the idea that teaching is a profession and not a casual occupation. I wonder whether they will have the same attitude towards their physicians, accountants, or lawyers.

Richard Sennett indicates that: "The more one understands how to do something well, the more one cares about it. Institutions based on short-term transactions and constantly shifting tasks, however, do not breed that depth" (Sennett, 2006, p. 105). To quote Sennett:

A key aspect of craftsmanship is learning how to get something right. Trial and error occurs in improving even seemingly routine tasks; the worker has to be free to make mistakes, then go over the work again and again. Whatever a person's innate abilities..., skill develops only in stages, in fits and starts... In a speeded-up institution, however, time intensive learning becomes difficult. The pressures to produce results quickly are too intense... time anxiety causes people to skin rather than to dwell (2006, p. 127).

While surely significant to the teachers who participate in the program, to their personal development, their social sensitivity and devotion, their feeling as an elite group, and their future career possibilities, it is not so clear that TFA is beneficial to the teaching profession or to the the pupils of TFA graduates.

Techniques-Based Teacher Education (RGSE)

A recent incarnation of the anti-academic tendency has a paradoxical feature. Let TEPs be conducted in a non-academic environment (i.e., in schools) which, nevertheless, gets the permission to award the student with a recognized second academic degree (MAT). The Relay Graduate School of Education (RGSE) suggests such an approved TEP (See: Appendix, Example 12).

RGSE, which begins its TEP in the fall of 2011, is the first stand-alone teacher education institute (after Bank Street) in NYC (and another branch will be opening in Newark). "It is designed to respond to the demand for effective teachers and includes an emphasis on concrete techniques and the use of video to share the leading practices of exemplary teachers". The program proudly claims that it is "the first ever to require its graduate students to demonstrate proficiency and student achievements while teaching full-time in their K-12 classrooms to earn a MAT degree" (RELAY/GSE press release, July 30, 2011)[41].

The name, Relay, was deliberately chosen. It reflects "a core belief that new teachers are best taught by master teachers with a track record of results in urban classrooms. Instructors at Relay School of Education are experienced exemplary teachers and not academicians. They will relay what they have learned to their graduate students, and these new teachers will, in turn, instill a love of learning in their students" (http://www.relayschool.org/press-releases/2011/2/15/new-york-board-of-regents-charters-relay-school-of-education.html).

The Admission Guide to the Newark program (RSE) enlists 10 programmatic features:

1. Learn and execute. RSE focuses on teaching its enrolled teachers concrete techniques that they can immediately implement as teachers, more so than on learning theory and research.

2. Be trained by professors who are themselves "champion" teachers. RSE faculty is comprised of some of the highest performing urban teachers and leaders who themselves have had success teaching low-income students. Instructors teach students by modeling precisely the techniques and strategies that can be implemented immediately and effectively in K-12 classrooms.

3. Watch and analyze teacher "game" film. RSE enrolled teachers learn to perform in their own classrooms the moves of model teachers by first witnessing moments of exemplary execution. Video is the best way to do this because (a) it allows enrolled teachers to virtually visit hundreds of teachers and their classrooms across the country; and (b) it precisely captures particular moves and techniques, enabling enrolled teachers to isolate them for clear viewing.

4. Receive multiple instructional and management "at-bats." Core assignments at RSE involve practicing the teaching techniques in the classroom. Armed with a Flip video camera and tripod, RSE students film themselves in action and then receive feedback from their instructors on how well they are "hitting the ball" in their classrooms.

5. Demonstrate it in the classroom and move on. RSE's program is competency-based. Some enrolled teachers may take longer than others to get through the material and show their competency. On the other hand, experienced individuals with previous training may demonstrate their mastery of various techniques and to engage in a professional development program that is tailored to their needs, thereby more efficiently fulfilling the program requirements.

6. Engage in high-quality online learning sessions. RSE is pushing the envelope in online instruction, delivering videos and practice exercises that develop skills and enhance learning. The blending of in-person learning with online learning gives enrolled teachers the flexibility and convenience to learn at their own pace.

7. Experience an aligned community of professors, principals, deans, and coaches. Based on its partnerships and experience in the charter school world, RSE professors – more than at many other programs – ensure that they teach their enrolled teachers a mindset and set of skills that are strategically and purposely aligned with the approaches and strategies utilized by the instructional leaders and mentors at the schools at which our enrolled teachers are employed.

8. Drive instruction with data. Through its programs, RSE trains novice teachers to assess their students in a way that generates meaningful information about their learning, which – in turn – will improve their instruction. By setting ambitious goals for students, investing students in those goals, regularly checking for their students' understanding, delivering aligned interim-assessments, effectively analyzing the outcomes of those assessments, and re-planning on the basis of that analysis, RSE enrolled teachers will be in a strong position to produce and track meaningful student learning.

9. Exemplify the character strengths you want your students to develop. At RSE, enrolled teachers are taught that both intelligence and character are malleable. They also learn to construct lessons that incorporate both

academic and character objectives while also receiving guidance on how best to serve as role models for their students.

10. Close the achievement gap. RSE enrolled teachers who complete the program, having learned all of the modeled and instructed techniques, are expected to demonstrate that their students have made at least a year's worth of academic growth in a year's time. Teachers who successfully complete the Alternate Certification program and demonstrate proficiency in concrete techniques and strategies and who generate student achievement gains in their classrooms will then be eligible to earn their master's degree after a second year of committed effort. Consequently, everyone will know – current and future employers, as well as the teachers themselves – that RSE certification counts for something fundamental and critical: teachers' ability to lead their students to meaningful student achievement gains. (http://tumirror.info/?a=w; retrieved 8.2011).

Teaching is seen as a craft in which the teacher has to master a set of techniques in order to be able to perform a good job. The techniques were formulated by Doug Lemov (2010), and they include 49 specific tools that the good teacher should master[42]. Lemov focuses on public schools, primarily those serving the inner city, and through hours of observations finds out what successful teachers (i.e., teachers whose students succeed in the exams) do. Champion teachers are using the techniques, which are all about efficient delivery methods. Lemov acknowledges that what makes a good teacher is not only the mastery of the techniques. The art of teaching is the implementation of the right technique in the appropriate context. But the first step of learning to teach is to acquire these techniques. A good TEP trains students to master them. Instead of courses, the NY RGSE curriculum comprises some 60 modules, each of them focused on a different technique. Forty percent of the coursework is online, and meetings are held in small groups for expanding on a core practice (Otterman, 2011) (See Appendix example no. 12). Theoretical knowledge in education is superfluous. One size fits all, and quick-fix- teach-by-the-numbers effective techniques are all that is needed[43].

Lemov's techniques are marked by a strict technical-rationality approach. Thus for example, Technique 6 (**Begin with the End**) (the bold words indicate the techniques' titles) states that great teachers:

1. Progress *from* unit planning to lesson planning.

2. Refine and perfect the lesson objective based on the degree of mastery from the day before.

3. Plan a short daily assessment to determine whether the objective was mastered.

4. Plan the sequence of activities that lead to mastery of the objective.

Technique 7 (**4MS**) tells the teachers that it is vital to design effective objectives.

To do so, use the criteria below to determine if your objective is effective:

1. Manageable: An objective can't be effective if you can't teach it in a single lesson. Of course you want your students to master larger skills, but this can take weeks so you need to break them into steps your students can master in one period.

2. Measureable: Effective objectives can be measured. This is often done at the end of the period with an exit ticket (a short activity or question students complete to show they learned the material).

3. Made first: An objective should guide the activities you use in the lesson and not simply be an afterthought.

4. Most important: Choose an objective based on what is *most* important for students to learn on the path to college. (Lemov, 2010).

The pedagogy of teaching the techniques has its own technique. Abbreviated as IPPA, it consists of four steps:

1. INTRODUCE – Help teachers understand the rationale behind it, especially since many of these ideas seem to contradict the latest educational theories. You can refer to the rationale for the technique described in the book, show a video clip if there is one for the technique you are introducing, or have teachers look at how successful they already are in this area.

2. PRACTICE – Before trying the technique in the classroom, have teachers practice it. This can be in the form of a role-play as teacher and student(s) or it might involve practicing writing a powerful lesson HOOK or writing STRETCH IT questions.

3. PLAN/PUT INTO PRACTICE – If the technique is conducted *spontaneously* in class (like responding to a student) then the teacher should plan to implement it for an entire week, perhaps asking a colleague to observe for it. If the technique is something that needs to be planned *ahead of time* into a lesson (like what the students should be doing in DOUBLE PLAN), the teacher should incorporate it into a lesson plan to be implemented within the next week.

4. ASSESS – Teachers will more rapidly progress in their command of these techniques if they get feedback on their implementation. In addition to their own self-reflection (which can happen at a future staff meeting), teachers should invite visitors to observe and give feedback on the technique, or even better, consider video taping themselves so they and others can watch multiple times to give feedback. Obviously, any feedback should be used by the teacher to improve her practice next time (Lemov, 2010).

According to Technique 9, "activities should be chosen based on how fast and how well they get students to master the objective. It is time to stop thinking of Socratic seminars or lectures as good or bad. Instead, take the SHORTEST PATH to your objectives in designing activities" (Lemov, 2010). Indeed, efficiency and accountability demand that all the techniques are "on the path to college". No other aim is even mentioned. Not surprisingly, the RGSE's main criterion to earn the master diploma is the student's practical accomplishments. To earn his degree he must submit a portfolio showing that his own students made at least one year of academic progress in a subject.

This kind of requirement might be seen as a diminution of what counts as an academic degree. Lin Goodwin, the associate dean at Teachers College, says that: "What they are doing is teacher training, to follow a protocol, to be able to perform in a particular context, to know how to work in this way. What that does is that it dumbs down teaching, and takes us back a few steps, in terms of our struggle in the profession for teachers to be seen as professionals" (Quated in Otterman, 2011).

Alternatively, it might be seen as a suggestive adaptation of the academic world to society's needs. Both ways, it is a purely technical-rationality approach to teaching (on the edge of "teacher proof teaching") and a complete dominance of the HAVING MoE. That measurable achievement is the only recognized outcome of the TEP clearly shows its adherence to the achievement principle of social esteem.

Maybe this top-down strategy is not that promising. The McKinsey Report (2010) claims that there is a direct correlation between the quality of the educational system and the amount of autonomy given to teachers and schools. The "great to excellent" systems emphasize "peer-based learning through school-based and system wide interactions" (p. 20). They decentralized "pedagogical rights to schools and teachers" (p. 28). They "unleash the creativity and innovations of its teachers" (p. 42). They give "their teachers the time, resources, and flexibility to reflect upon and try out new ideas to better support student learning" (p. 42). On the other end, "transparency and accountability" and designing a "learning model" for raising students capabilities characterize mediocre educational systems (p. 35). The focus of RGSE is in accordance with these mediocre stages. Even on its own standards, it cannot bring the teachers and the children to be innovative, and creative. It cannot prepare them for a democratic world in which they should be more than passive children who know the (only one) right answers to the teachers' questions. It can hardly meet the new ICT world for all the techniques are "chalk and talk" ones, in which the teacher (or the video) relays everything to the obedient students for their benefit. Again, Sennett's concern that "time anxiety causes people to skim rather than to dwell" is not taken into account (Sennett, 2006, p. 127).

Urban Teacher Residencies (UTR)

The Teacher Urban Residencies can be seen as a suggestive compromise between the inclination to minimize the role of the academia in teacher preparation and emphasize the field, and nevertheless to stay professional. The UTR, founded in

Chicago in 2001 and Boston in 2003, is one of the favorite models of the NCATE report (2010, p. 8). Residencies are proposed as an important option that policymakers, practitioners, and the public should consider in their efforts to ensure that they have a teaching workforce that is diverse and prepared to be successful (See: Appendix example 11).

According to Berry et al., in UTRs, "aspiring teachers – known as Residents – are selected according to rigorous criteria aligned with district needs. They integrate their master's level course work with an intensive, full-year classroom residency alongside an experienced mentor. In their second year, they become a teacher with their own classroom while continuing to receive intensive mentoring" (2008, p.5).

As stated by Berry et al.:

> The power and potential of UTRs lies in their commitment to address the real teacher supply and quality needs of urban school districts, leverage the best K – 12 educators as mentors and teacher leaders, and promote redesigned schools organized for students and teachers to learn. As such, they provide a potential entry point for significant improvements, not just in teacher preparation, but in the full human capital systems of urban school districts (p. 6).

> Somewhat mimicking the medical residency model that pairs professional course work and embedded clinical experience, UTRs are founded on the belief that new teachers in urban schools should enter the classroom with a minimum of one year of guided clinical experience in an urban classroom. Residents integrate their master's level coursework with an intensive full-year classroom residency alongside experienced, prepared mentors before becoming teachers of record in their own classrooms (p. 7).

Once again teaching should follow the footsteps of medicine in order to establish proper professional preparation program.

UTRs are distinctive in that they:

• Tightly weave together education theory and classroom practice;

• Focus on Residents learning alongside an experienced, trained Mentor;

• Group candidates in cohorts to cultivate professional learning community and foster collaboration;

• Build effective partnerships among school districts, higher education institutions and nonprofit organizations;

• Serve school districts by recruiting and training teachers to meet specific district needs;

• Support Residents once they are hired as teachers of record;

• Establish and support differentiated career goals for experienced teachers (p. 11).

Supported by the Obama administration, UTRs are spreading in the USA. Zeichner (2010) hopes that they will be more attenuate to the democratic challenge of reducing social gaps, because they may facilitate an environment of cooperation and discourse between the academia and the "field". Nonetheless, residencies based on uncritical "best practices", are really preserving the present. Attempting to meet the "here and now" problems and challenges, they might accept the current terms of reference (i.e., accountability through measurement), without asking whether the system is the problem and not the solution of the state of education.

TEPs in the US were usually criticized for their strong anti-intellectual bias, enhanced by a total lack of imagination. It is far from clear that the present tendency to emphasis practice is a proper response to this accusation. While "the courses, created specifically for the program and tailored to the instructional needs of the district, are taught by practitioners, consultants, and other experts drawn from colleges and universities, public schools, and community organizations" (Levine, 2006, p. 129), it also flatters the academic weight of the program.

The programs presented in this chapter are all designed to meet the emphasis on academic achievements as they are measured by standardized exams. They do not address the substantive question of the target's worth. They do not question its moral value. They do not ask whether they can really foster academic learning in a climate which is rigid, dictated, and enforced. Instead of an autonomous individual teacher, who is able to self-create his world-view, they produce a 'fit-for-purpose' obedient teacher, whose "knowing how" is very remote from the enlightenment ideal of the teacher as a pedagogue who can serve as a living model for his students. Teachers become mere instruments. TEPs become production-machines. As such, they can be liable to privatization and commercialization. They can be standardized and measured, as they conform to the *Homo Economicus* notion of rationality.

QUESTIONING THE REASONABLENESS OF THE *HOMO ECONOMICUS*

It is time to question this version of instrumental reasoning . There can be two responses to this line of thinking. The first is to say that some of the above TEPs adopt a distorted version of the *Homo Economicus* ideal. The second is to cast doubt on the ideal itself. The first response claims that even from the *Homo Economicus* point of view, many of the achievement-driven TEPs are too restrictive, counterproductive and ineffective. Instead of preparing the adaptive expert needed for the 21st century, they prepare a routine expert which cannot adjust himself to a changing world (Bransford et al. 2005). For example, the consortium "Route 21", established by many leading commercial corporations (including Apple, Intel, Microsoft, Lego or Ford), suggests that our society future requires a very different type of formal education than the one suggested in the TEPs above (Partnership, 2007a). The consortium defines a set of "21st century skills" which should be learned in the educational system. The list contains "core subjects and interdisciplinary themes" (the latter includes Global Awareness, Financial Economic, Business and Entrepreneurial literacy, and Civic Literacy); Learning and innovative skills (such as critical thinking and problem solving, and communication and collaboration); Information, media and technology skills; and life and career skills including: Flexibility and Adaptability; Initiative and Self-Direction; Social and Cross-cultural skills, Productivity and Accountability; Leadership and Responsibility (Partnerships for 21st century [Route 21], 2007a). In a supplementary document, entitled "21st century skills professional development" (Partnerships, 2007b), Route 21 describes the characteristics of an effective professional development that supports 21st skills. Economic success requires that practical rationality incorporates critical thinking and creativity, and it cannot ignore substantive issues. Thus, though deeply anchored in the technical-rationality mode of thinking, the "what works" approach, which concentrates on the present, should be replaced by a broader look on society and its challenges. From this point of view, TEPs like RELAY simply misses the *Homo Economicus* ideal. The lure of these TEPs will resemble the CBTE. Adherence to a set of techniques cannot infuse flexibility or creativity. At the end, society will regret its reliance on the one-dimensional criteria of success.

But the very ideal of the *Homo Economicus* is contested. In itself, it is claimed, it is not adapted to the 21st century needs. Martha Nussbaum (1995) finds four major difficulties with the ideal of *Homo Economicus*. First, it reduces differences of quality to differences of quantity. What cannot be mathematically formulized cannot be accounted for. This is a mistaken generalized view of human nature. Second, the statistical bias of the approach which tends to form a picture of "general" or "average" or "normal" utility, disregards personal qualitative differences between individuals. Third, by way of "maximization" it seeks an exact and definite solution to man's problem, thus disregarding life complexities and mysteries. Four, it supposes that humans act only because of interests and these interests are predefined.

The consequences of this approach are straightforward as all four difficulties are part of the "achievement driven" education system. Only exams, usually multiple choice ones, are accounted for; standardization demolishes any possibility of especially poor children to develop themselves in different areas; it sees academic success as the only remedy to the child's problems; and it supposes that without exams and grading, there will be no learning[44]. This has an influence on every aspect of the school's environment. It reificates the relationships between teachers and pupils, among the pupils, among the teachers, and between teachers and parents. The end (high grades) becomes more important than the means. It leads to cheating and corruption. The teachers become merely instruments whose assessments and esteem entirely depends on how their pupils are doing.

Other *Homo Economicus* definitive features have been challenged even within economics:

1. In classical economic theory, *Homo Economicus* deploys perfect rationality, in the sense that he strictly and unfailingly obeys all the laws of logics and statistics, and has complete knowledge about the world.[45] These two assumptions do not represent any "real" person. Although they portray an ideal type, it is clear that no human being can have these two characteristics. Tversky and Kahaneman convincingly demonstrate that human deliberations are often logically (or statistically) invalid, being affected by various psychological biases (e.g., Kahaneman, Slovik, Tversky; 1982; Rubinstein, 1998; Arieli, 2008). It is evident that no one can have a perfect knowledge. Even if it has been feasible, the price to pay in order to achieve it would violate the utility maximization principle, for achieving perfect knowledge will be too costly. Nevertheless, classical economics theorists usually assume that these assumptions are both factually true and normatively appealing (Hahn & Hollis, 1979, p. 12 – 13). They are factually true, in the sense that this idealization provides the best possible explanation of how humans actually behave. They are normatively appealing because they suggest how humans should behave if they want to maximize their utility. Thus, *Homo Economicus* possesses what is usually called "perfect" or "unbounded" rationality" (Watkins, 1970; Simon, 1976).

Teacher educators do not possess perfect rationality. They neither have complete knowledge nor unmistakable logical abilities. Nevertheless, the confidence of the adherences of TEPs like TFA, or RSGE (like that of the former CBTE) is enormous. With no hesitance, they claim that they have a "ground breaking" program which "will create a new generation of excellent teachers" (RSE). For the next few years, the innovative last word approach will spread until it is found that, after all, it does not provide the magic solution.

A different approach is to assume that the "rationality" in question is much more restricted. As suggested by Kirchgassner, "Rationality... means only that the individual, following his intentions, is principally in a position to assess and evaluate his action range and then to act accordingly ...without being fully informed..." (Kirchgassner, 2008, pp. 15 – 16). In other words: "the individual behaves as a 'satisfier' and not as an 'optimizer', he searches so long among the alternatives at his disposal until he meets a 'sufficient' acceptable one..." (p. 28).

TEPs act like satisfiers and not like optimizers, but it is crucial that they address the question of what counts as a satisfier and why it is so. This takes us to the second point.

2. The distinction between aims and means is usually connected with the assumption that values are inherent in the first, but not in the latter (Kirchgassner, 2008, p. 13). In this sense, "orthodox pure [economic] theory cannot admit any serious sense in which preferences may be irrational" (Hahn & Hollis, 1979, p. 10).

This suggestion follows the ideas of Max Weber (1947, pp. 184 – 186). Weber analyses the principles of economical thinking and differentiates between formal and substantive reasoning. Formal reasoning, which is based on quantifiable formulas, aims to maximize the possible material profit in a given situation. Substantive reasoning takes into account the social values of the action and the its social aims. Weber's concept of formal rationality has been given a precise formulation in Game Theory. A behavior is rational if:

> Of two alternatives which give rise to outcomes, a player will choose the one which yields the more preferred outcome, or more precisely, in terms of the utility function he will attempt to maximize expected utility (Luce & Raiffa, 1957, p. 50)

This assumption is problematic, since it is evident that when someone "pursues a certain goal it is important to him how this goal is achieved. When he wants to travel from Munich to Zurich, it is also important for him how and by which means he will reach this destination" (Kirchgassner, 2008, p. 13; cf. Back, 1987). "Thus, it may be postulated that instead of profit maximization, which ignores the issue of how the profit is achieved, the only one single purpose left, which in itself is no longer a means, is that of utility maximization" (Kirchgassner, 2008, p. 14). This shift also means that *Homo Economicus* "is generally not only financially motivated" (p. 14).

The problem is that the notion of a rational agent is ambiguous. It can refer either to (a) an individual who wants to achieve a certain end (usually happiness) or (b) an individual who chooses the best available action. But, the second definition does not guarantee that the chosen action will necessarily contribute to his happiness. The idea, that the rational man maximizes a function which is a mathematical expression of his happiness, is confusing (Rubinstein, 2009, p. 49 – 50). (Winning a lot of money does not necessarily improve one's chances of attaining happiness.) According to the second definition, maximizing utility becomes the end of the rational process. In such a case, happiness might be detached from the process, for it becomes a constraint on the preferences of the action (see: Kirchgassner, 2008, p. 12 – 13). If the means (e.g., material wealth) are not a precondition of the ends (happiness), it is necessary to examine the connection between the two (Bruni, 2007). Formal rationality is not enough, and some economists (e.g., Sen, 1979, 1986) suggest that the definition of the rational man as *Homo Economicus* is, in itself, irrational.

These observations point to a serious flaw in the logic of the last discussed TEPs: their rational is based on an ambiguity between (a) choosing the best available action (e.g., training the teacher to use a technique)) and (b) achieving the end of preparing an efficient teacher. The aim is detached from the process, and what is seen as the best available action becomes an end in itself. It is not the case that the TEP tries to follow Dewey's ideas about the importance of the end-in-view. Quite the opposite, it is the total absence of any critical discussion about the ends or the preferences of the program. Thus, for example, in RGSE, the question of what kind of impact the chosen techniques have on the teachers' identities, and what kind of citizens these authoritarian techniques enhance, is not even mentioned (being, supposedly, too theoretical).

3. Instrumental rationality does not always lead to utility maximization. A famous game-theory example, the "prisoner dilemma", demonstrates that while there are cases in which there is no other action available to the agent, the consequence of which he prefers to that of the chosen action (so the action is

formally rational), the preferred action does not achieve the best possible outcome. The story is well known, but merits another repetition:

> Two prisoners are accused of having committed a series of crimes (including an armed bank robbery). The public prosecutor's evidence is weak: Without confessions, he can convict both of them only on minor infractions... So he proposes to each of them the following deal (the prisoners cannot communicate which each other): If both confess, each of them will be punished severely with ten years of imprisonment. If neither confesses, they will both get off with a relatively light punishment of two years. If only one of them confesses, he will get off without punishment as chief witness, whereas the other one will be severely punished with 20 years of imprisonment.

In this situation, it would be reasonable for both prisoners to co-operate and not to confess. But each of them could regret this choice because neither can be sure that the other prisoner will not incriminate him. To behave rationally, he has to confess. But since both of prisoners are rational, each of them prefer to confess (because in the best case scenario he will be released and in the worst case he will be in jail for 10 years, while if he does not confess he will be in jail for 2 to 20 years). Since both of them are rational, they end up with 20 years in jail instead of 4. Behaving rationally is not the same as being reasonable. For the benefit of both, cooperation should be enforced on them...

The implications of the prisoner dilemma are far-reaching. They demonstrate that in a completely laissez-fair economy, based on free competition (what is called zero-sum game), in which each individual is rational, his situation is worse than could have been given some kind of co-operative arrangement. (This conclusion remains the same in versions of the game in which it runs a couple of times and the partners are allowed to discuss their possible strategies. As soon as the game is finite, the outcomes of the game are the same.)

What is important to note is that in this picture of the rational economic individual, there is no place for any 'moral' considerations.

The famous French writer Jean de La Fontaine introduces his famous fable *The Wolf and the Lamb* with the sentence: "The strongest reasons always yield to reasons of the strongest." La Fontaine's wolf, which devours the lamb, is not original. He is a devotee of the ethic of Callicles, one of Plato's heroes in the dialogue *Gorgias*, who believes that:

> ...nature herself makes it plain that it is right for the better to have the advantage over the worse, the more able than the less. And both among all animals and in entire states and races of mankind it is plain that this is the case – that right is recognized to be the sovereignty and advantage of the stronger over the weaker (Plato, Gorgias, 483 c-d).

Hence, "The more powerful, the better and the stronger are the same" (488 d) and therefore:

> Luxury and intemperance and license, are... virtues and happiness (492 c).
> The naturally noblest should suffer his appetites to grow to the greatest extent

and not check them, and through courage and intelligence should be competent to minister them at their greatest and to satisfy every appetite with what it craves (492 a).

In a world with limited resources, this unrestricted desire cannot be fulfilled without hurting others. But for Callicles, there is no problem. "Might is right" is the only legitimate moral principle he recognizes, and any imposed constraint is a plot of the majority of weak people against the natural rights of the few powerful nobles. Callicles is not aware that without restrictions even the powerful can suffer. There is always the possibility of someone more powerful appearing. To date, neo-liberalists share the same problem.

In this kind of thinking, *phronetic* thinking loses any respectable place and means-ends (or utility maximization) rationality becomes an end in itself. From a moral point of view, says Kirchgassner, "One of the strategies in economic or social theory to handle the problem of moral behavior is to show that all behavior which is usually called 'moral' is indeed performed out of self-interest; one has to look only somewhat more carefully to detect that this is the case" (Kirchgassner, 2008, p. 155). Thus, "it is a meaningful strategy to set the incentives for individual behavior in such a way as to make moral behavior (as far as possible) unnecessary, i.e., that the individuals show the desired behavior if they follow their self-interest" (p. 155). But this aim cannot be achieved if self-interest is defined in purely egoistic terms. The idea that the prisoner may want to tell the truth is not a possible consideration in the game. Mutual trust is unimportant as such. It is the dead end of the game, from a purely egocentric utility maximization assumption, which raises the question about the definition of rationality and its relations to morality. However, morality might provide the needed barrier which insures that reason will be reasonable and carry genuine utility for the individual who seeks happiness and well-being.

The last mentioned point is applicable to school systems and TEPs. Competition is a zero-sum game. If the self-interest of the institution is to survive, it will do whatever it can, regardless of the morality of the means it deploys. Nichols and Berliner (2007) and Ravitch (2010) expose the collateral damage that this policy imports to education: concealing data and cheating spread all over the system. A climate of suspicion and accusation replaces cooperation and trust. The image is more important than the real thing, or maybe, like in any simulacrum, the image replaces the real thing. The image of learning replaces learning. The teachers who have to "play the game" feel that they are not in the right vocation. They feel that they have to rescue the children from the system.

This line of thought illustrates that instrumental rationality does not guarantee a better lure to the human race. For the Frankfurt School, instrumental rationality is a recipe for disaster. The separation between means and ends, which is an essential feature of such thinking, and its pretense to be "value neutral", lead to the utilization of reason in the service of the worst immoral powers. Technology leads to alienation and loneliness. The Nazis, as Adorno and Horkheimer remind us, excelled in using instrumental reasoning to murder millions of people efficiently and effectively. Enlightenment, they say, is "indefatigable self-destructive". It leads humanity into "a new kind of barbarism" (Adorno & Horkheimer, 1972, p. xi).

These difficulties, which are reflected in the to-date economic crisis around the globe, suggest that the whole neo-liberal approach is mistaken. Hence, it is difficult to detect the legitimization of the view that teaching should be a kind of business, that for profit or non-profit NGO's are better suited to deal with it, in way that will ensure social justice, and that the children will be better educated if all they have on their mind is how to gain higher grades on the exams. At the same time, the devaluation of the teachers' role, and the transformation of TEPs into institutions which train new teachers to prepare their children to learn for the exams, seems to change the prospective teachers' identities. No longer is the teacher seen as a well-educated *phronimon*. Not even the well-prepared reflective practitioner. The new teacher is a short-term, temporary employee who is devoted to the children's grades and not to their lives. That is, however, the way he is examined and evaluated in order to attain his certificate.

SUMMARY

In the last three chapters we traced the enlightenment inspired TEPs. At first the TEPs move from non-academic ST and AT through the technical-rationality phase to the reflective-practitioner phase. At this point the path bifurcates. One direction leads to intensification of the reflective approach towards the teacher as researcher stance. The other direction takes them towards the teacher as clinician approach. While the first direction depends on substantial rationality, and is more *phronetic* oriented, the second direction returns to instrumental rationality. Both directions tend to be utilitarian, though the interpretation of what counts as utility is different. In one direction it is broad enough to cover many aspects of humanity. In the other, utility gets a very restricted, one dimensional interpretation.

These options describe various possibilities of teachers' identities within the enlightenment stance. They indicate, as well, the possible identification of the TEP. Depending on whether the TEP endorses instrumental or substantial rationality, on whether it emphases the technical, the *techne* or the *phronetic* aspects of teaching, and on whether it is more oriented towards HAVING than on either BEING or DOING and focuses on the achievement principle as its compass, it has distinctive features which define its identity.

The last phase of TEPs, especially in the US, is, for me, a distorted and destructive development. It devalues the teachers, and teaching profession, and impedes the traditional conceptions of what education is all about. This conclusion might be contested by the protagonists of the neo-liberal agenda, although even they can agree that education is more than high achievements in standardized exams, and that the students deserve something more. Nevertheless, the neo-liberals' argument is false. Slavoj Žižek identifies the basic paradox of liberalism:

> An anti-ideological and anti-utopian stance is inscribed into the very core of the liberal vision: liberalism conceives itself as a "politics of lesser evil," its ambition is to bring about the "least worst society possible", thus preventing

a greater evil, since it considers any attempt to directly impose a positive good as the ultimate source of all evil... However, the more its program permeates society, the more it turns into its opposite. The claim to want nothing but the lesser evil, once asserted as the principle of the new global order... clearly presents itself as the best of all possible worlds; its modest rejection of utopias ends with the imposition of its own market-liberal utopia which will supposedly become reality when we subject ourselves fully to the mechanism of the market and universal human rights. Behind all this lurks the ultimate totalitarian nightmare, the vision of a New Man who has left behind all the old ideological baggage" (2011, p. 38).

The neoliberal agenda becomes a secular religion. The enlightenment paradise turns into hell, and as we have seen, it influences TEPs the way religion does: it imposes a certain ideology and way of thinking which are immune to any critic, suspicion, or doubt.

The problem of the enlightenment is not restricted to instrumental rationality. As we realize today, after more than five hundred years of modern science, we still do not possess even one scientific theory which may be regarded as evidently true.

To wit:

1) Mathematics tells us that, in principle, man is limited in his ability to build consistent and complete systems which organize his knowledge. This is the impact of Russell's Paradox, and of Gödel's incompleteness theorem.

2) Modern Physics (quantum mechanics) tells us: (a) that it is impossible, in principle, that our knowledge will ever be complete (The principle of uncertainty); (b) that in order to understand reality we have to use conflicting theories (The complementary Principle); (c) that the observer influences what he sees; and (d) that (Pace Kant) the way we perceive the world (through the filter of Euclidean Geometry) is wrong. This is, by the way, a general feature of modern science as a whole. From as different domains such as Physics and Psychoanalysis, Linguistics and Biology, we hear the claim that "things aren't what we sense".

3) Modern Physics states that Newtonian Physics is false (being only an "approximation" to the new set of principles). Thus, we have to face the brute fact that even physics is defeasible. In general we may say that every scientific theory is accepted only temporally, its truth being accepted "for the time being", that it is the best option to date.

4) Many sciences (e.g., Physics, Biology, Psychology, or Economy) base their theories upon statistical generalizations. This move decreases the possibility to provide genuine explanations, and we have to remain satisfied with sophisticated descriptions of reality. Einstein once said that he cannot believe that God plays dice, but this is exactly how the world looks like to the eyes of modern science. As science gives up the interesting questions "why" and "what for", its raison d'être becomes open to hostile discussions.

5) Epistemologists (following Quine (1960) and Kuhn (1970)) tell us that theories are underdetermined by facts. Not only is perception "theory-laden", but any class of facts might give rise to different theories, each consistent by itself, but inconsistent with each other.

6) Post-Modern Philosophy of Science tells us that theories are relative to environmental influences. Since Kuhn's book, *The Structure of Scientific Revolution* (1970), it is common wisdom to claim that scientific changes are due to sociological, rather than logical factors, that scientific progress is an illusion, and that we have to pay attention to the deprived wisdom of females or of other cultures and societies (e.g., Harding, 1998).

7) Ethics tells us that the very demarcation between facts and values, so central to modern science, is highly dangerousMaybe, it is time to question the relationship between science and violence. What was socially successful in the last centuries was not science as such, but technology. The divorce between science and ethics, leads to a divorce between technology and ethics. The results, as we all know, were disastrous, the very future of the human race is in danger, and it is the proper time and almost the last opportunity to stop the whole process and to have a new evaluation of its foundations (Serres, 1995). Even if some of these points are controversial or too extreme, their overall effect is, nevertheless, clear:

1. Enlightenment, in the instrumental rationality interpretation, is problematic because ignoring the reasonableness of the aims may lead to disasters. Though,

2. Substantial rationality is questionable as well because there is no way to absolutely legitimize its claims about the nature of the true and the good. There is no valid procedure to ensure that what we think about is correct although it is possible (and rational) to be involved in a constant process of error elimination (including the possible error that reason is our only moral source).

Both ways it seems that reason alone is too dangerous to rely on.

DOING: DUTY AND FULFILLMENT

Enlightenment has been a reaction against the belief in external authority. It discards the individual who believes that he has a divine mission to fulfill the duties imposed on him by his faith. The believer, however, recognizes these obligations as his own. He internalizes and strives to realize them, believing that his actions will bring salvation to himself and to the entire world. Usually, this faith has been a specific religion, and the transcendental authority is God. But, there can be a secular faith (such as Communism), if it entails absolute obligations toward the fulfillment of a definite ideology.

The individual is "good", or behaves correctly, if he fulfills his duties sincerely and full-heartedly, without doubt or hesitation. Every human action is judged according to its agreement with these divine duties. This notion of the "good" reflects non-utilitarian ethics. To be evaluated as "good", an action does not have to contribute to a state of happiness in this sinful world. Good and bad are not defined according to any criteria of utility, although it is possible to take into account one's lure to heaven. Thus, for example, some religions held that what happens to any human being in the "next" world, after the death of his corporal body, depends on his behavior in this world. His entire life is examined before his eternal location, heaven or hell, can be decided. The human being is judged as a whole: he is "good" or "bad", "sinful" or "just", heretic or believer.

THE RELIGIOUS BELIEVER

The Jewish *Halakhic Man*, as it is described and analyzed by Rabbi Joseph B. Soloveitchik (1944/1983), illustrates the religious version in one of its purest manifestations. The *Halakha* is the collective body of the Jewish law. It is a comprehensive guide to all aspects of life, both material and spiritual, whose commandments and guidelines are elaborations of the 613 laws prescribed in the Old Testament.

The *Halakhic* Man is the Jewish individual who devotes his entire life to implementing this divine set of laws. According to Rabbi Soloveitchik:

a. The *Halakhic* Man strictly obeys all of the laws as they appear in the Bible and the extensions and interpretations given to them throughout the centuries. His unconditioned compliance is guided by the principle that "action precedes thinking". In all the behaviors of the *Halakhic* man "listening" comes after "doing"[46]. First of all he obeys the laws and only later he attempts to comprehend them.

b. Similarly to the scientist:

> [The] *Halakhic* man explores every nook and cranny of physical-biological existence... He is interested in sociological creations... he is involved with psychological problems... (Soloveitchik 1944/1983, p. 22 – 23)

But unlike the scientist, the *Halakhic* man holds an *a priori* world-view which dictates all his activities:

> *Halakhic* man orients himself to the entire cosmos and tries to understand it by utilizing an ideal world which he bears in his *Halakhic* consiousness. All *Halakhic* concepts are *a priori*, and it is through them that *Halakhic* man looks at the world... his world is similar to that of the mathematician: *a priori* and ideal. Both the mathematician and the *Halachist* gaze at the concrete world from an *a priori*, ideal standpoint... There is one question which they raise: Does this real phenomenon correspond to their ideal construction? (p. 23)

For example,

> When *Halakhic* man comes across a spring bubbling quietly, he already possesses a fixed *a priori* relationship with this real phenomenon: the complex of laws regarding the *Halakhic* construct of a spring... and he uses the statutes for the purpose of determining normative law: does the real spring correspond to the requirement of the ideal *Halakha* or not? *Halakhic* man is not overly curious, and he is not particularly concerned with cognizing the spring as it is in itself. Rather, he desires to coordinate the *a priori* concept with the *a posteriori* phenomenon...
>
> [Similarly] ...when *Halakhic* man looks at the western horizon and sees the fading rays of the setting sun... he knows that this sunset... imposes upon him anew obligations and commandments... They make the tome fit for carrying out of certain *Halakhic* practices... (p. 20 – 21).

In a nutshell:

> There is no real phenomenon to which *Halakhic* man does not possess a fixed relationship from the outset and a clear, definitive, *a priori* orientation (p. 22).

c. The *Halakhic* man obeys the laws for themselves and not because of any utilitarian motive. The fulfillment of the laws is, for him, an end by itself. He knows that obeying the law is the only way to love the deity. This recognition is an outcome of an educative process in which, at its beginning, stands the principle that action precedes understanding, but at its end the individual realizes that to obey the *Halakha* is the only way to approach God.

d. What interests the *Halakhic* man is the ideal world in which the divine commandments are fulfilled:

> *Halakhic* man cognizes the world in order to subordinate it to religeous performances... Cognition is for the purpose of doing (p. 63).

The mission of the *Halakhic* man is to bring redemption to the earthy world, a redemption which depends on the realization of the *Halakha*. The *Halakhic* man feels responsible that the world corresponds to the *Halakhic* commendments. The desire to bring redemption to the world is his own.

e. The individual (Jew) who lives in accordance with the *Halakha* will find personal redemption (p. 38). The power that motivates him is internal. He internalizes the *Halakhic* norms and sees them not as a cohersion but as an expression of his humanity:

> "He does not experience any consciousness of compulsion accompanying the norm... He discovered the norm in his innermost self, as though it was not just a commandment imposed upon him, but an existential law of his very being" (p. 63 – 64).

f.   The *Halakhic* man is not impulsive. He is not Romantic (p. 40 – 41; p. 139 –140). His deep religious experience "only follows upon cognition, only occurs after he has acquired knowledge of the *a priori*, ideal *Halakha* and its reflected image in the real world" (p. 83). He does not wish to replace this earthly world for any "deeper" or "highier" one. "He wishes to purify this world, not to escape from it" (p. 41). His religiosity is not based on ecstatic or mystic experiences but on knowledge. He is deeply involved in a constant process of learning, devoted to extract the moral and spiritual principles upon which the *Halakha* is based, believing that these principles convey the ideal human society and describe the ideal human person.

g. The *Halakha* is not a static set of laws. The changing contexts, in which it has to be implemented, require the *Halakhic* man to reinterpret the divine commandments so that they will be relevant to the current state of the world. This hermeneutic labor represents one of the *Halakhic* man important duties. The *Halakhic* man acknowledges that after the *Halakha* was given to man in Mount Sinai, "it is not in heaven" (80; elaborating on the *Talmudic* understanding of *Deut.*, 30, 12). Through his continual interpretations, the *Halakhic* man has the power to "create" the world, to become "partner to the almighty in the act of creation" (p. 81).

h. Repentance is the highest sign of the creative power of man. Man's actions define his personality, and by changing his actions, so that they will accord more faithfully with the *Halakha*, the individual recreates himself.

> "The severing of one's psychic identity with one previous "I", and the creation of a new "I", possessor of a new consciousness, a new heart and spirit, different desires, longings, goals – this is the meaning of that repentance compounded of regret over the past and resolve for the future" (p. 110).

Repentance is an ongoing process. Every day the *Halakhic* man faces new challenges, and he has to identify himself day-to-day as one who behaves according to the *Halakha*.

i. Repentance is dependent on man's free will.

Indeed, man's entire spiritual existence is enhanced by his unique privilege to create himself and make himself into a free man… [His glory] grounded this creative power in man's will. The will outwits the structured lawfulness of the species; it creates a new, free mode of being in man, one which is not enslaved by the rule of structured lawfulness of the universal but which it ascends to the very heavens and cleaves to the divine overflow. The will is the source of repentance, providence, prophecy, and the freedom of the spirit. However, this whole process of development unfolds in an ethical-*halakhic* spirit. The intellect, the will, feeling, the whole process of self-creation, all proceed in an ethical direction (p. 137).

In this sense, "Man must create himself" (p. 109) regularly and constantly.

In sum, the *Halakhic* man has a DOING-type mode of existence. It is based on an ethics of duties, and on externally imposed laws, which should be obeyed strictly and unconditionally. However, by obeying the law and learning their particularities, the individual realizes, gradually and step by step, that they present an ideal reality. This realization makes him feel free, and enables him to interpret the given commandments so that they will be relevant to the context he lives in. This creative activity ensures that through a process of permanent repentance, the *Halakhic* man takes part in a divine mission whose aim to bring salvation to the entire world.

There is second characteristic of the *Halakhic* man which Rabbi Soloveitchik explores in a later article (1965). The religious man realizes that although his mission is huge and sublime, he is a finite being with limited power. He feels terribly weak, and he is anxious that he is too lonely and weak to fulfill the assignment. What gives him the power to perform his mission is the community of believers to which he belongs. The individual cannot live in accordance with the *Halakha* unless he belongs to a community of believers (some of its laws can be performed only in a group). He can fulfill his duties only as a member of a community in which there is a mutual responsibility of each of the members for the behavior of any other, so that every individual has to see that any other member will obey the laws. This membership in a *Gemeinschaft*[47] lessens the individual fear of loneliness. It makes room for an encounter with the other with a feeling that they both belong to something sublime and divine which has a great past and promising future.

The individual is identified as a member of this community. (In Hebrew, the words "individual" (*yakhid*) and "together" (*yakhad*) are constructed from the same ;lexical origin, and both are connected to the word "one" (*ekhad*). This identity depends on the supposition that the individual is a conformist. In order to be accepted, the individual has to be obedient and sacrifice his personal preferences. He has to identify himself completely and resolutely with the ideals he attempts to enact and with the group which endorses them. But total conformity might lead to the loss of personal identity. This issue raises contradictory requirements. On one hand, according to the *Halakha* itself, it is necessary that the individual will keep his own personal identity. Man is born in God's image, and this means that each individual is unique, and has to fulfill his own essence, by finding his own original way towards God. However, any investigation is within definite limits and cannot lead to doubt or to heretic thinking. The genuine believer cannot agree to any concession. Critical thinking can be done only by the very few whose faith is strong and stable.

There is an obvious downside to the communal characteristic of the believer attitude. It leads to a sharp division of the world into "we" and "they". Usually, "they", the others, are against us. We are better or preferred because we recognize the truth which they deny. At the end, they will go to hell, but in meantime they are dangerous because they are heretics. They may prevent our salvation. Moreover, they pose an alternative to our faith, and this can harm our young generation. Either we enclose ourselves and limit our connection with them (like the Amish community in the USA), or try and convince them to be on our side. The many religious wars demonstrate how the second alternative might be disastrous. It even compels many individuals to become secular.

Modernization poses a special threat to the *Halakhic* ultra-religious community. For example, a need arises to educate women, so that they will contribute to the family's income. But general education threatens the closed traditional society because once educated, the women might join the secular society. This fear encourages the founding of orthodox religious schools for girls, and with it grows the need to educate teachers for these institutions. The idea had been to provide young women with the "education and training they needed to resolve their sense of alienation from the host Jewish community, encourage marriage within that community, thus enabling them to transmit the concepts and precepts of Judaism to successive generations of their children" (see: Gold, 2003).

THE SECULAR BELIEVER

It is possible to have a secular version of the external believer attitude. The modern secular believer finds a replacement for God. Science can reveal the necessary laws of society and discover the unavoidable aim it must reach. It describes society's necessary path of development, and consequently enables to specify the individual's absolute duties whose fulfillment will bring the sought after earthy heaven.

An example of such a secular faith is the Communist ideology, which regards Dialectical-Materialism as a valid scientific theory about the historical laws which dictate social, economic and political spheres of human behavior. Human society, which develops according to certain dialectical laws, has reached the stage in which the working class (the proletariat) should fight against the abusive capitalistic economic system. Man can bring salvation to himself and his society if he will transform his personality, realizing that only if he will join his fellow comrades, and feel solidarity with them, he will bring the long awaited release from any kind of repression. What makes this stance an instance of the believer MoE is that the theory is taken as ideology: its truth is uncontestable, universal, necessary, and absolute.

The believer, who accepts the Marxist Theory as dogma or as "religion", in the sense that it is a necessary truth, behaves like the *Halakhic* Man. When he interprets the world, the Communist New Man has the characteristics of the ultra-orthodox Jew. Karl Popper observes that "a Marxist could not open a newspaper without finding on every page confirming evidence for his interpretation of history; not only in the news, but also in its presentation – which revealed the class bias of the paper – and especially of course in what the paper did *not* say" (Popper, 1969, p. 35).

Like the *Halakhic* Man, the Communist Man knows that he cannot be satisfied with mere analysis of reality. He has an obligation to change it. He has to do something to provide a better future for himself and his society. Praxis, however, should be based on knowledge, so that the discussion and study of Marxist theory is an essential part of the development of every activist.

The activist knows the Marxist-Leninist doctrine, recognizes the principles of the dialectical-materialism theory and acknowledges the appropriate behavior implied by them. He internalizes the theory's maxims and turns its commandments into inner norms. In Isaiah Berlin's (1958) terms, he has a positive liberty. He chooses to behave according to a true and just ideal. Being an activist is, of course, a DOING oriented mode of existence in a society, which honors its members according to their loyalty "in action" to the official ideology.

In a famous poem written in 1924, and devoted to Lenin, the communist poet Vladimir Mayakovsky states that "the individual – is senseless, the individual is null"[48]. The meaning of the self's life is founded on his being part of the collective effort. He has to be fully assimilated in the society, and behave strictly according to its norms. It is better, of course, that he will be convinced that the collective way of life is the best possible, but if not, there is room for reeducation for his own sake and for the sake of the entire society.

EXTERNAL-BELIEVER TEACHER EDUCATION

The similarities between the religious and the secular versions of the DOING oriented believer are striking. Both share the same features for their respective TEPs:

1. The TEP has a distinct, clear and principled world-view, which expresses its definite faith. This world-view is formulized by the appropriate authorities (Rabbis, the Party), which address all levels of individual practices. Teacher educators cannot criticize or change this attitude or its pedagogical implications.

2. The teacher educator prepares the next generation to fulfill his duties. He represents society and has the responsibility for the way his students behave and the strength of their faith. He should provide a personal example of the ideals' implementation. He is personally committed to obey all its prescriptions. He has an obligation to see that his students faithfully perform all their obligations.

3. The mission of teacher educators is to prepare proper educators. They highlight the loyalty to the faith and the recognition in its absolute validity.

4. The TEP forms a strong community which is built on collaboration, belongingness, solidarity, caring, and mutual support. The community endorses a collective "I", which has its own narrative.

5. The TEP has a holistic, cohesive and coherent curriculum (formal, hidden, and null), which is directed towards the implementation of its ideology.

6. There is a strict recruitment process for faculty, students and administrators of the TEP to ensure that only suitable individuals will enter its door.

For instance, the TEPs in the ultraorthodox Jewish school chain "Beit-Yaakov" are restricted to women who graduate from the high school of the chain. Continuing with the same high-school cohort, the course of studies lasts for two additional years and its aim is to learn in order to teach. The curriculum is mainly devoted to religious studies (Bible, Jewish law, Jewish world-view). Secular studies are learned presupposing that any piece of scientific knowledge already has a hint in the *Torah* (The first part of the Old Testament), and the Jewish sages knew it thousands of years before the modern scientists. Literature includes only ultra-orthodox writers, and holocaust survivor memoirs. The history of the Jewish people is an important sacred subject. Other parts of the curriculum include Teaching, Practicum, and Subject specialization (See: Appendix, example 13).

Each TEP of Beit-Yaakov has a strict code of behavior (including how to dress and how to speak in public) which has to be obeyed. The library contains only religious books, and the students are not allowed to read other books or to use other libraries. The use of TV and cell-phones is forbidden. The students are not allowed to go to restaurants, secular events, or theaters. Their entire family has to keep each and every *halakhic* law.

In the secular HAVING culture, which encircles the ultra-religious society, it is quite difficult to teach modesty, humility, and austerity. To fight against the external culture, many class lessons in Beit-Yaakov are devoted to explaining the religious restrictions, which are viewed as providing the precondition for a proper education. Most of the religious studies are devoted to the importance of the mission young women should take upon themselves. (Every woman is seen as an educator in her family and neighborhood.) Thus, the DOING mode of existence is the only legitimate behavior she can pursue.

The seminar's teachers are experienced women-teachers and distinguished male rabbis. First and foremost, they are formative educators. Their most important mission is to keep the seminar code of behavior and to respond to any violation of its dictates. The code is seen as an armor which keeps educational "purity". Especially important issues that the teacher-educators have to address are prayer, personal integrity and honesty, sensitivity, gratefulness, modesty and humility. The educational value of the Jewish holidays and the prayers are highly emphasized.

Almost from an opposite ideology, one can find a very similar attitude in the pedagogical institutes in the former Soviet Union. Education in the USSR is primarily a political tool for the construction of a communist society (Grant, 1964, p. 23):

> The Soviet teacher is first and foremost, as an ideological educator, responsible for developing among young people a scientist, social, political and civic outlook. To be equal to this task, the teacher, in addition to receiving a through specialized and professional training, should acquire a broad philosophical and socio-political outlook (Torniak, 1972, p. 111).

The Soviet authorities do not view subject matter knowledge as the primary objective of education, but the development of the "New Soviet Man" who internalizes the "socialist morality." According to Bronfenbrenner (1962), optimal personality development can occur only through productive activity in a social collective. The first collective is the family, but this must be supplemented early in life by other collectives specially organized in schools, neighborhoods, and other community settings. The development of socialist morality is accomplished through an explicit regimen of activities, mediated by group criticism, self-criticism, and group-oriented punishments and rewards[49].

The role of the teacher is to faithfully implement all the dictates. "When teaching in schools, teachers had to inculcate their students the political thoughts of Marxism-Leninism and the moral principles of communism (Yan Man Kit, 2001, p. 83). Teachers are expected to "quote Lenin's work in class instruction; be ideal persons…; teach students the Soviet structures of government society; shape the mind of the students, but not teach them to think independently" (p. 83).

Teacher Education has to verify that the teacher is able to create the appropriate environment, in which the class, as a collective, functions to fulfill this type of social morality. The TEP in pedagogical institutions[50] lasts for five years. The curriculum is divided into three areas: political and general courses, education theory, and special subjects (Grant, 1964, p. 134 – 135) (See: Appendix, Example 14)[51]. But this division is a bit misleading because every course of the TEP is taught from a Marxist-Leninist point of view.

The two examples of the external believer TEPs have different foci in terms of their Modes of Existence. The Communist TEPs one is more DOING>HAVING MoE, although it is directed towards the HAVING of the collective and not that of the individual. On the other hand, the Jewish orthodox TEPs are more strictly DOING oriented.. Beit Yaakov TEPs openly oppose the HAVING MoE, which is seen as heretic behavior. But Beit Yaakov is not interested in the BEING of the individual women they educate but in their being loyal and faithful.

In addition to these two types, it is possible to find a DOING>BEING type of TEP. A striking example of this type was the TEP of the Kibbutzim movement in the 1940s. This TEP implements all the above mentioned six features the external-believer TEPs (Back, in press b). All the students were relatively old Kibbutz members, who were sent to the seminar by their communities because of their devotion to the ideology of the movement. They saw teaching as a sacred devotion, and their personal development was seen as enhancement of the cultural environment of their communities. The course of studies in "Seminar Ha-kibbutzim" was similar to a regular ST program, with a special emphasis on biology, nature studies, Jewish studies and the arts. Educational studies comprised mainly of developmental psychology, Freud, and the relations between work and society. The teacher educators were prestigious academics. There were no method courses and barely a practicum, and most of the studies had been infused with the enlightenment's *Bildung durch Wissenschaften* spirit. The emphasis was on self-learning, and one of the program's graduates characterized it as "formation more than information" (Segal, 1981). Unlike the academic course of studies, those of the seminar focused on general knowledge in a certain domain and on the relations between this knowledge and actual practice, without a detailed discussion of data or research methods. The primacy of a doing MoE came from the fact that, though located in Tel-Aviv, the seminar was a residence, a kind of closed community in which the life was organized as if it was a genuine Kibbutz, and the students were involved in every aspect of the program. Thus, the ideology was a form of life. It elevated many discussions but, unlike the communist example, ideology *per se* had not been learnt in any formal course (Segal, 1981).

Waldorf TEPs can present another example. Based on Rudolf Steiner's Anthroposophy, these TEPs are devoted to prepare teachers for Waldorf schools (See: Appendix, Example 15). By its adherents, Anthroposophy is seen as the science of the spirit. As theorized by Steiner, humans grow through a certain path of development, comprised of phases in which, in each of them, another human faculty is placed at the center. The physical body is the focus of the first, preschool (ages 0-7) phase, the emotional soul is the center of the second (primary school) phase (7-14), and the rational spirit is the center of the third (high school) one (14-21). The physical body is responsible for willing. Its physiological locus is the metabolic/limbic system (located in the abdomen). From a social point of view, its social attribute is fraternity, and its sphere is economy. The soul is responsible for feeling. Its physiological system is the Rhythmic (located in the chest). From a social point of view its social attribute is equality, and its sphere is politics (legal rights). The Spirit is responsible for thinking. Its physiological system is the nerves/senses, and it is located in the head (Mazzone, 1999, p. 52). From a social point of view, its social attribute is liberty and its sphere is (spiritual) culture. (Steiner believes that many of society's problems are the outcome of discrepancies between the social attribute and the social sphere.)

The development of each phase occurs in different ages and obeys different rules. The development of the spirit is the least predictable and more individual than either that of the body or the soul. For a proper education, each phase calls for different emphasis on the content and method of what happens in education. The knowledge of the spirit can include a conception of God, which is the recognition of a transcendental realty that stands behind the entire Cosmos. (As we shall see in the next chapter, this is also one tenet of the Romantic world-view which influences Steiner's thoughts, although his interpretation is Christian, and includes the ideas of karma and reincarnation).

Steiner himself develops a very detailed system of "dos" and "don't dos" for teachers. Thus, for example, in primary school, which should deal with the child's emotional world, the teacher should devote his energy to the arts. The child should reveal his creative imagination through art. However, to gain proper results, the arts should be exercised in a prescribed manner (e.g., certain color combinations are more appropriate than others, certain rhythms are preferred, etc.). The schools have a fixed daily schedule of studies, beginning with a main morning lesson, and include many rituals which aim to foster reflection and meditation by the individual upon his life. The primary class teachers receive their students in the first grade and then proceed with the same children for their entire primary education (six to eight years). The class teacher normally teaches almost all the subjects. He is expected to be engaged in a continual process of inner discussion with Steiner's anthropology and train himself to develop the intuitive faculty of knowing what to do with an individual child at a particular juncture of his development (Mazzone, 1999, p. 177).

Steiner enlists four basic principles which should characterize the teacher's work. The teacher:

- must be a person of initiative in everything that is done...

- should be one who is interested in the being of the whole world and of humanity

- must be one who never makes a compromise in his or her heart with what is untrue

- must never get stale or grow sour. (Mazzone, 1999, p. 109)

The TEPs are usually either standalone programs or special programs for certified teachers who want to teach in a Waldorf school. The major components of the TEPs are Anthroposophy, Waldorf pedagogy, Arts and Crafts.

Although Waldorf TEPs are BEING oriented, for they want to develop individual freedom, the road to BEING is highly prescribed and fixed. It is a DOING MoE which wants to attain BEING, in a very definite method.

SUMMARY

The external-believer moral source has a definite influence on every aspect of the TEP, because the teacher has the highly important role of the missionary who brings the light to the younger generation. Hence, devotion, personal example, and strict adherence are virtues that the TEP should inculcate in a formative manner. Each of the TEPs has its own holy books (the bible, Marx-Lenin, or Steiner), which have to be learned and cited. Each of them prescribes a very strict code of behavior. Right and wrong, true and false, are absolute, eternal, and beyond dispute. DOING is the dominant MoE, and the traditional mode of honor is the mode of recognition given to the loyal devotee.

The Enlightenment moral source aims to abolish this kind of dogmatic and uncritical thinking. As we have seen, its success has not been plain. First, both Marx and Steiner are modern thinkers which try to construct scientific world-views. Second, the enlightenment itself might become an ideology, and thus be dogmatic and totalitarian.

BEING: ROMANTICISM AND BEYOND

BEING ROMANTIC

The label Romanticism refers to an intellectual and cultural movement in Europe in the late 18th and throughout the 19th century. It is manifested primarily in philosophy and the arts (poetry, prose, drama, painting, music), but it has a widespread influence on the entire world-view of the time (including religion, politics, and education). For example, this movement is the origin of ideals such as "romantic love", "authenticity", or "meaningful learning". The label Romanticism refers to many different and conflicting ideas, and it is quite difficult to understand what makes all of them belong to the same movement (Berlin, 1999, chap. 1). It is even arguable that the very attempt to define the movement goes against its spirit (Thurley, 1983, p.1; Halpin, 2007, pp. 18 – 20)[52].

Nevertheless, David Halpin characterizes Romanticism as endorsing five definitive features:

> (1) A rejection of all kinds of strict rationalistic reductionism, being hostile to any suggestion that a single ideological or moral outlook or dogma or method can be successfully applied to the solution of anything but simple problems...; (2) A rebellion against attempts to underplay the role of feelings in understanding and interpreting human experience... [Especially crucial is the experience of love]; (3) A negative attitude towards all attempts to drive a wedge between reason and imagination; (4) An oppositional attitude about all forms of traditionalism for its own sake; And (5) An insubordinate, heroic sometimes, commitment to challenging the ugliness, spiritual emptiness and crude materialism of modern life (2007, pp. 22 – 23).

These are all "negative" features. While they emphasize what the Romantics were fighting against, and reveal the Romantics' aversion to the enlightenment emphasis on reason and method, they do not disclose the "positive" agenda of what the Romantics were aiming at. Towards this end, Halpin suggests a list of five Romantic ideas: childhood, love and friendship, heroism, imagination, and criticism (2007, p. 10). Even this list is not comprehensive. It is possible to add to it other ideas such as authenticity, integrity, and spontaneity (see: Heath, 2005, p. 5), as well as self-realization, and the German notion of *Bildung* (see: Beiser, 1998; 2003).

Loyal to Romanticism's spirit, I will expose its "positive" tenets by looking at a piece of art. Although published more than a century and half after the height of the Romantic era, the seemingly naïve book, *The Little Prince*, written by the

French author Antoine de Saint-Exupéry (1943), can be seen as a manifesto of its worldview. The book, disguised as children fairy-tale, presents many of the main Romantic ideas, and advocates their current viability.

The book narrates the story of the meeting between the author and The Little Prince in the Sahara Desert. It begins with an unusual dedication. The author dedicates his book to Léon Werth, but he feels the need for an apology, which can be seen as a motto to the entire story:

> I ask the indulgence of the children for dedicating it to a grown-up. I have a serious reason: he is the best friend I have in the world. I have another reason: this grown-up understands everything, even children's books. I have a third reason: he lives in France where he is hungry and cold. He needs cheering up. If all these reasons are not enough, I will dedicate the book to the child from whom this grown-up grew. All grown-ups were once children– although few of them remember it ...

So as not to offend the children, but remain loyal to his own feelings, the author corrects his dedication: "To Léon Werth when he was a little boy" (The book's dedication).[53]

This uncommon dedication, which expresses the reversal of the conventional relationships between children and adults, conveys three Romantic themes: (a) the difference between adults and children and the primacy of childhood; (b) the all importance of love and friendship; and (c) the ideal of authenticity as the proper way of life. The book elaborates these themes, which, as we shall see, are closely connected. The first suggests that the adults have a distorted world-view, and as a result, they are inauthentic and their life is meaningless and lonely. The second discloses that love and friendship can prevail over these shortcomings. The third theme connects the first two: children are authentic, while authenticity both depends on and leads to love and friendship.

THE PRIMACY OF CHILDHOOD

The book starts with an introductory chapter. The author remembers that when he was a child, he used to draw a boa constrictor digesting an elephant. The grown-ups respond unimaginatively to his drawings, misinterpreting them as a hat. They advised the child "to lay aside [his] drawings of boa constrictors..., and devote [himself] instead to geography, history, arithmetic, and grammar." The author followed their advice and becomes a pilot. Ironically, he admits, geography has been useful to him. "At a glance I can distinguish China from Arizona. If one gets lost in the night, such knowledge is valuable". Since his childhood, he believes that "grown-ups never understand anything by themselves, and it is tiresome for children always and forever to give them explanations" (chap. I). As an adult, he examines this belief by showing his drawings to every "sensible" grown-up he meets. Usually, the adult would respond that "it is only a hat," and the author would bring himself "down to his level, [and] would talk to him about bridge, and golf, and politics, and neckties. And the grown-up would be greatly pleased to have met such a sensible man" (chap. I)[54].

This experiential exam is puzzling. Why does the author expect that other adults will understand him? Why does he believe that they can guess what he is thinking about? Developmental Psychology tells us that the very young infant is egocentric. He believes that everybody else knows everything he has in his mind (Berk, 2008, p.325; 343). While he grows up, the child learns to differentiate between his self and others, and learns that his thoughts are hidden from them unless explicitly expressed. So, is the author just a developmentally arrested toddler or maybe he has something else in mind?

The book endorses the second option. In its second chapter, the Little Prince meets the author and recognizes the meaning of his drawing the minute he sees it. (Chap. II)[55]. How can he? How is it possible that he recognizes the boa constrictor without the need for any explicit explanation? What makes him so unique? The answer is that the Little Prince is a child. The author only expects children (or children-like adults like Léon Werth) to understand him. In his opinion, there is something distinct about the children's outlook that makes it possible for them to immediately penetrate and comprehend his imaginative world.

In a nutshell, the crucial difference between adults and children is that they have two totally different world-views. For the child, the world has an invisible, hidden dimension, while the adult denies its reality. It should be emphasized, however, that according to the author, to be a child is a state of mind and not a state of being a certain chronological age (see the dedication).

The hidden dimension of the world is imagined. It is an invention of the individual subject. Nevertheless, it is as real and objective as the visible one. Moreover, it is much more important than the visible dimension because it encloses universal, durable and viable ideals about humanity, and about the purpose and meaning of life. The principle, that "the thing that is important is the thing not seen" (Chap. XXVI), is repeated once and again throughout the entire book.

The hidden dimension of the world is accessible only by what the fox, which represents the genuine sage, calls "seeing with the heart" (chap. XXI). Any attempt to explicitly (i.e., verbally) describe it will nullify or flatten its meaning. The author believes that only children can penetrate this dimension. They alone can see with their heart, and this idea echoes the slogan written by the Romantic poet Novalis, "The heart is the key to life and the world" (cited by Beiser, 2003, p. 133).

Adults, adversely, believe that only the visible dimension of the world is real. They deny the reality of the imaginative dimension, and take it to be far-fetched. They hold that only rational, scientific and calculative reasoning, which deals with what is visible, can discover the truth about the universe we live in. Adults believe that "seeing with the eyes" is the single legitimate source of knowledge.

Thus, while the adults, who "see with their eyes", rely on and use their *logos* (the Greek equivalent for both 'reason' and 'word'), the children know that "...words are the source of misunderstandings" (chap. XXI.)[56]. They acknowledge that, as Wittgenstein puts it: "There are, indeed, things that cannot be put into words. They *make themselves* manifest. They are what is mystical" (Wittgenstein, 1922/1963, §6.522)." Children who "see with their hearts", rely on their feelings and use their imagination, and a result, they can penetrate the hidden dimension of the world.

The idea that the children have a different understanding of the world originates by Jean-Jacque Rousseau. For him, the child's conception of the world is based on immediate experiences. The child does not analyze the world, nor does he verbalize or quantify it. He feels it. In the first pages of his *Confessions*, Rousseau remembers himself as a toddler, and says "I feel before I think; it is the common lot of humanity" (Rousseau, 1789/2000, p. 8). Similarly, he declares in his book *Emile or On Education* (1762/1977) that "Childhood has its own ways of seeing, thinking, and feeling" (p. 54).

The message of *The Little prince* is cut and clear. The children's state of mind is preferable to that of the adults. It endows their life with meaning. It enables them to live authentically, and to attain genuine self-fulfillment. Since the adults acknowledge only what can be seen, their world is shallow, one-dimensional and meaningless. Their thin outlook causes them to ignore the really significant aspects of their life. As a result, "they have no roots" (chap. XVIII), their life is meaningless, and they feel alienation, despair, and loneliness. The author devotes many chapters of the book (especially chaps. IV, X-XV, XXII-XXIII) to descriptions of various adults who "do not understand life" (chap. IV)[57]. They waste their entire lifetime running from one place to another, performing pointless activities without knowing why or what for (e.g., chap. XXII).

In his account of the modern adult world-view, Saint-Exupery agrees with the Romantic critique of the enlightenment. (As Halpin's list of the Romantics' five definitive features presented at the beginning of this chapter can attest.) The Romantics, as well, believe that the imaginative and subjective outlook of the child reveals something real and objective about our human existence. "In our earliest childhood", philosopher Charles Guingon learns from the novel *Hyperion* (written in 1797-1799 by the Romantics Friedrich Hölderlin), "we are in touch with a primal truth... prior to the distancing relations and hardening of experience brought by growing up" (Guignon, 2004, p. 53).

What is the essence of this "primal truth"? What makes it so different from the adults'? Briefly said, the adults, who live in the modern era, ignore the spiritual dimension of reality. They comprehend the world as a huge mechanism (a "universe"), while the children, like our premodern ancestors, grasp it as a giant organism (a "cosmos") (Guignon, 2004, p. 20; Taylor, 2007, p. 59 – 61). (Though unlike our premodern ancestors, the modern child is secular. He does not believe in witches and magicians, in angles and devil. He does not mistake the world of Harry Potter to be the real one.)

For the modern adult, the world resembles a mechanical clock. It is a gigantic machine, divided into very small constituents (atoms), which are, at least in principle, visible. To him, the world seems a spiritless matter. It is possible to analyze its structure and discover the causal "laws of nature" which dictate what happens. There is no hidden reality. What cannot be seen does not exist. There are no concealed mysteries. There is no sublime essence which influences his life, and which the human being can search after and be part of.

The idea that the world is a huge organism has totally different implications. The world is alive. It changes and develops. It may be healthy or sick. It has power and will. It has passions and desires. It can love or hate. It can create and destroy. Within such a conception, it makes sense to address the world's spirit, aim (*telos*), or will, and it is sensible to look for their possible impact on our own being. Furthermore, it is appropriate to regard the individual human being as a cell of this cosmic organism, whose existence, health, and well-being depends on the entity as a whole, while its functioning affects the organism's life as well.

Such a world-view endows humans with the meaning of life. Moreover, only this view can explain the mystical feeling that humans are part of a sublime, infinite, and eternal entity (be it Nature, Spirit, or God – for those who remain religious). Immersing in this substance, they can forget that they are mortal and overcome their death anxiety (their lives are connected to something eternal and sublime). This world-view has another aspect. It alone explains why humans are influenced by ideas such as the true, the good, and the beautiful. This is a distinguished Romantic idea. According to Cecil M. Bowra, who studies the *Romantic Imagination*,

> ...in different ways each of the [Romantics] believed in an order of things which is not that which we see and know, and this was the goal of their passionate search. They wish to penetrate to an abiding reality, to explain its mysteries, and by this to understand more clearly what life means and what it is worth. They are convinced that, though visible things are the instruments by which we find this reality, they are not everything and have indeed little significance unless they are related to some embracing and sustaining power (1950/1961, p. 9).

> The great Romantics agreed that their task was to find... some transcendental order which explains the world of appearances and accounts not merely for the existence of visible things but for the effect which they have on us, for the sudden, unpredictable beating of the heart in the presence of beauty, for the conviction that what then moves us cannot be a cheat or an illusion, but must derive its authority from the power which moves the universe (p. 22).

The mysterious well, discovered by the author of *The Little Prince* toward the end of the book, is an appropriate metaphor of this world-view. The thirsty author, accompanied by the Little Prince, finds the well "at daybreak" (chap. XXIV), after a tiresome search. Strangely enough, it was not like the standard wells of the Sahara, for it looks "like a well in the village" (chap. XXV). "I thought I must be dreaming", the author says, and continues: "It is strange, everything is waiting for us". The well is singing for them, and its water, which symbolizes the affluent source of life, "was as sweet as some special festival treat. This water was indeed a different thing from ordinary nourishment. Its sweetness was born of the walk under the stars, the songs of the pulley, the effort of my arms. It was good to my heart, like a present" (chap. XXV).

The metaphor of the well enables the author to deal with the disturbing question: How do we know that we have reached the "real" hidden dimension? In other words, it is now possible to address the question of what makes the imaginative dimension objective? If we do not suppose an "external" kind of divine revelation, we need a secular criterion of the sublime reality. Saint-Exupery shares with the Romantics the idea that the criterion of reality is esthetical. The hidden dimension is real if we feel excited by its beauty. The Little Prince says that if something "... is beautiful, it is truly useful. What makes the desert beautiful," he continues, "is that somewhere it hides a well..." (chap. XIV)]. These words arouse the author's memory:

> When I was a little boy I lived in an old house, and legend told us that a treasure was buried there. To be sure, no one had ever known how to find it; perhaps no one had ever even looked for it. But it cast an enchantment over that house. My home was hiding a secret in the depths of its heart...
>
> "Yes," I said to the little prince. "The house, the stars, the desert – what gives them their beauty is something that is invisible!" (chap. XIV).

"Looking with the heart" provides a mystical, enchanted and imaginative experience, in which humans can be connected to the deep source of their existence.

According to Bowra, "the essence of the Romantic imagination is that it fashions shapes which display those unseen forces at work" (1950/1961, p. 10): "...far from thinking the imagination deals with the non-existent, the Romantics believe that, when it is at work, it sees things to which the ordinary intelligence is blind and that it is intimately connected with a special insight or perception or intuition" (p. 7)[58]. "Imagination" is a power which "creates and reveals, or rather reveals through creating" (p. 15). The knowledge revealed by the power of imagination does not lead to scientific generalizations. It is gained through "particular examples, because only then do we see them in their true individuality... [and] begin to understand their significance and their appeal." (pp. 10 – 11) The paradox is that as far as this imaginative journey is more individual, subjective, and personal, it discloses more general, universal and eternal truths about humans and their world (Schlegel, 1982, p. 16; cf., Nussbaum, 1995).

While imagination creates the hidden reality, it is through the arts that it is expressed and conveyed. Art does not provide an unequivocal picture of reality. It tries to show its infinite essence in a finite means, open to never-ending interpretations and meanings (Berlin, 1999). Artistic creations have endless depth and can convey the symbolic dimension of what is hidden. Therefore, art alone (and especially poetry and music) enables humans to understand their world and their life. As the fox insists, words (logos) cannot convey it without misunderstandings (chap. XXI). As Wittgenstein acknowledges, in the last sentence of the *Tractatus*, "what we cannot speak about" (i.e., what is invisible) "we must pass over in silence" (Wittgenstein, 1921/1961, §7). For the Romantics, art replaces science as the vehicle to truth and the genius replaces the scientist as the hero who reveals the true, the good, and the beautiful. The human genius replaces God as the creator and bearer of the human spirit.

FRIENDSHIP AND LOVE

In another of Saint-Exupery's themes, there is an additional factor that contributes to the meaninglessness and aimlessness of adults' lives. Their outlook makes them lonely. As the snake informs the Little Prince, "it is also lonely among men" (chap. XVII), and the fox agrees: "...men have no friends anymore" (chap. XXI)[59]. They are lonesome and disparate.

Love and friendship are extremely important because they render something common to something unique; endowing it with special significance that affects humans' entire lives. One of the climaxes of the book is the dialogue between The Little Prince and the fox. The fox wants to befriend The Little Prince. In his language, he wants to be "tamed" by him, because "...one only understands the things that one tames" (chap. XXI). He informs the Little Prince that:

> If you tame me, then we shall need each other. To me, you will be unique in all the world. To you I shall be unique in all the world. My life is very monotonous. I hunt chickens; men hunt me. All the chickens are just alike, and all the men are just alike. And, in consequence, I am a little bored. But if you tame me, it will be as if the sun came to shine on my life. I shall know the sound of a step that will be different from all the others. Other steps send me hurrying back underneath the ground. Yours will call me, like music, out of my burrow. And then look: you see the grain-fields down yonder? I do not eat bread. Wheat is of no use to me. The wheat fields have nothing to say to me. And that is sad. But you have hair that is the color of gold. Think how wonderful that will be when you have tamed me! The grain, which is also golden, will bring me back the thought of you. And I shall love to listen to the wind in the wheat . . . (chap. XXI).

The feeling of having a meaningful life depends on love and friendship: "If someone loves a flower, of which just one single blossom grows in all the millions and millions of stars, it is enough to make him happy just to look at the stars" (chap. VII). Without love the world is senseless. Everything in it has the same importance, hence nothing is really important.

In order to be able to love, one has to leave the utilitarian race of life and devote one's time to reflect and construct the meaning life. "Men, [explains the fox]... buy things all readymade at the shops. But there is no shop anywhere where one can buy friendship" (chap. XXI).The taming process between the fox and The Little Prince takes time and requires effort, but it has far-reaching consequences. Only after it takes place, The Little Prince understands that in his star, he "was too young to know how to love [the rose]" (chap. VIII). Only then, under the fox's guidance, he realizes that: "It is the time I have wasted for my rose that makes my rose so important (chap. XXI)."

The meaning of life is revealed through establishing a deep relationship with others. After The Little Prince and the fox become friends, The Little Prince understands what love is. He now realizes that although there are thousands of roses, his rose is unique because of the special relationship he feels toward it. The fox can now instruct The Little Prince to return to the garden where he had found thousands of roses. Now he can tell them:

You are beautiful, but you are empty. One could not die for you. To be sure, an ordinary passerby would think that my rose looked just like you—the rose that belongs to me. But in herself alone she is more important than all the hundreds of you other roses: because it is she that I have watered; because it is she that I have put under the glass globe... Because she is *my* rose (chap. XXI).

Similarly, love enables the author himself to endow new meaning to his own life: "...nothing in the universe can be the same if somewhere... a sheep that we never saw has – 'yes or no' eaten a rose... Look up at the sky... And you will see how everything changes..." (chap. XXVII). It is of no wonder that "it is a good thing to have a friend." (XXIV).

It may be questionable whether the love relationships in *The Little Prince* are "romantic", because they are asexual. Following Soble (1989), Raja Halwani (2010, p. 7 – 8) suggests that the concept of love may refer to three kinds of relationships, whose old Greek labels are *Eros, Philia,* and *Agape. Eros* refers to sexual love; we can also call it "erotic love," "passionate love," or "romantic love." *Philia* refers to friendship love, which includes friendship and any friendship-like love, such as that between siblings, colleagues and co-workers, parents, and children, and even husband and wife (depending on the type of marriage they have and at which stage it is). *Agape* is not based on the qualities of the beloved. Whereas in relations of *eros* or *philia* we (supposedly) love others because of who they are, in the *agape* relation we love others gratuitously; it is a love that "does not depend on our own attraction" (Halwani, 2010, p. 8), for example, the kind of love that God is said to have for His children.

According to these definitions, the love relationships in *The Little Prince* are instances of *philia.* Although they are between certain individuals, they lack any erotic dimension. However, Halpin (2006, 2007) defines *eros* much more broadly: "While *eros* is often interpreted as sexual craving, this is only a minor part of the story..." For him, the crucial feature of *eros* is having "a passionate intense longing for something". Following Plato's *Symposium, eros* can be "conceived a common desire that passionately seeks out the particular beauty of an individual person, thing, or image in order to anticipate or remind us of the true Beauty that exists only in the world of Forms of Ideas. In this tradition, love has a metaphysical and transcendental status, the ultimate object of which is an appreciation of the Beauty or the Good" (Halpin, 2006, p. 328).

We can now understand the all importance of love as one of Romanticism's most salient features (Halpin, 2006; 2007). For some Romantics love is the principle of all human life (e.g., Coleridge, Shelly, Wordworth). According to Beiser, Schlegel believes that "We can remystify the world, we can discover its lost beauty, mystery and magic, only if we see all things in the spirit of love. It is through love that we see ourselves in nature and others, and so reindentify with the world and become at home with it again" (Beiser, 1998, p. 296). For Coleridge as well, love has a transcendental dimension: "[It] is a desire of the whole being to be united to some thing, or some being, felt necessary by its completeness, by the most perfect means that nature allows, and reason permits" (quoted in Halpin, 2006,

p. 331). This concept makes evident the interdependency between Romanticism's two main themes. Imagination and love both aim at the appreciation of the hidden, sublime reality.

Moreover, as Beiser explains, "The Romantics saw it as their mission to restore the sovereignty of love to the realms of morals, politics, and art." For them, "it is love rather than reason that provides the sources and sanction of the moral law" (Beiser, 1998, p. 296). The last quotation suggests that love has an essential ethical dimension. The mutual dependency, which results from friendship and love, is the gateway to ethics. The fox explains the inherent ethical implication of love to The Little Prince: "You become responsible, forever, for what you have tamed. You are responsible for your rose..." (chap. XXI). The last part of *The Little Prince* highlights this ethical responsibility when the friendship between The Little Prince and the author becomes a key to their mutual survival (chap. XXIV – XXV). Both are desperately thirsty, and at the Little Prince's initiative, the pilot, who develops a 'need of protecting' the prince (chap. XXIV), finds, against all the odds, the mysterious well (chap. XXV). It seems that the very feelings of love, caring, and loyalty enable the author to find the well and access its mystical reality.

The Little Prince exposes the importance of love and friendship as the vehicle for moral life. Similarly, the Romantics believe that:

> We realize our common humanity, and develop our unique individuality, only through love... It is also through love that I fulfill my individuality because love derives from my innermost self, from my unique passions and desires, and it consists in a unique bond between myself and another... in loving someone I act on the rational principles of duty from, rather than contrary to, inclination (Beiser, 2003, p. 133).

The feeling of love carries with it the responsibility to the other, and therefore love becomes a moral source or an ethical compass. This moral source recommends a new type of ethics, based on "duty from inclination", which is neither the utilitarian ethics of ends and means nor the deontic ethics of principles and duties. When I examine my actions, I do not ask what their costs/benefits will be, and I do not examine whether there are instances of some general moral principle. Instead, I question what is appropriate to do in the specific situation in which I intend to carry the actions out.

Duty arising out of inclination is distinctive because it is directed only toward certain individuals (the beloved ones) in a given context. As such, it cannot be justified by reason alone (Honneth, 2007, p. 171 – 179). It represents "particularistic" ethics (Stout, 2008, p. 853), based on notions such as caring or empathy (Slote, 2009). It recommends behaviors which cannot be generalized or transferred to other contexts or to people other than the beloved ones. This ethical approach is disputed, because it seems to go against a major moral intuition according to which ethics cannot be situational or particular (Nussbaum, 1990, p. 50 – 53). The Little Prince explicitly differentiates between "his" rose and all the other roses to which he feels no duties or responsibility. Thus, it can be argued that the specific attitude of The Little Prince to his rose cannot be morally justified because he seems to discriminate against the other roses.

Nevertheless, such an ethics can have its own justification. For, as Schiller believes, love, freedom, and justice are closely related (Armstrong, 2002, pp. 120 – 122). Schiller, says Armstrong, "believes that love requires the integration of all our powers: we have to be sensual, but also understanding… devouring, sexual desire has to be tempered with respect…" (p. 122). According to bell hooks (2000, pp. 87 – 101) love ethics means "showing care, respect, knowledge, integrity, and the will to cooperate" (p. 101). Seen from this angel, love is the cornerstone of moral behavior. As already mentioned, it is a prerequisite for self-fulfillment (Honneth, 1995). The adult's inattentiveness to the needs of the author of *The Little Prince* renders his life meaningless, and only his love to the Little Prince restores his ability to be a painter. This line of thought introduces the idea of authenticity to the discussion.

AUTHENTICITY AS A "GIVEN"

The notion of authenticity is not mentioned in *The Little Prince*. Nonetheless, the author's life can be characterized as suffering from lack of authenticity. Due to his frustration, he gave up his promising career as a painter to become a pilot (chap. I). For him, maturation has been a process of decline. Socialization has a price. It demands the author's concession of his creative aspirations (chap. II). All his life he regrets this loss (chap. IV) and conceals, from other adults, his genuine self (chap. I). In other words, the author's behavior has been inauthentic, and he feels that he has to apologize for his wasted life. Since he does not get the opportunity to express his hidden self, he has not been able to attain his self-realization. He did not become an artist.

What happens to the author violates Rousseau's ideal of proper education. Rousseau opens his book *Emile* with the famous sentences:

> God makes all things good; man meddles with them and they become evil. He forces one soil to yield the products of another, one tree to bear another's fruit… He loves all that is deformed and monstrous; he will have nothing as nature made it, not even man himself, who must learn his paces like a saddle-horse, and be shaped to his master's taste like the trees in his garden… (Rousseau, 1762/1977, p. 5).

Society forces the child to give up his creative potential, but this creates a gap between the child's authentic self and his outer behavior, and annuls his chances for self-fulfillment.

For Rousseau, every human being has a unique inborn nature, so that everything should be "brought into harmony" with his natural tendencies. The individual should be loyal to his "given" self: "…to be something, to be himself, and always at one with himself, a man must act as he speaks, must know what course he ought to take, and must follow that course with vigor and persistence" (p. 8). This "idea of authenticity presupposes a conception of a true self lying within the individual, a self that contains resources of understanding and purpose that are worth access" (Guignon, 2004, p. 12). All one's personality, one's body and mind, emotions and reason, passions, and actions, should form a unified holistic substance, whose aim should enhance one's self-realization.

The idea that humans are born with an inner self they have to be loyal to, is not novel. What is original to Rousseau is his belief that this inborn nature refers to the person *qua* individual (and in a later Romantic transformation *qua,* a component of a certain nation, race, state, or spirit) and not to the person *qua* human being. This is a distinctive modern idea. Aristotle, for example, believed that every human being has a certain essence, but this essence is common to all humans. It defines the *Homo sapiens* as rational species. In order to gain happiness (*eudemonia*), humans have to enact all their capacities, turning them over from mere potentiality to actuality. This principle refers especially to the reasoning faculty, both theoretical and practical, since reason defines them as humans (Aristotle, 1984, DA; EN). Similarly, the monotheistic religions believe that humans have an innate divine nature ("in the image of God created He him"; Genesis, 1, 27), to which they have to be loyal if they want their soul to return to paradise. In both cases, this divine nature finds itself in conflict with the human inclination to pursue earthy happiness, and ignore the chosen way of life, so that being authentic in this context (i.e., authentic to the prescribed "true" nature) means almost the opposite of the term's current usage. The shift from the universal human essence toward the individual person is something that the Romantics take as axiomatic: "I will be/want to be mine" says Goethe in *Wilhelm Meister Lehrejare*[60], and expresses the Romantic ideal of self-realization, which emphasizes that any individual has distinctive personal traits (Beiser, 2003).

Beginning with Rousseau, being authentic has two main ingredients. The first is self-knowledge. The human being should be sincere. He has to be 'true to himself', and as a prerequisite he must bravely and sincerely explore and be sensitive to his inner voice. The second ingredient of authenticity is self-expression. We have to meet the requirement "to express that unique constellation of inner traits in our actions in the external world – to actually *be* what we *are* in our ways of being present in our relationships, careers, and practical activities. ... [Since] only by expressing our true selves, we can achieve self-realization and self-fulfillment as authentic human beings" (Guignon, 2004, p. 6). The reason for the requirement of self-expression is that any human being could truly *be* such-and-such a person only if others see him as being that person. Others reactions are necessary to confirm and stabilize one's self-identity (Honneth, 1995; Guignon, 2004, p. 66).

According to Rousseau, authenticity is "given" because it has a biological source (Golomb, 1990, p. 244). Each individual is born with a unique predefined nature, and like a plant, he has to actualize the potential inherent in his seed. He will be authentic as long as his actions will be sincere and loyal to his innate nature[61]. This loyalty can be highly demanding. It may lead even to self-sacrifice because the self cannot compromise his genuine emotions or beliefs (see the suicide of young *Werther* or the widespread phenomena of duals, usually due to romantic affairs or wounded honor) (Berlin, 1999). Self-sacrifice is morally better than concession. One has to fight for one's truth even if it means that one has to destroy the entire world or to commit horrible crimes (like Raskolnikov, the hero of Dostoievsky's (1866/1996) *Crime and Punishment*), because such behavior may lead to the destruction of a wicked society. Life should be worth living. It is more important how to live than to live. Reason cannot solve unsolvable problems (like unrequited love). The readiness to suffer and die for what you are attests that you are sincere and authentic. This, of course, is a very different ideal than happiness or well-being.

Sincerity, however, is not enough. Authenticity, as Trilling explores, suggests a "more exigent conception of the self and of what being true to it consists in, a wider reference to the universe and human's place in it, and a less acceptant and genial view of the social circumstances of life." (Trilling, 1972, p. 11) What the last sentence conveys is the core of authenticity as an ideal. As Guignon explains:

> ...gaining access to the inner self will get us in touch with something of profound significance. The innermost self is experienced as a doorway to a context of meaning that is greater than either the social world or the passing psychological occurrences within us. The turn inward is supposed to lead us to a dimension of the self that transcends our particularity. It is deep within myself that I find that I am part of Nature or The World Spirit or Humankind or the realm of imagination, creativity and beauty... By turning away from the pretense and deceptions of society, I find the place where I truly belong: my natural home as a spiritual or childlike or creative or quasi-divine being. ... [T]urning inward is all about getting in touch with something greater than ourselves, even though this "something greater" is no longer God (Guignon, 2004, p. 60)[62].

Living an authentic life is the sign that one's imagination and self-expression have been fully exercised.

It is possible, now, to see the linkage between the various Romantic themes. The gate to the hidden dimension of the world is found in our inner self. Authenticity is important because it liberates our imagination and creativity. It enables us to enter the cosmos, and to have meaningful relationships with it and its habitants. As we shall later see, according to a certain interpretation authenticity also enables us to love our fellows.

By a way of summarizing the Romantic world-view, I want to mention a complementary idea. Existential Psychologist Carlo Strenger (2010, pp. 28 – 30; 72) suggests that the main force, which drives humans, is their fear to die. In all their behavior they try to suppress the idea that they are mortal. Three strategies help them to overcome this anxiety: Having emotional connection with meaningful others; endorsing a world-view which specifies their "place" in the world, and give their life meaning and aim; a feeling of self-esteem which is derived both from the esteem they acquire from others and from their feeling of self-fulfillment.

The Romantic world-view captures these three strategies. The authentic individual imagines the hidden dimension of the world in a way which captures eternal human values, of which love and friendship are constitutive feelings. If he is a genius, he can creatively convey this imagined world to others, so as to influence their meaning of life.

PROBLEMS AND CAVEATS

Romanticism can be highly perilous. The ideal of "Given" authenticity, faces two major problems. The first results from those Romantics who go one-step further, and introduce the idea of a "national character" as a racist ideology. The second comes from the idea that looking inward may reveal a "heart of darkness", since the "innermost self" is home to morally intolerable instincts, drives, and passions.

For some Romantics (notably the German ones), the organic unit, humans seek to get in touch with, is not the entire cosmos (i.e., Nature, World-Spirit, or God). They postulate an intermediate level, such as the Nation, the Race, the State, the National Spirit, or some combination of them, to which the individual belongs. This level defines his identity, and frames his given authenticity. For Herder, Fichte, Schelling or Scliermacher, the Nation is a kind of such an organism (Reiss, 1955, p. 23; p. 34; Berlin, 1999, p. 83ff.; Siegel, 2005, p. 385). To be authentic, the individual has to be absorbed within the unique spirit of his nation. He has to adhere to the nation's *Volkgeist* (national genius, sometimes symbolized by its leader), because "the *Volkgeist* alone is able to express the will of that spiritual community, the nation which possesses a natural unity" (Reiss, 1955, p. 39, referring to Friedrich Carl von Savigny).

Authenticity in this context is defined not in individual terms but in terms of the larger organic entity to which the individual belongs. To be authentic means to be loyal to this entity, to embrace its spirit, to absorb its tradition, language, norms of conduct, and world-view, and to conceive of them as divine and sublime. This kind of authenticity endows the individual's life with meaning. He can find for himself a proper place in the world, have a sense of belonging, and transcend his mortal being[63].

Although the notion of "national character" may be conceived of as purely sociological (Luth, 2000, 69), it may signify a threat. As noted by Klafki, the classical perspective of Humboldt and Herder, which has been "progressive-liberal, republican and cosmopolitan", has been transformed into a "narrow nationalism", which "even gave ideological support to the initial preparations for, and later takeover of, Germany by the Nazis..." (2000, p. 95).

This transformation begins as a search for a unifying principle on which the German nation could be built. For the German Romantics this principle has been the notion of *Volksseele* (national soul) (Bauman, 1978, p. 23ff), which characterizes any genuine nation, and manifests itself in the nation's language, the vehicle of its identity. The slippery road towards Nazism started when the organic soul of the Nation/Race had not been taken simply as being one soul among others but as superior to them. By their very existence, the other Nations or Races threatened the Nation's "purity", which had to be protected by all possible means. This move became highly dangerous when this protection had not been passive (i.e., when one isolated oneself from "others") but active, when one tried to eliminate those others: to exile them or to murder them (as was the case in Nazi-Germany).

In 1941, Peter Viereck clarifies the connection between Romanticism and Nazism:

At first glance, there may seem scant connection between the earlier German romanticism and nazism. But the former evolved step by step into the latter over the complex period of a hundred years. We can enter the ideological house that Hitler built only by entering through the underground passage – apparently far off, apparently un-Nazi – of romanticism (1961, p. 16)[64].

A well-known philosopher, which represents this connection, is Martin Heidegger, whose search for authenticity culminates in his support of the Nazis (Adorno, 1974; Seigel, 2005, pp. 42, 582 – 585). Thus, for example, in 1934-1935 he devoted a seminar to the Romantic poet Hölderlin in which he presented his poems as prophesizing the "new German" (Faye, 2009, p. 103 – 123)[65].

The Romantic ideal, of the authentic human being who strives to find and express his inner self, by feeling part of the hidden dimension of the world, might lead to racism, extreme nationalism and fascism. Quite paradoxically, the *Wondervogel* ("The migratory bird" – the romantically inspired German youth movement of the early 20th century) lends in Auschwitz.

The idea of "given" authenticity raises a problem regarding the moral nature of the given self. While Rousseau believes that man is born innocent and morally good, after Freud, this very supposition becomes suspicious. Freud advances the theory that humans are born with an *id* full of unrestricted, self-destructive and morally suspicious passions and desires, so much so, that for society to exist, humans should cultivate their emotional world. Far from finding that their inner-self can provide humans with a moral compass, they discover a "heart of darkness" that has to be restrained by their civilization.

Moreover, this inner-self resides in an unconscious layer of the self to which the human being usually has no access. One's sincere confessions are no more than after the fact rationalizations one gives to one's behavior. As Nietzsche famously claims: "one's own self is well hidden from one's own self" (1882/1974, IV, §335). Contrary to what Rousseau believes, the inner look misdirects humans, deceives them, and cannot function as a reliable moral source.

"Given" authenticity looks like a self-deception and has to be discarded. Rousseau notwithstanding, it seems that it cannot serve as an educational ideal. Yet, we must ask what about the Romantic ideals of friendship and love, of the significance of imagination and of art, the reality of the hidden dimension of the world? Is it necessary to abandon the idea of authenticity or to get rid of the entire Romantic world-view? Is it possible to maintain the Romantic spirit, and its inner irrational moral source, without falling into its extremely dangerous traps? While for many Romantics, religion provides the shield against falling into barbarism, for those who do not accept the religious way out, a humanely anchored way to promote these ideals has to found.

"CREATED" AUTHENTICITY

One such account presupposes a different concept of authenticity according to which it is not "given" but "created". Instead of being loyal to a predefined inner self, each individual can become 'the author of his own life', capable to invent his own identity (Taylor, 1991, p. 61). In this concept, the individual does not discover who he is, but rather invents it.

One of the first protagonists of this concept of authenticity was Friedrich Nietzsche (Golomb, 1990, p. 244). In one of his famous aphorisms, Nietzsche says: "*will* a self and thou shalt *become* a self" (Neitzche, 1880/1986, II.1, §366). In another famous slogan he declares: "You should become who you are" (1882/1974 §270). Alexander Nehamas suggests that Nietzsche's basic intuition is that "everything that one has done actually constitutes who one is" (Nehamas, 1983/2001, p. 272). He believes that it is possible to define who one is by looking at all one's actions (and not by looking at what one possesses).

The notion of invented self-identity raises the problem of the self's stability. Human actions are by no means consistent. Life experiences are constantly changing, and require humans to behave differently in different contexts. They have to be flexible and adaptable for their sustainability. If every action can change the self's identity, self-identity is in a state of flux and cannot be something stable. Nevertheless, humans do strive for some feeling of coherence, integrity and continuity in their lives. They consider themselves to be the "same" beings. They try to find a meaningful and consistent account of their existence, which will preserve their unity.

The main strategy to achieve a relatively stable self-identity is to tell an autobiography which enables " ... the creation, or imposition, of a higher-order accord among one's lower-order thoughts, desires and actions" (Nehamas, 1983/2001, p. 272). This higher order is relatively steady and consistent. It develops, as MacIntyre suggests, a concept of a self "whose unity resides in the unity of a narrative which links birth to life to death as narrative beginning to middle to end" (MacIntyre, 1984, p. 205). This narrative is, inevitably, invented and subjective, because there can many different stories telling the same course of events, but still, it is this meaning that gives one's life-story continuity and consistency. Each action becomes intelligible only as a "possible-element-in-a sequence" within a given story (1984, p. 209).

Nietzsche believes that "...we want to be the poets of our life," (1882/1974 §299). Consequently, "To become one's own self – to 'become who you are' – is to take the task of creating oneself as a work of art" (Guignon, 2004, p. 131)[66]. "...Artistic creation becomes the paradigm mode in which people can come to self-definition" (Taylor, 1991, p. 61).This ideal has a Romantic flavor because of the central role it assigns to the arts. It conveys the message that looking at life as a work of art can provide them with meaning.

According to Nietzsche, the inventive life-narrative, the story in which humans tell themselves and others their life histories, carries with it an important moral attitude toward their life:

> It is the development of the ability or the willingness to accept responsibility for everything that one has done and to admit what is in fact the case, that everything that one has done actually constitutes who one is...

The self-creation, Nietzsche has in mind, involves the acceptance of everything one has done and, in the ideal case, its harmonization in a coherent whole (Nehamas, 1983/2001, p. 272).

For MacIntyre as well, "Human beings can be held to account for that of which they are the authors" (1984, p. 209).

There are three different scenarios in this type of authenticity, depending on the relationships between the individual and the society. According to one extreme, the invented self is idiosyncratic and individualistic, antagonistic to the society and its norms. To the extreme opposite, the invented self may reflect the common opinion of how an authentic individual should look. He is conformist and obeys the society's norms. In between is the moderate authentic individual, who remains an integral part of his society without abandoning his unique way of thinking and behaving.

1. Authenticity is the ability to go beyond your limits and constraints, without taking any physical or social restrictions into account. In that case:

–   You can become whoever you want to. You can overcome all the physical and social limitations which encircle your life, and become free to do whatever you really strive to, and thus redefine your identity. To be authentic just means to enact this total freedom.
–   Authenticity, i.e., the realization of your desires, is your ultimate goal in life. It leads to self-fulfillment and happiness. Although it may be achieved at the price of loneliness, in the long run this price is negligible for your well-being[67]

A free individual, being unrestricted by any social limitations of tradition, nationality, race, or social class, can choose what to do and thus to define his own identity according to his wishes. This individual is what Nietzsche calls *Übermennsch* (*Overman*). For Nietzsche,

The *Overman* is that type of human being who does not need to ask whether the world provides a structure within which to act, because he feels his own existence as the sole and sufficient basic of action. He never looks for stable being or significance in the world, his own will bears all the meaning, and all the power, he needs. Thus he sets no limits in advance to what the world might be, or to the ways he may find to express his life (Siegel, 2005, p. 556).

The major puzzle is whether humans can really attain life which is "free from the conflicting unreasonable demands of the mind" (as is promised in the back cover of Tolle, 2000), or whether, inevitably, human life cannot but contain a tragic element (as is the Existentialists' tenet). In the eastern philosophies, a "pain-free existence" requires the elimination of the illusion of the self (e.g., Ricard, 2006). To the western mind, to maintain such an ideal may result in another all-encompassing happiness-promising ideology whose unforeseen impact can be highly dangerous. This possibility brings us straight back to the problems of the given authenticity (to wit, the Nazis' use of the term *Übermenench*). Too easily, Bach's (Bach & Munson, 1970) "great seagull" may become Orwell's (1949) "big brother", despite its message of becoming free. It is preferable, maybe, to reject any and every "grand" ideology, which promises, once and for all, to get rid of human suffering and sorrow. Maybe it is better to maintain a piecemeal improvement instead of having a revolutionary shift in our ways of being.

2. A different extreme position of created authenticity admits that human constraints are unavoidable but contends that humans are completely free to choose how they interpret them and react to them. In a popular Australian best-seller, "*The Beginner'$ Guide to wealth*", the authors explain that "you live your life as you see it. Therefore, you can change your life by changing the way you look at it"... (Whittaker & Whittaker, 2010, p. 30). Everything in life is just a state of mind. Change it, and you will see the difference at once.[68] Authenticity in this position means that the individual sincerely attempts to give "his" unique meaning to his life.

This position faces a difficulty. It is questionable whether such a freedom is not a sheer illusion. As Sartre points out, the "free" will, itself, may be causally determined (cf., Guignon, 2004, p. 143 – 144). What can be experienced as a free choice (from a first person point of view), may be a predetermined action (from a third person perspective of the same person looking at himself from the outside). What you want to be may not reveal any genuine inner self but reflect an internalized version of what the general public values (e.g., "financial freedom"). In an age in which the things you possess define who you are, the inner self may be the reflection of the latest fashion. Zygmunt Bauman cites a TV ad, showing a group of women, whose subtitle is "All unique, all individuals, all choose [to buy] X" (Bauman, 2000, p. 84). Even the social pressure to be authentic may be just another fashion (Potter, 2010). As Walter Benjamin analyses it, in *The Work of Art in the Age of Its Technological Reproducibility*, the very idea of authenticity becomes problematic in an age of reproduction.

3. Despite the advice to "ignore your background" (Whittaker & Whittaker, 2010, p. 11), life is a quest to which we do not arrive as *tabula rasa*. Any journey is done by a living person whose beliefs and values influence the way he understand what's going on in his life. It is this set of beliefs and attitudes which enable him to enact the process of interpretation. It infuses the meaning of what he encounters. These beliefs are accordingly influenced by his socio-cultural "background" (or "horizon", or "habitus"). They encompass the overall influence of history and tradition upon the individual. We all carry a backpack, which contains a certain cultural signature that influences our journey and our experiences within it:

> ...we all approach our own circumstances as bearers of a particular social
> identity. I am someone's son or daughter, someone else's cousin or uncle.
> I am a citizen of this or that city, a member of this or that guild or profession.
> I belong to this clan, that tribe, this nation. Hence what is good for me has to
> be the good for one who inhabits these roles... (MacIntyre, 1984, p. 220).

The question is what you can do to be free and authentic in spite of this given background. According to Gadamer, you can see the given horizon as a pre-supposition, or a "prejudice". This prejudice functions like a scientific hypothesis, which has to be recognized and constantly checked against the available data, preferably with the intent of refuting it. The person can question its legacy, and probe its grand narrative.

To be authentic is to be able to decide which of these "given" presuppositions are really "yours" in the sense that you want to embrace and carry them forward. It is the critical assessment of the culture and the tradition you are born into (or live in) in order to define yourself in relation to this heritage. It is like finding your voice in the chore you belong to. Infrequently, it means to leave the chore. Some individuals, like Jonathan Livingstone Seagull (Bach & Munson,1970), may wish to throw away their past, and become entirely new people. For most of us, this is not something we strive for.

Creating a new persona is only one side of the coin. To be authentic in this sense means that you want the interpretation you give to the events in your world to be valid. That it is somehow correct, otherwise it is a case of self-deception. The only way to verify your interpretation is to check it against other possible interpretations. Someone else (including yourself in a different context) can read the same event differently and suspect the interpretation you give it. To reach a genuine understanding of your life, your interpretation of them has to be compared to the interpretation given to them by others. And for that to happen, you have to be in a constant dialogue with those others.

According to Taylor, authenticity should meet two conflicting sets of constraints. One the one hand it involves:

(A) (i) creation and construction as well as discovery, (ii) originality, and frequently (iii) opposition to the rules of society and even potentially to what we recognize as morality (Taylor, 1991, p. 66).

On the other hand, it also requires:

(B) (i) openness to horizon of significance (for otherwise the creation loses the background that can save it from insignificance) and (ii) a self-definition in dialogue (p. 66).

The difference between the extreme and the moderate positions of authenticity is that the first one endorses either condition (A) or (B), and the second has them both.

A genuine dialogue is not only a cognitive discussion about one's presuppositions. In itself, it presupposes certain relations of trust between those who are involved in it. According to Buber, the individual cannot "become what only he can become", without developing "*I-Thou*" relationships with others (see: Friedman, 1955, p. 198). Self-fulfillment can be attained only through genuine *I-Thou* dialogical relationships with other human beings (and for Buber also with God, the absolute Thou to which humans have to be responsive[69]). It is realized when man is able to "make the other present" (Buber, 1965, p. 70; 1968, p. 96 – 97). "Making the other present means to imagine quite concretely what another man is wishing, feeling, perceiving, and thinking." (Friedman, 1967, p. 174) When this "making present" is reciprocal, it creates a sphere of "the between" (Buber, 1965, p. 72 – 75). A dialogue develops in which "seeing through the eyes of the other", and mutual responsibility, are the basis for one's ethical decisions (see Friedman, 1967, p. 175).

Commentating on the philosophies of Buber and Marcel, Levinas says that in their view "the source and the model for the meaningful are sought in interhuman relations" (Levinas, 1993 Martin, p. 14). "All real life is meeting", Levinas cites Buber, and acknowledges that the "inverse of which should also be true" (p. 26). For Buber, the *I-Thou* relation is characterized in terms of being. " 'Between' is a *mode of being*: co-presence, co-esse... being and presence remain the ultimate support of meaning" (p. 16).

There is, however, a crucial difference between Levinas and Buber. For Levinas,

[T]he approach to others is not originally in my speaking out to the other, but in my responsibility for him or her... That is the original ethical relation. That responsibility is elicited, brought about by the face of the other person... described as... an order to me not to abandon the other..." (Levinas, 1993 Apropo, p. 33).

For Levinas, this responsibility does not presuppose reciprocity (Levinas, 1967, 147). Thus, Levinas quotes the profound truth of Dostoevsky's *Brothers Karamazov*: "We are all guilty of everything and everyone, towards everyone, and I more so than all the others" (Levinas, 1993 Apropo, p. 33):

The face forces itself on me, without it being possible for me to remain deaf to its summons or forget it, that is to say making it impossible for me to cease being responsible for its helplessness... to be I, means from now on to be unable to escape responsibility, as though the whole of creation rested on my shoulders... No-one can be made responsible in my place (Levinas, 1972/2003, p. 32 – 33).

This ethics is based on the presence of the other. Its main tenet is that "...caring for others is the whole point of our lives at all; it is to respond to the 'secret tears' of the other" (Morgan, 2007, p. 234; referring to Levinas, 1962/1996, p. 23). The author of *The Little Prince* agrees. As he reminds us, "one must run the risk of weeping a little, if one lets himself be tamed..." (chap. XXV).

Levinas' ethics may seem to be too demanding, because one can never fulfill one's obligation towards the other. "For Levinas each of us is called to compassion and concern for the other, for each and every other person, all the time, in every way" (Morgan, 2007, p. 417). This is an impossible mission, so, at the same time, "... because our social lives are always complex and varied... we always are faced with dilemmas, always involving compromises and accommodations..." (Morgan, 2007, p. 417).

Both Buber and Levinas advance an ethics which has a strong religious flavor. However, it is possible to have a secular version of this kind of ethics, for example the ethics of caring advocated by Nell Noddings. According to Noddings, "Ideally, another human being should be able to request, with expectation of positive response, my help and comfort" (1984, p. 101). So that "ethicality is determined in part by the degree of receptivity one has affectively exercised" (p. 114).

Noddings believes that, humans share a "sentiment of natural caring" (p. 79). "When my infant cries in the night, I not only feel that I must do something but I want to do something. Because I love this child, because I am bonded to him, I want to remove his pain as I want to remove my own" (p. 82). This natural, inborn sentiment should be supplemented with another, second-level, feeling, which arises "from an evaluation of the caring relation as good, as better than, as superior to, other form of relatedness" (p. 83). Noddings calls this second feeling "ethical caring". For her, it is a "response to a remembrance of the first" natural feeling:

> [The] memory of our own best moments of caring and being cared for sweeps over us as a feeling – an "I must"– in response to the plight of the other and our conflicting desire to serve our own interest... I recognize the feeling and remember what has followed in my own best moments. I have a picture of those moments in which I was cared for and in which I cared, and I may reach towards this memory and guide my conduct by it..." (pp. 79 – 80)

It is that "feeling for and with that best self" (p. 80) which should direct our activities.

Noddings characterizes her ethics of caring as feministic (1984, subtitle and pp. 95 – 98), but this is somewhat misleading (Slote, 2009)[70].

BILDUNG

Let us turn now to the educational implication of these world-views. In order to be authentic one has to know himself. Being self-aware presupposes a process of becoming self-aware. This educational process, in which the individual develops self-awareness and expresses what he "really" is, is the process of *Bildung*.

Both *The Little Prince* and *Jonathan Livingstone Seagull* are instances of the Romanic literary genre called *Bildungsroman*. Beginning with Goethe's *Wilhelm Meisters Lehrejare* (published in 1795-1796), this genre narrates a personal story of a self-education process one undertakes in order to become authentic and be capable of self-realization. The German term *Bildung* has no exact equivalent in English. In German, there is a difference between two words whose English meaning is 'education': *Erziehung* and *Bildung*. According to one interpretation, *Erziehung* denotes a process of personal formation guided by external influences like parents and teachers, while *Bildung* denotes a process of personal formation guided by reason (Gundem & Hopmann, 1998, p. 2). For two reasons, this is a controversial characterization. First, it is possible, and to some degree even mandatory, that the *Bildung* process has a mentor (see, for example the role of the Castle in Goethe's *Wilhelm Meister Lehrejare* (cf.: Bruford, 1975, p. 50 – 57; Armstrong, 2006, p. 273 – 274)). Second, for the Romanticists, *Bildung* refers "not just to formal education, but more generally to the process of personal formation that wider experience of the world helped to bring about" (Siegel, 2005, p. 302).

Life experience, and especially its social and cultural aspects, augment and even replace reason.

The *Bildungsroman* genre provides narrative examples of this process. In the *Little Prince*, The hero experiences a *Bildung* process. He leaves his planet and visits other asteroids "in order to add to his knowledge" (chap. X). He wants to examine how various adults give meaning to their life. His disappointing meetings with adults reflect that the *Bildung* process is difficult and demands persistence and determination. On Earth, the fox takes the guidance role and becomes The Little Prince's coach. He teaches the Little Prince the Romantic ideal that love is the secret of life. When the Little Prince has absorbed the lesson, he is ready to return to his planet, more mature and ready for love and life.

For Michel Serres, the journey is the only way to learn: "Certainly, I never learned anything unless I left, not taught someone else without inviting him to leave his nest… Whoever does not get moving learns nothing (Serres, 1997, p. 7).

At first sight, it seems unlikely that a process like *Bildung* can be part of the current educational system. What had been apt to a minority of aristocrats in 18th century Europe, who had the resources and the time to carry it on, cannot be applied to modern day mainstream schools. Nevertheless, many contemporary teachers believe that their main aim is to foster the process of *Bildung* in their pupils. Many of them are frustrated when they cannot accomplish in schools this vision of their vocation. As early as the beginning of the 20th century, a young Scottish schoolmaster in a rural school writes in his diary:

> My work is hopeless, for education should aim at bringing up a new generation that will be better than the old. The present system is to produce the same kind of man as we see to-day. And how hopeless he is. [A day later, however, he continues the log in a different spirit.] I am hopeful because I have found a solution. I shall henceforth try to make my bairns realise. Yes, realise is the word. Realise what? To tell the truth, I have some difficulty in saying. I think I want to make them realise what life means. Yes, I want to give them, or rather help them to find an attitude. Most of the stuff I teach them will be forgotten in a year or two, but an attitude remains with one throughout life. I want these boys and girls to acquire the habit of looking honestly at life… I wonder how many of them have sat down saying: "I must examine myself, so that I may find out what manner of man I am". I hold that self-knowledge must come before all things. When one has stripped off all the conventions, and superstitions, and hypocrisies, then one is educated.

This young schoolmaster was A.S. Neill (1915/1986, p.13), who, a couple of years later, founded the school named Summerhill, but in the meantime had to resign from his office because of his revolutionary views.

PREPARING A BEING WHO TEACHES

The main question that a Romantic inspired, *Bildung*-oriented, TEP should address is "who the teacher should be?" Following the ideas discussed in the previous chapter, the program should enhance a process that will enable the prospective teacher to define the personal meaning he gives to his becoming a teacher. The program should be structured as a journey, which takes the students through different experiences upon which they can reflect. It demands from them to creatively express their inner feelings and thoughts about what happens to them, and to receive feedback from others on their interpretations and attitudes. The educational environment of the program should promote a community of learners, based on love and caring. It should promote a reflective and critical dialogue between all those who are involved.

Romanticism emphasizes authenticity and caring, feelings and spontaneity, creativity and dialogue. Most TEPs, however, are part of the academic establishment, which, as we have seen, enlightenment driven. So, those TEPs, which want to maintain a Romantic stance, face a problem. They cannot base the programs solely on the irrational or the emotional aspects of life, because this will exclude them from the academic culture. Maybe the French philosopher Michel Serres is correct when he says that:

> *The goal of instruction is the end of instruction, that is to say invention.* Invention is the only true intellectual act... The rest? Copying, cheating, reproduction, laziness, convention, battle, sleep. Only invention awakens... The institutions of culture, of teaching, or of research, those that live on messages, repeated images, or printed copies, the great mammoths that are universities, media, and publishing, the ideocracies also, surround themselves with a mass of solid artifacts that forbid invention or break it, that fear it like the greatest danger... Do you want to create? You are in danger (1997, p. 92 – 93).

Romantic inspired TEPs have to find ways to overcome this hindrance, incorporate some Romantic aspects into "normal" programs, and adjust their vision with the dominant pathway. That there are TEPs who manage to do just this attests that it is possible to conduct BEING inspired programs even in universities and academic colleges.

It was easier to implement the Romantic stance in the pre academic ST . According to German educator Georg Kerschensteiner, the teacher is an educator who influences the being of young humans. The teacher's influence is conscious. The educator is not a bearer of values. He does not have selfish interests, and does not function as a creator of cultural heritage. He is a social person who has a unique inclination whose motives are purely pedagogical. He has a natural disposition to the other as a human being. "At the beginning, the middle and the end of education are both neither the intellectual, theoretical recognition, nor the subject-matter knowledge, but the heart, the love, the passion, the *eros*, of the educator" (1965, p. 34). According to Kerschensteiner, an individual becomes an educator not because of his pedagogical knowledge or because he has a comprehensive scholarship in a certain subject matter. The rational, theoretically inclined individual, who wishes to understand the world, is rarely the social person, who is directed by irrational feelings and has an intuitive understanding of the other. It is impossible to educate without an innate ability to penetrate into a different soul, and without the capability to do something proper with this understanding. Although innate, these abilities can be cultivated and developed, and TEPs should be designed to perform this task. But since it is a matter of enhancement of natural tendencies and not of knowing theories, the preparation process cannot be an academic enterprise. The university is not the proper place to educate educators because it is too cognitive oriented and cannot grasp the whole person. Hence, Kerschensteiner suggests that TEPs should be conducted in specially designed institutions, which can foster "communities of life and work directed to the wholeness of the students" (p. 34). At the center of these communities should stand the practice of pedagogy, i.e., the *Bildung* of the teacher educator who defines his personal identity as a pedagogue.

This is clearly a Romantic stance, which requires the TEP to prepare the authentic pedagogue who can cultivate his innate authentic talents, and become an educator who is interested in the development of his students' authentic life. A current version of this approach is a TEP named HOFFEN.

HOFFEN

HOFFEN (Hebrew acronym for Open Experimental Education, and also a word meaning 'handful') was established in 1989, as an independent TEP, at David Yellin Teachers College in Jerusalem. The program, which is still in operation, is a postgraduate, one year TEP. It is especially designed to address ideas of empowering the student BEING MoE. Two of its teachers, Eisenberg and Litvak, define the principles of the open experimental education:

a. At school and in the classroom the child is related to as a person. The education process focuses equally on the areas of intellectual knowledge and achievements as well as area of social, emotional and creative development.

b. The plan of studies is integrative; it employs different and varied methods of teaching with an emphasis on interdisciplinary thinking.

c. The school is a community whose members include the pupils, the teachers and the parents. The interpersonal relationships, the work framework and the discipline within the school are established through discussion and mutual agreement between members of the community.

d. The starting point for the educational process is the child (or the teacher-student) as an individual and as a part of the group, and the developing needs of the individual and the group (Eisenberg and Litvak, 1994, p. 137 – 138).

To these, another teacher educator, Svidovski-Vengosh, adds the creative dimension:

A good teacher is a creative teacher. He can use his knowledge to develop new things... To be novel, not to repeat what he had done before... The teacher must have a presence (Cited in Gover, 1994, p. 57).

To one of the program's students, this principle is exemplified in the *Little Prince*. The Little Prince, she says, "welcomes the painting of the sheep which leaves room to his imagination. He prefers the painting in which the sheep can change its appearance to his will, the free, always fresh, not painted, not commemorated and not fixed sheep" (Cited in HOFFEN, 1994, p. 124).

The program is designed to enable the student to explore his identity in terms of his abilities, domains of interest, priorities, and points of strengths and weaknesses, in a safe and friendly environment. This will help him to develop self-confidence (in accordance with Honneth's first (love) mode of recognition). In the program, the student is open to a process of *Bildung* in which he always has to choose between alternative possibilities within an emerging curriculum in which he actively participates in its construction (See Appendix, example no. 16). Consequently, he will be able to define for himself the priorities of his educational work.

The program emphasizes that:

1. *Bildung* is more important than techniques. In the long run, developing the student's personality will be more beneficial than giving him specific instructional tools.

2. For education, the individual and the group are both highly important. The program has to provide both personal and group opportunities for development.

3. It should be a model for what happens in (open) schools. It should encourage an open environment.

4. The educational process is an end in itself. It is impossible to predict its long-term outcomes, so it requires a lot of patience from all the involved participants.

5. Choice means responsibility. Though it might be frustrating (nobody else to blame), it is highly conducive in enhancing the teachers' autonomy.

6. Subject-matter courses have a very limited place in the program, because disciplinary knowledge can be acquired when needed. The intent is to focus on a detailed exploration of "who am I" as an individual, and to experience and cognize different aspects of group dynamics.

7. There is an intimate connection between personal traits, mode of teacher preparation and teaching styles.

8. The faculty and the students share responsibility on the curriculum. Together they have to address issues such as involvement, cooperation, authority in education (Eisenberg & Litvak, 1994, p. 20 – 22).

These principles assume that the teacher is a permanent student. He constantly participates in a journey of self-discovery, of open minded inquiry on his educational experiences. In this journey the paramount activity is the dialogue, the dialogue with himself, with his peers, with his teachers and with his students. The educational process really interests him. The *bildung* of free, autonomous students becomes the devotion of his professional life.

In sum, for the romantic inspired TEPs:

1. Teaching preparation is a lengthy process, with no ending point. Its main aim is to construct the professional identity of the student.

2. The student is at the center of the process. There should be a *bildung* of the student, who has to give, in an authentic and creative manner, a personal meaning to his becoming a teacher.

3. Caring about the students and recognition of their worth as individuals and as novice teachers is a prerequisite for successful preparation.

4. Constant dialogues occur between all the partners (students-teacher educators; students-students; teacher educators-students-schools, etc.) of the TEP.

5. A learning community enables a personal reflection and learning about the self in a secure environment.

6. A holistic mandatory curriculum, usually in stable learning groups.

7. There is a special place for the nonverbal aspect of the teachers' work. Special attention is given to the students' self-expression ability and their understanding of the world.

The Romantic inspired programs are BEING oriented. They are designed to deal with the teacher's identity. For them this factor is the most important mission that any TEP should perform.

HOFFEN is a unique program. Its students are those who accept the Romantic point of view. Its adherents act like a sect of believers, and unless you fully accept its presuppositions or are at least ready to examine and embrace them, you will not be welcomed to join it. This raises the question whether such a program is restricted to "believers" only, or can it, somehow, be converted to a mainstream program. If the Romantic point of view has a place in education, it should be present in "normal" TEPs, and not be enclosed in a separate space. Either open education might offer some cure to the educational crisis, or it will become a kind of refugee camp for those (pupils and teachers) who can no longer stand the system. By serving as a pressure valve, it may give an excuse for the rest of the system to ignore the Romanic import.

Even those TEPs, intrigued by Romantic ideas, have to face the problem of their place in to-date kind enlightenment inspired programs. Given the hegemony of the instrumental-rationality programs, and the dominant HAVING MoE, it is very rare to find TEPs such as ĦOFFEN which are "purely" Romantic. It is more common to find programs which incorporate Romantic themes into their world-view. For example, these programs ask the question, "Who is the teacher?" within the enlightenment inspired TEP's framework. Such programs might belong to the "applied science" or to the "practical occupation" phase discussed in chapters four and five. Unlike ĦOFFEN, these programs are TEPs "for all". Their graduates are supposed to teach in ordinary schools, so their students are not ideological devotees. They have to be persuaded that a different preparation will make them better teachers.

Humanistic Teacher Education

At the very same time in which the CBTE had been a dominant approach to teacher education in the US (see chapter 4), an alternative possibility attracted considerable attention. Simply change the applied science theory from Behaviorism to Humanistic psychology, and the outcome will be a program with quite a different atmosphere, curriculum, and structure. Such a TEP has been implemented at the University of Florida in the 1960s (Combs, 1965; 1972; Combs et al. 1974; For a detailed description of this model of TEP, see: Appendix, Example no. 17). The theory, called by Combs "Perceptual Psychology", postulates that a person's behavior is "the direct result of 1) how he sees himself; 2) how he sees the situations, in which he is involved; and 3) the interaction of these two" (Combs, 1965, p. 12). The implication of this theory is straightforward: it signifies a shift from a "mechanistic" to a "personal" view of teaching. This alteration means that TEPs "must concern themselves with persons rather than competencies" (p. 9), in order to cultivate "creative individuals, capable of shifting and changing to meet the demands and opportunities afforded in daily tasks" (p. 9).

The teacher becomes an intelligent human being "who has learned to use himself as an effective instrument... to solve the problems for which he is responsible" (p. 8). Thus emerges the concept of the "self as instrument" (p. 115). According to Combs, "...we may define the effective teacher formally as *a unique human being who has learned to use himself effectively and efficiently to carry out his own and society's purposes in the education of others"* (p. 9).

Combs suggests a set of seven propositions which emerges from this theoretical basis, and the experience it triggers:

1. The production of an effective teacher is a highly personal matter, dependent primarily upon the development of an appropriate system of beliefs[71].

2. The production of an effective teacher must be regarded as a problem in becoming. (It is question of helping a person to find his own unique ways of operating as an effective teacher.)

3. The process of becoming must start from security and acceptance.

4. Effective teacher education must concentrate its efforts upon meanings rather than behavior.

5. If sensitivity and empathy are prime characteristics of effective helpers, and if behavior is the product of perception, teacher preparation programs must shift their main concerns from objectivity to subjectivity.

6. The dynamic importance of need in learning must be fully exploited.

7. If the self-concept is as important a determiner of behavior as research suggests, teacher education must actively apply what is known about it (Combs, 1972).

Therefore:

...Teacher education must be deeply concerned about the developing self of the fledgling teacher. How a teacher behaves after he leaves the portals of his college will be very largely determined by how he has learned to see himself and his relationships with his students, his subject matter, and the teaching profession itself. Teacher education must thus become as student-centered as we hope the teachers we are currently producing will be in their own classrooms (1965, p. 15).

The main thesis of Perceptual Psychology is that learning is a "discovery of meaning by the student". It is a "highly personal matter involving the way he sees himself and his experience" (p. 27). It demands active involvement and personal commitment.

Combs presents the structure of the TEP in the following figure, which puts the learner in the center:

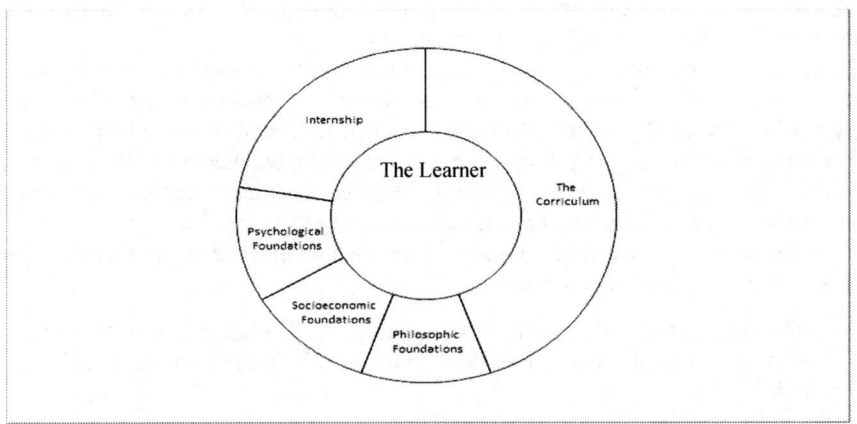

(Combs, 1965, p. 113)

The leading idea is that:

All educators [of the program] are concerned with the middle of the pie. The 'nature and condition of the learner' has invaded every course. With everyone concerned about the learner, subject matter that formerly was the exclusive prerogative of the course in human growth and development has now invaded the entire curriculum. *Everyone* now teaches human growth and development. Similarly, with the learner at the center of the problem, everyone must teach the relationship of the individual to society, the purposes of education, and the utilization of effective methods (1965, p. 113 – 115)..

According to Combs, an efficient program must:

1. Permit the movement of students at different speeds;

2. Provide content and experience in response to student needs;

3. Provide simultaneous, rather than sequential, experience for the learner;

4. Place much more responsibility upon the student himself (p. 115).

Humanistic TEP is a kind of *Bildung*. It is an open system. It assumes only "that the general direction of the desired growth is evident beforehand, and as the student becomes more and more a teacher he will have more to say about the kind of teacher he wants to be" (Combs et al., 1974, p. 148). The length of time students spend in the program varies with the individual (usually 4-7 quarters). The third point in the above list reflects the belief that the self of the teacher is an "interdependent organization, not a series of isolated boxes which can be dealt with one at a time" (Combs, 1965, p. 116). Therefore, "a problem-oriented, personal-growth-oriented program flows over all boundaries" (p. 116).

At the core of the program is the "seminar", a weekly meeting of two class periods, comprises 15-30 students and one faculty member. The seminar is the "home base" of the student. When he enters the program, each student is assigned to a seminar and he keeps this assignment throughout the program. When he leaves the program he is replaced by a novice student, so that the group consists of students at all levels of progress. In the seminar, in a safe environment of care and concern, "the student would be given opportunities to discuss, experiment, explore ideas, techniques, concepts, and the like with the friendly assistance of the permanent staff leader... (p. 119). The primary purpose is "for each student to discover his own personal meaning through exploration of himself and the ideas and experiences he has been exposed to in the previous week in an atmosphere designed to further such exploration and discovery" (Combs et al., 1974, p. 157). The seminar is devoted to plan the students' work and chart their own direction of learning. The particular program of the seminar depends on the needs of the students in the group (Combs, 1965, p. 121). "The activities in the seminar range from discussions of field experiences to communications labs and social gatherings..." (Combs et al., 1974, p. 157). The seminar leader serves as the personal counselor and academic adviser for the students.

The program should be designed in a way that maximizes the available resources of the community and the faculty for exposing ideas to the students. This may include a college-wide lecture series (planned by a student-faculty committee), special workshops, exhibits of educational resources, or trips (Combs, 1965, p. 121 – 124). Practice teaching depends upon the student's needs and the particular skills he has already acquired, beginning from his first day in the program. The student begins as an assistant-teacher (half day a week) and gradually increases his experience to take full charge of a classroom for a four-month period. In addition, there is a program of observation, involvement in professional affairs (like professional meetings and other school activities) and involvement in educational research.

Humanistic Teacher Education shows that applied science can support a BEING-type TEP. However, in a curious manner, it sees the teacher personality as an "instrument", thus remaining in the technical-rationality culture, in which the teacher is a problem-solver professional. Despite its "openness", the program is highly structured around the teacher's activities. The question of the children's outcome is not yet addressed, and neither is the Didaktik vision of cultivating their development. The question of how the preparation can be a model of teaching remains problematic (certainly, the aim is not that the children will see themselves as instruments for something else). So there is an inherent paradox in the program.

Doyle (1990) points out that Combs' suggestion is problematic. On one hand It requires open-mindedness and flexibility in teachers' perceptions, because "any one situation is compatible with multiple, and possibly incompatible, interpretations" (p. 48). On the other hand, Comb himself argues that:

> If we can be sure the teacher's ways of perceiving are accurate and constructive, it may not be necessary to know precisely how he will put his concern into effect. There are thousands of ways to express either of the above perceptions in action. The crucial question for teacher education is not which behavior but how to bring about appropriate shifts in perception (Combs, 1972, p. 288).

These ideas implies (1) that there is "a correct and constructive" interpretation, and (2) that once the teacher holds such an interpretation he knows how to transfer it into plans and means that fits his individual character and the specific situation (See: Doyle, 1990, p. 48). The first point is counter-intuitive. The second seems to be nonrealistic. In an era of technical rationality, it had not been enough to leave the technical solutions to the teacher students.

The next phase of the Romantic inspired TEPs regards teaching as *techne*, and follows the footprints of Aristotle's concept of practical knowledge.

FOLLOWING ARISTOTLE'S FOOTPRINTS

Realistic Teacher Education

As we move to the reflective-practitioner phase, there are few programs which direct the reflection towards the self-identity of the teacher. One such program, implemented at Utrecht University, in the Netherlands, is called "Realistic Teacher Education". It is a one year program designed for both undergraduate and graduate students (See: Appendix, example 18).

In real contexts, thinking is not that rational, logical, or analytical. It is a result of a *gestalt*, "the personal conglomerates of needs, concerns, values, meanings, preferences, feelings, and behavioral tendencies guiding action". The program aims to develop a *gestalt* which enhances self-directed learning (Korthagen et al. 2001, p. 49). To construct the teacher's *gestalt*, a pedagogical procedure, named ALACT, is implemented throughout the program. The idea is to design "an ongoing process of learning by reflection, defined as the mental process of trying to (re)structure an experience, a problem, or existing knowledge or insights" (p. 265). The ALACT process is based on cycles of the steps: Action – Looking back on the action – Awareness of essential aspects – Creating alternative methods of action – Trial (another Action) (p. 44).

Realistic Teacher Education is an attempt to bridge the gap between theory and practice. The appeal to educational theories is sometimes needed (in the Awareness step), but it is always done with regard to the issues in question. "What teachers use in practice is... situation specific principles, context dependent, that help them to rapidly arrive at decisions that solve practical problems" (p. 255). The later kind of theory with a small "t" is distinct from the theoretical theory (theory with capital "T"), and is much more perceptive (*nus*) than conceptual (*episteme*).

Korthagen believes that Realistic Teacher Education is based on sound psychological theories: learning from practice and (reforming) gestalts. He further believes that it has an important moral outcome, because it prepares teachers who can help pupils "to take responsibility for the position they will occupy in society" (p. 259): "Preparing children for the responsibility of using knowledge for the benefit of society means helping them to become reflective thinkers, able to use subject-matter in real situations, and confident that their actions can make a difference" (p. 261). As children have to learn to cope with many challenges, the teacher's role is changed from a transmitter of knowledge to a guide in a joint search process.

This utilitarian approach to knowledge is not the whole endeavor. Korthagen maintains that at the core of the ability to deal with the rapidly changing society stands the idea that:

> If people not only want to survive in such a world, but also wish to create meaningful life with a sense of contributing to the world, they have to stay in contact with their own personal *identity*. I believe that it is of paramount importance that they acquire a sense of *self-understanding* as a basis for developing their own unique potential, to direct themselves in realizing that potential and to relate to other people... The search for a moral basis in education should start with helping students to develop a sense of identity (p. 263).

Hence, "Teacher identity – what beginning teachers believe about teaching and learning and self-as-a-teacher – is of vital concern to teacher education; it is the basis for meaning making and decision making... Teacher education must begin, then, by exploring the teaching self" (Bullough, 1997; cited in Korthagen et al. 2001, p. 265).

Korthagen insists that "it is a teacher's task to guide children in... the development of self-understanding and a sense of interconnectedness" (Korthagen et al. 2001, p. 263). But this task requires an I-Thou relationship between teacher and student, "genuine personal encounters in which both are, within the here-and-now, in contact with their inner selves" (p. 264). Korthagen approvingly cites Bullough and Gitlin's claim that "teaching is a relationship, a way of being with and relating to others, and not merely an expression of having mastered a set of delivery skills", and adds: "This view requires from teachers courage, enthusiasm, and commitment (to students and to their own values), but also a respectful way of communicating" (p. 264). In a revealing endnote, Korthagen elaborates the last phrase:

> I believe *respect* is a keyword. Respect for others and their needs, as well as respect for one's own identity and needs, is in my view the foundation of a healthy society and a necessary requirement for classroom or school environments supporting learning and development. The notion of respect refers to a thoughtful, accepting way of caring for what is present in the encounter between human beings, and a willingness to critically examine and adjust one's own prejudice, in contrast to a preoccupation with the wish to change the other (p. 280).

This ideal presupposes the *love* mode of recognition (Honneth, 1995). The ethics of care becomes a dominant aspect of teaching. However, as noted above, Korthagen finds that some teacher-students do not fit in such a program, thus arises the question whether successful participation in such a program is a prerequisite for good teaching.

Realistic teacher education has only a few of the characteristics of the Romantic stance. It does not emphasis creativity and authenticity, it does not pay special attention to the child as a child, and it does not focus on feelings as a moral source. Reason is not its antagonist but its main weapon. Awareness to the teacher's BEING is not seen as a MoE, but as an important ingredient of his *technitas'* way of acting. Nevertheless, this TEP does concentrate on the hermeneutic of being in the world and on the importance of a dialogue in a caring environment. A somewhat different approach provides the rationale for the MT program.

The MT program

The MT program, University of Calgary[72], characterizes itself as "Learner-Focused, Inquiry-Based, and Field Oriented"[73]. Thus it might be classified under the reflective-practitioner stance. It is different from Realistic Teacher Education because it is openly focused on the teacher's identity. MT pedagogy emphasizes case studies and autobiographical narratives. Within a community of learning and backed by practical experience, it concentrates on the teacher as *phronimon*, and it wants the student-teacher to reinvent himself (Phelan, 2005, p. 71). It is expected, for example, that the student work in a climate of ambiguity, which requires "on-going inquiry, reflection and conversation". He should become a life-long-learner of "children, curriculum, and context". He should have "passion, trust, and interest". And he should respect diversity and recognize that teaching "cannot be divorced from the larger social, cultural and political contexts which frame what teachers do in classrooms." And although the program advances a constructivist view about teaching and learning[74], it is expected that the prospective teacher will formulize his own theory about teaching and learning. Therefore, MT is not grounded on "university course work on theoretical/research-based knowledge followed by short-term field experiences", but on "learning and teaching (of interrelated field-based and campus-based) experiences" (See: Appendix, example 19).

MT relies on two main philosophical insights. The first is the already discussed Aristotelian notion of practical reason. The second is Gadamer's conception of self-self-understanding. For Gadamer (1960/1989), any understanding is an act of interpretation. The major problem that confronts any interpretation is that of the "hermeneutic circle". It seems that any understanding presupposes itself. As Plato claims in *Meno*, one can understand something only if he already knows what is it all about. (Take a linguistic sentence. While you cannot understand the sentence without a prior understanding of each of its constituents, it is equally clear that you cannot grasp the meaning of these constituents without the context of the whole sentence.) This mutual dependency poses the question of how to "penetrate" the circle: how to begin the process of understanding without begging the very question it has to solve. Gadamer's answer to this question consists of a rehabilitation of the notion of presupposition. Interpretation does not begin with a state of *tabula rasa*. Any interpretation is done by a living person whose beliefs and values influence the way he understands what is happening. It is this set of beliefs and attitudes which enable one to begin the process of interpretation. It infuses the meaning of what he encounters. It defines his "horizon". But, this set of beliefs and desires is only a **pre**-supposition, or in Gadamer's term, a "prejudice". It functions like a scientific hypothesis, which has to be constantly checked against the available data, preferably with the intent of refuting it. This horizon reflects the socio-cultural environment of the agent. It encompasses the overall influence of history and tradition upon the individual. Yet, the person can question this legacy and probe its grand narrative.

One important feature of this line of thought is its holistic character. Every ingredient of the agent's belief-system is connected to all the other ingredients, and gets its meaning from the particular web of beliefs in which it is located. Therefore, one of the major steps towards a better understanding is self-self-understanding, which involves a conscious reflection upon one's own "background" presuppositions. This background has two dimensions which were neglected by Aristotle. It includes a historical dimension, which provides the cultural and social context of the interpreter. The type of questions that he regards as problematic, the paradigms he takes for granted, the kind of answers he accepts as legitimate, the power-knowledge relationships which dominate his world. It further includes a linguistic dimension, since any interpretation is a kind of conversation between the interpreter and the "text". Any interpretation is in some sense practical. Its aim is to promote the agent's self-understanding, while critically reflecting upon his tradition and habits. Its goal is to influence his actions through an ongoing process of discovering the meaning of the agent's world. It is, however, equally important that the agent's knowledge will become public, for only then it can be surface from his subconscious and be critically discussed. This move from tacit to overt knowledge (Polanyi, 1962), or from personal to local knowledge (Rönnerman, 2005), necessitate that the agent will participate in a community of practice (Wenger, 1998).

The main task of any TEP is to develop a process of reconstructing, redesigning or creating the prospective teachers' professional-identity. Note that the key words in the last sentence are the verbs "construct", "design" and "create". Although they seem to indicate the opposite, identity is not "something" that is objectively given, waiting to be discovered. It is the result of a meaning giving process in which the human agent explores his world and identifies his place in it. It is hermeneutical, developmental, and contextual. (One can have many identities depending on the context.) Moreover, it can be developed only in a community through a collaborative effort with other people, preferably with the help of an experienced mentor (Wenger, 1998).

In order to achieve this end in view, the MT program has the following features:

1. The program is a whole entity and not an amalgam of courses. The student does not participate in a series of separate courses but has to attend an interconnected and interrelated set of workshops, each of which contributes its specific tone to the melody. The program is centered upon predefined "themes" which pervade all the courses in a certain period. (E.g., in each week of semester 1 there is a lecture that introduces the subject of the week, which is further discussed in the various courses: the professional seminar, the case workshop, the practicum seminar and the practicum itself).

2. In order to cultivate reflection and deliberation, a special emphasize is devoted to construct learning communities in which meaningful learning takes place.

3. The program is for postgraduates. Disciplinary knowledge is not part of the TE program but its prerequisite. The underlying assumption is that the teacher is not an expert in the subject he teaches but in teaching subjects (students). He should master enough subject-matter knowledge for his teaching, but the core of TEP is pedagogy and methodology: the "why" and "who" and not the "what".

4. Since the theory with T is relatively less important to the prospective teacher, it is not delivered to the students in any systematic (e.g., introduction course-like) way. The student will encounter the theory when it will be needed by his needs.

5. Practice is the key to develop practical knowledge. And therefore about half of the program is devoted to practical experience "in the field". This experience is mentored, discussed and analyzed in special workshops, in a community of learners.

6. Meaningful learning occurs when the process is connected to real questions of the learners. Thus, individual inquiry is the main vehicle of learning. It is the cornerstone of Life Long Learning, and a model for the prospective teachers to follow in their future work.

7. Learning occurs not only in schools. The students should experience learning in various settings (adult education, informal education, work-sites etc.) to see how life-long-learning is enacted.

8. A key supposition of the program is that refection is the way to cultivate the inner *nus* and to formulate the theory with t, and that this process of reflection is done by writing. To write (field journal, independent inquiry, Biography of learning, Case studies, narrative assessments, inquiry project, exit presentation...) is to learn, because writing is creating. It explores the texts that have to be interpreted, negotiated and discussed by the self, and by the community of learners. And again, the reflective process is mentored both individualistically and within communities.

9. The program deals openly and deliberately with the 'identity' question. It regularly and constantly demands that every student will reflect on his own identity (in the biographies), and it culminates in an exit presentation which is devoted to the issue "Who am I as a teacher".

10. Evaluations of students are not numeric and are based on self-evaluation, and on on-going conversation between the teacher educator and the students about what constitutes good work in teaching and learning to teach.

The MT belongs to the reflective-rationality type of programs. It is case-based and problem based. Especially in the first year, its cases are found in the program's handbooks, and there is a structured method to deal with them. Nevertheless, the focus is on the question "what does it mean for me to be a teacher?" And teacher education is seen as a journey of search and research. The emphasis on creating a narrative is very close to the Romantic notion of *Bildung*, the attention is given to dialogues and to collaboration based on the idea of collegial friendship. Teacher educators see themselves as mentors, as pedagogues in the original sense of the word.

In a world in which hugging a first grade child could be interpreted as a sexual harassment, the very essence of the profession becomes problematic. What am I working for? What is the worth of my work? What is "right" or "wrong" to do, and who decides? What is the rationale for doing X or Y? Do I really help children? How do I know that I do not hinder their proper development? Am I causing damage or improving things? How do I know that I am a professional, responsible, moral and useful agent? And who cares? These are frightening questions. They are fear-provoking because there is no clear cut acceptable answer available to them. They are scary because they raise the identity question of who am I as a professional agent. No sincere teacher can escape them and remain influential in the educational process. The MT program assumes that no teacher can ignore them, continue as if "things remain the same", and still be relevant to his students' life.

Thus, the MT program advances a post-modern world-view. To the Aristotle's theory of "practical wisdom", it adds the centrality of inquiry, based on reflective thinking, as derived from Dewey. From the existentialists it gets the notion of meaningful learning, and from Gadamer it adopts the hermeneutical stance and the primacy of the dialogue. Its critical attitude to the knowledge-power relationships, as it is embodied in the technical-rationality teaching model, is a heritage of the Frankfurt school and Foucault.

But nevertheless, MT faces some critical difficulties:

1. The holistic nature of the program is impaired by the lack of congruence with the reality of schools. The message of the program is quite different from the attitude of both politicians and teachers about the nature of profession. Many of them still conceive of it as an applied-science, technical-rationality occupation. In an era of standardization and measurable achievements, there is an immense difficulty to find a suitable "field placement" in which the program's students practicum can take place. The difficulty is that the student, who cannot see 'in the field' that the program's pedagogical ideas are viable, might get the impression that they are too idealistic and unworkable. One possible solution to this problem could have been the establishment of a PDS environment, in which the school and the program promote the same educational agenda. Because of many practical reasons, the MT program has not been able to develop such an environment.

2. The missing PDS environment has another drawback on the program. Although it advances learning communities, they are not communities of practice. Moreover, throughout the program, the student finds himself in a number of workshops and practical placements, each consists of a different student body. While it is beneficial for the students to encounter as many colleagues as possible, it is possible that a 'cohort' structure of the learning group would be more beneficial to the students in the program.

3. The emphasis on *phronesis* and on dialogue decreases the *techne* element in the program. The idea is that if you know who you are and what you bring to teaching you will be able to be a good teacher. Nevertheless, according to the MT's critiques, there are some specific skills of "knowing how" that are crucial to teaching, because they contribute to the survival stage of the novice teacher (Dreyfus & Dreyfus, 1986). It is necessary that the student acquire some class management tips, some strategies of teaching-learning, some methods of evaluation etc., even if the idea is that at the end, as an expert, he would dispose of all these scaffolds.

4. The MT program developed from practice. While in itself this is not an obstacle, the problem has been that the faculty does not form a community of learning in which the program can be discussed and its message negotiated. Mainly because of practical time difficulties, there wasn't any continuation of the learning process which infused and fueled the program in its inceptions years. This state of affairs has two main effects on the program. The first is that once the program was fixed, very few changes were made to accommodate it to the practical wisdom that developed around it. The second has much more serious implications for the MT's future. Since the inauguration of the program, its faculty has changed. The rapid growth in the number of the students leads to a similar growth in the number of its staff. But without a learning community, it has been difficult to keep the spirit of the program. The problem intensified because most of the field advisors are not part of the tenured staff, and they are recruited on a temporary basis. Unless all the teachers of the teachers form a community devoted to develop its own practical

wisdom, it is hard to expect that the program will be able to keep the vitality, reflection, creativity, and energy which characterizes its first years.

5. The ideal teacher of the program has been very different from the ideal teacher of its students. "Tell us what to do as teachers?" has been a prevalent request of the students, especially in the first year of the program. This demand has been met by various workshops, but it was mainly a cognitive endeavor. The program lacks other means of (artistic) expressions, and learning remains mostly verbal. Thus, though very significant, for many students the creative aspects of learning to teach leaves them in the declarative phase in which they express what they believe their teachers want to hear. In the end, the rational approach remains the main vehicle for change, and it is not always enough to persuade minds.

These problems had a strong influence on the program. External and internal pressures (such as new faculty in administration, complaints that the program is too remote from the standards and accountability culture, and weaker commitment of the faculty) result in the closure of the program in 2011. This state of affairs raises some principled questions: is it possible, in an era of standardization and accountability to maintain a program which is BEING oriented? Is it feasible to change the prevalent conception of teaching and learning in an institution whose culture tends to emphasis individualism, competition, and measurable achievements? Is it fair to blame the TEP's teacher educators for being exhausted in their permanent struggle to redefine the achievement principle and support a dialogical concept of education? Or maybe the problem is that, after all, the program was not revolutionary enough. Maybe the seeds of the Romantic stance could not flourish in a program which, from its very beginning, had been dominated by the rational mood of case studies and reflection, of problem-based learning and critical thinking and not by irrational creativity or by encouraging spontaneous I-Thou relationships.

Hans Smits, one of programs leaders, attests that:

> In its emphasis on inquiry-based and collaborative learning, the eschewing of letter or numerical grades, the blurring of traditional disciplinary boundaries, and the challenge to the dominance of a professor's knowledge in favor of celebrating learner generated knowing, the program provoked starkly divided responses and often deeply seated resistances to reconceptualizing the role and responsibilities of professors (Smits; in press).

Smits, disappointed but still hopeful, insists that "what we need, critically, I think, is a focus on what Alain Badiou calls "the conditions of existence rather than just improving its methods". It is never too late to engage in that work" (Smits, 2011). The promise of the MT remains, for the time being, local and without any durable and lasting effect .

Active Collaborative Education (ACE)

ACE presents a somewhat different model of how to deal with these issues. Inspired by MT and ḤOFFEN, ACE (whose Hebrew acronym is SHAḤAF which mean seagull) presupposes that the issue of teachers' identity is the building block of their professional work. Based on social activity learning theories, it places a bigger stress on active collaboration (between the faculty members, between them and the students, among the students and between the college and the PDSs).

ACE is a two-year teacher education program at Kaye College of Education, Beer-Sheva, Israel (See: Appendix, Example 20, and Barak & Gidron, 2009). It is a two years (30 pts.) postgraduate program for k-12 and special education teachers. ACE offers a multicultural learning environment in which the participants are: Jews and Bedouin-Arabs, Hebrew and Arabic speakers, secular and religious, new *immigrants, and Israeli born citizens.*

ACE views learning to become a teacher as an active collaborative educational process, with threads of practice and personal experience mutually interweaving a web of practical knowledge that nourishes a growing sense of professional identity. This TEP acknowledges its debt to the Aristotelian notion of "*phronesis*", and regards teaching as a type of knowledge that emerges through the unique dialectic discourse between action and interpretation. Becoming teachers from this standpoint calls for a curriculum that allows student teachers to be actively engaged and become active participants in the narration of their professional identities.

The ACE's conceptual framework regards educational praxis in terms of BEING in schools with children in varied situations. It assumes that in order to understand teaching one has to learn how to self-navigate within the complex web of emotions, perceptions, interactions, and socio-cultural backgrounds which influence the learning processes.

ACE offers an holistic learning environment – a habitat – in that it is not an aggregate of courses but a set of intertwined workshops, most of them co–taught by members of the same team of teacher educators. Learning within this environment is based upon participation in a community of practice through shared ideas and experiences, reflection upon practice, critical thinking, and self-study of questions and dilemmas that emerge throughout this learning process. ACE curriculum, as presented in the following diagram, can be described as a dynamic web (see the figure in the next page).

At the core of ACE curriculum are two consecutive 'Wisdom of practice" yearly workshops in which students' practice is studied through narrative texts of their school experiences. Learning to teach is based upon the living experiences of the participants as they are related to their cultural and social backgrounds. These experiences become multifaceted narrative texts that invite the students to explore new arenas of learning and creation and expand their professional landscape. Participating in this process of telling and retelling practice stories is an ongoing activity of negotiating and renegotiating meanings. In the second (and last) year in the program, the students are being asked to make use of the narrative skills they have acquired, and accompany their teaching with a 'narrative self-study of practice' - a personal written work done within a collaborative community.

Another two workshops, Personal and Professional Identity, deal with the cultural background of the participants, within an atmosphere that encourages sharing and discussing different upbringing traditions, cultural norms and habits, issues of gender, personal world views etc., as they influence the person as well as the school context and life. This multicultural dialogue allows the participants to experience the meaning of being part of a diverse community of learners, and to develop their professional ways of action. Becoming a teacher, in this respect, is a process in which the personal and the professional experiences intertwine, and practical ways of being are told, retold, and develop. This workshop encourages hermeneutical processes to take place and, by that, enables the consideration of each individual's "t"-theory .

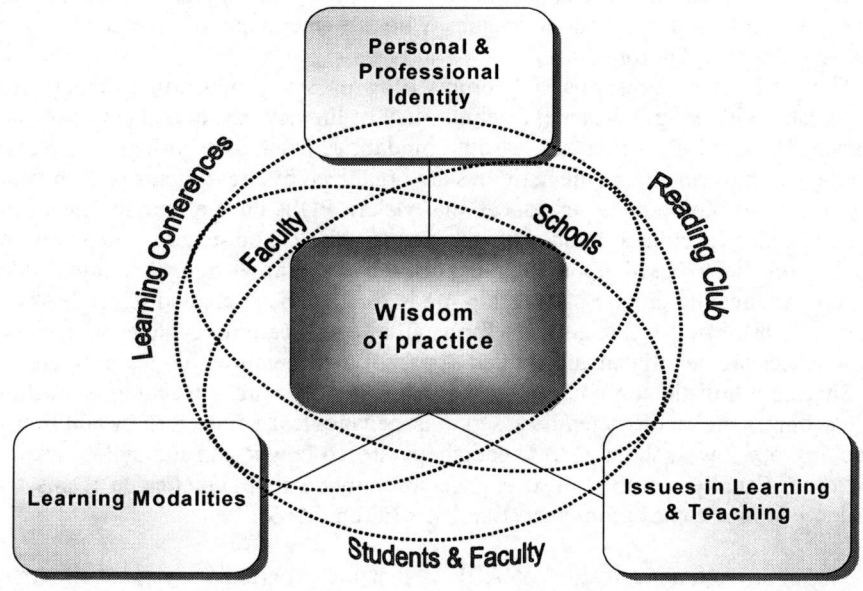

(Barak & Gidron, 2009, p.40)

The ways in which we identify ourselves and distinguish ourselves from others raise deep ethical questions. This workshop offers opportunities to approach identity not as fixed, but as a fluid process of continual redefinition and conflict. The students learn to interpret cultural evidence in order to transform their day-to-day experiences into educative ones and, by that, develop personal and professional ethical attitudes. Accordingly, each activity is designed to help the students represent their cultural experiences in various ways and then to reflect and deliberate on and about their thoughts and feelings. The act of representing their interpretation of cultural aspects and events makes it possible for each student to reconsider ideas, images, or feelings that are relevant to their experiences (Back & Mansur, 2009). Thus it encourages the development of the students' *phronesis.*

In ACE, the practical and the ethical are weaved together, and affect the kind of action the teacher will be engaged in. It also demonstrates how "telling identities" make us aware of the guiding lines which direct how we evaluate others and act upon this evaluation. Multiculturalism is an attitude that recognizes the legitimacy of different cultural patterns within society that is ready to mutually accept and respect them. The problem with such a multicultural attitude in practice is embedded in the limited ability of human beings to grasp the other in terms different than their own, and of humans as 'cultural beings' to extend their cultural horizons of understating beyond the boundaries shaped by their own contextually situated life stories. The need to work on widening our horizons to include the other in one's realm of understanding is crucial to people who want to work with other people in general, and is enhanced when working in a multicultural community. Within this context, educators should not be viewed as knowledge transmitters or cultural mediators alone, but mainly as engaged in educational dialogue with students and colleagues who are members of a community of learners (Mansur, Gidron, 2004).

The program's workshops and forums offer a variety of learning experiences that relate to learning issues and teaching such as literacy, social and psychological aspects. It includes a variety of learning modalities (such as paintings, sculptures, drama, and movement). Some activities are organized by the students (e.g., reading club meetings, conferences or educational visits). PDSs have a unique role within this program; in collaboration with the faculty, the school-teachers develop and teach workshops based upon their experience and knowledge. A unique 'edge culture' frames the unique partnership mode that has been created (Gorodetsky & Barak, 2008). The ACE team itself forms an integral learning cycle as its faculty's experiences are negotiated and studied as part of their being within the program.

Sharing a holistic approach to teacher education in which "teaching is teaching is teaching," all faculty members serve as pedagogical counselors in addition to teaching other workshops. Most workshops are co-taught and the syllabi are co-authored. Faculty members also engage in studying their practice in teams that coalesce around topics of interest (Barak & Gidron, 2009).

The main Romantic feature of ACE is that the program is seen as a journey. Each student is required to delve in a *Bildung* type quest about their personal, cultural and professional identity. Collaboration and dialogue are seen as the main educational ends-in-view which can foster a better understanding of the self's way of understanding his world. According to an unpublished research, many of the program's graduates claim that for them teaching is devotion. They want to make a difference in their students' lives. The subject-matter is just a mean for *Bildung*. They think that for that they need courage and prowess (especially in the more traditional Bedouin tribe societies), and they estimate the program's journey enables them to undertake that mission. Other graduates find that they love their occupation, and doing what they love energizes their daily struggles. It gives them joy of creation, interest, and satisfaction. They feel self-efficacy and self-fulfilled, and they attest that the program makes them sure that teaching is what they want to do. The graduates mention that their ability to see the "other" has been developed throughout the program. Nonetheless, there are some problems that the program faces. According to its graduates, the main obstacle they face is the inability of the school system to give them appropriate space to develop their own initiatives. The system is afraid of their spirit of independence and responsibility. Sometimes the other teachers do not accept their deep devotion because it makes them feel guilty (we are not like them). Another obstacle, that some of them feel, is that instead of infusing them with unrealizable expectation, the program should have given them more "tools" to deal with concrete problems. They feel that a more extensive attention to subject method courses would have rendered them better teachers.

In this chapter we explore Romantic inspired TEPs. However, the Romantic impact has been quite limited. The TEPs still favor the enlightenment emphasis on reasonable and rational behavior. However, some Romantic ideas are incorporated into the TEP's framework, such as love and friendship (especially to the other), caring and the pivotal acceptance that the meaning of life emerges out of journey and dialogue. This highlights the BEING MoE as an important alternative to HAVING. The process is more important than its end, the whole than its part, and the subjective than the objective. But maybe such a stance is too weak amid the troubled times we face. It might be that the (Aristotelian) submission of the passions and the emotions under the rule of reason is too dangerous in our post-modern era. It might be that the little room we have for literature, arts, and creativity, the neglect of humanity, even in the human sciences, is the reason for our social failures and for the sufferings which pervade the world. In that case, the TEPs in this chapter might be too little too late, and we need other kinds of TEPs altogether.

CHAPTER 10

THE END OF THE JOURNEY: THE FUTURE OF TEACHER EDUCATION

Throughout the book we have seen how various moral sources influence TEPs. In this chapter I will revisit the meta-theory and offer a generalized overview of the book, thus showing its fruitfulness for the analysis and evaluation of different kinds of TEPs. In the second part of the chapter I return to the three challenges discussed in the first chapter and discuss the possible ways that teacher education can meet them. This book has two aspects: it is descriptive as far as it suggests a way of analyzing existing TEPs. It is normative because it raises the question 'what should characterize a proper TEP'. Although the two aspects are inseparable, I begin with the descriptive import of the theory.

TEPS' IDENTITY

TEPs from all over the spectrum share a basic structure of their curriculum. While the length of the programs, the proportion between its ingredients and their interdependence, and their specific structure, content, and methods of teaching and learning, are widely divergent, they all have the following commonalities: (i) some theoretical studies in education; (ii) practicum; and (iii) subject-matter knowledge (usually learned outside of the TEP, but presupposed by it). In some programs (iii) includes a significant amount of general studies (liberal-arts courses). In other TEPs, usually of the External-believer type, religious or ideological courses form a necessary component of the program.

Each TEP operates in a certain context of teacher educators, students, learning environment, and institutional and external regulations. In this context the program adopts a moral source and deploys a specific MoE combination. Each TEP has a unique identity, defined by its specific blend of the moral source and the MoE it adopts. As far as its identity conforms to the hegemonic Mode of Recognition, it might get support and respect. As far as its identity does not confirm to this Mode, its graduates are less welcomed by the educational system, and it has to struggle for its persistence.

As we have seen, it is possible to define three broad families of TEPs: the Enlightenment oriented TEPs; the Romantic oriented TEPs; and the External Believer oriented TEPs. Within these three big families, TEPs can have different dominant Modes of Existence (HAVING, BEING, or DOING). Hence, it is possible to analyze a given TEP by answering two questions:

–   Which moral source it presupposes?

–   What is the specific Mode of Existence it pursues (for example, is it HAVING>DOING>BEING, BEING>DOING>HAVING or DOING>BEING>HAVING)?

Different TEPs have different identities because they offer diverse answers to these two questions. Based on the answers to these questions, it is possible to suggest the following generalizations:

1. Enlightenment: Most TEPs are conducted within the academic environment. They presuppose the enlightenment moral source, with its reason-based way of thinking. Reason is bifurcated into instrumental or substantial rationality.

a. Instrumental Rationality: This kind of TEP deals mainly with the technical aspects of the profession. It emphasizes the "how" of the teacher's activities, and takes for granted the hegemonic "why" and "what for" of the educational system, without opening them to critical discussion throughout the program. This option has two variants:

– The TEP might adopt the view that teaching is an applied science profession (techni). It incorporates the pyramid structure of the teachers' knowledge base and constructs field experiences in which the student-teacher is required to implement this theoretical knowledge [examples no. 4, 5, 17]. The final exam of such a program might be a practical project in which the student teacher demonstrates that he masters the sequence of planning-executing-evaluating in a unit of studies.

– Alternatively the TEP might hold that teaching is a reflective practice (*techne*) [examples no. 6-8]. It focuses on a 'learning from experience' process, monitored by personal supervision, practical workshops, and theoretical courses. The final exam of such a program might be an action research or a self-study, which presents and discusses the student's insights about his work.

According to both variants:

– The dominant MoE is HAVING. Utilitarian ethics dictates that the aim of the TEP is to prepare an efficient professional teacher. Even TEPs which deal with the BEING of the student-teacher do it for instrumental reasons: developing the teacher as a human being (enhancing his dialogical abilities, creativity, etc.) might develop a more efficient teacher (see example no. 17). In other TEPs, the theoretical part of the knowledge-base of the program might function like a dogma. In these cases a DOING-like MoE might be detected. The student teachers are expected to follow the program's practical dictates (see examples no. 5, 12). Yet, again, this is for the sake of being efficient. If the presupposed theory is no longer valid, it will be replaced.

– The *phronetic* level of the TEP is usually quite marginal. The TEP mainly addresses the question of how it can best serve the hegemonic concept of social justice and marginalizes the question of whether it should serve them in the first place. Such TEPs are conservative. They prepare teachers for the existing system, and the teacher is seen as a practitioner and not as a *praxitioner.*

In the current neoliberal climate, the dominant HAVING MoE has a narrow interpretation. The *Homo Economicus'* way of thinking, which characterizes the consumer society, demands that measurable achievements are the overriding sign of success, as they provide the dominant principle of social esteem. To receive recognition, the TEP must beoutcome driven, and the outcomes are the short-term accomplishments of student teachers and their pupils. Since only quantitative data can serve as evidence for success, the TEP is evaluated according to measurable criteria based on standardized exams [see examples no.9, and 12]. If such a TEP tolerates no heretic (i.e., against the current) thoughts or behaviors, it behaves in a DOING-like MoE.

b. Substantial Rationality: The TEP might address the reasonableness of the system's fundamental presuppositions. The supposition is that the techne of teaching cannot be value-free, and the teacher should always take into account the societal context in which he operates. A vital part of the teacher's job is to deal with questions, such as "why", "what for", and "for whose sake", in every decision he makes (see examples no. 7, 18-20). His deliberations have to take into account the long-term implications of his actions towards the students and society. For example, it is necessary that the TEP addresses the normative issues of competition vs. equity, justice vs. charity, excellence vs. equality, the individual vs. the community, etc. Hence, *phronetical* knowledge is a major focus of such TEPs, and it is present in various aspects of their structure and activities.

A Substantial Rationality TEP does not have to be rebellious or critical. It is possible for the students to find out that, after all, the given society is quite OKAY, even if it calls for some alterations or modifications. Although, of course, a more radical enlightened TEP might question the educational system and find that it needs a major revision. (For example, such a TEP may challenge the achievement principle or insist on a different relations between the different modes of recognition.) Thus, it is possible to differentiate between "dogmatic" TEPs, which presuppose a certain "correct" philosophy which has to be implemented, and "open" TEPs which deal with moral issues but have no predefined solutions for them. (There are, of course, TEPs which take only some of their presuppositions for granted.) The dogmatic option may lead to a DOING MoE, (the more "ideological" the TEP is, the more it tends to be authoritative and closed).

In today's climate, because of the hegemony of the achievement principle of social esteem, any TEP which openly rejects the HAVING MoE, is an instance of a radical approach. It is immediately labeled as "irregular" and it risks its social status (e.g., the MT program, example no. 19, which had been closed). The actual features of such an anti-HAVING TEP depend on whether it emphasizes BEING or DOING as its dominant MoE. A BEING oriented TEP endorses the program as a journey, and adds to the reflective practitioner stance a focus on the self as educator who wishes to enhance a non-utilitarian, but reason based *Bildung* process (see example no. 8). A DOING oriented TEP regards the program as an initiation process, and adds to the reflective practitioner stance a focus on the teacher as a missioner of certain supposedly valid ideology. While the last option is an instance of the external-believer TEPs (see appendix example 14), it does follow the footprints of the enlightenment quest for eternal and absolute conceptions of "true" and "good". To date, such a quest is usually delegitimized (e.g., it is not seen as politically correct, because it is not tolerant and "multi..."). It is not legitimate for the TEP to have a definite ideology unless it is publicly known as being part of a certain ideological movement.

2. *External-believer*. A genuine External-believer TEP can hardly be conducted within the free academic environment, because it rejects any source of knowledge which is not congruent with its world-view (see: example 13). Usually it is a DOING MoE program, which stress its missionary devotion and its contribution to the implementation of a sacred faith. The external believer TEPs deal with character formation, and teacher education has to ensure that the teacher will deploy the "correct" virtues. The very existence of this kind of TEPs presupposes a community of believers within which each of them operates, and for each, it is critical to receive the community's recognition, and support, for otherwise they will not have students, schools to practice etc.

There can be two slightly different versions of the DOING oriented external believer kind of TEP: the DOING>HAVING variant and the DOING>BEING one. Some TEPs look at HAVING (especially if it is supplemented by a material achievement principle) as a bitter enemy (it suggests a threatening seduction). Others see HAVING as a means to implement their ideology (a kind of stick and carrot approach). The DOING>HAVING possibility is more outcome driven and focuses on living in a society which conforms to its DOING ideology. Sometimes it reduces the place of the individual to a mere instrument in the service of the collective. The DOING>BEING possibility is more process driven (like the TEP of the Kibbutzim movement in the 1940s mentioned in chapter 7). It requires the individual to bring his own voice to the collective orchestra and emphasizes the hermeneutical aspects of being a believer.

3. Romantic inspired TEPs usually endorse the BEING MoE. Such a stance gains a limited legitimization in the academic world. But it is possible to find a BEING oriented program, which emphasizes the individual and the way he gives meaning to his world within the prescribed limits of the academic world (see examples 16-20). It is possible to encourage personal relationships, dialogue, and alternatives to the HAVING MoE. The negative effect of the academic environment is that it tends to weaken the non-rational ingredients of the Romantic stance. Everything should be verbalized, explained and discussed in a rational manner. Again, if the Romantic ideal becomes a dogma, it might turn into a DOING MoE, especially if authenticity becomes a kind of axiomatic, non-negotiated religion. As mentioned before, if BEING is used for utilitarian intentions (such as efficiency), it might become a mean in the quest for HAVING.

This analysis helps us understand the dilemmas in which any TEP can find itself.

1. It is commonly held that TEPs which make a difference are cohesive and consistent. They have a coherent and comprehensive world-view about the aims of education and the essence of the "good" teacher. This world-view, which includes,

aside from other factors, the moral source and the Mode of Existence, penetrates every aspect of the TEP: its recruiting criteria of faculty and students; its curriculum (formal, informal and null); its learning environment; its theory-practice relations, the ways it organizes the practicum; the teacher-student relations and the ways the TEP evaluates the students.

Many to date problems of the TEPs are due to the difficulty to sustain such a coherency in the academic environment in which they operate. For example, as we have seen, the subject matter studies are usually learnt outside the TEP. In most cases, the program presupposes that the subject matter is already known, or studied elsewhere, without any attempt to coordinate the subjects' course of studies with the education ones. Consequently, in most of the TEPs, a major element of teaching is poorly handled, that of using the subject-matter to educate (and not merely to inform) the students. At most, it is dealt within the educational studies without enabling the modeling or reflection of the student teacher about his own learning processes. Even within the TEP, it is difficult to preserve the integrity between the in-campus course of studies and the "field" experience, and between the theoretically and the practically oriented courses. Many attributes of the practicum are not tailored to the needs and orientation of the TEP. Schools have their own agendas, educational philosophies, and institutional identities. Unless a very thoughtful system of PDSs is in action, the theory-practice "gap" is unavoidable.

The problem of sustaining a cohesive program is also due to the academic freedom of the academic environment. On the one hand, it runs against any effort to coordinate, adjust or arrange the program according to a definite agenda. On the other, since teacher educators have their own vision about teaching and teachers, if the program runs against their beliefs they might be frustrated and non-cooperative.

2. Another difficulty arises from the need to adjust the TEP's vision to local regulations. External requirements (standards, exams) might run against the program's agenda, and require substantial compromises which threaten the program's integrity. Some combinations of moral source and MoE are seen as more legitimate or acceptable while others are seen as "experiential", exceptional, or even deviant or perilous, because they aim to prepare a different, non-standard, teacher. It is quite easy to maintain a TEP whose moral source and MoE coincide with that of the general public. It is quite demanding to sustain a TEP which runs counter to the hegemonic culture, especially if it is publicly supported.

The analysis of TEPs in terms of its moral sources and MoE might help detect these kinds of dilemmas and deal with them. For example, a detailed examination of the TEP's identity enables comparison between its vision and that of the public education system in which it operates. It highlights the points of congruence between the TEP and its social environment and poses the questions to what extent and to what price should the TEP be adjusted to "reality", and to what extent and to what price the TEP could be autonomous to pursue its own vision. The same analysis can be done regarding the academic environment in which the TEP operates. For example, stronger stress on academic research might lead to a faculty more remote from the realities of actual teaching, value neutrality might lead to pedagogical paralysis, and academic freedom of individual lecturers might impair the program's integrity and coherency.

Nevertheless, some of the examples examined in this book show that it is feasible to maintain a cohesive and consistent academic TEP. It demands an ongoing alertness to the difficulties and obstacles that such a TEP faces. It requires a continuous effort to keep the program going and developed, albeit the ever changing context and a constant evaluation of whether the TEP is still on the right track. The rise and fall of so many irregular TEPs demonstrates this is all but an easy task. This is especially true for the TEPs which try to make a difference; to insistently favor a moral source or a MoE which does not comply with the hegemonic ones.

3. TEPs are not "static" entities. They constantly change and develop. They are not "rational" in the sense of having a deliberate and conscious decision making process. One important aspect of their activity is that they do not operate in a vacuum. TEPs influence each other. Their academics interact, exchange ideas, methods, modes of thinking. As in other areas, there are fashions in teacher education. Training has been replaced by reflection, which, in turn is replaced by short-term outcome driven philosophy, which again, emphasizes training and competencies. At any given time, there are some "buzz" words which appear in every program, for otherwise it will not be "in", and up-to-date. In these circumstances, it is quite difficult to maintain a unique or different identity. For instance, one to date slogan is diversity. Actually, it means that all the programs should be standardized to incorporate diversity.

Thus, any TEP can incorporate a set of notions, ideas, methods, just for the sake of being updated. In many cases, this assimilation really changes the program's attributes. In other cases, there is only a vocabulary modification. For example, it is quite common to declare that the teacher should be "reflective". But, as we have seen, one can endorse reflection and remain in a very utilitarian HAVING MoE, so that no time is given to genuine reflection beyond "technical rationality" processes. Moreover, if the TEP adopts reflection and inquiry as a stance, without changing other attributes of the program, it is hardly going to change the students' minds (e.g., incorporating action research in the very last period of the program). One of the merits of the theory proposed in this book is that it enables an open and critical discussion of these points. Using the vocabulary of moral sources and MoE, it is possible, for instance, to address questions such as: How to make sense of all the ingredients of the program? Do they appear in the program only to please someone? What are the processes in which the program assimilates and accommodates new conceptions and methods of teaching and learning? How much of the program is there just because of tradition, habits, fashion, external influences, and how much the program is a result of continuous deliberate and informed discussion about the ways the students learn to teach?

The third challenge mentioned in the first chapter can be met simply by embracing the multi-faceted world of TEPs. If we do not want a one embracing ideology to conquer the entire world, we cannot aspire to have a consensus on education's aims and methods. This multiplicity is a blessing, not a threat. It enables invention and creation, cross fertilization, and critical thinking.

THE POSTMODERN HAVING

One of the salient features of the postmodern, consumerist culture is that in all three moral sources, the three MoEs are reduced to HAVING. We have already seen (chapter 6) how instrumental rationality might be understood as utilitarian means-end (or utility maximization) deliberation, where the end is defined in strictly materialistic terms. This approach has been elevated to the status of a common sense dogma, so that every critical attitude against it is seen as a betrayal. Enlightenment based alternatives to the utilitarian stance must come from substantial reasoning, albeit the many attempts to accomplish such a mission (e.g., Gewirth, Taylor, Honneth, Nussbaum or Sen), there is still a widespread fear that this line of reasoning will end up with a new "ideology", which might be as harmful as its predecessors (knowledge is power and power is oppressive). In a climate of relativism and diversity, "politically correct" behavior, and multicultural tolerance, any commitment to an eternal truth is suspicious and has to be avoided, even if the price is to live without an "ideology".

The "null" ideology becomes itself a new ideology. HAVING is elevated to a status of a new religion, consumerism becomes a new god, and the shopping malls become new temples. Buying replaces praying, rating and fashion replaces the priests and the rabbis. Paradoxically, for the individual to maintain a kind of self-identity, he has to be like anyone else (Bauman, 2007).

This reduction process happens to Romanticism as well. The HAVING MoE easily absorbs the romantic feelings and transforms them into a consumer-based ideal (Illouz, 1997). (If you love somebody, you have to spend a lot of money to please her/him). A distorted notion of a self, whose BEING is totally defined by what he possesses, reduces BEING into a mere instrument for HAVING. The widespread BE-DO-HAVE advice of many personal coaches is a good representative of this reduction:

> What would happen if you shifted the paradigm [from do-have-be] to be-do-have? By "being" happy, successful, loving, loyal, open, compassionate, a good lover and a good partner you will begin "doing" things differently which will allow you to "have" things you never would have had if you were running the process as a do-have-be paradigm.

> (http://www.yourdailylifecoach.com/be-do-have.html).

BEING becomes a means for HAVING, while the "what for" of this HAVING is not really discussed.

Recently, there has been a dramatic change in the way that HAVING is expressed. Its adherents use romantic terms like creativity, authenticity, empowerment, self-enhancement, or self-fulfilling, which are taken from the BEING vocabulary. But this is a sign that BEING has been surrounded by the interests of HAVING. A typical example of this process is what happens to the notion of quality (Pirsig, 1974). The notion changes its meaning from excellence or wholeness to fitness to/for purposes (Doherty, 2008). According to the first definition, "quality" is a primary notion which cannot be reduced to other notions and cannot be further analyzed. The recognition that something is high "quality" comes prior to the question what makes it so. The supposition is that something high quality is extraordinary and unique. A symphony has high quality, not because there are many like it, but because it is unique, because there is something special about it. Its holistic *gestalt* renders it unique. The feeling that nothing is missing and nothing can be added to it makes it perfect. An outstanding book or painting is recognized as such before any analysis to discover why they are so marvelous is performed. Even if one discovers why they are good, it is impossible to reproduce them. The whole is always more than its parts. On the other hand, the second definition – fitness for purposes – is functional and relational. Quality is understood in quantitative terms ('to be number one')[75]. This definition enables us to assess whether a given entity or process can perform a given role as good, better or best in comparison with others who do the same, but not whether it is genuinely "good'. The first definition is Romantic, the second is utilitarian, analytic, and follows the instrumental-rationality paradigm.

This example illustrates that the use of Romantic notions such as "quality" does not have to mislead, because it is possible to give them new meaning which is in agreement with HAVING and strengthens it. This also happens to the "self-fulfillment" notion. The individual's self-fulfillment means that he HAS more material resources, either because being rich is in itself self-fulfillment, or because self-fulfillment requires a lot of resources. For example, it becomes impossible to attain self-fulfillment without a cadre of advisors, coaches, or spiritual guides which charge a lot of money for their services. A prevalent attitude in our achievement driven society is that self-fulfillment is first of all a successful career, defined by measurable criteria. This attitude is a function of the amount of material resources one obtains. Again, this is another symptom of a general phenomenon. Everything is commercialized. Everything, personal identity included, becomes a commodity which can be merged in the world of HAVING. Along the way, identity changes its original meaning. As we have already mentioned, this modification of terms might characterize the TEPs as well.

Paradoxically, because everything is reduced to HAVING, the autonomous, authentic self has to resemble any other autonomous being. The modern quest of being autonomous ends up defining self-identity as being similar to others. As HAVING becomes the new secular religion, substantial, critical reason becomes suspicious and dangerous (for sure, it endangers the hegemonic world-view).

The External-belief DOING stance can also be reduced to HAVING. Two examples illustrate this process. Marx (1859/1971) famously postulates that "being determines consciousness", and by "being" he understands material conditions. Communism just aims to replace the individual HAVING with a collective understanding of the term. The ideal of DOING for communal HAVING might have reasonable reasons. Internal equality, among the community's members becomes the overriding ideal. The basic intention has been that no one will have more material resources than his fellows. This kind of HAVING is more important than freedom or individuality. Solidarity and comradeships are favored to competition and rivalry.

As for the religious believer, we have already seen that Max Weber (1905/1958) argues that the Protestant Ethics justifies the HAVING MoE[76]. Man cannot prosper without God's blessing, so having earthy wealth is a sign that the individual is morally good. Success depends on the individual's behavior. If he fails, that is if he is poor, it is a sign that he deserves punishment. Since the fate of the individual is dictated by his actions, he continuously has to reflect on his activities in terms of their impact on his eternal lure. This is a typical instrumental rationality mode of thinking. Again the external-believer adopts a HAVING driven MoE.

The implication of this state of affairs is that even TEPs which are BEING or DOING oriented are judged according to utilitarian criteria (e.g., they all must comply with the NCATE's 2010 standard that "evaluation of candidates must be based on students' outcome data..."). The HAVING MoE, with its tendency to standardize everything, so it might be measured, compared, and become a commodity, becomes the dominant model of the TEPs, although it is quite difficult to justify this transformation by any of the three moral sources.

The above discussion attests that the normative aspect is an essential component of any educational theory. I fully accept Honneth's argument that social theory necessarily has a normative aspect. We always judge social phenomenon "to be positive only when they point in the direction of a societal development that we can grasp as coming closer to our notions of a good or just society..." (Honneth, 2004, p. 354). Education is ideology laden. Its aims are prescribed by the society, and are justified by its notion of the "good". Neglect of this normative aspect, not only serves the existing system interests, but also hinders the possibility of thinking about various alternatives to them. It might harm the reasonable modern aspiration to improve our society.

The neo-liberal challenge to TEPs is serious and perilous. It might be that its only remedy is to get rid of this ideology all together. This is, of course, a normative stance. It might not be accepted by all, but as far as I can see it is more reasonable than any other option.

BEYOND ARISTOTLE'S PHRONESIS

The first challenge of teacher education, presented by the post-modern era, is difficult to deal with, and calls for further investigation.. However I do have some preliminary thoughts which can be of some help, although they indicate a total change in our conception of what teacher education should look like.

Interestingly enough, in all the programs discussed in this book, except those belonging to the external-believer stance, the *phronetic* level remains in the individual realm. It has not evolved to the social or political spheres level of human activity. The teacher remains a children's pedagogue, and has not become a guide for an improved society or world-order. This might be fine, but it raises the question of TEPs' prospects to educate the next generation of teachers.

The postmodern criticism makes it clear that none of the moral sources can provide a reliable and uncontestable compass to man's life. Though each of them has its own strengths, they fail to provide an undisputable "guide for the perplexed" in our ever-changing society. One of the reasons for this shortcoming is that we try to oversimplify the world. The very attempt to subordinate the right behavior to one cardinal moral source seems to be misguided. Simultaneously, humans are rational and emotional, skeptical and believers, individuals and communitarians, target oriented and spontaneous voyagers. The moral source cannot remain unique. It is not enough to acknowledge that each moral source is relative and, to some extent, suspicious. This will make any moral decision casual and caprice. It might be more prudent to seek for a kind of synthesis (in the Hegelian sense), in which the different sources will merge into a compound constitution of beliefs and desires, which takes into account the contradictory aspects of the human condition. Most humans are not one-dimensional. They possess decentralizing minds (Minsky, 1980), and they face the task of reconciling the various ingredients of their inner world by making a proper place for each of them. Humans have to deal with their inner voices and conflicts and still maintain their personal and professional identity. To elaborate this option, let us go back to Aristotle.

Aristotle claims that humans are compound organisms. They have physiological, emotional and reasoning faculties (e.g., Aristotle, 1984, E.N. I, 13) whose proper functioning is a necessary condition for their well-being (*eudemonia*). Human desires and passions can have multiple sources. They can be irrational (arising out of physiological, emotional, personal or social needs) or rational (cognitive needs). Neglect of any of these faculties may cause unhappiness. Each of them has to be nourished, enhanced and developed to its full competency.

Phronesis is the practical knowledge of sustaining the proper functioning of the human organism within his society. In Aristotelian terms, the virtue of reaching one's highest potential is called *arête.* The supreme aim of education is to nourish and enhance the development of the child's *arête*, so that he will become prudent and virtuous. Aristotle maintains that practical reason should guide the individual and resolve any kind of inner conflict he faces. It enables him to understand the long-term consequences of any specific behavior. Practical reason is not "against" passion or desire. It is a judging faculty, which evaluates the motives of human behavior in order to find the appropriate resolution in case they conflict. The supremacy of practical reason is not because it reveals general, universal and eternal truths; it comes from its ability to evaluate the pros and cons of a concrete activity in a given context and suggest its possible consequences. Thus it might render something one desires (e.g., smoking) to something less desirable, or stir an appetite for something which has not been previously wished for (e.g., to be "green" or eat healthy food).

Prudence means to feel and do "the right things at the right time, with reference to the right objects, towards the right people, with the right motive, and in the right way" (Aristotle, 1984, E.N. II, 6; cf.: III, 7, 1115^b 18; II, 9, 1109^a 27-28). At the center of the Aristotelian ethics stands the "Golden Mean" principle:

> Excellence, then, is a state concerned with choice, lying in a mean relative to us, this being determined by reason and in the way in which the man of *phronesis* would determine it (E.N., II, 6, 1107^a 1-2).

The principle can be applied to both *techne* and to *phronesis*:

…if ten pounds are too much for a particular person to eat and two too little, it does not follow that the trainer will order six pounds [the mathematical mean between two and six]; for this also is perhaps too much for the person who is to take it, or too little—too little for Milo [a famous wrestler], too much for the beginner in athletic exercises" (E.N., II, 6, 1106b 1-6; cf.: E.E., II, 3, 1120b 21-31, where Aristotle explicitly mentions the *techne* of gymnastics, medicine, building, and navigation).

Though in general:

…every art does its work well—by looking to the intermediate and judging its works by this standard (so that we often say of good work of art that it is not possible either to take away or to add anything, implying that excess and defect destroy the goodness of works of art, while the mean preserves it; and good *technitas*, we may say, look to this in their work), and if, further, excellence is more exact and better than any art… then it must have the quality of aiming at the intermediate. I mean moral excellence; for it is this that is concerned with passions and actions, and in these there ii excess, defeat, and the intermediate… (E.N., II, 6, 1106b 10-20).

It is impossible to characterize in advance what will count as the correct mean in a particular situation. First, because it is 'relative to us' (E.N., II, 6, 1107^a 1-2). Second, because any situation is unique and calls for a special deliberation. The virtuous individual has the ability to intuitively see that certain activity is the mean (II, 9, 1109^b 20-24) before he can act in the right way.

Neither theoretical reason nor irrational emotions can serve as unique moral sources. Morality, driven only by emotions, might cause the individual to be emphatically responsive to the other as a subject. A human being, motivated by feelings of love, caring, and friendship might restrain his actions so that they will be morally good. However, humans are also motivated by feelings of hatred, envy, or will to power. Both kinds of motives have to somehow be balanced by a reason which advances notions such as human rights, justice, fairness, and symmetry. On the other hand, morality, driven by "pure" reason alone, might lead to alienation and reification of the other. The moral law can be graceless and allow for no exceptions, but the Other is a living person. He has his own feelings, desires, beliefs and preferences which have to be taken into account. The whole point of ethics is to keep the other's rights within the community he is part of. *Phronesis*, as practical knowledge, enables humans to make context-sensitive balanced decisions.

The external belief source adds another dimension. It answers the human quest for a stable and secure meaning of life. However, the external moral source is best understood as an externalization of a basic human need. This need can be met by acknowledging that the mission of one's life is nothing else than life itself. According to Aristotle, The aim of life is internal to it. It is to see that all the ingredients of the individual's personality can flourish and achieve fruition. Only a way of life, which addresses the individual in a holistic manner, can advance well-being and happiness (*eudemonia*).

Although the prevalent image is that of the "professional", enlightenment driven teacher, the interaction between the teacher and the pupils cannot only be "professional". Education is also a romantic meeting between souls, and the teacher brings to the class his whole personality, including his *eros*. He cannot ignore his own world-view, feelings, and passions. He cannot disregard the pupils' beliefs and desires. He will not be meaningful to their lives if he does not wish to influence their lives. He will not be relevant to their maturation process if he does not touch their souls. Without a genuine dialogue with his pupils, he might find that his job is meaningless or redundant.

In current schools, the teacher, in his roles as in *locus parentis* and as a representative of the adult's culture, has to deal with moral issues. His everyday decisions must be a result of a practical knowledge type of thinking. Moreover, and this is one of my normative credos, as an educator, he has to develop the pupils' *phronesis*.

The aim of teacher education cannot be reduced to develop professional efficiency, to enhance the teacher's authentic self-fulfillment, or to advance the target of attaining agiven ideal society. In Aristotelian terms, its aim should be to prepare a pedagogue whose passion is to be *phronimon*, and who is able to instill this passion in the child.

Amid the unpredictable future, we know that the future will not resemble the past. All three types of TEPs can, at best, prepare the teacher of today. Those of the future will have different roles. They will work in a different learning environment, enhance different skills, and focus on different types of knowledge. In the changing world, flexibility and creativity will be major virtues. But albeit the attempts to define the 21st century skills, it might be questionable whether they really represent what will be needed in the years to come. No one can say what how the next generation of the technological devices will change our life, and nobody knows how to integrate teaching and learning into this fuzzy world. I deliberately say very little about the new technologies and the school environment, because it is premature to deal with this issue. Everything I can think of might be old fashioned a day after the publication of the book. However, one point seems to me to be of vital importance. The children of the future will need a responsible adult on whom they can rely. They need someone, with enough integrity and concern, who cares about their proper development, and will see that they have a kind of a compass to help them navigate in the world. Functioning as a teacher in the technical sense (even of techn*e*) will not be enough. The teacher of tomorrow should be a *phronimon*. He should not instruct but educate. For this to happen, I believe, any type of TEP should emphasize the BEING MoE. Some kind of a *Bildung* process is prerequisite to meet the future's needs.

Aristotle's *phronimon* is the individual whose reasoning faculty both dominates and is influenced by his irrational faculties such as feeling, imagination, and passion. An equilibrated human is, for him, a person who finds the "correct" balance between them. He has no inner conflicts because he already feels and desires the things that his reason will approve. The ideal picture is that of a "balanced" teacher whose head (theoretical knowledge), heart (caring and empathy) and hand operate harmoniously and lead to successful professional performance (Sullivan, 2005; 2006).

But even this might not be enough. For Aristotle, it is still the reasoning faculty which takes the lead and has the "last word" in cases of conflict. For Freud this "rationalization" is an illusion. It masks an inner chaotic and dangerous world, in which the attempt to repress unconscious motives cause humans to be mentally ill. Civilization is the outcome of this effort, but the price is too high. But maybe, the very quest to be rational is in itself irrational.

Michel Serres (1997) suggests a different way of overcoming the gap between the rational and the irrational, between the enlightenment and the Romantic, between science and art, between the secular and the sacred. For him the dominance of either the rational or the irrational is too hazardous. While in the enlightenment perspective reason is the unique center of human knowledge, and in the Romantic perspective feeling and emotion play the same role, Serres advises us to replace the idea of a circle with the idea of an ellipse. Unlike the circle, an ellipse has two foci, and the "third", the point in between them, is a kind of irreducible synthesis which is neither the one nor the other.

> In knowledge and instruction, [he says], a third place also exists, a worthless position today between the two others: on the one hand, the hard sciences, formal, objective, powerful; on the other, what one calls culture, dying. Whence the begetting of a third man: the third-instructed... We have to educate ourselves in the third place between these two foci (Serres, 1997, p. 45 – 46).

Reason at its best is critical. Feeling at its best is creative. Neither of them is redundant. Neither can be left alone. Both seem vital to a proper human life. Will it be possible to invent a TEP which will be both critical and creative? Will it be possible to have a TEP which will meet the next generations' needs? Should we invite ourselves to a new journey to a yet unknown territory in the quest to find a better, more viable and more sustainable teacher education program?

APPENDIX

EXAMPLES OF TEACHER EDUCATION PROGRAMS

Chapter 4

Example 1: ST

In one of the US first normal schools, opened in 1839 in Westfield, Mass., the curriculum included: "Reading of scripture daily, Orthography (Spelling), Enunciation and reading, Writing, Physiology, Drawing, Grammar, Algebra, Geometry, Philosophy, Phonography, The globes, Theory and Practice of Teaching, Vocal music, English composition" (Hunt, 1956, p. 24). A similar program characterizes the normal school in Lexington, Mass.: "the minimum course was one year, and included six basic areas: (a) a thorough review of the common subjects - spelling, reading, writing, geography, and arithmetic; (b) some secondary school academic subjects (e.g. geometry, algebra, philosophy, etc. - but no ancient languages); (c) the physical, mental, and moral development of children; (d) the principles and methods of teaching the common subjects ; (e) the art of school government; and (f) practice teaching" (Snyder, 1953, p. 222).

A typical example ST in Israel has been the "Curriculum for Preparing Primary School Teachers", which had been mandated by the Department of Education in Israel in 1950. The post-secondary, non-academic, two years program contains a total of 85 pts. (each pt. is equivalent to 30 hours), and has four components: Theoretical subject matter courses (merged with method studies), 26 pts., (31% of the program). (7 different subjects max. of 6 pts. each): (E.g., Literature, Language, Biblical Studies, Geography; History; Nature); Practical subject-matter courses, 21 pts., (25% of the program) (E.g., Physical Education, Music, Drawing, Crafts, Chorus); Educational Studies courses, 26 pts. (31% of the program) (E.g., Foundations and History, Psychology, Educational theory, General and Special method courses); including practical experience (7 pts.); and Miscellaneous courses, 12 pts. (13% of the program), including English, and Religious or Ideological courses (Department of Education, 1950). In 1954 the model has been abridged to only 60 pts., but the proportion between the components remains almost the same (32%, 32%, 30% and 8% respectively). The total number of the subject matter studies had been reduced from 20 to 13. Practical experience remains the same, so it comprises 12% of the new model (Nardi, 1956, p. 240). In addition to the 7 weekly field experience pts., each student has to be in school for two blocks (one per year) of three consecutive weeks. Within the elective courses, the religious or ideological courses have been eliminated and replaced by special education, adult education and other practical subject-matter courses).

Currently, one can still encounter the same model, for example in Austria, where the initial training programs [for primary school] go back to the "seminaristic tradition" (see: http://www.see-educoop.net/education_in /pdf/techer-educ-austria.pdf, retrieved 11/2010).

Example 2: AT

The Hebrew University in Jerusalem adopted the consecutive model, when it opened a teacher education program for high school teachers in 1935. The program lasted for two years after the student has completed at least two of his three years studies in a relevant-to-school subject matter faculty. The theoretical courses of the TEP had been delivered by the faculty of education, while the methods courses and the field experience had been supervised by experienced teachers. There had been an annual retreat: a week of visits in the educational system (Yaakobi, 2005, p. 489).

This is all but an historical example. In Ben-Gurion University (2003-2004), the two year consecutive TEP endures 17-19 pts. (in addition to the 60 pts. required for the BA degree). It includes: 3.5 pts. of method courses; 3.5 pts. practicum; 4 pts. of behavioral science courses; 1 pt. educational measurement; 1 pts. educational policies; 1 pts. curriculum and diversity; 1 pt. informal, social education; 1 pt. the teacher and the school-system; 2 pts. teachers' collaboration (and additional 2 pts. a special workshop for students who are already in-service). A similar program is carried on in the academic year 2010-2011 in Tel-Aviv University (http://go.tau.ac.il/index.php/ma/what-to-learn/education/diploma, accessed 10/2010).

Example 3: Towards academic ST

There is no difference between the 1950s "list of courses" (see: Appendix Example 1) and the 1970s list in terms of the amount of the theoretical studies (78 pts. for both) but they are much more disciplinary oriented: Disciplinary studies rise from 26 pts. to 45 pts. (including a specialization of 15-26 pts. in one subject-matter), while Pedagogical studies slightly decline from 26 pts. to 23 pts. Practical experience changes from 7 pts. to 8 pts. (In the third year of study the students begin to teach their own class. This practicum gives them an additional 10 pts.); Miscellaneous studies declines from 12 pts. to 10 pts. In other words, subject matter studies rise from 32% (in the fifties) to 45%, education studies rise from 32% to 43%, and various practical subject-matter courses and electives decline from 25% to 12%. Practical experience rise to 19% of the total (Ministry of Education and Culture, 1974).

The list of lessons, published by the Ministry of Education in the 1970s for elementary teachers contains 96 pts. It was divided into four parts: i. Basic disciplinary studies (19 pts.) (Hebrew: 3 pts.; Geography of Israel and history of the country and the people (4 pts); Basic science and math. (8 pts.); English (2 pts.) and Tradition (2 pts.); ii. Pedagogical studies (41 pts.): Philosophy and sociology (4 pts.); Psychology (6 pts); Teaching: general theory and methods (8 pts.); Special Ed. (2 pts.) Special domain didactics (2 pts.); Hygiene (1 pts.); and Field Experience (18pts.). iii. Domain Specialization [subject matter or special ed.] 26 pts. (minimum of 15 pts. for major); iv. Miscellaneous (10 pts.): Arts and Crafts (4 pts.); Physical Ed. (4 pts.) and an elective such as technology in teaching (2 pts.). (Ministry of Education and Culture, 1974). A very similar program characterizes the American State Normal School curriculum; see: Conant, 1964; p. 196; Ogren, 2005, p. 87; 103).

Example 4: The B.Ed. "guiding model"

In 1981, the Israeli Council For Higher Education (CHE) [MALAG: Hamoaztza Lehaskala Gvoha] published a *Guiding Model* which defines the curriculum of the newly established B.Ed. program (CHE, 1981). According to this model, academic TEPs should reach two aims: To give students the best possible preparation for their role as teachers and to meet the standards of a four year bachelor-degree academic program. To achieve these aims, the curriculum has three components: Education, Subject-matter and Auxiliary studies. The model has slight variations depending on the school-level and the subject-matter involved. The archetype example is primary school teacher preparation (in what follows, 1pt. is equivalent to 56 contact hours):

    A.   Educational studies (28 pts. theoretical studies + 18 pts. practicum):

        a.   Theoretical studies:

        i.   The Theoretical bases of Education and its basic sciences:

                Introductory courses which include: Introduction to the Philosophy of Education; Introduction to the Psychology of Education; Introduction to the Sociology of Education; Introduction to Statistics and Research Methods.

                It is recommended that the first three subjects be learned with direct link to educational activities and to the work of teaching. It is best to place them in the second year of studies, after some practical experience has been taken by the students. They should be taught by teachers who had been teachers themselves.

                It is possible, instead, to merge the content of these courses with the courses of section ii.

The introduction to Statistics and Methodology has to emphasize those research methods that the teacher can use in his class, in order to examine new teaching methods or examine curricular issues, even if these methods defy generalization.

ii. A systematic discussion of selected educational issues in which the focus will be on applied knowledge taken from the theoretical bases of education and its basic sciences. (Such issues can be: Modern conceptions of education; The family and education; Education and social diversity; Cognitive development of children; Teacher-Student interaction; Students psychological health in school; Aims and principles of the open class; The personality of the teacher as a factor in teaching; The Nature of Pedagogical deliberations; Principles of Educational Management; The Educators' role; The Psychological basis of learning of skills; Teacher-principle-superintendent Relationships; Teaching in heterogeneous classroom; Special problems of children from deprived socio-economical background, etc.)

b. Didactic and Practicum in schools:

Teaching didactical issues should facilitate an encounter of the student with various and diverse methods of teaching, and develop his ability to deliberate about the relative merits of each of them to different classes, students, etc. The practicum should enable the student to experience different methods and the transfer between them.

The didactic courses should be followed by practicum in schools in teaching various subject-matters or special teaching methods (such as learning for mastery of active learning). This frame should address the new curricula.

The practicum should be in a variety of schools (e.g., schools in deprived areas). Respectively, the theoretical studies should contain courses devoted to the special needs of children from deprived background.

c. Seminars:

The seminars will be of various types, such as: implementation of knowledge taken from the theory of education and its basic sciences to solve educational issues; Critical analysis of an educational theory; empirical study.

...A general remark: In the courses and especially in the seminars the intention is that the student will encounter the research literature and will be able to learn himself the research methods on which the theoretical knowledge, the basis of the practice of teaching, is grounded – in order to prepare a teacher which will be a critical consumer of new scientific innovations.

B. Subject-Matter (48 pts.):

The student will learn 4 subject-matter areas, all of them should be taught at primary schools. It is recommended that at least one of them will be a major (18 or 24 pts.). No one of the other three can be less than 6 pts. [A regular BA major has been 24 pts.]

C. Auxiliary Courses:

English for academic purposes (4 pts.); Physical education (4 pts.); Arts (6 pts.)

(CHE, 1981)

The *Guideline Model* requires that 43% of the total student's learning time will be devoted to education, (26% in academic courses and 17% in practicum), 44% to subject-matter studies, and 13% to auxiliary courses. [To this list of courses, the Ministry of Education adds another 12 pts. of Hebrew/Arabic language and cultural (Jewish/Arabic) studies.]

Example 5: CBTE

The TEP in the University of Houston posits five propositions specifying the teacher's role:

"The teacher is a liberal educated person with a broad background in his teaching field.

The Teacher reflects in his actions that he is a student of human behavior. Teaching is an applied behavioral science: knowledge alone is not sufficient. Teachers should demonstrate the full range of competencies derived from psychology, multicultural education, socio-linguistics, sociology, philosophy and anthropology. Further, such understandings are translated into actions which reflect a realistic understanding of self and others... These two program aspects – self-understanding and formal study of the behavioral sciences – support program elements derived from the premise that teachers who better understand themselves and others are likely to be more efficient teachers.

The teacher makes decisions on a rational basis. The rational approach to decision making, and its attending paradigm, permeates the training program so that the prospective teacher can analyze important functions of his roles and the consequences of actions. The actions of the professional constitute an interrelationship between theoretical considerations and behavioral manifestations. The process includes four stages. (1) Goals and objectives are delineated based on perceived needs. (2) Strategies for achieving these goals and objectives are planned. (3) Plans for achieving goals and objectives are implemented. (4) The extent to which goals or objectives are achieved is evaluated. This rational approach is predicated on the belief that when professionals systematically analyze important functions of their roles and evaluate the consequences of their actions, they are more likely to be effective.

The Teacher employs a wide variety of appropriate communication and instructional strategies. This proposition is drawn from the premise that teachers who have a wider repertoire of skills and techniques of instruction, management, and communication are more likely to be effective.

The teacher exhibits behavior which reflects professionalism. This includes the ability to work closely with other persons in solving problems, as well as continual self-assessment..." (Houston, Jones, 1974)

These characteristics are manifested by 16 basic competencies that the prospective teacher should exhibit. "The prospective teacher: Diagnosis the learner's emotional, social, physical, and intellectual needs; Identifies and/or specifies instructional goals and objectives based on learner needs; Designs instruction appropriate to goals and objectives; Implements instruction that is consistent with plan; Designs and implements evaluation procedures which focus on learner achievements and instructional effectiveness; Integrates into instruction the cultural background of students; Demonstrates a repertoire of instructional models and teaching skills appropriate to specified objectives and to particular learners; Promotes effective pattern of classroom communication; Uses resources appropriate to instructional objectives; Monitors processes and outcomes during instruction and modifies instruction on the basis of feedback; Demonstrates an adequate knowledge of the subject matter which she/he is preparing to teach; Uses organizational and management skills to facilitate and maintain the social, emotional, physical, and intellectual growth of learners; Identifies and reacts with sensitivity to the needs and feelings of self and others; Exhibits openness and flexibility in making rational decisions; Works effectively as a member of a professional team; Analyzes professional effectiveness and continually strives to increase effectiveness" (Houston, Jones, 1974). These competencies are further divided to many sub-competencies which will not be reproduced here.

The modules are divided into five content areas: emotional (teaching and myself); psychological (human behavior); socio-cultural; curriculum; and teaching. The order in which they are taught is justified by the "concern theory" suggested by Frances Fuller (1969). The entire program lasts two years (30 pts. out of a total of 122 pts. for a first academic degree), contains 4 stages, and has 27 different ingredients (Houston, Jones, 1974). (The disciplinary subject matter areas are studied in the relevant faculties). Examples of modules designed in Israel are: Higher cognitive questions; Instructional and learning objectives; Preparation of tests for the evaluation of achievements; Lesson planning for small group work; Dividing a classroom population into groups (Perelberg, Kremer, 1977, p.51).

Chapter 5

Example 6: Reflective Teacher at the University of Maryland

The "Master Certification Program at the University of Maryland" (McCaleb et al., 1992) is a post graduate, one calendar program, requiring 43-49 semester hours of work, two scholarly papers and a comprehensive examination. To reinforce reflection, the students, called "scholar teachers", are organized in cohorts. The courses are:

First Session (six week summer school): 1. Models of Teaching (3 credits), theory and research of teaching as applied to models of instruction, form a social criticism stance; 2. Cognitive basis of Instruction (3 credits); 3. Teaching as a profession (3 credits), including the knowledge base of teaching and schooling, Social issues that affect teaching and learning and the role of research.

Second Session (fifteen weeks): 4. Research on effective teaching (3 credits); 5. Teaching reading and writing (3 credits); 6.Quantitative research methods (3 credits); 7.Specific method course (3-6 credits); 8.Content specific courses (3-6 credits).

Third Session (fifteen weeks): 9. Action research project (improvement of educational practice) (3 credits); 10. Proseminar on teaching (1 credit); 11. Internship (8 credits).

Fourth session (six week summer school): 12, Trends in curriculum (3 credits) (includes attention to social and ethical concerns broader than the classroom and school level; 13. Independent study (3 credits) to complete the action research and prepare for exams (p. 48 – 49).

Field experience occurs throughout the program. In the first session it includes visits to various educational environments. In the second the scholar-teacher observes the beginning of school and, later, experiences are coordinated with assignments given in the university courses. The third session includes an internship in two different and diverse school sites, and the scholar teachers are encouraged to visit each other (p. 48).

Example 7: Research Based TEP

The TEP for class teachers (primary schools teachers) in the University of Helsinki is a five years MA program. It consists of 300 ECT credits (1 ECT = 27 hours of work), 180 ECT at the bachelor level and 120 at the master level. The TEP includes the following components:

Communication studies and orientation studies (25 CR; 5 of them in the M.Ed level) (8% of the entire program):

Basics of curriculum planning; Language and communication skills (including: mother language, foreign language, and second national language); Information and communication technology in studies; Introduction to media education.

Main subject studies in education (140 CR; 80 of them in the M.Ed level) (47%):

Cultural bases of education (15 CR); Psychological bases of education (15 CR); Pedagogical bases of education (20 CR).

Research studies in education (70 CR; including 10 CR Bachelor's thesis and 40 CR Mater's thesis). The topics of the master's thesis are usually school-related. (Jakku-Sihvonen 2008, p. 228).

Teaching Practice (20 CR) (Main subject 12 CR; Minor subject 8 CR, all of them in the master level) (6.7%)

Minor subject studies: Multidisciplinary studies in subjects and cross-curricular issues taught in comprehensive school (60 CR) (20%) (All of them in the B.Ed. level)

Mother tongue and literature education (8 CR); Mathematics education (7 CR); Arts education, Crafts education, Physical education, Music education (13 CR); Didactics in humanistic subjects (History, religious or ethics studies) (6 CR); Didactics in environmental and science studies

(Geography, Biology, Physics, Chemistry) (12 CR); Optional courses (in any of the last mentioned domains (14 CR, 3-4 CR in each)

Optional minor subject and optional studies (75 CR) (25%) (40 of them in the B.Ed level)

(The program for secondary subject-matter teachers requires a BA in a subject (60 CR). Usually the Master is in the subject area and the pedagogical studies component is a minor (60 CR.))

See:
http://www.helsinki.fi/teachereducation/education/classteacher/curriculum%20for%20class%20teacher%20education%202008.pdf; (retrieved 20.07.2011).

For a general presentation of primary TEPs in Finland see: Niemi & Sihvonen, 2011, 37-38.

Example 8: The Layouts Model

The NAEM approach was partially adopted by the new CHE layouts for TEPs in Israel in 2006 (CHE, 2006). The primary TEP layout serves, again, as a typical example. The first assumption of the layouts is that: The professional teacher acts systematically in an 'evidence-based' manner on the basis of disciplinary and pedagogic-didactic knowledge about his own teaching and his students' learning. His deliberations are based on the understanding of learning processes, curriculum, and his students' needs. He has the skills and competencies needed in today's teaching-learning environments, and he knows to reasonably use various teaching-learning methods. Issues of social values and creativity are important aspects of this professional conception.

Compared with the former CHE guidelines (see example no. 4), the layouts reduce the total amount of studies from 108 pts. to 90-96 pts. They reduce the amount of the Educational Studies in the former B.Ed. programs (30-34% instead of 43%, though, the proportion can rise up to 53% if education is taken also as a minor disciplinary subject matter). The "teacher preparation" ingredient of the program is called the "basic layout". It is assumed that "There is a common knowledge base to all teachers, irrespective to subject or educational level because a teacher is first of all an educator, and only second a teacher of a specific subject" (CHE, 2006, p. 6).

The "basic layout" is divided into two ingredients: (A). Theoretical studies: i. Educational studies (min. 4 pts); Theoretical and practical studies essential to the work of educating and teaching and to the formation of the teacher as an educational person. ii. Pedagogy and Methods (min. 4 pts); General pedagogy and disciplinary didactics (PCK), including curriculum studies, disciplinary teaching, learning and evaluation methods. iii. Research Literacy (min. 2 pts), concentrating on qualitative methods like action research or case study. (B). Practicum (9-15 pts.) Active participation in schools' activities, recommended in a PDS model (CHE, 2006, p. 10 – 11). (Thus, although the practicum is 16% of the student's entire B.Ed. program, it can be up to 50% of the "basic layout". (In fact, because of the reduction of the whole program, the extent of the practicum, which had been 18 pts., reduces as well.))

The surface similarity between the 1981 CHE guiding model and the 2006 CHE layouts should not mislead. The layouts presuppose a different approach, according to which: Teaching is an activity anchored in both theoretical research and practical-reflective knowledge. It is not an apprenticeship occupation and it cannot be based on recipes. The success of any TEP depends on an explicit integration between the program's various ingredients as in strengthening its relevance to the students while they learn. This success also depends on an ecological understanding of teaching – the individual pupil, groups, the school, the community, and society (CHE, 2006, p. 6). Thus, for example, according to the "basic layout" any TEP should address the following list, which is not intended to be a list of courses but a list of topics which should permeate the entire course of studies: Moral - social – normative aspects of educator's work; Language across the curriculum; Development theories (cognitive, emotional, and social); Learning and Teaching Theories (including ICT); Planning, organizing, and evaluation in learning, in view of the systems' policies; Diversity of students with different needs and different socio-cultural backgrounds (CHE, 2006).

The program's subject-matter ingredient (60 pts.) can be studied either concurrently with or after the "the basic layout". The prospective teacher has to study either one extended or two regular majors in primary school subjects. Instead of one regular major he may study either a regular major in education (e.g., special ed.; informal ed.; math ed.; science ed.; literacy, etc.) or 2 disciplinary minors (except science, math, or ESL).

Example 9: Outcome based TEP (TERI)

TERI has seven core areas of focus:

1. Student Learning; 2. Adaptive Teaching; 3. Diversifying the Teacher Workforce; 4. Enhanced Clinical Experiences; 5. Strengthening our Curriculum; 6. Improving Teacher Support; and 7. Measuring Effectiveness. The TERI project partners with schools and districts across Minnesota, which provides teacher candidates the opportunity to receive hands on training in the school, working directly with students. "The project aims to measure teacher effectiveness by using student achievement and one year of academic growth in one year of instruction as the basis, which aligns with the Bush Foundation's model, which also emphasizes performance-based salary pay structure for teachers, based on a standardized assessment (Omari, 2011).

Chapter 6

Example 10: Teach for America

The program begins with a five-week intensive training program (summer institute) "designed to set corps members up for success from their first day of teaching". After this course the novice teachers are placed in schools, and have one-on-one coaching throughout the two years and an "extensive bank of online resources" (all the citations are taken from: http://www.teachforamerica.org/why-teach-for-america).

In the summer institute, through "planning, practice, observation, coaching, study, and reflection, corps members develop the knowledge, skills, and mindsets needed to be highly effective beginning teachers." The institute's course work addresses the issues of "Instructional Planning and Delivery", which presents a goal-oriented, standards-based approach to instruction, including diagnosing and assessing students, lesson planning, and instructional delivery; "Classroom Management and Culture", which teaches how to build a culture of achievement to maximize student learning; "Diversity, Community, and Achievement", which examines diversity-related issues new teachers may encounter; "Learning Theory", which focuses on learner-driven instructional planning; "Literacy Development" which explores elementary and secondary methods for teaching literacy.

The activities in the summer institute include:

1. Teaching:

Corps members teach summer school students for approximately two hours each day, under the supervision of experienced teachers. For the first hour, most corps members work directly with four to five students to build skills in math and literacy, to gain experience in facilitating group work. For the second hour, corps members lead a full class lesson, which builds skills in delivering lessons and managing a classroom.

2. Observations and Feedback

Teach For America instructors observe every corps member several times each week, provide them with written feedback, and engage in debrief conversations to help them refine their teaching practice.

3. Rehearsal Sessions

Corps members gather in small groups to rehearse upcoming lessons and to respond to potential classroom management challenges. Rehearsal sessions provide a safe space to practice new skills and receive feedback from Teach For America instructors and other corps members.

4. Lesson Planning Clinics

Corps members receive extensive lesson planning instruction from Teach For America instructors. They work to deeply understand student learning objectives for the coming week, determine the assessments that will be used to evaluate student progress, select the appropriate instructional methods to meet their objectives, and develop their plans in greater detail.

5. Curriculum Sessions

Corps members study the fundamentals of teaching, practice instructional techniques, and engage in exercises designed to prepare them for all elements of classroom instruction, including how to manage a classroom, how to plan effectively, and how to structure learning so students can understand complex concepts. Curriculum sessions also explore issues of diversity and how they might impact corps members' approach in their classrooms and communities.

6. Reflection Sessions

Corps members gather in small groups to analyze student progress and discuss the feedback and observations of "Teach For America" instructors, veteran district teachers, and other corps members. Corps members walk away with clear action steps to improve their effectiveness.

Teach For Israel (HOTAM) comprises 24 academic credits (8 in a summer program in a dormitory setting, and 16 credits in one-day-perweek of academic studies and distance learning courses). The summer semester deals with class management, planning, and specific subject method workshops. The yearly course shadows the student's work, and includes observations of his work, meeting with school and academy mentors. It mainly comprises methods of specific domains workshops, case studies of authentic experiences, and small group activities (http://tfi.org.il/Pages/Chotameducationaltraining.aspx; Hebrew, retrieved 08/2010).

Example 11: Boston Residency

The Boston Residency program (BTR) lasts for 13 months. Residents learn:

Year 1: July-August: Classroom management and lesson planning courses, work in summer school classes or content classes (depending on need).

Sept.-June: Four days a week in host school with mentor teacher; continue graduate level coursework; develop a teaching portfolio, consisting of performance-based assessments aligned with program and district standards.

July (2nd summer): Residents complete coursework for master's degree and work towards Special Education Licensure.

Year 2: Graduates have a full-time, paid teaching position with induction support from BTR and BPS (Boston Professional school). Complete Special Education licensure.

The Resident Weekly Schedule in year 1 is four days a week with a mentor teacher; classwork all-day on Fridays and one afternoon a week (Berry et al. 2008, p. 39).

Example 12: Relay Graduate School of Education

RSE Newark is a 200 hour program in a combination of online and in-person course work. It lasts a full year and the first summer covers 80 hours of them. During the fall and spring semesters, teachers participate in 120 hours of instruction on two weeknights a month and one Saturday a month. Each course addresses the following elements: Student Growth and Achievements; Teaching Cycle; Classroom Culture; Content (English, Math., Science, Social Studies); Self & Other people (See: http://www.relayschool.org, retrieved 8.2011).

Chapter 7

Example 13: Beit-Yaakov

The two-year curriculum is based on the ST model (see example 1). It has two ingredients:

1. Jewish studies: mainly Biblical stories and laws (including traditional interpreters). All women-related commandments (especially regarding holidays, kosher food, praying, marital relations, etc.). At the end of the studies there is a comprehensive exam on the Bible (the Tora), and all the laws which the women, who intend to be an educator, should know and enact. Special courses are devoted to a lesson called "Point of View" which address the religious way of looking at the world (27 pts).

2. Teacher Education:

Education: psychology (4 pts.), didactics (4), computers (2), methods of holy studies (1) alternative teaching methods

Practicum: observations and guided teaching. Practical Experience (85-90). This ingredient culminates in a "teaching exam".

Basic Studies: Hebrew, educational visits, physical ed. (20 lessons)

Subject Specialization (18 pts. including methods): Subject matter specialization (Hebrew, English, computers, mathematics...)

(http://www.peopleil.org/details.aspx?itemID=7407&searchMode=0&index=4).

Example 14: Soviet Union Pedagogical Institutes

i) In the 1960th, pedagogical institute in Leningrad, the TEP lasts for five years. The Curriculum includes:

a. Political and general courses (6%). In the USSR higher education all students "must attend classes in philosophy and theory of history, the history of the Communist party and of the Soviet Union, and the principles of political economy" (Grant, 1964, p. 25). General courses include sport, physical education, and foreign language.

b. Educational theory (13-20%). Psychology (mainly Pavlovian); Pedagogy (aims, moral education, disciplines, general teaching methods; school hygiene, visual aids, extracurricular activities).

c. Special subjects (40-70%): Two majors.

d. Teaching Practice (16-18 weeks starting in the third or fourth year; plus 3 weeks in a summer camp as leaders in a Pioneer camp) (Grant, 1964, p. 133 – 136).

ii) In 1989, the program in Moscow, includes "socio-political cycle", in which the subject "Foundations of Marxism-Leninism" lasted from Second year to the fourth year. In each year there were 2 semesters with 2 hours per week throughout the 3 years. It was 198 total hours. Study of Marxism-Leninism was compulsory. These courses were organized in various ways with various forms for students who wanted to be teachers. Subjects took the form ranging from "Principles of Marxism" to "Foundations of Marxism-Leninism" to much more specialized subjects like The History of the Communist Party of the Soviet Union, Marxist-Leninist philosophy, Political Economy and Scientific Communism. (Yan Man Kit, 2001, p. 81) In the interviews in Moscow with the respondents who were asked about the study of Marxism-Leninism in pedagogical institutions, they all mentioned the different courses they had studied, depending on the type of institutes and faculties. But the courses were mainly a combination of the subjects as follows: a) History of the Communist Party of the Soviet Union; b) Scientific Socialism; c) Political Economy; d) Atheism; e) Philosophy of Socialism; f) Materialism; g) Marxist-Leninist philosophy. All student teachers should attend all of these lectures, taking notes which were to be submitted for assessment, and at the end of the semester to sit for the examination. Taking such courses were universal for them regardless of what subject specialty they studied and what grades in school they would teach. To pass was necessary; if the student failed three times, they were asked to withdraw (Yan Man Kit, 2001, p. 81 – 82).

Example 15: Waldorf TEP

The components of Waldorf TEP:

1. Anthropological Studies

   Epistemology and the Philosophy of Freedom; The threefold nature of the human being; The tripartite soul: Thinking, feeling and Willing; Developmental stages of growth; The human being and the Kingdoms of nature; Recapitulation and the evolution of Consciousness; Reincarnation and Karma; Universal (Cosmic) Christianity

2. Waldorf Pedagogy: Child development; Curriculum Development; Teaching Methodology (Who: body, soul, spirit; why: philosophical justification; How: Teaching methodology; What: Curriculum studies

3. The Arts

4. The Crafts

5. Movement (Eurythmy and Spatial dynamics), Games and Sport

6. School organization and Management: The threefold social order (the school belongs to the social order); The college of teachers (the plenary of the teachers manages the school); Social and community relations

7. Classroom management

8. Teaching Practice

9. Meditative Training

   This program is based on the Threefold Curriculum for students (Steiner's The Philosophy of Freedom):

The plastic element (body-imagination): Modeling Painting, Carving, Drawing, etc.

The element of imagination in language and literature (to make the student see and create inner visions); The plastic forces in the kingdoms of nature, especially in Geology and Botany; The plastic forces in Geometry; The power of imagination in Fairy tales, Sages, legends, and mythology.

The Musical Element (astral body – Inspiration):

Music, harmonics, Tone, Euryhmy (harmonious rhythm); The musical element in the kingdoms of nature, especially in Zoology, Chemistry; The musical element in Arithmetic; Rhythms in the evolution of the growing human being (7 year periods); Study group on teaching and education.

The Speech Element (ego- Intuition):

Speech Formation, Speech Eurythmy; The dramatic element in history (Methods of teaching history); The evolution of individuality in mankind (Biographies); Comparative study on the spirit of different languages; Health and illness (What the educator has to know about medicine)

A common model of a three-year training program:

Year 1: Orientation Year in Anthroposophy and the Arts: Anthroposophy; Art; Crafts; Group work and Social skills training; Visits to anthroposophically based institutions

Year 2: Pedagogical studies: Arts, Crafts, and Movement; school based Group work and Social skills training; Practicum (two periods of at least four weeks).

Year 3: Pedagogical studies: Arts, Crafts, Movement; Practicum (two periods of six to eight weeks); meditative practice; school administration; special project. (Mazzone, 1999).

Chapter 9

Example 16: HOFFEN: Open Experimental Education

The following account is based on Eisenberg and Litvak (1994). The program includes three basic ingredients: Theoretical Studies in Education, Practical Studies and Personal and group activities:

Theoretical Studies in Education (9 pts):

Creative Self-Education: Education self-constructing work, variable in its scope, time and options;

Philosophy of open education: To enable the student to build his own theoretical credo;

Humanistic Psychology and developmental psychology;

Personal and professional identity: The self as teacher and as learner;

Differential Teaching: Diversity and variability in the classroom and methods to deal with them.

Practical Studies (15 pts):

Practical experience: 10 weekly hours of field experience (preschool, elementary school, or middle-high school). The student gradually proceeds from being observant to be responsible to teach lessons. He is supervised by a school teacher and a College mentor visits him at work.

Supervision: A weekly meeting in cohorts to discuss issues which arise from the field experience.

Methods in Open Education: E.g., how to develop a topic, how to work in integrative manner, building projects, events, etc.

Good morning work: On morning a week in which the student works on a topic he wants to explore. This activity is supervised by program faculty members.

Learning Resources: Workshop to prepare various learning resources.

School's Competencies: A brief presentation in which the student encounters the aims, the curricula and the methods of each of the school subject-matter areas.

Personal and group activities (10 pts.)

Students' Workshop: Each week one of the students presents the cohort with something he chooses and receives feedback.

Weekly meeting: Open forum to discuss issues raised by the participants.

Self-education center: An open environment in which students share their concerns (e.g., how my learning is influenced by stress).

The Program Evening: in which the entire cohort and faculty (1) encounters new themes; (2) participate in social and learning activities organized by the students; (3) prepare and actualize various events

Enhancement Workshops: designed to fit the students' requests and each of them empowers the student's personality and enables a meaningful exploration of his strengths and weakness (e.g., music, nature, watching television, karate, yoga, or psychodrama)

The program is variable:

The courses last between 25 minutes to 4-5 hours;

The courses are conducted in different learning environments (including outdoor lessons);

The arrangement of the class (informal gathering, or sitting in a circle, with or without tables);

The cohort is divided in various manners;

Different instruction method;

Different level of required students' participation;

Varied responsibility to the lesson: the teacher alone, the teacher and the students, the students alone.

The Structure of the program:

First Semester:

The program begins with a marathon of 3-6 days in which the student experiences the program. An integrative topic is presented in a multidimensional manner.

The program includes mandatory and elective courses. It is presented to the students and for the next three weeks he is invited to participate in as many electives as he wishes so that he might choose among them.

After three weeks the student builds his own course of studies (He can choose 36 out of 50 hours). Though he has no choice on the mandatory courses, he still can have an influence on the special issues dealt within each of them and on the methods of teaching-learning they pursue.

At the end of the semester the students evaluate each course, and they can ask for new courses.

Between the semesters the students participate in marathons and journeys on their own initiative.

Second Semester:

Many of the mandatory courses become electives. The students can ask for workshops they want to include in the program (depending on the number of the interested students). Workshops from the first semester are continuous if students request them. After the first two weeks, the students build their course of studies. There are more marathons if the students request them. Three times a year the students present their projects to their peers.

Example 17: Humanistic Teacher Education

The program lasts 5 to 7 quarters, 16-18 academic hrs. It is divided into four large components:

1. The Substantive Panel and Field Experience. In the Substantive Panel, curriculum, foundations, and content experts provide: general presentations and demonstrations; programs for groups with common needs; consultation as needed on learning activities; individual counsel and aid; self-directed study.

2. Community Session (1 hr. per week)

3. Continuous Seminar (15 students; 2 hrs. per week): Guidance, Planning, Discussion and Evaluation.

4. An example on Student Z practicum studies:

Weeks 1-10: Observed 10 times in multi-age classes at school A (A rather modern well equipped campus school where flexible, open teaching occurred).

Weeks 1-10: Tutored a youngster at the same school.

Weeks 11-19: Teacher initiate in second-grade level at school B (a well-equipped suburban school in an affluent part of city where the student was exposed to a self-contained classroom taught by a rather authoritarian teacher).

Weeks 20-30: Assistant teacher on six-grade level at school C (a rather poorly-equipped school located in an inner-city ghetto area in which an open classroom was in operation).

Weeks 31-40: Assistant teacher at school D on the second-level (a "prestigious" school).

Weeks: 41-50: Associate teacher at school E in a third-grade classroom in a rural community.

Weeks 51-60: Student interns at school E (takes complete charge of same third grade classroom.

The amount of time between the substantive panel and the field experience is proportionally inversed as the program goes on.

In the program, there are three assessment points: at the entrance, at midpoint (for diagnosis and plan for progress), and a final evaluation (Combs et al. 1972, p. 149 – 150).

Example 18: Realistic Teacher Education

The following account is based on Korthagen et al. 2001. The program has been developed in close cooperation with school administrators and mentor teachers. The study load of the program is 56 cr. (1680 hours), half are "school-connected" activities and the other half on-campus activities. The school connected activities include at least 250 classroom hours, of which at least 120 hours have to be taught by the student teacher. 300 hours (in both campus and school) are devoted to inquiry-oriented activities (Korthagen et al. 2001, p. 34). The program is structured as an alteration of blocks of studies, on campus and in schools. It is combined of six phases, including an orientation phase (additional two months) designed for undergraduates students. It is presupposed that the graduate students have already studied this phase (p. 35).

1. The Orientation Course includes a sample of the entire program. It includes 4 weeks of on-campus activities and 4 weeks of practicum. The on-campus course of studies includes: training observation and discussion skills and social and communicative skills; practice in simulations of teaching and role playing; reflection on the important pedagogical and subject-related principles that surface during these experiences; and visiting schools (3 days).

2. The Introduction phase lasts for two weeks. It is intended as a reminder of the orientation course, and a preparation for the next phase. The students are involved in giving 5 to 10 minute lessons to each other, supervise group discussions, etc. They are required to reflect on those experiences and to formulate pedagogical principles.

3. Triad Teaching Practice Period (14 weeks). Three students work together as a group under the close supervision of a cooperative teacher and a university supervisor. This period contains two blocks of school practicum. In the first 2 1/2 weeks, student teachers proceed from teaching parts of lessons to a series of lessons. In the second block (5 weeks) they teach individual lessons, a series of lessons, and they take responsibility for teaching a certain subject during the week. Studies between the two blocks are intended for exchange and analysis of field experiences, and they include supervision conferences.

4. Reorientation (10 weeks) intended for reflection and deepening the insights. The prospective teachers write a paper about their experience, and study issues they want to explore, based on relevant research (a practice-oriented research program). To look at the teaching profession from a broader professional perspective, they study school organization.

5. Independent Final Teaching Practice (14 weeks). Held in a different school than the first practical period, the student functions like a regular teacher (10-12 hours a week), although the ultimate responsibility still lies with the cooperative teacher. This practicum, which addresses both the quality of work and the professional development of the prospective teacher, are supervised "at-a-distance". There are university supervisory conferences, and student teachers meet on a weekly basis with their cohort group to share experiences, problems, ideas, and resources.

6. Concluding phase (3 weeks). Final assessment of the student's competence based on his practice results, a submitted report or portfolio, and discussions.

Example 19: The MT at the University of Calgary

The following description in based on the handbook of the MT program (1997-1998). The MT is a postgraduate TEP, delivered over two academic years (4 semesters). Each semester has an organizing theme:

Learners and Learning (semester 1): Exploration of the phenomenon of learning in psychological, sociological, philosophical and pedagogical terms. Understanding of the self as learner is also emphasized.

Teaching and Teachers (semester 1): Exploration of the phenomenon of teaching in terms of its purpose, history, practices, theories, and its personal and ethical dimensions. Understanding of the self as teacher is also emphasized.

Curriculum Contexts (semester 2): Exploration of political, social and cultural contexts in which curriculum is enacted;

Curriculum Studies (semester 2): Exploration of curriculum development and teaching practices specific to early childhood, elementary and secondary education (in different groups);

Praxis (semester 3): Exploration of teaching as a collaborative, inquiry oriented reflective practice in the context of a 13 week practicum;

Integration (semester 4): Exploration of the ethical and moral dimensions of teaching.

The themes are studied in campus (Integrated lecture series; Case-based tutorials; Professional Inquiry seminars; Independent studies), and in the field (School-based Practice; Community-Work place experiences; Field based inquiry Seminar; Independent Studies). Over the entire program there is a regular and ongoing narrative assessment in each component.

The weekly schedule of the student includes:

Year 1: 2 days on campus (Independent study; Professional Seminar; Lecture; Tutorial Case work; Field Inquiry Seminar; Case Team Work, and Advisement) and two days of "field experience". The placements include schools (half semester) and community and workplace sites (half semester) each lasting for 5 weeks (15 hrs/week). In the middle of the semester there is a week devoted to independent work ("reading week"). In semester two, the entire field experience is in schools.

Year 2: Semester 1: 4 days of field experience; a day in campus: Advisement; Case team work, Independent study

Year 2: Semester 2: 2 days of field experience (usually devoted to the independent study); Professional Seminar (dealing with the professional identity of the student); Lecture (to be replaced by an elective); Case Team Work, Individual Study and Advisement.

Since 1998 there were very little changes in the program, though most of them were separate attempts to react to some criticisms. Thus, for example, the professional seminar of year 1 was shortened to accommodate an additional method course, and a special ed. course replaced the elective course in semester 4. (For a detailed description of the MT program see: Lund, in press.)

Example 20: ACE (Kaye College of Education)

Based on: Barak & Gidron, 2009. The program for primary teacher education is:

Year 1: Wisdom of practice I (4 pts.); Electives (2 pts.); Modes of learning (1 pts.); Literacy (1 pts.); Community of learning (1 pts.); Class environment (1 pts.); Field Experience (4 pts.); Identity (1 pts.); Children's world (1 pts.)

Year 2: Field Experience (6 pts.); Wisdom of Practice II (4 pts.); Community of learning (1 pts.) Elective (1 pts.); Subject Methods (1 pts.); Parents/children/teachers (1 pts.)

NOTES

[1]   See, for example the papers collected in Sandlin, Scultz and Burdick, 2010.

[2]   For some recent attempts to cope with these issues, see, for example: Berry et al. 2011; Salen et al. 2011; Selwyn, 2011; Facer, 2011.

[3]   See Saltman, 2009, for a similar account of what happens in the USA.

[4]   Private-Sector Teacher Education programs may have another advantage. As Sosale emphasizes, from a purely economic point of view, "The underlying principle is that strengthening the private sector's role in non-compulsory education will release public resources for the compulsory (primary) level. The private sector is emerging as a force governments, donors, and other technical assistance agencies cannot ignore" (Sosale, 2000). So private teacher education programs may be, after all both feasible and recommended. The threat to current public TEPs cannot be ignored.

[5]   The classical transmission model does not seem to work in a heterogeneous, all-inclusive, democratic educational environment (cf. Darling-Hammond, 2006, p. 10).

[6]   Similarly, Calderhead & Shorrock (1997, p. 2) remark that: "Teacher education, in effect, is too complex to be characterized by any one of these orientations alone, and inevitably encapsulates aspects of them all".

[7]   While each of the models presupposes a different meaning of the term 'professional', it may be questioned whether the above models, except the clinician, really warrant the label 'professional'. Abbott (1988), for one example, suggests that any profession deals with problem-solving activities which follow a three step process: diagnosis, routines or inferences, and treatment. This process can be properly found only in the clinician-professional model, the other ones seem to display different features.

[8]   For other psychological theories, which connect the notion of identity to that of morality, see the surveys of Bergman, 2004 or Lapsley, 2008. Both authors emphasize the ideas of Blasi for whom "the integration of morality and personality is key" (Bergman, 2004, p. 33): "The best answer to the question, Why be moral?, may thus be, because that is who I am, or, because I can do no other and remain (or become) the person I am committed to being" (p. 37).

[9]   Another website similarly insists that: "You have to be before you can do, and you have to do before you can have" (http://www.stacistallings.com/lifelessonbedohave.htm; 29/10/2010).

[10]   The German term *Bildung* is usually translated as 'education', but as we will see below, it is has both a more specific meaning (akin to self-formation) and more general meaning (akin to culture). In order to retain the original meaning of the term, I will not translate it. I will return to the notion of *Bildung* in chapters 5 and 8.

[11]   For example: the logical maxim called 'Modus Ponens' (if p than q, p and therefore q) is valid no matter who states it and what is the content of the specific statements that the variables p and q substitute (e.g., If there is rain (p) there are clouds (q); there is rain (p), and therefore there are clouds; If there is smoke (p), there is fire (q); There is smoke (p), and therefore there is fire (q); If I win the lottery (p) I buy a new house (q); I win the lottery (p) hence I buy a new house (q). Another example is the classical syllogism: "All the Greeks are mortal, Socrates is Greek; Hence, Socrates is mortal. It is possible to replace the three notions (Greek, Socrates, Mortal), with other notions (such as: , males ,smokers, , risk their life…) and as far as the statements which represent the argument's antecedents are true, the conclusion, which appears after the word 'hence' must be true).

[12]   Popper's full schema is much more complicated. TT is a shortened notation for a multiplicity of options, TT_1, TT_2,…,TT_n, which the scientists should check and find the one which is the closest to the truth (Popper, 1972, p. 243).

[13] The logic and the psychology of formal practical reasoning have been extensively discussed within the fields of logic, game-theory, psychology, decision-theory, and economics.

[14] The empirical research regarding the common idea of what is happiness is based on what interrogates say when they are asked about their SWB (subjective well-being, i.e., the amount of happiness they feel).

[15] This phenomenon is called the paradox of happiness. See for example the papers in the second part of Bruni & Porta, 2007, pp. 127 – 236.

[16] Hem and Haw, the heroes of "*Who Moved my Cheese*", decorate the walls of their maze with the slogan: "Having cheese makes you happy". "Finding Cheese", the author explains, "was the Little people's way of getting what they thought they needed to be happy… For some, finding Cheese was having material things. For others it was enjoying good health or developing a spiritual sense of well-being. For Haw, Cheese just meant feeling safe, having a loving family someday and living in a cozy cottage on Cheddar Lane. To Hem, Cheese was becoming a Big Cheese in charge of others and owning a big house atop Camembert Hill (Johnson, 1998, p. 9–10).

[17] In 1990 Feiman-Nemser finds that in the US TEPs "The balance between… the liberal and the technical seems tilted in the direction of the technical"… (p. 217). This inclination has been intensified in the last decades.

[18] See: Lieberman, 1956, p, 2; Shermis & Ollich, 1965, p. 293 – 294, Parsons, 1968, p. 537; Schön, 1983; Abbott, 1988.

[19] I will return to the notion of *Bildung* in chapters 5 and 8.

[20] For a detailed history of the American State Normal School see: Herbst, 1989; or Ogren, 2005.

[21] The Austrian case is representative. "For more than a hundred years, universities were only obliged to provide the theoretical foundations in two academic subjects and pedagogy for (prospective) teachers, who, after completion of their studies at university, had to take a state examination. Having passed this state examination, graduates had to go in for a practical training at schools, training that was organized and supervised by school administration as well" (based on: http://www.see-educoop.net/education_in/pdf/techer-educ-austria.pdf.). Typically enough, during the four-and-a-half year university training program, only 16 percent of the curricula are dedicated to special didactics, pedagogy, and school practice (Schratz & Resinger, 2003, p. 20).

[22] Such a curriculum was implemented in Israel in the 70s, when a third year of studies was added to the seminars to enable them to prepare teachers for the newly established junior high schools by incorporating a subject-matter specialization element to the program (See Appendix example 3).

[23] Not much has changed since 1946. In 2000, it is still the case that "The components of teacher education programs—collections of courses, field experiences, and student teaching—tend to be disjointed; they are often taught or overseen by people who have little ongoing communication with each other. Even when the components are efficiently organized, there may be no shared philosophical base among the faculty" (NCR, 2000, p.201).

[24] Cf.: "One alumnus reported the problem with his teacher education program: "I could talk about Carl Jung, scaffolding, cooperative learning groups,[and] the advantages of constructivism," but had no idea what to do "when Johnny goes nuts in the back of the class, or when Lisa comes in abused, or when Sue hasn't eaten in three days." What he described is a symptom of a serious underlying problem described by one education alumnus as "an abyss" between theory and practice" (Levine, 2006, p. 39).

[25] For a detailed analysis of the CBTE movement see: Back, 2005.

[26] In some of its versions P (Performance) replaces C (Competency). For the differences between the two versions, see: Kelly, 1974.

[27] The process of how the CBTE in Houston had been replaced by the reflective practitioner approach is described by Clift et al. (1992, p. 121 – 123).

[28] Loughran and others conceive of it as a distinct discipline. See the articles in the Journal *Teacher and Teaching: Teaching and Practice*, 2009, 15, 2.

[29] "...techne arises, when from many notions gained by experience one universal judgment about similar objects is produced. For to have a judgment that when Callias was ill of this disease this did him good, and similarly in the case of Socrates and in many individual cases, is a matter of experience; but to judge that it has some good to all persons of a certain constitution, marked off in one class, when they were ill of disease..., — this is a matter of techne" (Aristotle, 1984, Met., I, 1, 981[a] 6-12; cf., Pos. An., II, 19 100[a] 6-10; E.N., X, 9, 1180[b] 20-22).

[30] Aristotle reiterates the same point a few lines later: "...for it is from playing the lyre that both good and bad lyre-players are produced. And the corresponding statement is true of builders and all the rest; men will be good or bad builders as a result of building well or badly. For if this were not so, there would have been no need of a teacher, but all men would have been born good or bad at their craft" (E.N., II, 1, 1103[b] 8-12). And in another place he declares that: "...a man will not have the techne when he has ceased to use it" (Met., IX, 3, 1047[a] 3, and see also the preceding lines, beginning in 1046[b] 34).

[31] In *The Fragility of Goodness* (2001, p. 95 – 99), Martha C. Nussbaum discusses Aristotle's criteria of *techne*. She follows Metaphysics. I., 1, and finds that *techne* has four features: universality, teachability, precision, and concern with explanation. All but the third feature has to do with the productive-theory. The third acknowledges that in human affairs a precision (which means a rule which is always true) is unattainable.

[32] The TEP devised by Korthagen et al. (2001), to be discussed in chapter 9, provides another example of this approach (See: Appendix example 18).

[33] This concept of reflection is evident in official documents in the 1990s in the US. Porter et al. (2001) review three widespread teaching concepts and find that all of them "stress the need for teachers to engage in reflective practice. The content of the reflection is to plan the next step, to improve teaching skills over time, and to foster the collaboration with others" (p. 265 – 266).

[34] For a somewhat different classification see: Hatton & Smith, 1995, p. 59. Valli's first "technical" level roughly corresponds to the technical and descriptive types of reflection in Hatton and Smith. Dialogue, critical and intrapersonal types deal with hearing one's voice, taking account of social/political or cultural forces, and the effects of one's own biography and feelings.

[35] The idea of "Professional Development School", has been introduced in the US by the Holmes Group (1985, p. 66): "Unique and particularly intense school–university collaborations, PDSs were designed to accomplish a four-fold agenda: preparing future educators, providing current educators with ongoing professional development, encouraging joint school–university faculty investigation of education-related issues, and promoting the learning of P–12 students" (NAPDS, 2008). According to NCATE standards, PDS should be characterized by "I: Learning community – at the heart of the PDS, this represents the teaching and learning activities, philosophies, and environments created in these partnerships. II: Accountability and quality assurance – assessment of the partnership and its outcomes in ways that address the PDS's accountability to its various stakeholders. III: Collaboration – the partnership's formation and the development of an increasingly interdependent committed relationship. IV: Diversity and equity – how the PDS prepares a diverse group of educators to provide learning opportunities for all students. V: Structures, resources and roles – how the PDS organizes itself to support and do its work. (NCATE, 2001).Thus "PDS... are more than simply places where teacher candidates complete their clinical experiences. Instead, they are schools whose faculty and staff as a collective whole are committed to working with college/university faculty to offer a meaningful introduction to the teaching profession. As such, PDSs create a school-wide culture that incorporates teacher candidates as full participants of the school community" (NAPDS, 2008, http://www.napds.org/9%20Essentials/statement.pdf).

[36] This point has an empirical consequence. Reflection is both time consuming and faculty consuming, since it requires intensified supervision. If it is not effective, it may be easily relinquished in times of economic crisis.

[37] For Humboldt, the universal concept of humanity is found in the hidden dimension of the world (1793/2000, p. 59),which is part of the authentic self.

[38] This view is not without its problems, for teachers research is still suspected as a kind of scientific endeavor (Cochran-Smith & Lytle, 2009, p. 86 – 117).

[39] Art Levine, in a different survey of excellent TEPs, finds that "Each is committed to preparing excellent teachers and has clearly defined what an excellent teacher needs to know and be able to do. This is translated into a coherent, integrated, comprehensive, and up-to-date curriculum. The field experience component of the curriculum is sustained, begins early, and provides immediate application of theory to real classroom situations. There is a close connection between the teacher education program and the schools in which students teach, including ongoing collaboration between academic and clinical faculties. All have high graduation standards" (2006, p.81).

[40] According to Kirchgassner, "This means that an individual acts according to his own preferences (and not according to the preferences of others). Of course, he can take into account the interests of others in his preferences; in an extreme case, he can be envious or malevolent, but also altruistic and benevolent. As a rule, however, 'the axiom of self-interest' is presupposed: The individual acts exclusively according to his own interests. Thus, envy, malevolence, altruism, and benevolence are excluded. Of course, the individual knows that he does not live in isolation, but within a society. Corresponding 'social orientations', for example, the desire to live in a democratic society, are part of his preferences. The interests of other individuals are taken into account, however, only insofar as they influence the individual's range of action" (2008, p. 15).

[41] This is not entirely accurate, as can be seen from TERI (see: Appendix, example 9).

[42] Lemov's book is a compilation of the techniques and is presented as a toolbox for teachers who want to improve their craft. For example, Technique 1: NO OPT OUT. "In typical classes, when students don't know an answer, or don't want to try, they quickly learn the teacher will leave them alone if they respond to a question with "I don't know" or shrugging their shoulders. The teacher then moves on to another student. Instead, NO OPT OUT is a useful tool to get all students to the right answer, as often as possible, even if only to repeat the correct answer. For example, on day 1 to review you ask Charlie, "What is 3 times 8?" He mutters, "I don't know" and looks away. Many teachers don't know how to respond, and students come to use "I don't know" to avoid work all year long. Instead, at a minimum, you can turn to another student, ask the same question, and if you get the correct answer, turn back to Charlie, "Now you tell me what is 3 times 8." Charlie, and all of the students, have just learned that they can't get off the hook and must do the work in your class. In a more rigorous form of NO OPT OUT you or another student can provide a cue. For example, in a class where a student was unable to identify the subject of the sentence, "My mother was not happy" the teacher asked another student, "When I am asking you for the subject, what am I asking for?" The second student responded, "You are asking for who or what the sentence is about." Then the teacher turned to the first student and said, "When I ask for the subject, I am asking for who or what the sentence is about. What's the subject?" This time the student was able to respond correctly, "Mother." The sequence began with the student unable to answer and ended up with him giving a correct answer. Note that the tone in most classrooms that use NO OPT OUT is positive and academic and using it only reinforces the teacher's belief in students' ability to get the right answer." A summary of the book's main ideas, under the title "Teach like a champion" can be found in the website: (http://media.wiley.com/assets/3006/21/TeachLikeAChampion_TheMainIdea.pdf (Retrieved 06/09/2011).

[43] Lemov's techniques have also been adapted in the Teach For America and Boston Teacher Residence TEPs.

[44] If as Honneth (2008) suggests, cognition presupposes recognition, it becomes even more ifficult to achieve the aim that pupils will learn.

[45] Especially, he obeys the principle that the relations between his various preferences have the logical features of completeness, reflexivity, and transitivity (Hahn & Hollis, 1979, p.4).

[46] The translation of the Bible 'All that the Lord hath spoken will we do, and obey.' (Exodus, 24, 7) misses the Hebrew origin which is "we shall do and listen".

[47] Tönnies (1887/1957) differentiates between two forms of society, *Gemeinschaft* and *Geselleschaft*. *Gessellschaft* (often translated as 'society') is a social group in which the membership is sustained by some instrumental goal. Examples of *Gesellschafts* are the city or the state. *Gemeinschaft* (often translated as 'community') is like an organism which is structured around a non utilitarian ingredient (e.g., the family or the neighborhood). In this definition, *Gemeinschaft* has a strong Romantic flavor.

[48] "Единица — вздор, единица — ноль, Один – дажееслиоченьважный – неподыметпростоепятивершковоебревно"(Владимир Маяковский: *Владимир Ильич Ленин* .(Retrived, 07.07.09 from:http://mayakovsky.narod.ru/Mayakovsky_files/Poemy/Lenin.htm).

[49] Thus:

"1. The peer collective (under adult leadership) rivals and early surpasses the family as the principal agent of socialization.

2. Competition between groups is utilized as the principal mechanism for motivating achievement of behavior norms.

3. The behavior of the individual is evaluated primarily in terms of its relevance to the goals and achievements of the collective.

4. Rewards and punishments are frequently given on a group basis; that is to say, the entire group benefits or suffers as a consequence of the conduct of individual members.

5. As soon as possible, the task of evaluating the behavior of individuals and of dispensing rewards and sanctions is delegated to the members of the collective.

6. The principal methods of social control are public recognition and public criticism, with explicit training and practice being given in these activities. Specifically, each member of the collective is encouraged to observe deviant behavior by his fellows and is given opportunity to report his observations to the group. Reporting on one's peers is esteemed and rewarded as a civic duty.

7. Group criticism becomes the vehicle for training in self-criticism in the presence of one's peers. Such public self-criticism is regarded as a powerful mechanism for maintaining and enhancing commitment to approved standards of behavior, as well as the method of choice for bringing deviants back into line" (Bronfenbrenner, 1962).

These methods should ensure that the child would gradually internalize these ideas :

First Stage: Elementary ideas of good and bad; Love of the Motherland; Industriousness and frugality; Truthfulness, honesty, modesty, and kindness; Friendship and comradeship; Discipline; Love of studies and conscientiousness; Good social conduct (Grant, 1964, p. 51 – 52).

Middle stage: Soviet patriotism, and Solidarity with the working people all over the world; Realization of social duty; Discipline, persistence, and endurance; Friendship and comradeship (tell the truth to the other's face); Attentive and thoughtful attitude towards people; Truthfulness, honesty, and modesty, having a proper attitude to criticism, resist bad influences; Responsibility attitudes towards study and work (including concern for the study achievements of the whole class) (Grant, 1964, p. 53 – 54).

Senior stage: More stress on personal and social responsibility, and on the fitting of young people for their duties as adults, members of families, workers, and citizens of the USSR (Grant, 1964, p. 53 – 54).

[50] There were 3 types of TEPs in the USSR: 1. A four year course as a special high-school path (replaced later by a two year course for high-school graduates); 2. A five year academic course in Pedagogical Institutes; 3.Graduates of universities (five years of study concentrating on subjects and political subjects, with less pedagogical courses and practice).

[51] The 1950s Israeli model, described in Appendix Example 1, has many points of resemblance with the USSR one.

[52] For Anita Brookner, for instance, Romanticism is a movement in the literal sense of the word. Instead of providing a definition, she characterizes the Romantic as someone who believes that "it is better to travel hopefully than to arrive" (Brookner, 2001, p.1).

[53] Citations from *The Little Prince* (referenced by chapter number in Roman letters) refer to Catherine Woods' (1943) classical translation. I have corrected some mistranslations.

[54] This idea is repeated time and again in the book. For example, "Children should always show great forbearance toward grown-ups" (chap IV). In chap. VII, to talk like an adult is an offense. And one of book's last sentences is "And no grown-up will ever understand that this is a serious matter" (chap. XXVII).

[55] In chapter II., the Little Prince requests the author to draw a sheep. After some unsuccessful attempts, the author draws a box and says to the Little Prince: "This is only his box. The sheep you asked for is inside." To this, the Little Prince replies: "That is exactly the way I wanted it! Do you think that this sheep will have to have a great deal of grass". Later on, he even worries that the sheep will eat his rose and ask the author to add a bridle to the drawing.

[56] The Little Prince himself mistakenly believes that his rose does not love him because he attunes himself to what she openly says and not to how she feels deep inside (chap. VIII). He does not yet realize that "...words are the source of misunderstanding ..." (Chap. XXI).)

[57] Chapter IV explains the difference between the children and the grown-ups. The author discovers that The Little Prince comes from an asteroid known as B-612, and he continues:

> If I have told you these details about the asteroid, and made a note of its number for you, it is on account of the grown-ups and their ways. When you tell them that you have made a new friend, they never ask you any questions about essential matters. They never say to you, "What does his voice sound like? What games does he love best? Does he collect butterflies?" Instead, they demand: "How old is he? How many brothers has he? How much does he weigh? How much money does his father make?" Only from these figures do they think they have learned anything about him...

> The [grown-ups] are like that. One must not hold it against them. Children should always show great forbearance toward grown-up people. But certainly, for us who understand life, figures are a matter of indifference. I should have liked to begin this story in the fashion of the fairy-tales. I should have liked to say: 'Once upon a time there was a little prince who lived on a planet that was scarcely any bigger than himself, and who had need of a friend.' To those who understand life, that would seem to be much truer (chap. IV)

[58] This point of view is of no surprise. It has been a response to Kant's critical philosophy. According to Kant, reason is limited and can comprehend only what we perceive. Moreover, what we perceive is only phenomenal, so that the "world" is only our construction (for we cannot see the "things by themselves"). However, if Kant is correct, it is possible to conclude that our limited reason may not be the best guide to knowledge and understanding. Perhaps we have to turn to other human faculties that are better equipped to perform this job. Imagination turns out to be the required faculty that can bring meaning to our constructed world. After all, even the visible world is just a product of our imagination. Therefore, to attain the true, the beautiful, the good, one has to turn to one's own creative imagination.

[59] This is a recurrent theme in the book. The author confesses that he "lived his life alone, without anyone that [he] could really talk to" (chap. II). He is afraid that if he will forget The Little Prince he will resemble the grown-ups. He disparately regrets that "not everyone has had a friend" (chap. IV). The Little Prince himself, disappointed by the rose, embarks on his journey to look after a friend. While on Earth, he shouts from the height of the mountain to the echo of his own voice: "Be my friends, I am all alone", only to get the echo's response: "I am all alone - I am all alone - I am all alone" (chap. XIX).

[60] *"Ich will meinsein"*; quoted in: Armstrong, 2006, p. 262.

[61] In a famous Hasidic story, which Buber retells times and again, "Before his death, Rabbi Zusya said 'In the coming world, they will not ask me: Why were you not Moses? They will ask me: Why were you not Zusya?" (Buber, 1956, I, 251).

[62] This attitude reminds Humboldt's idea, mentioned above (endnote no. 41), about the universal concept of humanity (see: 1793/2000, p. 59).

[63] The Jewish philosopher Aharon David Gordon, who migrated to Palestine at the dawn of the 20th century, expressed this approach. For him, the Nation is like "a funnel, which from its broad side receives the [universe's] infinite existence and from the narrow side ... pours everything into one's soul ..." (Gordon, 1958, p. 1, §1, III). The Nation gets its living power from its connectedness to Nature, "which makes it a living body, apart from what is called society which is nothing but an artificial grouping, without the breath of life" (Gordon, 1958, p. 1, §1, V). For Gordon, the specific relation of each Nation with Nature distinguishes between the various nations because it is territory dependent. It comes "from a place of the unification of the nation's nature with the nature of its land of birth and growth (Gordon, 1958, p. 2, §1, VII). This is the source of life and creation, the source of the nation's top affluence and strength.

For Gordon, the individual *qua* individual does not lose his self-identity in this context. On the one hand, the "individual's personality is nothing but a cell in the collective personality of the nation" (Gordon, 1958, p.7, §4, XXI). However, on the other hand, like in any healthy organism,

> ...[T]he existence of a national "self" is dependent on the private "I" of the nations' individuals. The more the individuals of the nation are stronger and the more deep and solid is their individuality, that is, the more it is internal, and expresses quality of the their soul, instead of being the fruit of their brain or their reading, the more secure becomes the existence of the nation, the existence of the national "I"... (Gordon, 1958, p.15, §8, ILIII).

The Hebrew word "Nation" (*Ouma*) comes from the same lexical root of the word "mother" (*Ima*). The Nation forms a big family, to which each individual brings his own contribution. However, being part of a family does not mean that the individual loses his identity or his uniqueness. To love your family and to be devoted to it means to live more fully as an individual. The familial environment enables the human being to take part in the entire cosmos.

[64] Other authors are a bit more balanced. Frederick Hertz claims that "one can derive from Romanticism any political principle one pleases except a sober, calculating policy which gives no scope for imagination or emotion (Hertz, 1975, p. 53), but he cites Alfred Stein who admits that although "Romanticism has discovered new territory, full of the magnificent fruits... it has shown harmful seeds in many a fields and robbed healthy growth of air and light by its luxuriant tendrils" (p. 55).

[65] Moreover, as some scholars argue, authenticity is for Heidegger, "always the authenticity of the German people (*Volk*) understood as organic totality" (Rockmore, 2009, p. xvi; cf. Faye, 2009, pp. 15 – 18).

[66] Cf.: Every human becomes "a kind of artist who freely shapes one's self as a work of art" (Golomb, 1990, p. 244).

[67] For an illusstaration of this attitude, see, for example, the first part of *Jonathan Livingstone Seagull* (Bach & Munson, 1970)). Interesing enough, in the next parts of the book Bach passes from created authenticity to a given one, as the seagull finds that his created identity reflects his "true", inborn nature.

[68] In a similar fashion, a web-site suggests to the reader: "If it's financial freedom and happiness you are aiming for, then start being the person who is financially free and happy. Imagine that you are already financially free and start being that person. Walk like a person who is financially free. Make the choices that a person who is financially free will make. Do the things that a financially free person will do. Live like a financially free person will live. Feel like you are financially free!" (http://www.squidoo.com/BE_DO_HAVE_Principle; 29/06/2010).

[69] For Buber, every genuine dialogue is infused by a religious feeling which is one's personal answer to God's "Where art thou, Adam?" question (Friedman, 1967, p. 189). In Levinas' terms: "The 'responses' constituting the dialogue signify 'responsibility'.... This is an ethics of... the service of God through responsibility to your neighbor, in which I am irreplaceable" (Levinas, 1993 Martin, p. 25).

[70] Gabriel Marcel, Knud EljerLogstrup, and Stanely Cavell advance similar views. Nel Noddings, Martin Buber, and Emmanuel Levinas are all involved in education. Levinas had been a school principle in Paris, Buber directed a Teacher Education program and wrote various papers concerning education, and Noddings' *Caring* (1984) is subtitled "A Feminist Approach to Ethics & Moral Education."

[71] Note the principled similarity between Combs and the CBTE movement. Just replace the words "appropriate system of beliefs" with "appropriate system of competencies". The paradigmatic stance of teaching as an applied science is clearly there as the expression "production of an effective teacher" attests.

[72] For a detailed analysis of the MT program, see: the papers in: Lund et al. (in press), especially Back (in press a) and Smits (in press).

[73] All the citations in this paragraph refer to the first handbook of the MT program (1996-1997).

[74] The 1997-1998 first year handbook enumerates nine "principles of learning": "Learning is developmental; We learn in different ways; We learn at different rates; We learn through interaction with one another; We learn through observing; We learn more effectively when we have significant input into decisions about our learning; Learning is effective when we are motivated; We learn best that which has meaning, relevance and practical application; and Learning is more effective when structured for success." (I, 11). But since "Learning and teaching are the two faces of the pedagogical coin" (ibid), the second year handbook enumerates ten almost corollary principles of teaching: "Teaching is developmental; We ought to teach in different ways; We pace our teaching and reiterate when needed; We teach through interactions; We teach on the basis of what we observe; Teaching involves negotiation with learners; Intentionality is an essential aspect of teaching and learning; We best teach that which has meaning and relevance; teaching is effective when structured for success; and Teaching is always situated in a larger social context" (II, 10).

[75] See EFQM or Baldridge awards for high quality organizations.

[76] Similarly, Werner Sombart (1911/2001) suggests a controversial theory, which connects the rise of Capitalism with Judaism. According to Sombart, the relationship between God and the Jewish people depends on a contract in which the Jews should obey God's commandments and God has to see that they will prosper and flourish.

LIST OF REFERENCES

Abbott, A. (1988). *The System of Professions.* Chicago: The University of Chicago Press.

Adorno, T. W. (1974). *The Jargon of Authenticity* (K. Tarnowski & F. Will, Trans.). London & NY: Routledge.

Adorno, T. W., & Horkheimer, M. (1972). *Dialectic of Enlightenment* (J. Cumming, Trans.). London & NY: Verso.

Alexander, R. E. (Ed.). (2010). *Children, their World, their Education.* London & NY: Routledge; Esmee Fairbairn Foundation.

Anderson, J. (1995). Translator's introduction (J. Anderson, Trans.). In *The Struggle for Recognition: The Moral Grammer of Social Conflicts by Axel Honneth* (pp. x–xxi). Cambridge, MA: The M.I.T. Press.

Aoki, T. T. (2005). Teaching as indwelling between two curriculum worlds. In W. F. Pinar & R. L. Irwin (Eds.), *Curriculum in a New Key: The Collected Works of Ted T. Aoki* (pp. 159–165). Mahwah, NJ: Lawrence Erlbaum Associates.

Arieli, D. (2008). *Predictably Irrational.* USA: Harper Collins Publishers.

Aristotle. (1984). On the soul [D.A.] (J. A. Smith, Trans.). In J. Barnes (Ed.), *The Complete Works of Aristotle* (The Revised Oxford Translation ed., Vol. 1, pp. 641–692). Princeton: Princeton University Press.

Aristotle. (1984). Eudemonian Ethics [E.E.] (J. Solomon, Trans.). In J. Barnes (Ed.), *The Complete Works of Aristotle* (The Revised Oxford Translation ed., Vol. 2, pp. 1921–1985). Princeton: Princeton University Press.

Aristotle. (1984). Nicomachean Ethics [E.N.] (W. Ross, revised by J. Urmson, Trans.). In J. Barnes (Ed.), *The Complete Works of Aristotle* (The Revised Oxford Translation ed., Vol. 2, pp. 1729–1867). Princeton: Princeton University Press.

Aristotle. (1984). Metaphisics [Meta.] (W. D. Ross, Trans.). In J. Barnes (Ed.), *The Complete Works of Aristotle* (The Revised Oxford Translation ed., Vol. 2, pp. 1552–1728). Princeton: Princeton University Press.

Aristotle. (1984). Posterior analytics [Pos. An.] (J. Barnes, Trans.). In J. Barnes (Ed.). *The Complete Works of Aristotle* (The Revised Oxford Translation ed., Vol. 1, pp. 114–166). Princeton: Princeton University Press.

Aristotle. (1984). Rhetoric [Reth.] (W. R. Roberts, Trans.). In J. Barnes (Ed.), *The Complete Works of Aristotle* (The Revised Oxford Translation ed., Vol. 2, pp. 2152–2269). Princeton: Princeton University Press.

Armstrong, J. (2002). *Conditions of Love.* London: Pinguin Books.

Armstrong, J. (2006). *Love, Life, Goethe.* Cabmberwell, Victoria: Allen Lane.

Arnstine, D. (1973). The knowledge nobody wants: The humanistic foundations in teacher education. *Educational Theory, 23*(1), 3–14.

Ayers, W. (1993). *To Teach.* NY and London: Teachers College Press, Colombia University.

Bach, R., & Munson, R. (2006). *Jonathan Livingston Seagull* . NY: Scribner.

Back, S. (1987). *Sof Maasse Bemahshava Tehila* (Practical Reasoning and Human Conduct). Unpublished Ph.D. Thesis submitted to Tel-Aviv University (in Hebrew).

Back, S. (2005). *Tehna'ut kehazon behahsharat morim* (The Technical Rationality Vision: The case of Teacher Education). Beer-Seva: Hotsa'at ha-sefarim shel Universitat Ben-Gurion baNegev [Ben-Gurion UP] (in Hebrew).

Back, S. (in press a). Afterword: Master of Teaching: Phronesis and Beyond. In E. D. Lund, L. E. Panayotidis, Smits & J. Towers (Eds.), *Provoking Conversations on Inquiry in Teacher Education.* Peter Lang.

LIST OF REFERENCES

Back, S. (in press b) Hegionot Sotrim Behahsharat Morim (Contradictions in Teacher Education). In: R. Klawir & L. Kuzminsky (Eds.), *Havnayat Zehout Mikzoit* (Constructing Professional Identity: A Network of Research in Teacher Education). Tel-Aviv: Mofet Institute (in Hebrew).

Back, S., & Mansur, R. (2009). *Professional Identity and "The Good"*. Paper presented at the 3rd IAASC Conference, Stellenboch, SA.

Bacon, F. (1597). *Religious Meditations, Of Heresies.*

Barak, J. & Gidron, A. (Eds.). (2009). *Shahaf* (Active Collaborative Education (ACE)): A Story of Teacher Education). Tel-Aviv: Mofet Institute (in Hebrew).

Bates, R., & Townsend, T. (2007). The future of teacher education: Challanges and opportunities. In T. Townsend & R. Bates (Eds.), *Handbook of Teacher Education: Globalization, Standards and Professionalism in Times of Change* (pp. 727–734). Dordrecht, Holland: Springer.

Bauman, Z. (1978). *Hermeneutics and Social Science.* London: Huchinson of London.

Bauman, Z. (2000). *Liquid Modernity.* Cambridge: Polity Press.

Bauman, Z. (2003). Educational challenges of the liquid-Modern Era. *Diogenes, 50*(1), 15–26.

Bauman, Z. (2005). Education in liquid modernity. *Review of Education, Pedagogy, and Cultural Studies, 27*(4), 303–17.

Bauman, Z. (2007). *Liquid Times: Living in An Age of Uncertainty.* Cambridge: Polity.Bauman, Z. (2008). *Does Ethics Have a Chance in a World of Consumers?* Cabmridge, MA: Harvard University Press.

Beiser, F. C. (1998). A romantic education: The concept of bildung in early German romanticism. In A. O. Rorty (Ed.), *Philosophers on Education* (pp. 284–299). London & NY: Routledge.

Beiser, F. C. (2003). Romanticism. In R. Curren (Ed.), *A Companion to the Philosophy of Education* (pp. 130–142). Oxford: Blackwell.

Ben-Gurion University, Faculty of Humanities and Social Sciences. (2003). *Shnaton TShND* (Handbook for the Academic Year 2003–2004). Beer-Sheba: Ben-Gurion University (in Hebrew).

Bentham, J. (1780/1948). *The Principles of Morals and Legislation.* NY: Hafner Press.

Bergman, R. (2004). Identity as motivation: Toward a theory of the moral self. In D. K. Lapsley & D. Narvaes (Eds.), *Moral Development, Self, and Identity* (pp. 21–46). Mahhwah, NJ: Lawrence Erlbaum Ass.

Berk, L. E. (2008). *Infants and Children* (6th ed.). USA: Pearson.

Berlin, I. (1958). *Two Concepts of Liberty.* Oxford: Clarendon Press.

Berlin, I. (1999). *The Roots of Romanticism.* Princeton: Princeton University Press.

Bernstein, B. (1975). Class and pedagogies: Visible and invisible. In B. Berstein (Ed.), *Class, Codes and Control* (Vol. 3, pp. 116–156). London: Routledge and Kegan Paul.

Berry, B., & The TeacherSolutions 2030 Team. (2011). *Teaching 2030.* New York and London: Teacher College Press.

Berry, B., Montgomery, D., Curtis, R., Hernandez, M., Wurtzel, J., & Snyder, J. (2008). *Creating and Sustaining Urban Teacher Residencies: A New Way to Rectuit, Prepare, and Retain Effective Teahers in High-Needs Districts.* The Aspen Institue; Center for Teaching Quality.

Biesta, G. J. J. (2010). *Good Education in an Age of Measurement: Ethics, Politics, Democracy.* Boulder; London: Paradigm Publishers.

Biesta, G. J. J., & Burbules, N. C. (2003). *Pragmatism and Educational Research.* Lanham, Maryland: Rowman & Littlefield Publishers, Inc.

Bowers, C. A. (2005). *The False Promise of Constructivist Theories of Learning.* NY: Peter Lang.

Bowra, C. (1961). *The Romantic Imagination.* Oxford: Oxford University Press.

Bransford, J., Derry, S., Berliner, D. C., Hammerness, K., & Beckett, K. L. (2005). Theories of learning and their roles in teaching. In L. Darling-Hammond & J. Bransford (Eds.), *Preparing Teachers for a Changing World* (pp. 40–87). San-Francisco: Jossey-Bass.

Bronfenbrenner, U. (1962). Soviet methods of character education: Some implications for research. *American Psychologist,* 550–564.

Brookner, A. (2001). *Romanticism and its Discintents.* London: Pinguin.

Bruford, W. (1975). *The German Tradition of Self-Cultivation.* Cambridge, UK: Cambridge University Press.

Bruni, L. (2007). The 'technology of happiness' and the tradition of economic science. In L. Bruni & P. L. Porta (Eds.), *Handbook on the Economics of Happiness* (pp. 24–52). Cheltenham, UK; Northampton, MA, USA: Edward Elgar.

Bruni, L. & Porta, P. L. (Eds.). (2007). *Handbook on the Economics of Happiness.* Cheltenham, UK; Northampton, MA, USA: Edward Elgar.

Buber, M. (1956). *Tales of the Hasidim* (O. Marx, Trans.). London: Thames.

Buber, M. (1965). *The Knowledge of Man* (M. S. Friedman & R. G. Smith, Trans.). London: George Allen & Unwin LTD.Buber, M. (1968). *Between Man and Man* (R. G. Smith, Trans.). New York: The MacMillan Company.

Buchberger, F. (1998). Teacher education in Europe - Diversity versus uniformity. *European Education, 30*(1), 44–95.

Calderhead, J. (1992). The role of reflection in learning to teach. In L. Valli (Ed.), *Reflective Teacher Education* (pp. 139–146). NY: State University of New York Press.

Calderhead, J., & Shorrock, S. B. (1997). *Understanding Teacher Education: Case Studies in the Professional Development of Beginning Teachers.* London: Routledge.

CHE [The Counsil of Higher Education]. (1981). *Degem Manhe Letohnit Limudim Letoar Boger Behoraa* (Guiding lines for B.Ed. Studies). Jerusalem: The Counsil of Higher Education (in Hebrew).

CHE [The Counsil of Higher Education]. (2006). *Doh Havada Likviat Matvim Manhim Lehahshara Lehoraah* (Report of the Committee of Teacher Education Programs). Jerusalem: The Counsil of Higher Education (in Hebrew).

Christensen, D. (1996). The professional knowledge-research base for teacher education. In J. Sikula (Ed.), *Handbook of Research on Teacher Education* (2nd ed., pp. 38–52). NY: McMillan Publishing Company.

Ciriello, M. J., Valli, L., & Taylor, N. E. (1992). Problem solving is not enough: Reflective teacher education at the Catholic University of America. In L. Valli (Ed.), *Reflective Teacher Education* (pp. 99–115). NY: State University of New York Press.

Clifford, G. J., & Guthrie, J. W. (1988). *Ed Scool: A Brief for Professional Education.* Chicago: The University of Chicago Press.

Clift, R. T., Houston, W. R., & McCarthy, J. (1992). Getting it RITE: A case of negotiated curriculum in teacher preparation at the University of Houston. In L. Valli (Ed.), *Reflective Teacher Education* (pp. 116–135). NY: State University of New York Press.

Cochran-Smith, M., Feiman-Nemser, S., & McIntyre, D. (Eds.). (2008). *Handbook of Research on Teacher Education* (3rd ed.). NY: Routledge/Taylor & Francis Group; The Association of Teacher Educators.

Cochran-Smith, M., & Lytle, S. L. (2009). *Inquiry as Stance.* NY and London: Teacher College Press.

Combs, A. W. (1965). *The Professional Education of Teachers.* Boston: Allyn & Bacon.

Combs, A. W. (1972). Soms basic concepts for teacher education. *Journal of Teacher Education, 23,* 286–290.

Combs, A. W., Blume, R. A., Newman, A. J., & Wass, H. L. (1974). *The Professional Education of Teachers* (2nd ed.). Boston: Allyn & Bacon.

Conant, J. B. (1964). *The Education of American Teachers.* New York Toronto London: Mc Graw-Hill Book Co.

LIST OF REFERENCES

Cooper, J. M., & Weber, W. A. (1973). A competency based systems approach to teacher education. In J. Cooper, W. Webber, & C. Johnson (Eds.), *Competency-Based Teacher Education II: A System Approach to Program Design* (pp. 7–18). Berkeley, CA: McCutchan Publishing Corporation.

Cottrell, D. P. (Ed.). (1956). *Teacher Education for a Free People.* Oneonta, NY: AACTE.

Cottrell, D. P. (1956). Facing the future: Central ideas for teacher education. In D. P. Cottrell (Ed.), *Teacher Education For a Free People* (pp. 383–406). Oneonta, NY: AACTE.

Cremin, L. A. (1979). *The Education of the Educating Professions.* Washington: AACTE.

CTE [Commission on Teacher Education]. (1946). *The Improvement of Teacher Education.* Washington, DC: American Counsil on Education.

Darling-Hammond, L. (2000). Forword. In L. Darling-Hammond (Ed.), *Studies of Excellence in Teacher Eduation* (pp. v–xi). NY: AACTE.

Darling-Hammond, L. (2006). *Powerful Teacher Education.* San Francisco: Jossey-Bass.

Darling-Hammond, L. (2009). Steady work: How Finland is building a strong teaching and learning system. *V.U.E, Summer*(2009), 15–25.

Darling-Hammond, Banks, J., Zumwalt, K., Gomez, L., Sherin, M. G., Griesdorn, J., et al. (2005). Educational goals and purposes: Developing a curricular vision for teaching. In L. Darling-Hammond & J. Bransford (Eds.), *Preparing Teachers for a Changing World* (pp. 169–200). San-Francisco: Jossey-Bass.Darling-Hammond, L. & Bransford, J. (Eds.). (2005). *Preparing Teachers for a Changing World.* San-Francisco: Jossey-Bass.

Darling-Hammond, L., Bransford, J., & LePage, P. (2005). Introduction. In L. Darling-Hammond & J. Bransford (Eds.), *Preparing Teachers for a Changing World* (pp. 1–39). San-Francisco: Jossey-Bass.

Darling-Hammond, L., Hammerness, K., Grossman, P., Rust, F., & Shulman, L. (2005). The design of teacher education programs. In L. Darling-Hammond & J. Bransford (Eds.), *Preparing Teachers for a Changing World* (pp. 390–441). San-Francisco: Jossey-Bass.

Darling-Hammond, L., Holtzman, D. J., Gatlin, Su Jim, & Heiling, J. V. (2005). *Does Teacher Preparation Matter? Evidence about Teacher Certification, Teach for America, and Teacher Effectiveness.* Unpublished manuscript, Palo Alto.

Davis, M. (2008). *The Land of Plenty.* Melbourne: Melbourne University Press.

Department of Education. (1950). Maarechet sahot Achida 1949–1950 (List of lessons for the year 1949–1950). In Yonai (Ed.), (1991). *Hachsharat Ovdey Horaa* (pp. 6–12). (Teacher Education Documents). Jerusalem: The Ministry of Education and Culture (in Hebrew).

Dewey, J. (1916). *Democracy and Education.* NY: The MacMillan Company.

Dewey, J. (1922/1930). *Human Nature and Conduct.* NY: The Modern Library.

Dewey, J. (1939). Means and ends. [Means]. In G. Novack (Ed.), *Their Morals and Ours: Marxist Versus Liberal Views on Morality* (pp. 51–55). NY: Merit Publishers.

Doherty, G. D. (2008). On quality in education. *Quality Assurance in Education, 16*(3), 255–265.

Dostoyevsky, F. (1996). *Crime and punishment* (C. Garnett, Trans.). USA: Bantam Classics.

Doyle, W. (1990). Themes in teacher education. In W. R. Houston (Ed.), *Handbook of Research on Teacher Education* (pp. 3–24). NY: McMillan College Publishung Company.

Dreyfus, H. L., & Dreyfus, S. E. (1986). *Mind over Machine: The Power of Human Intuition and Expertise in the Era of the Computer.* NY: The Free Press.

Eisenberg, M., & Litvak, M. (1994). Ma meahorey maarehet hashaot behoffen? (What is behind HOFFEN's program?) *BamiHlala, 5,* 11–25 (in Hebrew).

Elam, S. (1971). *Performance Based Teacher Education: What is the State of the Art?* Washington, DC: American Association of Colleges for Teacher Education.

Evetts, J., Mieg, H. A., & Felt, U. (2006). Professionalization, scientific expertise, and elitism: A sociological perspective. In K. Ericsson, N. Charness, P. J. Feltovich, & R. R. Hoffman (Eds.), *The*

Cambridge Handbook of Expertise and Expert Performance (pp. 105–123). NY: Cambridge at the University Press.

Facer, K. (2011). *Learning Futures*. London & NY: Routledge.

Faculty of Education - The Division of Teacher Preparation. (1997). *Handbook for New Teacher Education Program*. Calgary: University of Calgary.

Faculty of Education - The Division of Teacher Preparation. (1998). *Handbook for New Teacher Education Program*. Calgary: University of Calgary.

Faye, E. (2009). *Heidegger: The Introduction of Nazism into Philosophy in Light of the Unpublished Seminars of 1933–1935*. New Haven & London: Yale University Press.

Feiman-Nemser, S. (1990). Teacher preparation: Structural and conceptual alternatives. In W. R. Houston (Ed.), *Handbook of Research on Teacher Education* (pp. 212–233). NY: McMillan Publishing Company.

Feistritze, C. E. (2011, February 22). What is the role of teacher education? *Education Week*.

Fenstermacher, G., & Soltis, J. F. (1998). *Approaches to Teaching* (3rd ed.). NY: Teachers College Press.

Flyvbjerg, B. (2001). *Making Social Science Matter*. Cambridge, UK: Cambridge University Press.

Fowle, W. B. (1867). *The Teachers' Institute*. NY: A.S. Barnes and Co.

Frey, B. S., & Stutzer, A. (2002). *Happiness and Economics*. Princeton and London: Princeton University Press.

Friedman, M. S. (1955). *Martin Buber - The Life of Dialogue*. London: Routledge and Kegan Paul.

Friedman, M. S. (1967). The bases of buber's ethics. In P. A. Schlipp & M. S. Friedman (Eds.), *The Philosophy of Marin Buber* (171-200). La Salle, Ill: Open Court.

Fromm, E. (1976). *To Have or to Be*. NY: Continuum.

Fuller, F. (1969). Concerns of teachers: A developmental conceptualization. *American Educational Research Journal*, 6(4), 207–226.

Gadamer, H.-G. (1960/1989). *Truth and Method* (J. Weinsheimer & D. G. Marshall, Trans., 2nd ed.). NY: Continuum.

Gandin, L. A. (2007). The construction of the citizen school project as an alternative to neoliberal educational policies. *Policy Futures in Education*, 5(2), 179–193.

Gergen, K. (1991). *The Saturated Self*. NY: Basic Books.

Gewirth, A. (1983). The rationality of reasonableness. *Synthese*, 57(225), 248.

Giroux, H. A. (1988). *Teachers as Intellectuals: Towards a Critical Pedagogy of Learning*. Bergin & Garvey Publishers, Inc.

Gold, M. (2003). A reflection on teaching and learning in a Jewish Day School: A review of practical pedagogy for the Jewish classroom: Classroom management, instruction and curriculum development, by Daniel B. Kohn, Westport, Greenwood Press, 1999. *Curriculum Inquiry*, 33(2).

Golomb, J. (1990). Nietzsche on authenticity. *Philosophy Today*, 34(3), 243–258.

Goodlad, J. I. (1984). *A Place Called School*. NY: McGraw-Hill.

Goodwin, A. L. (2008). Defining teacher quality. In M. Cochran-Smith, S. Feiman-Nemser, & D. McIntyre (Eds.), *Handbook of Research on Teacher Education* (3rd ed., pp. 399–403). NY: Routledge/Taylor & Francis Group; The Association of Teacher Educators.

Gover, N. (1994). Haani maamin shelanou (Our beliefs, discussion with HOFFEN's teachers). *Bamihlala*, 5, 27–66 (in Hebrew).Gordon, A. D. (1958). *Yalkut* (Selections). Jerusalem: The Zionist world organization (in Hebrew).

Gorodetsky, M., & Barak, J. (2008). The educational-cultural edge: A participative learning environment for co-emergence of personal and institutional growth. Teaching and Teacher Education, 24(7), 1907-1918.

Grant, N. (1964). *Soviet Education*. Harmondsworth, Middlesex, England: Penguin Books.

LIST OF REFERENCES

Greenfield, S. (2008). *i.d.* London: Sceptre.

Grossman, P. & Loeb, S. (Eds.). (2008). *Alternative Routes to Teaching.* Cambridge, MA: Harvard University Press.

Guignon, C. (2004). *On Being Authentic.* London and New York: Routledge.

Gundem, B. B., & Hopmann, S. (1998). Introduction: Didaktik meets curriculum. In B. B. Gundem & S. Hopmann (Eds.), *Didaktik and/or Curriculum* (pp. 1–8). NY: Peter Lang.

Hahn, F. & Hollis, M. (Eds.). (1979). *Philosophy and Economic Theory.* Oxford: Oxford University Press.

Halpin, D. (2006). Why a romantic conception of education matters? *Oxford Review of Education, 32*(3), 325–345.

Halpin, D. (2007). *Romanticism and Education.* London & NY: Continuum.

Halwani, R. (2010). *Philosophy of Love, Sex, and Marriage.* Routledge.

Hammerness, K., Darling-Hammond, L., Bransford, J., Berliner, D. C., Cochran-Smith, M., McDonald, M., et al. (2005). How teachers learn and develop. In L. Darling-Hammond & J. Bransford (Eds.), *Preparing Teachers for a Changing World* (pp. 358–389). San-Francisco: Jossey-Bass.

Harding, S. (1998). Is Science Multi-Cultural: Postcolonialism, Feminisms, and Epistemologies . Bloomington: Indiana University Press.Hargreaves, A. (2000). Four ages of professionalism and professional learning. *Teachers and Teaching: Theory and Practice, 6*(2), 151–182.

Hatton, N., & Smith, D. (1995). Facilitating reflection: Issues and research. *Forum of Education, 50*(1), 49–65.

Hautamaki, J., Harjunen, E., Hautamaki, A., Karjalainen, T., Kupiainen, S., Laaksonen, S., et al. (Eds.). (2008). *PISA06.* Helsinki: Ministry of Education, OECD, University of Helsinki, Centre for Educational Assessments.

Heath, D. (1999). *Introducing Romanticism.* Cambridge: Icon Books.

Heilig, J. V, & Jez, S. (2010). *Teach for America: A Review of the Evidence.* Boulder and Tempe: Education and the Public Interest Center & Education Policy Research Unit.

Hempel, K. (1935/1980). The logical analysis of psychology. In N. Block (Ed.), *Readings in Philosophy of Psychology* (Vol. 1, pp. 14–23).

Henson, K. T. (1996). Teachers as researchers. In J. Sikula (Ed.), *Handbook of Research on Teacher Education* (2nd ed., pp. 53–64). NY: McMillan Publishing Company.

Herbst, J. (1989). *And Sadly Teach: Teacher Education and Professionalization in American Culture.* Madison, WI: The University of Wisconsin Press.

Hertz, F. (1975). *The German Public Mind in the Nineteenth Century.* London: George Allen & Unwin LTD.

Hess, F. M. (2009). Revitalizing teacher education by revisiting our assumptions about teaching. *Journal of Teacher Education, 60*(5), 450–457.

Hobbel, N. (2009). Standards talk: Considering discourse in teacher education standards. In S. L. Groenke & J. A. Hatch (Eds.), *Critical Pedagogy and Teacher Education in the Neoliberal Era* (pp. 37–48). Springer.

HOFFEN Institute. (1994). Osef divrey talmidim oubogrim (Collection of HOFFEN's students and graduates sayings). *Bamihlala, 5,* 121–127 (in Hebrew).

Holmes Group. (1986). *Tomorrow's Teachers: A Report of the Holmes Group.* East Lansing, MI: The Holmes Group Inc.

Honneth, A. (1995). The struggle for recognition: The moral grammar of social conflicts (J. Anderson, Trans.). Cambridge, MA: The M.I.T. Press.Honneth, A. (2002). Grounding recognition: A rejoinder to critical questions. *Inquiry, 45*(4), 499–519.

Honneth, A. (2003). Redistribution as recognition: A response to Nancy Fraser (J. Golb & J. Ingram, Trans.). In N. Fraser & A. Honneth (Eds.), *Redistribution or Recognition?* (pp. 110–197). London & NY: Verso.

Honneth, A. (2004). Recognition and justice. *Acta Sociologica, 47*(4), 351–364.

Honneth, A. (Ed.). (2007). *Disrespect: The Normative Foundations of Critical Theory.* Cambridge, UK: Polity.

Honneth, A. (Ed.). (2008). *Reification: A New Look at an Old Idea.* Oxford: Oxford University Press.

Honneth, A., & Hartmann, M. (2004). Paradoxien des Kapitalismus. *Berliner Debatte Initial, 15,* 4–17.

hooks, b. (2000). *All about Love.* London: The Women's Press.

Houston, W. R. (Ed.). (1990). *Handbook of Research on Teacher Education.* NY: McMillan Publishing Company.

Houston, W. R., & Howsman, R. B. (1972). Change and challange. In W. R. Houston & R. B. Howsman (Eds.), *Competency-Based Teacher Education: Progress, Problems and Prospects* (pp. 1–16). USA: Science Research Associates, Inc.

Houston, W. R., & Jones, H. L. (1974). *Three Views of CBTE: II. University of Houston. Applying System Theory to Program Design.* Bloomington, IN: Phi Delta Kappa.

Howey, K. R., & Storm, S. (1987). Teacher selection reconsidered. In G. Katz & J. Rath (Eds.), *Advances in Teacher Education* (Vol. 3, pp. 1–34). Norwood, NJ: Abelex Pub. Co.

Howey, K. R., & Zimpher, N. L. (1989). *Profiles of Preservice Teacher Education.* Albany: NY State University of NY Press.

Hume, D. (1740/1978). *A Treatise of Human Nature* (2nd ed.). Oxford: Clarendon Press.

Hume, D. (1777/1975). *Enquiries Concerning Human Understanding and Concerning the Principles of Morals* (3rd, with text revised ed.). Oxford: Clarendon Press.

Humphrey, D. C., & Wechsler, M. E. (2008). Getting beyond the label: What characterizes alternative programs? In P. Grossman & S. Loeb (Eds.), *Alternative Routes to Teaching* (pp. 65–97). Cambridge, MA: Harvard University Press.

Hunt, C. W. (1956). Toward a profession of teaching. In D. P. Cottrell (Ed.), *Teacher Education For a Free People* (pp. 18–55). Oneonta, NY: AACTE.

Illouz, E. (1997). *Consuming the Romantic Utopia: Love and the Cultural Contradictions of Capitalism.* San-Francisco: University of California Press.

Illouz, E. (2002). *Tarbout Hakapitalism* (The Culture of Capitalism). Tel-Aviv: The Ministry of Defense Publishing Press (in Hebrew).

Jardine, D. (2006). *Piaget & Education.* NY: Peter Lang.

Jardine, D., Sharon, F., & Clifford, P. (2006). *Curriculum in Abundance.* Mahwah, NJ: Lawrence Erlbaum Associates.

Johnson, M. (1975). Conceptual confusion and premature policies. In R. A. Smith (Ed.), *Regaining Educational Leadership: Critical Essays on PBTE/CBTE, Behavioral Objectives and Accountability* (pp. 46–63). NY: John Wiley & Sons, Inc.

Johnson, S. (1998). *Who Moved My Cheese?* NY: Penguin Putnam.

Johnson, S. M., & Birkeland, S. E. (2008). Is fast-track preparation enough? It depends. In P. Grossman & S. Loeb (Eds.), *Alternative Routes to Teaching* (pp. 101–128). Cambridge, MA: Harvard University Press.

Joyce, B. (1975). Conceptions of man and their implications for teacher education. In K. Ryan (Ed.), *Teacher Education, the 74th Yearbook of the NSSE* (Vol. 2, pp. 111–145). Chicago: The University of Chicago Press.

Jyrhama, R., Kynaslahti, H., Krokfors, L., Byman, R., Maaranen, K., & Toom, A., et al. (2008). The appreciation and realisation of research-based teacher education: Finnish students' experiences of teacher education. *European Dimensions of Teacher Eduction, 31*(1), 1–16.

Kahaneman, D., Slovic, P., & Tverski, A. (Eds.). (1982). *Judgment under Uncertainty: Heristics and Biases.* Cambridge: Cambridge University Press.

LIST OF REFERENCES

Kansanen, P. (2003). Teacher education in Finland: Current models and new developments. In B. Moon, L. Vlasceanu, & L. C. Barrows (Eds.), *Institutional Approaches to Teacher Education Within Higher Education in Europe: Current Models and New Developments* (pp. 86–108). Bucarest: UNESCO CEPES.

Kansanen, P. (2004). The role of general education in teacher education. *Zeitschrift fur Erziehungswissenschaft*, *7*(2), 207–218.

Kansanen, P. (2006). Constructing a research-based program in teacher education. In F. K. Oser, A. Frank, & Ursula (Eds.), *Competence Oriented Teacher Training* (pp. 11 – 22). Rotterdam/Boston/Taipei: Sense Publishers.

Kant, I. (1785/1948). *Groundwork of the Metaphysic of Morals* (H. Paton, Trans.). London: Hutchinson and Co.

Kant, I. (1803/1964). *The Doctrine of Virtue* (M. J. Gregor, Trans.). NY: Harper & Row.

Kelly, E. A. (1974). *Three Views of Competency-Based Teacher Education: III University of Nebraska.* Bloomington, IN: Phi Delata Kappa Educational Foundation.

Kerschensteiner, G. (1965). *Nefesh Hamehanech* (The Educator's Soul). (Hebrew Translator: Y.Amir). Jerusalem: Hebrew University, School of Education (in Hebrew).

Kincheloe, J. L. (2003). *Teachers as Researchers* (2nd ed.). London & NY: RoutledgeFalmer.

Kincheloe, J. L. (2004). *Critical Pedagogy.* NY: Peter Lang.

Kirchgassner, G. (2008). *Homo Oeconomicus.* Springer.

Klafki, W. (2000). The significance of classical theories of bildung for a contemporary concept of Allgemeinbildung (R. MacPherson, Trans.). In I. Westbury, S. Hopmann, & K. Riquarts (Eds.), *Teaching as a Reflective Practice: The German Didaktik Tradition* (pp. 85–107). Mahhah, NJ: Lawrence Erlbaum Ass.

Klein, N. (2007). *The Shock Doctrine: The Rise of Disaster Capitalism.* NY: Metropolitan Books; Henry Holt and Company.

Korczak, J. (1929/1974). Ketzad Leehov Yeladim (How to Love a Child). In: *Ktavim* (Vol. I, pp. 279–352). (The Writings of Januaz Korczak). (Hebrew translation: Z.Arad). Tel-Aviv: Hotzaat Hakibutz Hameouhad (in Hebrew).

Korthagen, F. A. J., in cooperation with Kessels, J., Koster, B., Lagerwerf, B., & Wubbels, T. (2001). *Linking Theory and Practice: The Pedagogy of Realistic Teacher Education.* Mahwah, NJ: Lawrence Erlbaum Associates.

Kuhn, T. A. (1970). *The Structure of Scientific Revolutions* (2nd ed.).

Labaree, D. F. (2004). *The Trouble with Ed Schools.* New Heaven; London: Yale, University Press.

Lagemann, E. C. (2000). *An Elusive Science: The Troubling History of Educational Research.* Chicago: The University of Chicago Press.

Lam, Z, (2000). Keirouv Hahsharat Morim L"mitat" Hahoraa. (Narrowing the gap between teacher education and the "bed" of teaching) In: Harpaz. Y. (ed.) *Laxatz Vhitnagdout Bahinuh* (Pressure and Resistence in Education) (pp. 64-68). Tel-Aviv: Sifriyat Hapoalim (in Hebrew).

Lapsley, D. K. (2008). Moral self-Identity as the aim of education. In L. P. Nucci & D. Navarez (Eds.), *Handbook of Moral and Character Education* (pp. 30–52). NY & London: Routledge.

Layard, R. (2005). *Happiness - Lessons from a New Science.* NY: The Penguin Press.

Le Baron, W. (1973). System Analysis and Teacher Education. In M. V. De Vault, Andersen, D. W. & G. E. Dickson (Eds.), *Competency-Based Teacher Education I: Problems and prospects for the Decades Ahead* (pp. 15-31). Berekly, Cal.: McCutchan Publishing Corporation.

Lemov, D. (2010). *Teach Like a Champion: 49 Techniques That Put Students on the Path to College.* Wiley.

Levinas, E. (1962/1996). Transcendence and height (S. Critcheley, Trans.). In A. T. Peperzk, S. Critcheley, & R. Bernasconi (Eds.), *Emmanuel Levinas: Basic Philosophical Writings* (pp. 11–31). Bloomington: Indiana University Press.

Levinas, E. (1967). Martin Buber and the theory of knowledge. In P. A. Schlipp & M. S. Friedman (Eds.), *The Philosophy of Marin Buber* (pp. 133–150). La Salle, Ill: Open Court.

Levinas, E. (Ed.). (1972/2003). *Humanism of the Other*. Urbana and Chicago: University of Illinois Press.

Levinas, E. (1993). Apropos Buber: Some notes. In E. Levinas (Ed.), *Outside the Subject* (pp. 30–36). London & NY: Continuum.

Levinas, E. (1993). Martin Buber, Gabriel Marcel and philosophy. In E. Levinas (Ed.), *Outside the Subject* (pp. 14–29). London & NY: Continuum.

Levinas, E. (1997). Apropos Buber: Some notes. In H. Jodalen & A. J. Vetlesen (Eds.), *Closeness, An Ethics* (pp. 45–52). Oslo: Scandivian University Press.

Levine, A. (2006). *Educating School Teachers*. Washington, DC: The Education Schools Project.

Levine, A. (2010). Teacher education must respond to change in America. *Phi Delta Kappan, 92*(2), 19–24.

Lieberman, M. (1956). *Education as a Profession*. Englewood Cliffs, NJ: Prentice-Hall, Inc.

Lortie, D. C. (1975). *Schoolteacher: A Sociological Study*. Chicago: University of Chicago Press.

Luce, R. D., & Raiffa, H. (1957). *Games and Decisions*. NY: Dover Publications, Inc.

Lund, E. D., Panayotidis, L. E., Smits, H., & Towers, J. (Eds.). (in press). *Provoking Conversations on Inquiry in Teacher Education*. Peter Lang.Luth, C. (2000). On Wilhelm von Humboldt's theory of bildung (G. Horton-Kruger, Trans.). In I. Westbury, S. Hopmann, & K. Riquarts (Eds.), *Teaching as a Reflective Practice: The German Didaktik Tradition* (pp. 63–84). Mahhah, NJ: Lawrence Erlbaum Ass.

Lyotard, J. F. (1979). *La condition postmoderne*. Paris: Les Editions de Minuit.

MacIntyre, A. (1984). *After Virtue* (2nd ed.). Notre Dame, Indiana: University of Notre Dame Press.

Mansur, R., & Gidron, A. (2004). Ethnology in the service of education. *International Journal of Diversity in Organizations, Communities and Nations, 4*.

Marcuse, H. (1964). *One Dimensional Man*. London: Routledge.

Marx, K. (1932/2000). *Economic & Philosophic Manuscripts of 1844* (M. Milligan, Trans.).

Marx, K. (1859/1971). A contribution to the critique of political economy (S. Ryazankaya, Trans.). London: Lawrence and Wisshart.

Mazzone, A. (1999). *Waldorf Teacher Education*. Adelaide, SA.

McCaleb, J., Borko, H., & Arends, R. (1992). Reflection, research, and repertoire in the maters certification program at the University of Maryland. In L. Valli (Ed.), *Reflective Teacher Education* (pp. 40–64). NY: State University of New York Press.

McCourt, F. (2005). *Teacher Man*. NY: Scribner.

McKinsey&Company. (2007). *How the Best-Performing School Systems Come Out on Top*. McKinsey&Company.

McKinsey&Company. (2010). *How the World's Most Improved Shools Systems Keep Getting Better*. McKinsey&Company.

Mill, J. S. (1874/2000). *Essays on Some Unsettled Questions of Political Economy* (2nd ed.). London: Batoche Books. http://www.efm.bris.ac.uk/het/mill/question.pdf

Ministry of Education and Culture – The Department of Teacher Education. (1974). *Louhot Hasheourim* (Table of Lessons in teacher education institutions). Jerusalem: The Ministry of Education and Culture (in Hebrew).

Minsky, M. L. (1980). Decentralizing minds. *The Behavioral and Brain Sciences, 3*, 439.

Morgan, M. L. (2007). *Discovering Levinas*. NY: Cambridge University Press.NAPDS [National Association for Professional Development Schools]. (2008). *What It Means to Be a Professional Development School*. USA: NAPDS.

LIST OF REFERENCES

NCATE [National Council for Accreditation of Teacher Education]. (1970). *Recommended Standards for Teacher Education.* Washington, DC: NCATE.

NCATE [National Council for Accreditation of Teacher Education]. (2001). *Standards for Professional Development Schools.* Retrieved from http://www.ncate.org/public/standards.asp

NCATE [National Council for Accreditation of Teacher Education]. (2010). *Transforming Teacher Education Through Clinical Practice: A National Strategy to Prepare Effective Teachers.* Washington, DC.

NCTAF [The National Commission on Teaching & America's Future]. (1996). *What Matters Most: Teaching for America's Future.* NY: NCTAF.

NCTQ [National Counsil on Teacher Quality]. (2011). *NCTQ Standards and Indicators for National Review of Teacher Preparation.* NCTQ. Retrieved 6, 2011, from http://www.nctq.org/p/edschools/docs/standards_and_indicators.pdf

NMAP. [National Mathematics Advisory Panel]. (2008). *Foundations for Success: The Final Report of the National Mathematics Advisory Panel.* Washington, DC: Department of Education.

NRC [National Research Counsil]. (2000). *How People Learn* (2nd ed.). Washington, DC: National Academy Press.

Nardi, N. (1956). Hamore BeIsrael (The Teacher in Israel). In C. Richardson, H. Brule, & H. Snyder (Eds.), (1956). *The Education of Teachers in England, France and the U.S.A* (pp. 211–262). Tel-Aviv: Isreali Teachers Association in cooperation with UNESCO (in Hebrew).

Nehamas, A. (2001). How one becomes what one is. In J. Richardson & B. Leiter (Eds.), *Nietzsche* (pp. 255–280). Oxford: Oxford University Press.

Neill, A. (1915/1986). *A Dominie's Log.* London: The Hogarth Press.

Nichols, S. L., & Berliner, D. C. (2007). *Collateral Damage.* Cambridge, MA: Harvard University Press.

Niemi, H., & Jakko-Sihvonen, R. (2011). Teacher education in Finland. In M. V. Zuljan & J. Vogrinc (Eds.), *European Dimensions of Teacher Education - Similarities and Differences* (pp. 33–51). Ljubljana: Faculty of Education, University of Ljubljana, Slovenia and The National School of Leadership in Education, Kranji, Slovenia.

Nietzsche, F. W. (1880/1986). *Human, All Too Human. A Book for Free Spirits;* II 1: Assorted Opinions and Maxims (R. Hollingdale, Trans.). Cambridge UK: Cambridge University Press.

Nietzsche, F. W. (1882/1974). *The Gay Science* (W. Kaufman, Trans.). NY: Vintage Books.

Noddings, N. (1984). *Caring: A Feminine Approach to Ethics and Moral Education.* Berkeley: University of California Press.

Nussbaum, M. C. (1990). *Love's Knowledge.* NY, Oxford: Oxford University Press.

Nussbaum, M. C. (1995). *Poetic Justice.* Boston: Beacon Press.

Nussbaum, M. C. (2001). *The fragility of goodness* (Rev. ed.). Cambridge: Cambridge University Press.

Oancea, A., & Pring, R. (2009). The importance of being through: On systematic accumulations of 'What Works' in educational research. In D. Bridges, P. Smeyers, & R. Smith (Eds.), *Evidence-Based Education Policy* (pp. 11–35). West-Sussex, UK: Wiley-Blackwell.

Ogren, C. A. (2005). *The American State Normal School.* NY: Palgrave.

Omari, A. M. (2011). Race to the top funds: An uphill race for Minnesota. Retrieved 8, 2011, from http://conservancy.umn.edu/bitstream/90574/1/Race%20to%20the%20Top%20Funds.pdf

Orwell, G. (2003). *Nineteen Eighty Four .* USA: Plume.Otterman, S. (2011, July 21). Ed Scools' pedagogical puzzle. *The New York Times.*

Page, D. P. (1857). *Theory and Practice of Teaching* (15th ed.). NY: A. S. Barnes and Co.

Palmer, P. (1998). *The Courage to Teach.* San Francisco: Jossey-Bass.

Parsons, T. (1968). Professions. In D. Sills (Ed.), *International Encyclopedia of the Social Sciences* (Vol. 12, pp. 536–547). USA: The Macmillan Company & Free Press.

Partnership for 21st Century Skills. (2007a). The Intellectual and Policy Foundations of the 21st Century Skills Framework, from http://route21.p21.org/index.php.

Partnership for 21st Century Skills. (2007b). 21st Century Skills Professional Development, from http://route21.p21.org/index.php.

Patrinos, H. A., & Sosale, S. (2007). Public-Private partnerships in education. In H. A. Patrinos & S. Sosale (Eds.), *Mobilizing the Private Sector for Public Education* (pp. 1–9). Washington, DC: The World Bank.

Peck, R. F., & Tucker, J. A. (1973). Research on teacher education. In R. M. W. Travers (Ed.), *Second Handbook of Research on Teaching* (pp. 940–978). Chicago: Rand McNally College Publishing Company.

Perlberg, A., & Kremer, L. (1977). *Towards New Teacher Education Models.* Haifa: Technion - Israel Institue of Technology, Laboratory for Research & Development in Teaching and Learning.

Phelan, A. (2005). On discernment: The wisdom of practice and the practice of wisdom in teacher education. In G. F. Hoban (Ed.), *The Missing Links in teacher Education* (pp. 57–73). Dordrecht, Holland: Springer.

Pirsig, R. M. (1974). *Zen and the Art of Motorcycle Maintenance.* NY: Bantam Books.Plato. (1961). Gorgias (W. Woodhead, Trans.). In E. Hamilton & H. Cairns (Eds.), *Plato: The Collected Dialogues* (pp. 229–307). Princeton: Princeton University Press.

Polanyi, M. (1962). *Personal Knowledge: Towards a Post-Critical Philosophy* (2nd ed.). Chicago: The University of Chicago Press.

Popper, K. R. (Ed.). (1969). *Conjectures and Refutations* (3rd ed.). London: Routledge and Kegan Paul.

Popper, K. R. (Ed.). (1972). *Objective Knowledge.* Oxford: The Claredon Press.

Porter, A. C., Youngs, P., & Odden, A. (2001). Advances in teacher assessments and their uses. In V. Richardson (Ed.), *Handbook of Research on Teaching* (4th ed., pp. 259–297). Washington, DC: AERA.

Potter, A. (2010). *The Authenticity Hoax.* Melbourne: Scribe.

Quine, W. v. O. (1960). Word and Object. Cambridge, Mass.: The M.I.T. Press.

Rand, A. (1962). *Objectivism on One Foot.* Retrieved August 20, 2008, from http://aynrandlexicon.com

Rand, J. (2009). Sygnonot Kyom: Lyhyiot, Sheeye li, Laasot. (Modes of Existence: To Be, To Have and To Do). In J. Rand & D. Shkolnick (Eds.), *Sygnonot Kyom (Modes of Existence)* (pp. 41–94). Tel-Aviv: Mofet Institute (in Hebrew).

Rand, J., & Shkolnick, D. (2009). Divrey Hmehabrim (The authors' introduction). In J. Rand & D. Shkolnick (Eds.), *Sygnonot Kyom* (pp. 11–38). (Modes of Existence). Tel-Aviv: Mofet Institute (in Hebrew).

Ratner, J. (Ed.). (1939). *Intelligence in the Modern World: John Dewey's Philosophy.* NY: Random House: The Modern Library.

Ravitch, D. (2010). The death and life of the great American school system: How testing and choice are undermining education. NY: Basic Books.

Rawls, J. (1971). *A Theory of Justice.* Cambridge, MA: The Belknap Press of Harvard University Press.

Rawls, J. (2001). *Justice as Fairness - A Restatement.* Cambridge, MA: Belknap Press of Harvard University Press.

Reichenberg, R., & Sagi, R. (2003). *Sygnonot Kyoum: Mi Ata Ish Hahinuh* (Modes of Existence: Who is the educator?) Tel-Aviv: Mofet Institute (in Hebrew).

Reiss, H. (1955). Introduction. In H. Reiss (Ed.), *The Political Thought of the German Romantics 1973–1815* (pp. 1–43). Oxford: Basil Blackwell.Ricard, M. (2006). *Happiness: A Guide to Developing Life's Most Important Skill* (J. Browner, Trans.). NY: Little, Brown and Company.

Richardson, V., & Placier, P. (2001). Teacher change. In V. Richardson (Ed.), *Handbook of Research on Teaching* (4th ed., pp. 905–947). Washington, DC: AERA.

LIST OF REFERENCES

Ricoeur, P. (1992). *Oneself as Another* (K. Blamey, Trans.). Chicago and London: The University of Chicago Press.

Rockmore, T. (2009). Forward to the English Edition. In E. Faye (Ed.), *Heidegger: The Introduction of Nazism into Philosophy in Light of the Unpublished Seminars of 1933–1935* (pp. vii–xxi). New Haven & London: Yale University Press.

Rodgers, C. C., & Scott, K. H. (2008). The development of the personal self and professional identity in learning to teach. In M. Cochran-Smith, S. Feiman-Nemser, & D. McIntyre (Eds.), *Handbook of Research on Teacher Education* (3rd ed., pp. 732–755). NY: Routledge/Taylor & Francis Group; The Association of Teacher Educators.

Ronnerman, K. (2005). *Participant Knowledge and the Meeting of Practitioners and Researchers.* Paper presented at the ECER, Dublin.

Rorty, R. (1994/1999). Ethics without principles. In R. Rorty (Ed.), *Philosophy and Social Hope* (pp. 72–90). London: Penguin Books.

Rosenshine, B. (2009). The empirical support fo direct learning. In S. Tobias & T. M. Duffy (Eds.), *Constructivist Instruction: Success or Failure?* (pp. 201–220). NY & London: Routledge.

Ross, D. D., Johnson, M., & Smith, W. (1992). Developing a PROfessional TEACHer at the University of Florida. In L. Valli (Ed.), *Reflective Teacher Education* (pp. 24–39). NY: State University of New York Press.

Rousseau, J.-J. (1762/1977). *Emile* (B. Foxley, Trans.). London and Toronto: Dent, Everyman's Library.

Rousseau, J.-J. (1789/2000). *The Confessions* (P. Coleman & A. Scolar, Trans.). Oxford: Oxford University Press.

Rubinstein, A. (1998). *Modeling Bounded Rationality.* Massachusetts: MIT press.

Rubinstein, A. (2009). *Agadot Hakalkala* (The Legends of Economics). Or-Yehuda: Kineret-Zmora-Bitan (in Hebrew).

Saint-Exupery, A. de (1943/1959). Le Petit Prince. In O. D. Exupery (Ed.), *Oeuvres D'Antoine De Saint - Exupery* (pp. 407–497). France: Libraire Gallimard. (English translation: The Little Prince (1943) by Katherine Woods).

Sahlberg, P. (2011). Lessons from Finland. *American Educator,* 34–38.

Salen, K., Torres, R., Wolozin, L., Riufo-Tepper, R., & Shapiro, A. (2011). *Quest to Learn.* Cambridge, MA: The M.I.T. Press.

Saltman, K. J. (2008). Schooling in disaster capitalism. In D. Boyles (Ed.), *The Corporate Assault on Youth* (pp. 187–218). NY: Peter Lang.

Saltman, K. J. (2009). Corporatization and the control of schools. In M. W. Apple, A. Wayne, & L. A. Gandin (Eds.), *The Routledge International Handbook of Critical Education* (pp. 51–63). NY & London: Routledge.

Sandlin, J. A., Schultz, B. D., & Burdick, J. (Eds.). (2010). *Handbook of Public Pedagogy.* New York & London: Routledge.

Scheffler, S. (Ed.). (1988). *Consequentialism and Its Critics.* Oxford: Oxford University Press.

Schlegel, F. (1982). *Fragmentim* (Fragments) (Hebrew Translation: T. Rivner). Tel-Aviv: Sifriat Poalim Publishing House, Hotzaat Hakibutz Hameouhad (in Hebrew).

Schön, D. A. (1983). *The Reflective Practitioner.* USA: Basic Books, Inc.

Schön, D. A. (1987). *Educating the Reflective Practitioner.* San-Francisco: Jossey-Bass Publishers.

Schratz, M., & Resinger, J. P. (2003). Current models and new developments in teacher education in Austria. In L. Vlasceneau & L. C. Barrows (Eds.), *Institutional Approaches to Teacher Education Within Higher Education in Europe: Current Models and New Developments* (pp. 17–34). Bucharest: UNESCO.

Schwartz, D., Bransford, J., & Sears, D. (2005). Efficiency and innovation in transfer. In J. P. Mestre (Ed.), *Transfer of Learning: Research and Perspectives* (pp. 1–52). USA: Information Age Publishing.

Schwartz, H. (1996). The changing nature of teacher education. In J. Sikula (Ed.), *Handbook of Research on Teacher Education* (2nd ed., pp. 3–13). NY: McMillan Publishing Company.

Segal, M. (1981). Hareishit Oulahreha (The Beginning and Later). *Hahinuch Ousvivo* (Education and Around), *3–4*, 9–75 (in Hebrew).

Seigel, J. (2005). *The Idea of the Self.* Cambridge, UK: Cambridge University Press.

Selwyn, N. (2011). *Schools and Schooling in the Digital Age.* London & NY: Routledge.

Sen, A. K. (1979). Rational fools: A critique of the behavioral foundations of economic theory. In F. Hahn & M. Hollis (Eds.), *Philosophy of Economic Theory* (pp. 87–109). Oxford: Oxford University Press.

Sen, A. K. (1986). Behaviour and the concept of preference. In J. Elster (Ed.), *Rational Choice* (pp. 60 – 81). Oxford: Basil Blackwell.

Sennett, R. (1998). *The Corrosion of Character.* NY: W.W.Norton.

Sennett, R. (2006). *The Culture of the New Capitalism.* New Haven & London: Yale University Press.

Sennett, R. (2008). *The Craftsman.* London: Allen Lane.

Serres, M. (1995). *The Natural Contract* (E. MacArthur & W. Paulson, Trans.). Ann Arbor: The University of Michigan Press.

Serres, M. (1997). *The Troubadour of Knowledge* (F. Faria Glaser, Trans.). Ann Arbor: The University of Michigan Press.

Shaw, W. H. (1999). *Contemporary Ethics.* Oxford, UK: Blackwell Publishers.

Shermis, S. S., & Orlich, D. C. (1965). Teaching as a profession. In D. C. Orlich (Ed.), *The Pursuit of Excellence: Introductory Readings in Education* (pp. 288–314). NY: American Book Company.

Shulman, L. (1998/2004). Theory, practice, and the education of professionals. In L. Shulman (Ed.), *The Wisdom of Practice: Essays on Teaching, Learning, and Learning to Teach* (pp. 523–544). San-Francisco: Jossey-Bass.

Shulman, L. (2005). *The Signature Pedagogies in the Professions of Law, Medicine, Engineering and the Clergy: Lessons for the Education of Teachers.* Paper presented at the Teacher Education for Effective Teaching and Learning.

Shulman, L. (2007). Practical wisdom in the service of professional practice. *Educational Researcher, 36*(9), 560–563.

Sibley, W. (1953). The rational versus the reasonable. *Philosophical Review, 62*, 554–560.Sikula, J. (Ed.). (1996). *Handbook of Research on Teacher Education* (2nd ed.). NY: McMillan Publishing Company.

Simola, H. (1998). Decontextualizing Teacher's Knowledge: Finnish didactics and teacher education during the 1980s and 1990s. Scandinavian Journal of Educational Research, 42(4), 325-338.Simon, H. A. (1976). From substantive to procedural rationality. In S. Lastis (Ed.), *Method and Appraisal in Economics.* Cambridge: Cambridge University Press.

Slote, M. (2007). *The Ethics of Care and Empathy.* London and New York: Routledge.

Slote, M. (2009). Caring, empathy, and moral education. In H. Siegel (Ed.), *The Oxford Handbook of Philosophy of Education.* Oxford: Oxford University Press.

Smith, A. (1776/1904). *An Inquiry into the Nature and Causes of the Wealth of Nations.* London: Methuen & Co., Library of Economics and Liberty.

Smits, H. (2011). Is there an historical mission for teacher education? or Is it too late?. Keynote address presented at the Canadien Association for Teacher Education, Fredericton, NB.

LIST OF REFERENCES

Smits, H. (in press). Epilogue: Some reflections on the demise of a teacher education program and the importance of memory. In: E. D. Lund, L. E. Panayotidis, Smits & J. Towers (Eds.) (in press). *Provoking Conversations on Inquiry in Teacher Education.* Peter Lang.

Snyder, H. E. (1953). The education of teachers for the public schools of the United States. In C. Richardson, H. Brule, & H. E. Snyder (Eds.), *The Education of Teachers in England, France and the U.S.A* (pp. 212–341). Paris: UNESCO.

Soble, A. (Ed.). (1989). *Eros, Agape and Philia: Readings in the Philosophy of Love.* NY: Paragon House.

Sockett, H. (2008). The moral and epistemic purposes of teacher education. In M. Cochran-Smith, S. Feiman-Nemser, & D. McIntyre (Eds.), *Handbook of Research on Teacher Education* (3rd ed., pp. 45–65). NY: Routledge/Taylor & Francis Group; The Association of Teacher Educators.

Solomon, M. R., Dann, S., & Russell-Bennett, R. (2007). *Consumer Behavior: Buying, Having, Being.* Frenches Forest NSW: Pearson Education Australia.

Soloveitchik, J. (1944/1983). *Halakhic Man* (L. Kaplan, Trans.). The Jewish Publication Society.

Soloveitchik, J. (1965). The Lonely Face of Man. *Tradition, 7*(2).

Sombart, W. (2001). *The Jews and Modern Capitalism* (M. Epstein, Trans.). Kitchener, Ontario: Batoche Books.

Sosale, S. (2000). *Trends in Private Sector Development in World Bank Education Projects* (No. 2452). Washington, DC: World Bank.

Spencer, H. (Ed.). (1861/1911). *Essays on Education Etc.* London: J. M. Dent & Sons LTD.

Stout, R. (2008). Twentieth-century moral philosophy. In D. Moran (Ed.), *The Routledge Companion to Twentieth Century Philosophy* (pp. 851–882). London & NY: Routledge.

Stratemeyer, F. B. (1956). Relating the several parts of the teacher education program. In D. P. Cottrell (Ed.), *Teacher Education for a Free People* (pp. 231–272). Oneonta, NY: AACTE.

Strenger, K. (2010). *Ani, Proyekt Mitoug* (I, A Trade Marketing Project) Or-Yehuda: Kineret-Zmora-Bitan (in Hebrew).

Sullivan, W. M. (2005). *Work and Integrity* (2nd ed.). San Francisco: Jossey-Bass, The Carnegie Foundation.

Sullivan, W. M. (2006). Introduction. In C. R. Foster, L. E. Dahill, L. A. Golemon, & B. W. Tolentino (Eds.), *Educating Clergy: Teaching Practicies and Pastoral Imagination* (pp. 1–16). San Francisco: Carnegie Foundation for the Advancement of Teaching; Jossey-Bass.

Tabachnick & Zeichner, K. M. (Eds.). (1991). *Issues and Practices in Inquiry-Oriented Teacher Education.* London New York Philadelphia: The Falmer Press.

Taylor, C. (1989). *Sources of the Self: The Making of the Modern Identity.* Cambridge, MA: Harvard University Press.

Taylor, C. (1991). *The Ethics of Authenticity.* Cambridge, MA: Harvard University Press.

Taylor, C. (2007). *A Secular Age.* Cambridge, MA: Harvard University Press.Thomas, B., Fordham Foundation. (1999). *The Teachers We Need and How to Get More of Them.* Retrieved September 14, 2001, from http://www.edexcellence.net/library/teacher.html

Thurley, G. (1983). *The Romantic Predicament.* London: Macmillan Press.

Tobias, S. & Duffy, T. M. (Eds.). (2009). *Constructivist Instruction: Success or Failure?* NY & London: Routledge.

Tolle, E. (2000). *The Power of Now.* Sydney, Australia: Hachette Australia.Tom, A. R., & Valli, L. (1990). Professional knowledge for teachers. In W. R. Houston (Ed.), *Handbook of Research on Teacher Education* (pp. 373–392). NY: McMillan Publishing Company.

Tomlinson, P. (1999). Conscious reflection and implicit learning in teacher preparation, Part I: Recent light on an old issue. *Oxford Review of Education, 25*(3), 405–424.

Tönnies, F. (1887/1957). *Community and Society: Gemeinschaft und Gesellschaft* (C. P. Loomis, Trans.). Michigan: The Michigan State University Press.

Toom, A., Kynaslahti, Krokfors, L., Jyrhama, R., Byman, R., Stenberg, K., et al. (2010). Experiences of a research-based approach to teacher education: Suggestions for future policies. *European Journal of Education*, *45*(2), 332–344.

Torniak, J. (1972). *The Soviet Union*. Devon: David & Charles Publishers Ltd.

Trilling, L. (1972). *Sincerity and Authority*. London: Oxford University Press.

Valli, L. (Ed.). (1992). *Reflective Teacher Education*. NY: State University of New York Press.

Valli, L. (1992). Afterword. In L. Valli (Ed.), *Reflective Teacher Education* (pp. 213–225). NY: State University of New York Press.

Valli, L. (1997). Listening to other voices: A description of teacher reflection in the United States. *Peabody Journal of Education*, *72*(1), 67–88.

van den Brink, B., & Owen, D. (2007). Introduction. In B. van den Brink & D. Owen (Eds.), *Recognition and Power* (pp. 1–32). Leiden: Cambridge University Press.

van Manen, M. (1977). Linking ways of knowing with ways of being Practical. *Curriculum Inquiry*, *6*(3), 205–228.

van Manen, M. (1991). *The Tact of Teaching*. London, Ontario: The Althouse Press.

Viereck, P. (1961). *Metapolitics - The Roots of the Nazi Mind*. NY: Cpricorn Books.

von Humboldt, W. (1793/2000). Theory of bildung (G. Horton-Kruger, Trans.). In I. Westbury, S. Hopmann, & K. Riquarts (Eds.), *Teaching as a Reflective Practice: The German Didaktik Tradition* (pp. 57–61). Mahhah, NJ: Lawrence Erlbaum Ass.

Watkins, J. (1970). Imperfect rationality. In R. Borger & F. Cioffi (Eds.), *Explanations in the Behavioral Sciences* (pp. 167–217). Cambridge: Cambridge University Press.

Webb, J. (2006). *Organizations, Identities and the Self*. London: Palgrave.

Weber, K. (Ed.). (2010). *Waiting for "SUPERMAN"*. NY: Public Affairs.

Weber, M. (1905/1958). *The Protestant Ethic and the Spirit of Capitalism* (T. Parsons, Trans.). NY: Charles Scribners.

Weber, M. (1947). *The Theory of Social and Economics Organizations* (A. Henderson & T. Parsons, Trans.). London: The Free Press of Glenoce. Collier-Macmillan Limited.Weber, S., & Mitchell, C. (1995). *That's Funny, You Don't Look Like A Teacher*. London: The Falmer Press.

Weglinsky, H. (2004). From practice to Praxis: Books about the New Principal Preparatory. *Educational Researcher*, *33*(9), 33–37.

Wells, H. (1923). *Men Like Gods*. ebook; Project Gutenberg. Retrieved February 20, 2011.

Wenger, E. (1998). *Communities of Practice: Learning, Meaning, and Identity*. Cambridge, UK: Cambridge University Press.

Wesley Null, J. (2007). Curriculum for teachers: Four traditions within pedagogical philosophy. *Educational Studies*, *42*(1), 43–63.

Westbury, I. (2000). Teaching as a reflective practice: What might didaktik teach curriculum. In I. Westbury, S. Hopmann, & K. Riquarts (Eds.), *Teaching as a Reflective Practice: The German Didaktik Tradition* (pp. 15–39). Mahhah, NJ: Lawrence Erlbaum Ass.

Whittaker, N., & Whittaker, J. (2010). *The Beginner'$ Guide to Wealth*. Sydney, Australia: Simon & Schuster.

Wideen, M., Mayer-Smith, J., & Moon, B. (1998). A critical analysis of the research on learning to teach: Making the case for an ecological perspective on inquiry. *Review of Educational Research*, *68*(2), 130–178.

Wittgenstein, L. (1922/1961). *Tractatus Logico-Philosophicus* (D. Pears & B. McGuinness, Trans.). London: Routledge & Kegan-Paul.

Yaakobi, D. (2005). Reshita shel hahshara mikzoit baouniversita haivrit (The beginning of professional education in the Hebrew University in Jerusalem). In H. Lavski (Ed.), *Toldot Hauniversita haivrit byerushalaim I* (pp. 475–501) (in Hebrew).

LIST OF REFERENCES

Yan Man Kit, D. (2001). *Ideology and Teacher Education in Communist Russia amd Post-Communist Russia*. Unpublished M.Ed., The University of Hong-Kong.

Zeichner, K. M. (1983). Alternative paradigms of teacher education. *Journal of Teacher Education, 34*(3), 3–9.

Zeichner, K. M. (1992). Conceptions of reflective teaching in contemporary U.S. teacher education program reforms. In L. Valli (Ed.), *Reflective Teacher Education* (pp. 161–173). NY: State University of New York Press.

Zeichner, K. M. (2010). Rethinking college and university-based teacher education. *Journal of Teacher Education, 61*(1–2), 89–99.

Zeichner, K. M., & Liston, D. P. (1996). *Reflective Teaching: An Introduction*. Mahwah, NJ: Lawrence Erlbaum Associates, Publishers.

Žižek, S. (2011). *Living in the End Times*. London & N.Y.: Verso.

Zumwalt, K., & Craig, E. (2008). Who is teaching? Does it matter? In M. Cochran-Smith, S. Feiman-Nemser, & D. McIntyre (Eds.), *Handbook of Research on Teacher Education* (3rd ed., pp. 404–423). NY: Routledge/Taylor & Francis Group; The Association of Teacher Educators.

AUTHOR INDEX

SUBJECT INDEX

Lightning Source UK Ltd.
Milton Keynes UK
UKOW031116230812

197927UK00002B/7/P